Concepts of Athletic Training

Concepts of Athletic Training

Second Edition

RONALD P. PFEIFFER, Ed.D., A.T.C.-R.

Professor, Undergraduate Athletic Training Curriculum Director
Director, Human Anatomy Laboratory

Boise State University

BRENT C. MANGUS, Ed.D., A.T.C.

Chair and Professor, Department of Health Education
and Sports Injury Management

University of Nevada, Las Vegas

JONES AND BARTLETT PUBLISHERS

Sudbury, Massachusetts

BOSTON   TORONTO   LONDON   SINGAPORE

World Headquarters
Jones and Bartlett Publishers
40 Tall Pine Drive
Sudbury, MA 01776
978-443-5000
info@jbpub.com
www.jbpub.com

Jones and Bartlett Publishers Canada
2406 Nikanna Road
Mississauga, Ontario
Canada L5C 2W6

Jones and Bartlett Publishers International
Barb House, Barb Mews
London W6 7PA
UK

Copyright © 1998 by Jones and Bartlett Publishers, Inc.

Library of Congress Cataloging-in-Publication Data

Pfeiffer, Ronald P.
    Concepts of athletic training / Ronald P. Pfeiffer, Brent C.
Mangus.—2nd ed.
      p. cm.
    Includes bibliographical references and index.
    ISBN 0–7637–0235–8
    1. Athletic trainers. 2. Sports medicine. I. Mangus, Brent C.
II. Title.
    [DNLM: 1. Athletic Injuries—therapy. 2. Sports Medicine.   QT
261 P528c 1998]
RC1210.P45 1998
617.1'027—dc21
DNLM/DLC
for Library of Congress   97-20506
                                             CIP

Editor: TRACY MURPHY
Project Editor: CANDACE KOOYOOMJIAN
Manufacturing Buyer: JANE BROMBACK
Design: BOOKS BY DESIGN, INC.
Editorial Production Service: BOOKS BY DESIGN, INC.
Typesetting: MODERN GRAPHICS, INC.
Cover Design: LINDA WADE
Printing and Binding: COURIER COMPANY
Cover Printing: COURIER COMPANY

Photo credits: *Frontispiece:* Mark Gibson. *Chapter opening photography:* Chapters 1, 3, 18, 19, Mark Gibson; Chapter 6, Mark Philbrick; Chapters 2, 4, 5, 8, 12, 13, 16, Central Michigan University; Chapter 14, Boise State University; Chapters 7, 9, 10, 11, 15, 17, Stock Boston. *Cover photography:* Photodisc and Stock Boston.

Printed in the United States of America
00 99 98   10 9 8 7 6 5 4 3

B R I E F
C O N T E N T S

CONTENTS

Introduction

Coaches most often see an injury first. Their decisions often determine the outcome of the injury. Given this fact, it is essential that coaches receive specialized education in the immediate care, recognition, and management of sports-related injuries. This training must go beyond what is offered in the typical first aid class since they usually focus on, and are limited to, injuries resulting from natural calamities and vehicular accidents. This second edition of *Concepts of Athletic Training* includes information on medical terminology unique to sports medicine, injury psychology, the inflammatory process, and common intervention procedures. These topics, provide coaches and athletic trainers with the knowledge and skills to begin treating injuries as soon as they happen.

About the Book

While the primary audience for this text continues to be coaching and physical education majors, this text will also serve as an exceptional introductory resource for athletic training majors who are pursuing a career in the sports medicine field. The second edition has been modified to address feedback from readers and to include information that has only recently become available. Nearly every chapter has been updated to include information that was not available when the manuscript for the first edition was completed. Chapter 1 includes results from the most recent NATA high school sports injury study. Chapter 9 has been modified to include critical information generated from research that has been conducted and published in the past year on the topic of emergency management of the helmeted tackle football player with possible head or neck injury. In addition, the frightening and potentially lethal phenomenon known as second impact syndrome is also described. A section on the application of adhesive tape for prevention of ankle injuries has been added to Chapter 15. New appendices include an entire overview of exercise rehabilitation with sample programs, as well as guidelines for the safe construction of movable soccer goals. The most recent National Safety Council guidelines for CPR and Bloodborne Pathogens are also included.

New Features

In addition to new material, two important pedagogical aids have also been added throughout the text. Most college students have access to the World Wide Web (WWW) either through computer labs located on campus or by way of modems and their own personal computers. Over the past two years a plethora of interesting and educational Web pages have been placed "on-line" and offer a wealth of information. Each chapter in the second edition has one or more special features titled **"Information at your Fingertips"** that prompts readers to visit the Web site specifically selected to accompany the text. The *Concepts of Athletic Training* Web page features a chapter-by-chapter listing of Web addresses that will provide additional information to important chapter concepts. This Web site will be updated on a regular basis to ensure that the reader receives the most recent and pertinent information available on the Internet. In addition, "real-life" scenarios have been placed in each chapter in order to encourage the reader to work on critical decision making skills. These sections, entitled **"What If?,"** provide the sort of information typically available to coaching personnel when confronted with an injury or related problem. These scenarios can have many applications ranging from simple "decision making" practice sessions alone or with another student or, ideally, as the script for role play exercises in a sports injury class laboratory practice session.

This book is not meant to be a carry-on-the-field "cookbook" for care and management for sports injuries. Individuals charged with the responsibility of providing emergency care for student athletes must be trained to respond appropriately without having to rely on printed resources when confronted with an injury. In many situations there is not enough time to read through a manual to determine the proper course of action. Coaching personnel should also avoid the temptation to circumvent the knowledge and expertise of health professionals, such as NATABOC-certified athletic trainers and other medical personnel. This text is designed to give coaches the necessary skills to recognize and differentiate the minor from more serious sports injuries that must be referred to the appropriate health care personnel.

Ancillaries for the Instructor

We have developed the following supplements to support your efforts in the classroom.

1. **Instructor's Resource Manual**—provides the instructor with a chapter-by-chapter outline to assist with organizing and teaching the course.

2. **Instructor's Test Bank**—over 450 multiple choice, true/false, and short questions help evaluate student comprehension.

3. **Instructor's CD-ROM**—PowerPoint presentation provides a lecture outline for each chapter of the book and is designed to correspond with the text's organization and content. Additionally, **Web simulations** within each chapter demonstrate the benefit of the Internet without having a live Internet connection in the classroom. Your students will see how the various Web sites can enhance their knowledge and understanding of topics important to athletic training.

Acknowledgments

This text would not have been completed had it not been for those colleagues who reviewed and contributed to the manuscript:

Veronica Ampey
Assistant Director for Sports Medicine
Emory University
Atlanta, GA

Bill G. Bean
Head Athletic Trainer
University of Utah
Salt Lake City, UT

Debra Belcher
Assistant Athletic Trainer
University of Vermont
Burlington, VT

Professor George L. Borden
Virginia Commonwealth University
Richmond, VA

Dr. Bart Buxton
Sports Medicine Program Coordinator
Georgia Southern University
Statesboro, GA

Professor Ben Davidson
Southern Utah University
Cedar City, UT

Dr. Earlene Durrant
Athletic Training Education Program Director
Brigham Young University
Provo, UT

Doris E. Flores
Program Director for Athletic Training Curriculum
California State University, Sacramento
Sacramento, CA

Dr. Danny T. Foster
Head Athletic Trainer
University of Iowa
Iowa City, IA

Professor Gordon Graham
Athletic Training Education Program Director
Mankato State University
Mankato, MN

Professor Al Green
University of Kentucky
Lexington, KY

Rick Griffin
Head Trainer
Seattle Mariners
Seattle, WA

Professor Chuck Kimmel
Austin PEAY State University
Clarksville, TN

Kenneth W. Kopke
President, Athletic Training Services
Mt. Pleasant, MI

Rebecca A. Larkin
Assistant Athletic Trainer
University of Vermont
Burlington, VT

Richard Leander
Head Athletic Trainer
Moscow School District
Moscow, ID

Sue Lerner
Assistant Athletic Trainer
University of Southern California
Los Angeles, CA

Dr. Larry J. Leverenz
Director of Athletic Training Education
Purdue University
West Lafayette, IN

Dale Mildenberger
Head Athletic Trainer
Utah State University
Logan, UT

Debra J. C. Murray
Lecturer and Athletic Trainer
University of North Carolina, Chapel Hill
Chapel Hill, NC

Jayne E. Nelson
Director of Student Health Care Center
Boise State University
Boise, ID

Dr. Louis Osternig
University of Oregon
Eugene, OR

Professor Rod Poindexter
Athletic Training Education Program Director
California Lutheran University
Thousand Oaks, CA

Dr. Andrew Pruitt
Director, Western Orthopedic Sports Medicine and
    Rehabilitation Center
Denver, CO

Michelle Puetz
Assistant Athletic Trainer
Montana State University
Bozeman, MT

Dan Ruiz
Assistant Athletic Trainer
Carolina Panthers
Charlotte, NC

Dennis Sealey
Head Athletic Trainer
University of Washington
Seattle, WA

Mark J. Smaha
Director of Athletic Medicine
Washington State University
Pullman, WA

Professor Karen Smith
University of West Florida
Pensacola, FL

Barrie Steele
Head Athletic Trainer
University of Idaho
Moscow, ID

Dr. Christine Stopka
Athletic Training Education Program Director
University of Florida
Gainesville, FL

Jennifer Teaford
Adjunct Faculty
Whitworth College
Spokane, WA

Professor Clint Thompson
Northeast Missouri State
Kirksville, MO

Professor Deborah Warner
Greensboro College
Greensboro, NC

Nathan Yearsley
Ricks College
Rexburg, ID

Professor Carol Zweifel
Athletic Training Education Program Director
Washington State University
Pullman, WA

CHAPTER 1

The Concept of Sports Injury

MAJOR CONCEPTS

After reading and studying this chapter, the reader should be familiar with the scope and breadth of the topic of sports injury. The chapter presents the most recent data available in order to provide a quantitative perspective on the number of participants injured while engaging in sport activities. It discusses the most popular definitions of sports injury currently in use along with a variety of the most commonly used medical terms related to the type and severity of injury. These terms will be used throughout the remainder of the book and will also prove useful to the coach when communicating with members of the medical community about sports injuries. The last section introduces the concept of epidemiology as it applies to the study of sports injury.

Organized competitive sports continue to be extremely popular among American children. Recent reports indicate that approximately 7 million public-school children are involved in these activities annually (Stanitski, 1989). For example, tackle football (Figure 1.1) attracts about 1.5 million high school and junior high school participants, wrestling (Figure 1.2) garners 245,000, and baseball and track involve 407,000 and 829,000, respectively (Mueller and Cantu, 1993). With the implementation of the Title IX Education Assistance Act of 1972, the growth in participation of female athletes within the United States has been 700% (Stanitski, 1989). Ironically, due to unfounded fears within both the lay and coaching communities that girls were not tough enough to play sports, many young female athletes were historically discouraged from participation. Even more disturbing is the fact that such negative stereotypes persist within some sports organizations. Fortunately, researchers have produced data demonstrating clearly that injuries to female participants are sport specific (Figure 1.3), not gender specific (Collins, 1987). These data support the premise that females are at no greater risk for injury when involved in organized activities than are their male counterparts (Figure 1.4).

In spite of the best efforts of parents, coaches, and officials, **injury** continues to be an unavoidable reality for a significant number of these young participants. To date, two large-scale, comprehensive studies of injuries among young athletes have been completed and their findings support the premise that injuries are a constant problem associated with sports participation (NATA, 1989; Foster, 1996).

Results from the latest (1995) National High School

FIGURE 1.1 Some 1.5 million students in junior and senior high schools participate in tackle football annually. (Courtesy of Boise State University.)

FIGURE 1.2 Each year wrestling attracts as many as 245,000 participants in secondary schools. (Courtesy of Boise State University.)

FIGURE 1.3 Data clearly indicate that injuries to female athletes are sport specific. (Courtesy of Boise State University.)

FIGURE 1.4 Females are at no greater risk for injury when involved in sports than are their male counterparts. (Courtesy of Boise State University.)

Injury Survey sponsored by the National Athletic Trainers' Association (NATA) found that national injury rates have remained close to those documented by the same group for the three-year period 1986 to 1988. In a similar study of high school injuries in the state of Pennsylvania, Grollman and associates found an overall 3,069 reportable injuries from 10 sports (boys and girls) across 40 high schools for the 1994–1995 school year. The sport with the highest percentage of injuries was tackle football (46.7%), followed by boys' basketball (10%), and wrestling (9.68%). The sport producing the highest percentage of injuries for girls was basketball (7.5%).

A study of 87,000 Massachusetts children revealed that 1 out of every 14 admitted to a hospital emergency room was admitted as a result of a sports-related injury. To put this in perspective, the same study found that accidents involving motor vehicles accounted for 1 out of 50 admissions within the same group (Gallagher, 1984). In a similar study of Illinois children, Zaricznyj and colleagues (1980) found that over a period of one year 6% of the school-aged youngsters suffered a sports-related injury serious enough to require first aid. Interestingly, organized school sports accounted for only 15% of these injuries; unorganized sports and physical education classes produced 40% and 38% of the injuries, respectively. In a study of emergency room admissions in urban hospitals in Ottawa, Canada, Pelletier, Anderson, and Stark (1991) found that 66.5% of the admissions for sports- and/or leisure-related injuries were among patients 20 years of age or younger. The vast majority of these injuries (94.5%) was classified as acute—with touch football, tackle football, ice hockey, and soccer producing over half of all injuries reported.

Definition of Sports Injury

Though logic would seem to argue that determining what constitutes a sports injury would be simple, just the opposite is the case. In spite of the efforts of many within the sports medicine community, a single, universally acceptable definition of sports injury remains unavailable. Debates about precise definitions among academicians may seem petty to the injured athlete; however, from a clinical and scientific viewpoint, having a standard set of definitions would greatly improve the usefulness and impact of future injury studies. Several definitions are currently in use by sports medicine personnel. Injuries continue to be defined and described in terms of such variables as body area involved, type of tissue involved, severity of damage, and time lost to the athlete.

Most current definitions of sports injury incorporate the length of time away from participation (time lost) as the major determinant (DeLee and Farney, 1992). Using this definition, an injury is said to have occurred when an athlete is forced to discontinue play and/or practice for a predetermined length of time—for example, 24 hours. In 1982 the National Collegiate Athletic Association (NCAA) established the Injury Surveillance System (ISS), which established a common set of injury and risk definitions for use in their tracking of collegiate sport injuries. To qualify as an injury under the ISS, that injury must meet the following criteria:

1. Occurs as a result of participation in an organized intercollegiate practice or game.
2. Requires medical attention by a team athletic trainer or physician.
3. Results in restriction of the student athlete's participation or performance for one or more days beyond the day of injury (Benson, 1995).

The NCAA monitors injuries at division I, II, and III institutions across all regions of the country and produces an annual report of the findings.

Information at your fingertips

The World Wide Web—you can find more information about the NCAA. Go to http://www.jbpub.com/athletictraining and click on Chapter 1.

The NATA has conducted national surveys of high school sports injuries spanning a three-year period from 1986 to 1988. A second study is currently under way with data recently collected for the 1995 academic year. The injury definitions used are similar to the ISS because they rely on estimates of time lost from play as the indicator of injury severity (Foster, 1996).

Even though time lost is a convenient method for identifying an injury, such a definition does not lend itself to an accurate reflection of the severity of the injury. Such determinations may be made by a variety of people, including the coach, sports medicine personnel, and perhaps even the athlete. The problem is that no standard is currently in use by all organizations monitoring sports injuries for the amount of time—hours, days, weeks, or months—that must be lost in order to qualify as an injury. Furthermore, opinions regarding the severity of a given injury may vary considerably among sports medicine personnel such as physicians, athletic trainers, and sports physical therapists.

From a scientific standpoint, using the amount of time lost as a definition of sports injury is subject to significant error as described above, depending upon the method of data collection and injury definitions employed. However, once an injury is identified, several qualifiers are available to enable sports medicine personnel to better describe the precise characteristics of the injury—i.e., tissue(s) involved, location, severity, type, and mechanism of injury.

A commonly used medical classification system for injuries uses two major categories: acute and chronic. **Acute injuries** have been defined as those "characterized by a rapid onset, resulting from a traumatic event" (AAOS, 1991). Acute injuries are usually associated with a significant traumatic event (Figure 1.5), followed

immediately by a pattern of signs and symptoms such as pain, swelling, and loss of function. In the case of an acute injury, **critical force** has been defined as the "magnitude of a single force for which the anatomical structure of interest is damaged" (Nigg and Bobbert, 1990). The potential for critical force, and subsequent acute injury, is clearly seen in tackle football. Estimates demonstrate that the vertebral bodies in the human cervical spine have a critical force limit of 340–455 kilograms. Researchers, using devices to simulate a typical tackle, have estimated that compressive forces acting on the cervical spine can exceed these limits (Torg, 1982).

Chronic injuries have been defined as those "characterized by a slow, insidious onset, implying a gradual development of structural damage" (AAFP, 1992). Chronic sports injuries, in contrast to acute ones, are

FIGURE 1.5 Acute injury to the hand in baseball.

FIGURE 1.6 Chronic injuries are common in high-impact sports such as running.

tellar tendon, and rotator cuff tendon in the shoulder (Hess et al., 1989). The Achilles tendon is subjected to tremendous stress during running and jumping (Figure 1.7). Research indicates that these forces may exceed the physiological limits of the tendon, thereby resulting in damage (Curwain and Stanish, 1984). Likewise, the patellar tendon must absorb repeated episodes of stress during sports. For instance, the act of kicking a soccer ball (Figure 1.8) generates forces within the tendon that are many times greater than those produced during normal gait (Gainor et al., 1978). The rotator cuff tendon, specifically the supraspinatus, is also vulnerable to injury from overuse. Any activity requiring repeated overhead movements of the arm, such as overhead strokes in tennis (Figure 1.9), places significant stress on this tendon. This is especially true during the deceleration phase of a swing or throw, after the arm has reached peak velocity. It is during this period of movement that muscles

FIGURE 1.7 Injuries to the Achilles tendon are common in track and field events. (Courtesy of Boise State University.)

not associated with a single traumatic episode; rather, they develop progressively over time. In many cases, they occur to athletes who are involved in activities that require repeated, continuous movements, such as in running (Figure 1.6). Consequently, such injuries are sometimes called overuse injuries, implying the athlete has simply done too many repetitions of the given activity. Overuse injuries in tendons occur when the workload from exercise exceeds the ability of musculotendinous tissues to recover (Hess et al., 1989). Thus, activity serves to cause a progressive breakdown of the tissue, leading eventually to failure. Common sites for overuse injuries are the Achilles tendon, pa-

FIGURE 1.8 Kicking a soccer ball subjects the patellar tendon to stress.

FIGURE 1.9 Overhead strokes in tennis place significant stress on the rotator cuff.

are undergoing **eccentric contraction,** a type of contraction identified as a causative factor in tendon injury (Curwain and Stanish, 1984). Such stress can cause damage in the supraspinatus tendon, resulting in a chronic injury.

Probably the most commonly used terms for differentiating tissues involved in a given injury are soft and skeletal. **Soft tissue,** as a category, includes muscles, **fascia,** tendons, **joint capsules,** ligaments, blood vessels, and nerves. Most soft-tissue injuries involve contusions (bruises), sprains (ligaments/capsules), and strains (muscles/tendons). Skeletal tissue includes any bony structure within the body. Therefore, under this system, a common ankle sprain would qualify as a soft-tissue injury; a fractured wrist would be deemed a skeletal injury. These injuries, and the forces that produce them, are discussed further in Chapter 8.

A notable exception to the general confusion in defining a sports injury has to do with injuries so severe that they are known as catastrophic. **Catastrophic injuries** are those that involve damage to the brain and/or spinal cord and are potentially life threatening or permanent. In the context of high school and college sports, catastrophic injury has been defined as one "incurred during participation in a high school/college sport in which there is permanent severe functional neurological disability (nonfatal), or transient but not permanent functional neurological disability (serious)" (Mueller and Cantu, 1990). Mueller and Cantu have defined direct catastrophic injuries as those that resulted directly from participation in the skills of a given sport. Indirect catastrophic injuries are defined as those caused by systemic failure resulting from exertion while participating in a sports activity, or by a complication that was secondary to a nonfatal injury (Mueller and Cantu, 1993). Given these definitions, a catastrophic injury can occur as either a direct result of participation (sustaining a neck fracture during a tackle in football), or can happen indirectly (suffering a systemic heat stroke during a cross-country run). Though catastrophic sports injuries account for a small portion of all sports-related injuries, their potential for serious complications has resulted in an increased awareness by members of the sports medicine community.

Injury Classifications

Regardless of the specific force involved in producing an injury, it is critical that the coach or physical educa-

Athletic Trainers Speak Out

"The proper management of acute sports injuries is paramount, especially during the first few minutes [after the injury has occurred]. The ability to properly treat an acute musculoskeletal strain or ligamentous sprain immediately following occurrence can aid in reducing the athlete's recovery time and expedite the athlete's return to safe, healthy participation. In the case of a potentially catastrophic injury, the precise acute management and treatment can mean the difference between life and death for an injured athlete."

—*Bart Buxton, A.T.C., Ed.D.*

Dr. Buxton is the Athletic Training Education Program Director at the University of Hawaii at Manoa.

Bart Buxton

tion teacher be familiar with the basic terminology of connective tissue injury. It is essential that any injury be correctly identified and described when dealing with other members of the sports medicine team, e.g., the team physician or athletic trainer. It is also vital that a vocabulary of standardized terms universal to all members of the sports medicine team be mastered. In 1968, the Committee on the Medical Aspects of Sports, a branch of the American Medical Association (AMA) published *Standard Nomenclature of Athletic Injuries*

(*SNAI*). This text provides clearly defined, standardized terms that can and should be utilized by those providing care for sports injuries.

Since the vast majority of sports injuries involve damage to connective tissue, the terms that apply to these common conditions are listed below. Obviously, a certain degree of variability is unavoidable within any clinical definition. However, these terms, when used properly, will greatly reduce the confusion that so often exists regarding specific injuries.

Sprains

Sprains are injuries to ligaments, which surround all synovial joints within the body. The severity of sprains is highly variable depending on the forces involved. *SNAI* describes three categories of sprains, based upon the level of severity.

■ First-Degree Sprains
According to *SNAI*, first-degree sprains are the mildest form of sprain; only mild pain and disability occur. There sprains demonstrate little or no swelling and are associated with minor ligament damage.

■ Second-Degree Sprains
Second-degree sprains are more severe: they imply more actual damage to the ligament(s) involved, with an increase in the amount of pain and dysfunction. Swelling will be more pronounced, and abnormal motion will be present. Such injuries have a tendency to recur.

■ Third-Degree Sprains
Third-degree sprains are the most severe form of sprain and imply a complete tear of the ligament(s) involved. Given the extensive damage, pain, swelling, and **hemorrhage** will be significant and associated with considerable loss of joint stability.

Strains

Strains are injuries to muscles, tendons, or the junction between the two, commonly known as the musculotendinous junction (MTJ). The most common location of a strain is the MTJ; however, the exact reason for this is unknown. As is the case with sprains, there is tremendous variability with respect to the severity of strains seen in sports. *SNAI* presents three categories of strains.

■ First-Degree Strains
SNAI describes first-degree strains as the mildest form with little associated damage to muscle and tendon structures. Pain is most noticeable during use; there may be mild swelling and muscle spasm present.

■ Second-Degree Strains
Second-degree strains imply more extensive damage to the soft-tissue structures involved. Pain, swelling, and muscle spasm will be more pronounced, and func-

tional loss will be moderate. These types of injuries are associated with excessive, forced stretching or a failure in the synergistic action within a muscle group.

■ Third-Degree Strains
Third-degree strains are the most severe form and imply a complete rupture of the soft-tissue structures involved. Damage may occur at a variety of locations, including the bony attachment of the tendon (avulsion fracture), the tissues between the tendon and muscle (MTJ), or those within the muscle itself. A defect may be apparent through the skin and will be associated with significant swelling. Obviously, this type of injury will involve significant loss of function.

Contusions

In all probability, common bruises or **contusions** are the most frequent sports injury, regardless of activity. Contusions result from direct blows to the body surface, which cause a compression of the underlying tissue(s) as well as the skin (O'Donoghue, 1984). They can occur in almost any activity; however, collision and contact sports such as tackle football, basketball, and baseball are more prolific in this regard. Curiously, many athletes and coaches view contusions as routine, minor injuries, but they can be serious, even life-threatening, injuries when the tissues involve vital organs such as the kidneys or brain.

Contusions are typically characterized as being associated with pain, stiffness, swelling, **ecchymosis** (discoloration), and **hematoma** (pooling of blood). If not treated properly, such injuries to muscle tissue can result in a condition known as **myositis ossificans,** which involves bone-like formations developing within the muscle tissue.

Fractures

Fractures and dislocations represent two categories of injuries involving either bones or joints of the body. Though such injuries can occur in any activity, they are more common in collision sports in which large forces come into play. **Fractures** have been defined by the National Safety Council (NSC, 1991) as "a break or crack in a bone." The NSC recognizes two types of fractures: closed (i.e., bone ends not breaking the skin) and open or compound (i.e., bone ends breaking through the skin surface). Compound fractures are potentially more serious due to the risk of infection related to the open wound. Furthermore, control of bleeding may be necessary depending upon the severity and location of the wound. Acute fractures are relatively uncommon sports injuries. When they occur, however, appropriate first aid is essential in order to prevent complications such as shock, excessive blood loss, or permanent damage. Fortunately, with modern diagnostic procedures identifying traumatic fractures is relatively easy. The NSC has provided the following descriptions of signs and symptoms:

■ *Swelling.* Caused by bleeding; it occurs rapidly after a fracture.

■ *Deformity.* This is not always obvious. Compare the injured with the uninjured opposite body part when checking for deformity.

■ *Pain and tenderness.* Commonly found only at the injury site. The athlete will usually be able to point to the site of pain. A useful procedure for detecting fractures is to feel gently along the bones; complaints about pain or tenderness serve as a reliable sign of a fracture.

■ *Loss of use.* Inability to use the injured part. Guarded motion occurs because movement pro-

duces pain, and the athlete will refuse to use the injured limb. However, sometimes the athlete is able to move the limb with little or no pain.

■ *Grating sensation.* Do not move the injured limb in an attempt to see if a grating sensation called **crepitation** can be felt (and even sometimes heard) when broken bone ends rub together.

■ *History of the injury.* Suspect a fracture whenever severe forces are involved, especially in high-risk sports such as tackle football, alpine skiing, and ice hockey. The athlete may have heard or felt the bone snap.

Fractures may also be described in terms of the specific nature of the break in the bone. The major types of traumatic fractures are shown in Figure 1.10.

■ **Stress Fracture**

A stress fracture is most usually linked to sports since it develops over a relatively long time period, as opposed to other fractures caused by a single trauma. **Stress fractures** occur when a bone is subjected to repeated episodes of overloading (stress) that exceed its rate of recovery. In effect, the bone starts to break

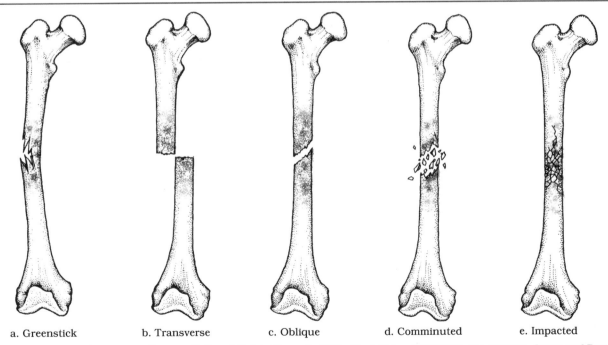

a. Greenstick   b. Transverse   c. Oblique   d. Comminuted   e. Impacted

FIGURE 1.10 Types of fractures. (Source: National Safety Council. 1991. *First Aid and CPR* (1st ed.). Boston: Jones and Bartlett. Reprinted with permission.)

down and eventually begins to fail. Since stress fractures take time to develop, the signs and symptoms are easily confused with other, less serious sports-related problems. This is especially true for stress fractures of the lower leg bones, which are often confused with shin splints. Although stress fractures can occur throughout the body, the majority occur in the lower extremities. Athletes at high risk for stress fractures are those who are in poor physical condition or overweight. However, even well-conditioned participants may develop such a fracture, particularly when they have made a recent and sudden increase in the intensity of their training program. Stress fractures may even be related to diet: a regimen low in calcium may predispose athletes, particularly females, to this problem (Nelson, 1989).

The symptoms of a stress fracture are nebulous at best; nevertheless, certain factors are usually present when one is developing:

■ **Pain/tenderness.** Athlete complains of pain and/or tenderness. A constant ache is not relieved with rest.

■ **Absence of trauma.** Suspect such a fracture when there is no history of traumatic event, yet the symptoms persist.

■ **Repetitive activity.** Athlete is involved in an activity that subjects the suspect area to repeated stressful episodes.

■ **Duration.** Symptoms have slowly developed over a period of days, weeks, or even months.

this healing process, known technically as a callus, that signals that a fracture has occurred. As a result, the physician must base the diagnosis on the factors listed previously. The best approach is to treat athletes as if they have a stress fracture and repeat the X-ray evaluation on a weekly or biweekly basis until a callus is seen. In difficult cases, bone scan or magnetic resonance imaging may be used to obtain a positive diagnosis. Treatment of stress fractures involves rest and splinting or casting when necessary, followed by a slow, gradual return to participation. Athletes are often encouraged to maintain their fitness levels during recovery by cross training—i.e., riding a stationary bike, jogging in shallow water, or swimming. All of those activities provide good stimulation of aerobic fitness while reducing stress on the skeletal system. Any program of recovery must be structured on an individual basis by the coach, athletic trainer, and physician.

Dislocations

Dislocations have been defined as "the displacement of contiguous surfaces of bones comprising a joint" (Booher and Thibodeau, 1989). Two types of dislocations can occur, based upon the severity of the injury. A **subluxation** takes place when the bones of a joint are only partially displaced. A **luxation** happens when the bones of a joint are totally displaced. In a sense, any dislocation, whether it is a subluxation or luxation, should be viewed as a severe type of sprain. Recall that sprains involve damage to the tissues surrounding

W H A T   I F ?

A student athlete asks you to explain the differences between a subluxation and a luxation of a joint.

Stress fractures often present the physician with a difficult diagnosis since, during the initial phases, X-ray examinations may not show the fracture. This is because stress fractures develop slowly and rarely result in large, visible cracks in the bones (O'Donoghue, 1984). Most stress fractures are not visible on standard X-rays until they actually begin to heal. It is

joints—i.e., capsules and ligaments. As such, dislocations present many of the same signs and symptoms as those seen in sprains. First-aid treatment for dislocations combines care given for both sprains and fractures. Dislocations can occur within any articulation; however, specific joints seem to be more vulnerable. Two joints in the shoulder complex, the glenohumeral and the acromioclavicular, are injured frequently in sports such as tackle football and wrestling. The small joints in the fingers are commonly dislocated in baseball and softball. Fortunately, such dislocations are relatively easy to evaluate; if treated properly, full recovery typically occurs. *It is important to note that at no time should the coach attempt to reduce (put back in place) any dislocation, no matter how minor it may appear to be.* All dislocations should be diagnosed and reduced by a physician after a complete medical evaluation.

Injury Recognition

From a practical standpoint, learning to recognize injury, regardless of the classification system used, is an essential skill to be mastered by the coach. To a great extent, the athlete's health and safety are determined by the decisions and subsequent actions of the coach. In addition, the dramatic increase in sports-injury litigation should serve as further incentive for coaching personnel to be prepared for emergencies. The premise that most injuries are best treated with the "run-it-out" approach is dangerous, to say the least. Today's coach should treat all possible injuries as such, until proven otherwise. It is imperative that coaching personnel develop the knowledge and skills to discriminate injuries requiring medical referral from those not necessitating such evaluation. Moreover, it should be noted that such decisions are best left to qualified health specialists such as athletic trainers certified by the National Athletic Trainers' Association Board of Certification (NATABOC). Every effort should be made to have such a specialist employed, either permanently or part-time, by the school or agency sponsoring the sports program.

Epidemiology of Sports Injury

Scientific sports-injury research is a relatively recent phenomenon. The majority of the early studies, sometimes known as case-series studies, were based on information collected by medical personnel at hospitals or clinics (Walter et al., 1985). Although these data have provided valuable information, there are significant problems associated with this type of data collection. Typically, only athletes with significant injuries will seek medical attention at a hospital or clinic. Thus,

a large number of athletes with injuries of minor to moderate severity may not be included in the study. Another problem with case-series research is the inability to accurately identify the cause or causes of a specific injury. For example, researchers at a particular clinic might conclude that less experienced athletes are more susceptible to injuries. However, without knowing the general level of experience of all athletes, injured as well as uninjured, it is impossible to determine what constitutes inexperience.

A better approach to sports-injury research involves the application of the principles of epidemiology. The science of **epidemiology** is the "study of the distribution of diseases, injuries, or other health states in human populations for the purpose of identifying and implementing measures to prevent their development and spread" (Caine, Caine, and Lindner, 1996). The sports epidemiologist collects information in an effort to identify causative agents or **risk factors** that may have contributed to a particular injury. Hypotheses are then developed and tested to confirm a statistical relationship. Risk factors, such as collisions in tackle football or ice hockey, may be inherent in the sport. Equipment may increase the risk of injury—e.g., a football helmet with a faulty design or a diving board set too close to the pool deck. The athlete may also possess risk factors—e.g., muscle imbalances, obesity, or any of a variety of congenital conditions.

By determining statistical relationships between suspected risk factors and specific injuries, sports regulatory organizations can implement strategies designed to reduce or eliminate the risk of sports injuries. The incidence of spine injury in tackle football was significantly reduced by a rule change implemented in 1976 that made the practice of **spearing** (tackling and/or blocking with the head as the initial point of contact) illegal (Torg, 1982). In this case, the available data indicated that the technique of spearing placed the cervical spine (neck) of athletes at risk.

Several national injury surveillance systems are currently active throughout the country. One of the oldest is the National Athletic Injury/Illness Reporting System (NAIRS), which was instituted in 1975. More recently, the National Collegiate Athletic Association Injury Surveillance System (NCAA/ISS), the National High School Injury Registry, and the National Sports Injury Surveillance System (NSISS) have been implemented. The National Center for Catastrophic Sports Injury Research began operation during the early 1980s with a focus on the documentation of catastrophic injuries at the high school and college level (Mueller and Cantu, 1993). It is hoped that the informa-

TABLE 1.1 Classification of Sports by Strenuousness

HIGH TO MODERATE INTENSITY			LOW INTENSITY
High to Moderate Dynamic and Static Demands	**High to Moderate Dynamic and Low Static Demands**	**High to Moderate Static and Low Dynamic Demands**	**Low Dynamic and Low Static Demands**
Boxing*	Badminton	Archery	Bowling
Crew/rowing	Baseball	Auto racing	Cricket
Cross-country skiing	Basketball	Diving	Curling
Cycling	Field hockey	Equestrian	Golf
Downhill skiing	Lacrosse	Field events (jumping)	Riflery
Fencing	Orienteering	Field events (throwing)	
Football	Ping-pong	Gymnastics	
Ice hockey	Race walking	Karate or judo	
Rugby	Racquetball	Motorcycling	
Running (sprint)	Soccer	Rodeoing	
Speed skating	Squash	Sailing	
Water polo	Swimming	Ski jumping	
Wrestling	Tennis	Water skiing	
	Volleyball	Weight lifting	

*Participation not recommended.
Source: American Academy of Pediatrics. 1994. Committee on Sports Medicine and Fitness. Medical conditions affecting sports participation. *Pediatr.* 94(5):757–760. Reprinted with permission.

WHAT IF?

A student athlete asks you the classification of her three favorite sports, e.g., softball, golf, and soccer.

tion collected by these organizations will lead to continued reductions in both the frequency and severity of sports injuries.

Classification of Sports

Just as injuries can be defined and described using a variety of medical and scientific terms, sports can be classified based upon their strenuousness (intensity). The American Academy of Pediatrics has recently revised their classification system for many popular sports and has placed them into one of four separate categories using these criteria (See Table 1.1). The reader will note that the AAP has stated that participation in boxing is not recommended (AAP, 1994).

Sports medicine personnel, coaches, administrators, and parents can use this information when athletes are found to have specific health-related problems during their preparticipation physical evaluations. For example, a child with a history of recent head injury would be ill-advised to participate in a contact/collision sport such as football. However, contrary to popular belief, noncontact sports can represent a risk to athletes as well. For example, a child with an identified, clinically significant congenital heart disorder might be advised to avoid aerobic activities such as track, swimming, or aerobic dance.

Extent of the Injury Problem—Some Examples

In spite of rule changes, proper supervision, and improved coaching, experts report that from 3% to 11% of all children will suffer some type of sports injury

FIGURE 1.11 Up to 36% of participants in interscholastic tackle football can expect to be injured. (Courtesy of Boise State University.)

every year (Goldberg, 1989). These data indicate that the type and severity of these injuries are sport specific. That is, every sport tends to generate specific types of injuries unique to that sport. In this section, current statistical information will be presented on injuries in six popular interscholastic sports, beginning with tackle football.

Tackle Football

Tackle football (Figure 1.11) continues to be popular with approximately 1.5 million athletes participating at the high school level annually in the United States. Of these, about 36% can expect to be injured, based upon research by the National Athletic Trainers' Association (NATA, 1989). Recent research sponsored by the NATA suggests that the percentage of high school

level players injured annually may be increasing—the figure reported for 1995 was 39.70% (Foster T, 1996). Many of these injuries are directly attributable to the fact that participants obviously collide with one another as part of the game. However, recent research has found that the incidence of injury is variable, based on position played. The NATA study mentioned above reported that running backs had the highest overall injury rates and offensive linemen had the lowest. Sprains and strains are the most common injuries: 4% require surgery, the majority of which involve the knee (Goldberg, 1989). In a recent study of high school football in Texas, a similar pattern of injury was noted (DeLee and Farney, 1992). For example, out of their sample of 4,399 players, approximately 23% sustained sprains to the knee during the 1–year study period. The most recent data available (1995 season) indicate sprains and strains continue to be the most common

Information at your fingertips

The World Wide Web—You can find more information about the Consumer Product Safety Commission (CPSC). Go to http://www.jbpub.com/athletictraining and click on Chapter 1.

types of injuries to these young athletes and, further, 1.4% of all reported injuries in this group required surgery (Foster T, 1996).

Basketball

Nearly 1 million high school students, boys and girls, participated in basketball programs within the United States during the 1994–1995 school year. Research has found that basketball places the lower extremities at risk. Reported injury rates range from a low of 6% to a high of 31% annually of all school-aged participants. Ankle sprains are the most frequent injury, followed by knee and leg trauma. It has also been learned that female players (Figure 1.12) tend to suffer more knee injuries than do their male counterparts (Goldberg, 1989).

FIGURE 1.12 Basketball places the lower extremities of female players at particular risk. (Courtesy of Boise State University.)

Baseball

Baseball, softball, and teeball continue to be very popular, with approximately 6 million league participants between the ages of 5 and 14, and an additional 13 million young participants in "non-league" play (CPSC, 1996). According to a recent study by the Consumer Product Safety Commission (CPSC) of baseball injuries in the United States, 162,000 children were treated in hospital emergency rooms for baseball-related injuries in 1995. Of these, 33% were found to be severe injuries involving fractures, concussions, internal injuries, and dental injuries (CPSC, 1996). These injuries were caused by being hit by a ball or hit by a bat, and through collision, tripping, and sliding. The CPSC has made several recommendations regarding safety equipment, which it estimates could reduce the number of these injuries by 36%.

In addition, the CPSC studied the reports of 88 baseball-related fatalities that occurred between 1973 and 1995. It was determined that 68 deaths were related to ball impacts and 13 related to bat impacts. Of deaths caused by ball impacts, 38 were caused by blows to the chest and 21 by blows to the head (CPSC, 1996).

Another area of concern has involved the possibility of chronic injuries to the elbow related to adolescent pitchers throwing too many times per game. Research by Adams (1965) raised serious concerns about elbow injuries among little-league pitchers. This condition, dubbed **little-league elbow,** created a considerable amount of worry among parents in the late 1960s. In response to these widespread concerns, sports medicine researchers began to investigate the problem. Two large-scale studies found no relationship between pitching and elbow damage (Gugenheim et al., 1976; Larson et al., 1976). However, research conducted by Michlei and Fehlandt endeavored to identify what caused injuries to tendons and apophyses (bony attachments of tendons) in a population of 445 children aged 8 to 19. Their conclusion was that for boys, baseball was associated with the highest occurrence of injury. Further, softball was the fourth most commonly associated sport for injury in girls. Overall, they found that in their study group the most common injuries were to the elbow (Micheli and Fehlandt, 1992). It has also been reported that those pitching with a sidearm technique (Figure 1.13) are three times more likely to develop elbow problems than those who pitch using the more traditional overhand style (Stanitski, 1993).

FIGURE 1.13 The correct pitching technique can spare little-leaguers possible elbow damage.

FIGURE 1.14 In wrestling, takedown and escape maneuvers can result in injuries. (Courtesy of Boise State University.)

Wrestling

Wrestling has averaged approximately 245,000 participants at the high school level for the past 10 years (Mueller and Cantu, 1993). Its continued popularity is no doubt partly due to the fact that participants are matched by body weight. However, given the nature of the sport, collisions with opponents and mats do result in various injuries. In addition, joint injuries occur in takedown and escape maneuvers as well as holds (Figure 1.14) that are essential parts of the sport. Few studies on wrestling injuries are available; however, studies of high school wrestling have reported injury rates ranging from 23% to 75% per year (Goldberg, 1989; McGuine, 1989). Sprains and strains are the most common types of injuries, and they occur throughout the body. Interestingly, interscholastic wrestling is second only to tackle football when it comes to knee injuries requiring surgery (Requa and Garrick, 1981). Other injuries common to wrestling are **friction** burns to the skin, skin infections, and irritation of the outer ear (sometimes referred to as cauliflower ear). Mandatory head gear that provides ear protection, improvements in mat surfaces, and vigilant cleaning and maintenance of facilities have signifi-

cantly reduced the incidence of these problems. As wrestling incorporates specific weight categories, the sport has historically been plagued with problems associated with rapid and excessive weight loss by participants. This issue will be discussed further in Chapter 6.

Gymnastics

The sport of gymnastics continues to be extremely popular in the United States, particularly among girls (Figure 1.15). Currently, there are approximately 2 million children actively participating in schools and clubs within the United States (DiFiori et al., 1996). Although there are far fewer male than female gymnasts, there are slightly less than 6000 high school and over 700 collegiate level male participants within the U.S. (Samuelson, Reider, and Weiss, 1996). In the few studies that have been done, injury rates ranging from 12% to 22% annually have been reported in adolescent participants (Goldberg, 1989). Historically, the sport has a reputation for being dangerous due to the relatively high incidence of severe head and neck trauma among participants. Many of these injuries happened on the trampoline. In 1976 the trampoline was eliminated as an official event, leaving floor exercise, the balance beam, uneven parallel bars, and vaulting as women's events. The incidence of severe head

FIGURE 1.15 In gymnastics, tumbling routines place repetitive stress on the lumbar region of the spine.

FIGURE 1.16 The most common injuries among soccer players involve the knee, shin, and ankle.

and neck injuries dropped dramatically as a result of this change. The available data indicate that injuries to the lower extremities are the most common, with sprains and strains of associated tissues being the most frequent. Due to the nature of the sport, repetitive stress is placed on the lumbar region of the spine. Research has documented a significant increase in the number of lumbar spinal problems in female gymnasts when compared with nonathletes. McAuley et al. (1987) reported that the overall incidence of injuries to gymnasts seemed to increase with both skill level and amount of practice time. This finding is supported by a recent NCAA report indicating that, when compared with college-level wrestling, football, men's lacrosse, women's volleyball, baseball, and women's lacrosse, women's gymnastics produced the most injuries requiring surgery: it was second only to wrestling in injury rates per capita of participants (Duda, 1987).

Soccer

Soccer (Figure 1.16) has grown in popularity throughout the United States; there are over 12 million participants under the age of 18. Soccer ranks as the fourth-highest participation sport in the United States, behind basketball, volleyball, and softball (CPSC,

1995). According to the National Federation of State High School Associations, during the 1994–1995 school year, 272,810 boys and 191,350 girls participated in soccer programs at their respective high schools (NFSHSA, 1995). Although soccer does not involve intentional collisions between players, incidental collisions frequently occur. Protective equipment is limited, with most body areas being exposed to external trauma. Not surprisingly, contusions are the most common type of injury; however, the majority are minor. Injuries involving extremities are most common to the knee, ankle, and shin. The majority, however, are not severe. A unique aspect of the game involves the skill known as heading, in which a participant contacts a kicked ball with the head. Some medical experts have hypothesized that this practice may

WHAT IF?

A parent asks you for advice about which high school sport is the safest for his daughter. Based upon available data, what would you tell him?

lead to possible head injury. No reliable research has been conducted to date confirming this hypothesis (Smodlaka, 1984; Jordan et al. 1996).

In recent years, a number of deaths and severe injuries have been related to improperly constructed, movable soccer goals. For the period 1979 to 1994 at least 21 deaths were reported; an additional 120 nonfatal injuries occurred, directly related to movable goals (CPSC, 1996). The majority of these injuries and fatalities occurred when the goals tipped over and struck the victims. As a result, numerous soccer organizations—such as the Federation of Internationale De Football, the National Federation of State High School Associations, and the National Collegiate Athletic Association—have all established strict criteria for the construction of soccer goals. In addition, the CPSC has published guidelines for the design and construction of movable soccer goals. (Please refer to Appendix 7.)

Review Questions

1. Which popular sports were found, in one study, to be responsible for producing over half of all reported injuries?

2. What are the most commonly used criteria for defining a sports injury?

3. Describe briefly two major problems that arise regarding the most commonly used definitions of sports injury.

4. What are the three criteria necessary for an injury to be classified as such under the NCAA's Injury Surveillance System (ISS)?

5. Define and differentiate between acute and chronic forms of injury.

6. What constitutes a catastrophic sports injury?

7. What specific tissue types are involved in sprains and strains? How is the severity of these injuries defined?

8. What makes a stress fracture unique when compared with other types of fractures?

9. Define and differentiate between subluxation and luxation.

10. What is the science of epidemiology?

11. According to a recent NATA study, which player position in tackle football had the highest injury rate?

12. *True or false:* Offensive linemen in football were found to have the highest frequency of injury compared with all other positions, according to NATA.

13. What is the most frequent injury in basketball?

14. According to the Consumer Product Safety Commission, what percentage of reported baseball injuries was found to be severe?

15 What piece of equipment related to soccer has been found to play a direct role in the majority of deaths related to this sport?

References

Adams JE. 1965. Injury to the throwing arm: a study of traumatic changes in the elbow joint of boy baseball players. *California Med.* 102:127–132.

American Academy of Family Physicians. 1992. *Preparticipation Physical Evaluation* (1st ed.). Chicago: American Academy of Family Physicians.

American Academy of Orthopaedic Surgeons. 1991. *Athletic Training and Sports Medicine* (2d ed.). Park Ridge, Ill.: American Academy of Orthopaedic Surgeons.

American Academy of Pediatrics. 1988. Committee on Sports Medicine. Recommendations for participation in competitive sports. *Pediatr.* 81(5):737–739.

American Medical Association. 1968. *Standard Nomenclature of Athletic Injuries* (1st ed.). Chicago: American Medical Association.

Benson M. 1995. *1995–96 NCAA Sports Medicine Handbook* (8th ed.). Overland Park: The National Collegiate Athletic Association.

Booher JM, Thibodeau GA. 1989. *Athletic Injury Assessment.* St. Louis: Times Mirror/Mosby.

Collins RK. 1987. Injury patterns in women's intramural flag football. *Am J Sports Med.* 15(3):238–242.

Caine DJ, Caine CG, Lindner KJ (eds.). 1996. *Epidemiology of Sports Injuries.* Champaign: Human Kinetics.

Consumer Product Safety Commission (CPSC). 1996. CPSC releases study of protective equipment for baseball. *CPSC Document #96–140.*

Consumer Product Safety Commission (CPSC). 1995. Guidelines for movable soccer goal safety. *CPSC Document #4326.*

Curwain S, Stanish WD. 1984. *Tendinitis: Its Etiology and Treatment.* Lexington, Mass.: D. C. Heath and Company.

DeLee JC, Farney WC. 1992. Incidence of injury in Texas high-school football. *Am J Sports Med.* 20:575–580.

DiFiori JP, et al. 1996. Factors associated with wrist pain in the young gymnast. *Am J Sports Med.* 24:9–14.

Duda M. 1987. NCAA survey shows injury trends. *Phys Sportsmed.* 15:30.

Foster T. 1996. NATA releases results from high school injury study. *NATA News.* April.

Gainor BJ, et al. 1978. The kick: biomechanics and collision injury. *Am J Sports Med.* 6:185–193.

Gallagher S. 1984. The incidence of injuries among 87,000 Massachusetts children and adolescents: results of the 1980–81 statewide childhood injury prevention program surveillance system. *Am J Pub Health.* 74:1340–1346.

Goldberg B. 1989. Injury patterns in youth sports. *Phys Sportsmed.* 17:175–186.

Grollman LJ, Irrgang JJ, Dearwater SD. 1996. Statewide surveillance of interscholastic sports injury: PATS, Inc. Injury reporting system (PIRS). Poster presentation at the annual meeting of the National Athletic Trainers' Association, Orlando, Fla.

Gugenheim JJ, et al. 1976. Little-league survey: the Houston study. *Am J Sports Med.* 4:189–199.

Hess GP, et al. 1989. Prevention and treatment of overuse tendon injuries. *Sports Med.* 8:371–384.

Jordan SE, et al. 1996. Acute and chronic brain injury in United States national team soccer players. *Med Sci Sports and Exerc.* 24:205–210.

Larson RL, et al. 1976. Little-league survey: the Eugene study. *Am J Sports Med.* 4:201–209.

McAuley E, et al. 1987. Injuries in women's gymnastics—the state of the art. *Am J Sports Med.* 15:558–565.

McGuine T. 1989. Injury frequency during a one-day collegiate wrestling tournament. *Athletic Training.* 24:227–229.

Micheli LJ, Fehlandt AF. 1992. Overuse injuries to tendons and apophyses in children and adolescents. *Clin Sports Med.* 11:713–726.

Mueller FO, Cantu RC. 1990. Catastrophic injuries and fatalities in high-school and college sports, fall 1982–spring 1988. *Med Sci Sports and Exerc.* 22:737–741.

Mueller FO, Cantu RC. 1993. *National center for catastrophic sports injury research—tenth annual report—fall 1982–spring 1992.* Unpublished manuscript. Chapel Hill: University of North Carolina, Department of Physical Education.

National Athletic Trainers' Association. 1989. 3–year study finds "major injuries" up 20% in high-school football. *Athletic Training.* 24:60–69.

National Federation of State High School Associations. 1995. *1995 High School Athletics Participation Survey.* Kansas City: National Federation of State High School Associations.

National Safety Council. 1991. *First Aid and CPR* (1st ed.). Boston: Jones and Bartlett.

Nelson RA. 1989. Nutrition for the athlete. In Ryan AJ, Allman FL (eds.). *Sports Medicine.* San Diego: Academic Press. 165–182.

Nigg BM, Bobbert M. 1990. On the potential of various approaches in load analysis to reduce the frequency of sports injuries. *J Biomech.* 23:Suppl. 1, 3–12.

O'Donoghue DH. 1984. *Treatment of Injuries to Athletes.* Philadelphia: W. B. Saunders.

Pelletier RL, Anderson G, Stark RM. 1991. Profile of sport/leisure injuries treated at emergency rooms in urban hospitals. *Can J Sports Sci.* 16:99–102.

Requa R, Garrick JG. 1981. Injuries in interscholastic wrestling. *Phys Sportsmed.* 9:44–51.

Samuelson M, Reider B, Weiss D. 1996. Grip lock injuries to the forearm in male gymnasts. *Am J Sports Med.* 24:15–18.

Smodlaka V. 1984. Medical aspects of heading the ball in soccer. *Phys Sportsmed.* 12:127–131.

Stanitski CL. 1989. Common injuries in preadolescent and adolescent athletes—recommendations for prevention. *Sports Med.* 7:32–41.

Stanitski CL. 1993. Combating overuse injuries—a focus on children and adolescents. *Phys Sportsmed.* 21:87–106.

Torg JS. 1982. *Athletic Injuries to the Head, Neck and Face.* Philadelphia: Lea & Febiger.

Walter SD, et al. 1985. The aetiology of sport injuries—a review of methodologies. *Sports Med.* 2:47–58.

Zaricznyj B, et al. 1980. Sports-related injuries in school-aged children. *Am J Sports Med.* 8:318–322.

CHAPTER 2

The Sports Medicine Team

MAJOR CONCEPTS

The cornerstone of providing optimal care to those suffering sports injuries is the sports medicine team, which is made up of a variety of highly trained medical and allied medical personnel. This chapter provides an overview of the principal members of the team and reviews the evolution of the field of sports medicine. In addition, it describes specific services to be provided by the sports medicine team, giving special attention to the team physician and the NATABOC-certified athletic trainer. It also outlines educational requirements for NATABOC certification and employment options for athletic trainers.

As the name implies, the field of **sports medicine** is concerned with the medical aspects of sports participation. However, sports medicine is an umbrella term that today reaches beyond the traditional bounds of medicine as it relates to athletes. In fact, the practice of sports medicine is inclusive of professionals with diverse academic backgrounds and is not the exclusive domain of medical doctors. Nor is the study of sports medicine concerned only with injuries and diseases associated with competitive athletics.

According to Ryan (1989), the discipline of sports medicine is concerned with:

1. medical supervision of the athlete

2. special (adapted) physical education

3. therapeutic exercise

4. exercise aimed at the prevention of chronic and/or degenerative disease.

Although both special (adapted) physical education and preventative exercise are important, professionals directly involved with sports most frequently deal with medical supervision of the athlete and therapeutic exercise. Ideally, both include a variety of health services and personnel. At the professional level, today's athletes typically have access to a wide variety of sports medicine services. These include comprehensive preseason physical examinations; proper instruction on sports skills; supervision of conditioning programs; psychological assessments; nutrition education and dietary counseling; help with preventive taping, strapping, and bracing; acute injury care with medical referral; and injury rehabilitation. Sports medicine services at the interscholastic level are much more limited, but usually include some type of preseason physical examination. Additionally, an increasing number of high schools employ a certified athletic trainer, certified by the National Athletic Trainers' Association Board of Certification (NATABOC). In some instances, however, in the absence of an athletic trainer, athletic events may be supervised by a medical doctor or other health professional.

With few exceptions, the health care of professional and college athletes was traditionally the domain of the **orthopedic surgeon.** This was logical since many of the serious injuries involved bones and joints. However, with the increased popularity of sports across all age groups, and a subsequent rise in demand for services, many different medical specialists are now providing sports medicine services.

It is generally acknowledged that more sports medi-cine services in the future will be offered to the athletic community by primary care physicians, a group that includes family practitioners, internists, **pediatricians,** osteopaths (D.O.), and others. In fact, sports medicine fellowships lasting one to two years are now available to physicians; these can lead to an additional credential, the Certificate of Added Qualifications in Sports Medicine (CAQ). The CAQ is available to any primary care practitioner and is awarded upon successful completion of an examination as well as completion of either a sports medicine fellowship or five years of practice, 20% of which must have involved sports medicine (Rich, 1993).

The field of sports medicine has grown rapidly in the past two decades, and as a result many other professionals are now included on the sports medicine team. These include neurosurgeons, physical medicine practitioners, gynecologists, cardiologists, **podiatrists,** dermatologists, **chiropractors,** dentists, and nurses (Lawrence, 1983; Rich, 1993). Exercise physiologists, physical therapists, sports-massage specialists, sports psychologists, nutritionists, physical educators, and administrators may also be part of the modern sports medicine team.

Key Members of the Team

Although each member of the sports medicine team is important, two are essential: the team physician and the NATABOC-certified athletic trainer. **Team physicians** are medical doctors who agree to provide (either voluntarily or for pay) at least limited medical care to a particular sports program or institution. These services range in scope from a pediatrician who volunteers to be present for home football games at the local high school to the team orthopedic surgeon who is under contract with a professional football program.

According to Ball (1989), the team physician should provide the following services to the athletic program:

1. Participate in in-service training for nonmedical staff members.

2. Be aware of the qualifications and capabilities of staff members in dealing with injury problems.

3. Be familiar with the layout of the athletic facilities and the equipment available for handling injury emergencies.

4. Take part in the design of the emergency medical plan.

5. Serve as liaison with other members of the medical community, i.e., hospitals, emergency medical services, and specialists who may provide services to the athletes.

6. Implement an effective program for the administration of preparticipation physical examinations.

7. Design a record-keeping system for the purposes of monitoring injury histories, rehabilitation progress, and subsequent return-to-play decisions.

8. Attend any athletic event at which physician attendance is particularly important.

A qualified team physician has an understanding of sports injuries that most other doctors simply do not possess. Furthermore, a team physician generally knows the common risk factors regarding sports injuries, is familiar with the athletes, and should have a genuine interest in the welfare of each participant. These attributes are a great advantage to both coaches and athletes. Acquiring the services of a team physician may not be an easy task, especially in rural communities and in situations where little or no money is available. However, team physicians report that the major reason they become involved with sports is because of a strong personal interest (Rogers, 1985). Thus, it may be possible to obtain a team physician on a volunteer basis, at least for the purposes of providing medical care at athletic events. To expect more will, in all likelihood, require that some sort of contractual payment plan be arranged. Contacting your state medical association may provide information on how to locate interested physicians. Also, if a university is nearby, its team physician may be willing to provide services to your program as well. If not, he or she may know of other physicians in the area who would be willing to do so.

A variety of continuing education programs are currently available to team physicians through workshops, seminars, and postgraduate courses offered by hospitals, medical schools, and professional groups.

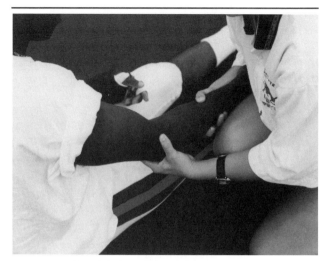

FIGURE 2.1 An athletic trainer evaluates an acute elbow injury.

In addition, numerous medical organizations exist that promote the study of sports medicine through membership. Some of these include the American Medical Society for Sports Medicine, the American Orthopedic Society for Sports Medicine, the American College of Sports Medicine, the American Osteopathic Academy of Sports Medicine, and the Canadian Academy of Sports Medicine (Rich, 1993).

Perhaps the best way to provide comprehensive medical care for athletes (during both practice and games) is to hire a NATABOC-certified athletic trainer who works in conjunction with the team physician. Athletic trainers are recognized allied health-care professionals who complete a bachelor's degree with extensive academic and clinical training in the broad area of care and prevention of sports injuries. Including a NATABOC-certified athletic trainer on the high school staff can greatly enhance the overall quality of sports medicine services (Figure 2.1). The practice of athletic training includes all of the following areas of expertise (Heavner, 1995):

Information at your fingertips

The World Wide Web—You can find more information about the American College of Sports Medicine (ACSM). Go to http://www.jbpub.com/athletictraining and click on Chapter 2.

1. Prevention of athletic injuries

2. Recognition, evaluation, and immediate care of athletic injuries

3. Rehabilitation and reconditioning of athletic injuries

4. Health care administration

5. Professional development and responsibility

The National Athletic Trainers' Association (NATA) is the national governing body for athletic training in the United States. Becoming a NATABOC-certified athletic trainer requires qualifying to sit for, and passing, the NATABOC examination, which is offered five times per year at various sites around the United States. In order to qualify to sit for the examination, one must have completed an undergraduate educational program accredited by the Joint Review Committee–Athletic Training (JRC-AT) or through an Internship, which is recognized by the NATABOC as adequate for the entry-level preparation of an athletic trainer. It should be noted that an educational task force (ETF) was established by the NATA in 1995 to examine the educational needs for the future of professional education in athletic training. The ETF concluded that several significant changes in the educational preparation are needed. Perhaps one of the more controversial recommendations of the ETF was to eliminate internships as a means to NATABOC certification, effective in the year 2004. In December of 1996, the NATA board of directors approved all 18 ETF recommendations. Beginning in 2004, only graduates from JRC-AT accredited programs will be eligible for the NATABOC examination.

educational program.) The purpose of the clinical training is to prepare students in the psychomotor skills necessary to function as athletic trainers. JRC-AT accredited curriculums must include formal instruction in the following areas:

1. Prevention of athletic injuries/illnesses

2. Evaluation of athletic injuries/illnesses

3. First aid and emergency care

4. Therapeutic modalities

5. Therapeutic exercise

6. Administration of athletic training programs

7. Human anatomy

8. Human physiology

9. Exercise physiology

10. Kinesiology/biomechanics

11. Nutrition

12. Psychology

13. Personal/community health

The formal class instruction, as well as the 800 hours of clinical instruction, must provide the student with the appropriate information to master 191 specific education competencies as designated by the JRC-AT. These competencies are derived from the three educational domains—cognitive, affective, and psychomotor—and consist of the specific knowledge and skills required of the entry-level athletic trainer.

The internship route to NATABOC certification requires a bachelor's degree with less specific course work, but a minimum of 1,500 hours of clinical educa-

Information at your fingertips

The World Wide Web—You can find more information about the NATA. Go to http://www.jbpub.com/athletictraining and click on Chapter 2.

The JRC-AT accredited undergraduate curriculum offers specific courses designed to prepare students in essential cognitive, affective, and psychomotor domains. In addition, students are also required to complete a minimum of 800 hours of clinical education, 400 of which must be in traditional athletic training settings. (These are generally the athletic training rooms at the academic institution that sponsors the

tion. The internship route requires at least one formal course in each of the following areas:

1. Health (i.e., nutrition, drugs/substance abuse, health education, pathology, personal health)

2. Human anatomy

3. Kinesiology/biomechanics

4. Human physiology

5. Physiology of exercise

6. Basic athletic training

7. Advanced athletic training

Once the requirements for the bachelor's degree are completed and the student graduates from either the JRC-AT accredited program or from an institution sponsoring an internship in athletic training education, the student may apply to the NATABOC to sit for the certification examination. In order to become a NATABOC-certified athletic trainer the candidate must successfully pass a rigorous, three-part (written, written-simulation, oral-practical) refereed examination in order to become NATABOC certified. To remain certified an athletic trainer is required to earn continuing education credits (CEUs) by attending and participating in professional meetings, writing articles for journals, making presentations, and enrolling in college classes that pertain to sports medicine.

Recently, the profession of athletic training received recognition as an allied health profession by the American Medical Association (AMA), and accreditation of educational programs in athletic training is now supervised by the Commission on Accreditation of Allied Health Education Programs (CAAHEP). NATA oversees all professional educational programs through JRC-AT and makes recommendations regarding program accreditation to CAAHEP. These recent changes represent significant steps forward in the evolution of athletic training as an allied health profession in the United States.

NATABOC-certified athletic trainers signify a marked improvement in the health care services provided to athletes, regardless of the level. This is partly due to the fact that even under the best of circumstances team physicians are typically available to athletes on only a part-time basis. The NATABOC-certified athletic trainer can provide a direct link between the injured athlete and the appropriate medical services. In this way, the coach is relieved of much of the responsibility of providing care for injured participants.

FIGURE 2.2 Since 1980 there has been a 300% increase in the number of sports medicine centers in the United States.

Sports Medicine Delivery

Professional and Recreational Levels

At the professional and university levels, it could be said that today's athletes enjoy a somewhat pampered lifestyle. If they become depressed they can consult the team psychologist; if they wish to gain or lose weight, they can meet with the team nutritionist; questions regarding weight training can be directed to the conditioning coach. In short, at the upper levels of competitive athletics, sports medicine services are highly sophisticated.

Likewise, access to sports medicine services has been made easier for the recreational athlete as well. With the increased emphasis on fitness in the United States, there has been a significant increase in the number of adults participating in recreational sports, both at home and at work. It has recently been reported

WHAT IF?

A high school senior asks you for information on the academic requirements and certification process to be an athletic trainer.

that over 50% of adult Americans take part in some form of regular exercise. In an attempt to take advantage of this developing market, many physicians have established practices in sports medicine. Since 1980, there has been a 300% increase in the number of registered sports medicine centers in the United States (Figure 2.2). A broad range of services is provided by these centers, including fitness evaluation and exercise prescription, lifestyle counseling, evaluation and treatment of injuries, and even sports medicine research (Weidner, 1988).

Interscholastic Level

Sports medicine services at the interscholastic sports level, although slowly improving, remain woefully inadequate. Hossler (1985) reported that in the majority of cases less than half of all high schools have contracts with physicians to provide services for athletic events. The situation is worse during practice sessions, when athletes spend most of their playing time without a physician in attendance. Most schools reported that most first aid for injuries was provided by the coaching staff. This is a particularly sobering finding in light of recent research, which determined that the majority of coaches are poorly trained with respect to care and prevention of sports injuries (Rowe and Robertson, 1986). Powell (1987) reported that less than 10% of U.S. high schools offering interscholastic football retain the services of a certified athletic trainer. This produces a ratio of one trainer for every 5,500 student athletes in secondary schools. In contrast, virtually any professional or college player has direct access to such services (Stopka and Kaiser, 1988).

■ How to Improve the Situation

"Why doesn't your school employ an athletic trainer?" When asked this question, most administrators respond that they cannot afford to hire such a person. This argument is no longer as valid as it once may have been. Today, schools have a variety of options available to them if they want to hire a NATABOC-certified athletic trainer (Stopka and Kaiser, 1988). The most cost-effective approach appears to be employing one individual as both teacher and athletic trainer. This person is typically hired as a teacher and in addition provides athletic training after school. Ideally, classroom loads can be adjusted in order to give the teacher/athletic trainer time in the afternoons or mornings to see athletes before practice. This allows an opportunity for rehabilitation, evaluation of injury recovery,

counseling, and any other tasks that cannot be effectively completed otherwise. Administrators find this option to be very affordable since the teacher/athletic trainer can be given a standard teaching contract and can provide educational services to the general student population. Additional monetary stipends, often similar to those given a head coach within the same school or district, are sometimes negotiated in order to pay for the athletic training services provided. A recent study found that the national average annual salary for high school athletic trainers was $31,730 (Rankin, 1992).

A less affordable but more effective option is for the school to hire a full-time athletic trainer. This individual has no formal teaching responsibilities at the school, but is responsible for implementing a comprehensive sports medicine program. This can include follow-up care and rehabilitation of injured athletes during the morning hours prior to practice (during study hall, for example). In addition, the full-time athletic trainer may be able to arrange a schedule so that it more closely approximates the normal number of hours per week provided by other personnel at the school. Though this option often results in the best health care for student athletes, school districts are generally reluctant to commit to the initial financial outlay necessary to develop such a position. Given the financial realities of many school districts around the country, this option may not see significant growth in the foreseeable future.

Other options are available to schools; however, they all offer fewer services to both the school and the student athletes. Some alternatives include hiring a part-time athletic trainer or a graduate student/athletic trainer if a university is located nearby, contracting for services with a local sports medicine clinic, or using a substitute teacher/athletic trainer. Though all of these alternatives will save the school money, they obviously shortchange student athletes with respect to the availability of sports medicine services.

Having a NATABOC-certified athletic trainer on staff provides many indirect benefits to the school. From a legal standpoint, it will be less vulnerable to tort claims related to sports injuries. This is because such claims are often based on the premise that the school failed to provide adequate medical care to the athletes. Moreover, by hiring a NATABOC-certified athletic trainer, the school has demonstrated a commitment to providing the best possible care for student athletes (Stopka and Kaiser, 1988). A qualified athletic trainer also offers many unique educational opportunities for the school. For example, such a professional can teach classes in basic sports injury care, first aid and CPR,

Athletic Trainers Speak Out

"Athletic training has been a very rewarding career for me, despite the lack of an abundance of ethnic minority peer support. As our country becomes increasingly multicultural, it is disheartening to note that there is a noticeable absence of ethnic minorities in athletic training. Recent demographic data from the National Athletic Trainers' Association indicates a membership that is predominantly Caucasian with total ethnic minority membership at around 7%. The African American NATA membership totals less than 1% (77 females and 132 males). Based on these statistics alone, there is clearly a need within both the association, and the profession in general, to recruit and produce more ethnic minority athletic trainers.

Perhaps, there are many sociological reasons for the lack of multicultural diversity in athletic training. A primary reason is that the NATA at its conception was a predominantly Caucasian male organization, although, historically, many of the pioneers providing care to athletes were ethnic minorities. In addition, the under-representation of ethnic minority athletic trainers may be a reflection of the world of athletics at large. Beginning in 1990, the National Collegiate Athletic Association conducted a four-year study focusing on the race demographics of member institutions. It was determined that in 1992–1993, 25.6% of all Division I athletes were African American. However, in regard to revenue sports, the percentage of African American athletes escalates to 49.4%. This same study shows that in regard to administrators from all divisions, less than 9% are of African American descent. The broad description of administrators in-

Veronica Ampey

cluded 19 different positions, including athletic directors, equipment managers, coaches, and athletic trainers.

Hopefully, through the commitment of influential individuals, and the introduction of programs by both the NCAA and the NATA, ethnic minority representation at the administrative level will rise and we will begin to see a more ethnically diverse population of athletic trainers."

—Veronica Ampey, M.S., A.T.C.

Veronica Ampey is the Assistant Director for Sports Medicine at Emory University.

nutrition, and physical conditioning. The athletic trainer can also implement a student athletic trainer program at the school in order to provide educational opportunities for high school students interested in a career in sports medicine. High school student athletic trainers wishing to continue their education at the university level may qualify for scholarships or other types of financial aid. Such funds are typically made available through the sports-medicine program at the sponsoring institutions. Finally, the athletic trainer can provide in-service training on various aspects of sports-injury management for the coaching staff. Obviously, the school can realize many returns on its investment when hiring a NATABOC-certified athletic trainer.

Once the decision is made to hire a certified athletic trainer, potential applicants can be located by contacting the NATA national office in Dallas, Texas, at (214) 637–6282. Employers can also contact a professional placement service, such as the Athletic Training Registry in Mt. Pleasant, Michigan. Another option is to contact universities that offer either NATABOC-approved curriculums or internship routes in athletic training for a listing of their recent graduates. A listing of all universities with NATA-approved curriculums is available by contacting the NATA national office.

Review Questions

1. List the major components of the general discipline of sports medicine. Which of these is most pertinent to organized sports today?

2. What kinds of services are available to the professional athlete?

3. List the specific services that should be provided to the athlete by the team physician.

4. What are the six areas that comprise the role of the NATABOC-certified athletic trainer?

5. What are the two types of academic programs currently available that lead to NATABOC certification as an athletic trainer?

6. At present, what percentage of U.S. high schools employ an athletic trainer?

7. Briefly describe seven different employment options for a NATABOC-certified athletic trainer in the school setting. Elaborate on the advantages and disadvantages of each option.

8. *True or false:* JRC-AT accredited curriculums in athletic training require a minimum of 1,500 clinical hours for graduation.

9. *True or false:* According to this chapter, over 50% of adult Americans participate in some form of regular exercise.

10. *True or false:* It is generally acknowledged that sports medicine services in the future will be provided by medical specialists rather than primary care physicians.

11. List the 13 specific areas that are required by the JRC-AT for accredited curriculums in athletic training.

References

Ball RT. 1989. Legal responsibilities and problems. In Ryan AJ, Allman FL (eds.). *Sports Medicine.* San Diego: Academic Press. 447–489.

Heavner S (ed.). 1995. The National Athletic Trainers Association Board of Certification, Inc.—Role Delineation Study. Raleigh: F.A. Davis. 17.

Hossler P. 1985. How to acquire an athletic trainer on the high-school level. *Athletic Training.* 20(3): 199–228.

Lawrence RM. 1983. Foreword. In Appenzeller O, Atkinson R (eds.). *Sports Medicine: Fitness, Training,* *Injuries.* Baltimore: Urban & Schwarzenberg. xiii–xiv.

National Athletic Trainers' Association. 1992. *Competencies in Athletic Training.* Dallas: NATA-PEC.

Powell J. 1987. 636,000 injuries annually in high-school football. *Athletic Training.* 22(1):19–22.

Rankin JM. 1992. Financial resources for conducting athletic training programs in the collegiate and high-school settings. *Journal of Athletic Training.* 27(4):344–349.

Rich BSE. 1993. "All physicians are not created equal":

understanding the educational background of the sports-medicine physician. *Journal of Athletic Training.* 28(2):177–179.

Rogers CC. 1985. Does sports medicine fit in the new health-care market? *Phys Sportsmed.* 13(1): 116–127.

Rowe PJ, Robertson DM. 1986. Knowledge of care and prevention of athletic injuries in high schools. *Athletic Training.* 21(2):116–119.

Ryan AJ. 1989. Sports medicine in the world today. In Ryan AJ, Allman FL (eds.). *Sports Medicine.* San Diego: Academic Press. 3–20.

Ryan AJ, Allman FL (eds.). 1989. *Sports Medicine.* San Diego: Academic Press.

Stopka C, Kaiser D. 1988. Certified athletic trainers in our secondary schools: the need and solution. *Athletic Training.* 23(4):322–324.

Weidner TG. 1988. Sports-medicine centers: aspects of their operation and approaches to sports-medicine care. *Athletic Training.* 23(1):22–26.

CHAPTER 3

The Law of Sports Injury

M A J O R   C O N C E P T S

As with medicine in general, the field of sports medicine has witnessed a dramatic increase in the amount of litigation related to sports injuries over the last decade. This chapter introduces the reader to legal terminology and outlines what constitutes the coach's duty when working with athletes. It provides a listing of the major forms of coaching liability along with information on how to reduce the risk of litigation. It also presents appropriate steps to take in the event of a lawsuit and concludes with a discussion on the ethics of sports injury care.

The coach is often the first on the scene when a sports injury occurs. The coach's decisions and actions at the time of the injury are critical to the welfare of the athlete (Figure 3.1). Moreover, inappropriate decisions and actions may jeopardize the injured participant and lead to legal action by the athlete and/or parents or legal guardians (in the case of minors). A recent study of 104 high school athletic coaches found a significant percentage lacked adequate first aid knowledge in accordance with nationally recognized guidelines. Perhaps even more alarming was the finding that when a close game was at stake a significant percentage of the coaches reported a conflict of interest when a starting player was injured (Dunn and Ransone, 1996). Perhaps at no other time in the history of sports has the potential for legal action against coaching personnel been as great as it is today.

There are several reasons for this increase in the number of lawsuits. They include an increase in the number of participants; greater visibility of sports through the media; rising expectations regarding legal negligence; improved accessibility of legal services; more acceptance by the courts of comparative negligence settlements; and greater consumer awareness about sports services and products (Baley and Matthews, 1989).

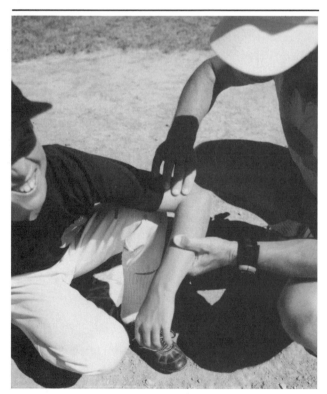

FIGURE 3.1 A coach evaluates an injured athlete.

■ The Concept of Tort

A **tort** is harm, other than a breach of contract, done to another for which the law holds the wrongdoer responsible (Ray, 1994; Schubert, Smith, and Trentadue, 1986). In the context of sports, an injured athlete may argue that an injury resulted from someone else's behavior—that of an opponent, an official, or a coach—or the lack of such behavior. Tort cases involving sports-related injuries generally seek to recover money to compensate the athlete for damages resulting from someone's alleged negligence. Essential to proving a tort is establishing that someone, other than the athlete, acted in a negligent manner, which resulted in an injury. **Negligence** is a type of tort and is defined as the failure to do what a reasonably careful and prudent person would have done under the same or like circumstances, or, conversely, doing something that a reasonably careful and prudent person would not have done under the same or like circumstances (Baley and Matthews, 1989; Ray, 1994). Negligence involves either an act of **commission** (acting in an improper way) or an act of **omission** (failure to act). A typical scenario is the high school football player (plaintiff) who claims that permanent **quadriplegia** resulted from improper first aid rendered by the coach (defendant) at the time he sustained a neck injury during a game. In such a case, the athlete might claim the coach's actions caused additional spinal damage that would not have occurred if proper first aid had been rendered. In this case, the athlete would argue that the coach's actions constituted negligence. The defendant would then be judged, in part, on the basis of what a similarly trained person would have done in the same situation.

In school sports cases, tort claims often name as many defendants as possible. For example, in the scenario above, the list of defendants might include the coach, an official(s), the athletic director, the school district, and perhaps even the state high school athletic association. Tort claims generally ask for monetary rewards; therefore, it is only logical that defendants would be selected, in part, based upon their ability to pay such awards. This is commonly referred to as "going for the deepest pocket."

Appenzeller (1978) identifies four elements that must be present in order to prove negligence. They are listed in Box 3.1.

According to Appenzeller (1978), proving the absence of one or more of the four elements in Box 3.1 is the best method of defense in a negligence suit. Other ways of defeating a negligence suit involve showing proof of one of the following legal doctrines:

BOX 3.1   Four Elements of Negligence

1. **Duty:** an obligation recognized by the law requiring a person to conform to a certain standard of conduct for the protection of others against unreasonable risks.
2. **Breach of duty:** a failure to conform to the standard required.
3. **Proximate or legal cause:** a reasonably close causal connection between the conduct and the resulting injury.
4. **Damage:** actual loss resulting to the interests of another.

- **Contributory negligence.** The plaintiff is found to be responsible for the injury, in part or totally.

- **Comparative negligence.** This allows for the plaintiff to receive partial compensation on a prorated basis, dependent upon a judgment regarding the extent of contributory negligence. In other words, if a monetary reward is given, it will be based only on the percentage of negligence assigned to the defendant.

What Is Your Liability?

Anyone serving in a coaching capacity, whether voluntarily or paid, bears considerable responsibility for the health and safety of athletes. Historically, a coach employed by government institutions such as school districts or universities has enjoyed a certain degree of immunity from tort litigation under the doctrine of sovereign immunity. This in essence protects government institutions and their personnel from liability claims. However, some states have determined through legislative action that tort litigation against such agencies may be possible, depending upon the specific circumstances. Consequently, more injury liability cases are now being contested successfully against coaching personnel. Therefore, it appears that protection under the doctrine of sovereign immunity is no longer guaranteed (Berry, 1986). The coach must always use reasonable care to avoid creating a foreseeable risk of harm to others (Schubert, Smith, and Trentadue, 1986). Whether on staff or volunteer, a coach should have some sort of written contract outlining specific duties (Graham, 1985). Such a document pro-

Information at your fingertips

The World Wide Web—For a listing of additional resources on the topic of sports law, go to http://www.jbpub.com/athletictraining and click on Chapter 3.

- **Assumption of risk.** This means that the plaintiff assumes responsibility for injury. In other words, the plaintiff agrees to participate in the sport knowing that there is a chance of suffering an injury. For this defense to work it is essential that the athlete (plaintiff) be fully informed of the potential dangers related to participation. Failure to warn the athlete of such dangers has been found to constitute negligence (Graham, 1985).

- **Act of God (act of nature).** This concedes that the injury occurred as a result of factors beyond the control of the defendant. Being injured or killed by an earthquake that occurs during a cross-country running event would, in all probability, be considered an act of God.

vides a level of protection from litigation as long as the coach functions within the context of the contract. Schubert, Smith, and Trentadue (1986) outline seven potential actions for which a coach may be found negligent. These are explained in Box 3.2.

Are You Protected?

The best protection a coach can have against the risk of litigation is to avoid the problems listed in Box 3.2. Today's coach must be constantly aware of potential risks to athletes and must take appropriate action to reduce or eliminate those risks.

Athletic Trainers Speak Out

"The coach is still the primary provider of health care to the majority of student athletes in secondary schools. Because of this charge that coaches have been given, it is imperative that they stay abreast of current coaching and athletic-training techniques, ideas, training regimes, and injury-prevention skills. This will not only help coaches provide safe and efficient care, but also help reduce the possibility of putting themselves in a potentially litigious situation."

—Barrie Steele, M.S., A.T.C./R

Barrie Steele is the head athletic trainer for the athletic department at the University of Idaho.

Barrie Steele

Since most tort claims seek monetary rewards, it is obvious that a coach's personal assets may be in jeopardy in the event of an unfavorable court decision. Therefore, it is imperative that the coach be protected by some form of liability insurance. A coach in an interscholastic or intercollegiate setting is generally covered by insurance provided by the employer. However, it is wise to ascertain the specific type of coverage provided. Don't assume you are protected. A volunteer coach may not have any liability coverage, in which case the purchase of personal liability insurance is advisable.

A good rule of thumb is never to assume that you are covered. Before beginning the playing season, contact your employer, sponsoring organization, or an insurance company representative to determine what type of coverage you have and whether it offers the best protection.

BOX 3.2 Potentially Negligent Actions by Coaches

- **Failure to provide competent personnel.** When a head coach hires an assistant, he or she assumes some responsibility for the competence, or lack thereof, of that assistant. If the assistant coach fails to give proper instruction to the athlete, the head coach could be found to be negligent.

- **Failure to provide instruction.** This involves providing proper instruction on the fundamental and advanced skills required for participation, as well as those for injury prevention. The coach must make sure that the participants receive adequate conditioning exercises and use the appropriate protective equipment. The coach must also instruct athletes on the rules and regulations regarding participation.

- **Failure to provide proper equipment.** As the coach may be responsible for the selection and purchase of protective equipment, he or she must make sure that any such equipment does not place an athlete in jeopardy. The coach may also be held responsible for failure to maintain and/or replace damaged equipment.

- **Failure to warn.** The coach has the obligation to warn participants of any dangers that may not be obvious. It may be advisable, in light of recent cases, to warn athletes *in writing*, even of dangers that appear obvious (Graham, 1985). When dealing with minors, any written warning should be given to the parent(s) or guardian.

- **Failure to supervise.** The coach is required to supervise activities to an extent that is determined, in part, by the age, skill, and experience of the participants. Thus, inexperienced children involved in a high-risk sport such as football require a higher level of supervision than do senior varsity athletes in the same sport. Anytime children are involved, regardless of the activity, the coach is responsible for providing supervision.

- **Moving or improperly treating an injured athlete.** The coach is required to provide medical care to an injured athlete. Given this mandate, the prudent coach should have basic training in proper first aid procedures for common athletic injuries. Coaches have been found liable for failing to provide appropriate first aid as well as for having applied inappropriate procedures. It is also critical that a coach remove a child from participation if there is any question about immediate health status.

- **Selecting participants.** The coach is responsible for ensuring that an athlete is ready to play—i.e., the athlete possesses an adequate level of physical fitness, or if recently injured, is ready to resume participation. In most cases, examination by a medical doctor should be required before an athlete is allowed to resume participation after an injury.

Source: Schubert GW, Smith RK, Trentadue JC. 1986. *Sports Law*. St. Paul: West Publishing Company. Reprinted with permission.

How to Reduce Your Chances of Going to Court

The following is a list of nine important preventative steps a coach can implement in order to reduce the chances of being sued:

1. **Written contract.** This document should state in detail the expectations and limitations of your service as a coach. (It is advisable to have an attorney examine any contract to determine what liabilities may be included.)

2. **Certification in basic or advanced first aid and CPR.** Make sure your certification is current and that you periodically practice your skills. Such training is available through the National Safety Council.

3. **Emergency plan.** It is essential that a formal emergency plan be developed for both home and out-of-town contests. These plans should be in written form; all parties involved with their implementation should have copies. Furthermore, any emergency scheme should be periodically rehearsed in order to ensure that it will function effectively during a real crisis. It is advised that the plan be examined by an attorney to ensure that it meets all legal requirements (Baley and Matthews, 1989).

4. **Parental consent form** (for athletes under 18 years of age). These forms provide an excellent opportunity to inform both the athlete and parents/guardians regarding the potential for injury inherent in participation.

5. **Comprehensive preparticipation physical examination.** Such an examination must be a requirement of all participants. This exam should be administered by a medical doctor, and all pertinent information should be recorded on an appropriate form. Athletes should not be allowed to participate in sports activities until they have undergone the physical. Most school districts and colleges and universities have standard forms for these physical exams. Information collected should be on file with the athletic administrator and handled confidentially.

   New comprehensive guidelines for the preparticipation physical evaluation (PPE) have recently been published by a consortium of medical groups, including the American Academy of Family Physicians, the American Academy of Pediatrics, the American Medical Society for Sports Medicine, the American Orthopaedic Society for Sports Medicine, and the American Osteopathic Academy of Sports Medicine. A complete document, *Preparticipation Physical Evaluation,* can be purchased by phoning the American Academy of Family Physicians at (800) 944–0000. Physicians who administer PPEs should consider following these new guidelines; doing so is likely to be interpreted by the courts as exercising reasonable care towards athletes under their care. A detailed description of a PPE is given in Chapter 4. A sample format of the exam is presented in Appendix 3.

6. **Document all injuries.** Regardless of severity, a detailed description of the initial care and treatment—as well as the cause(s)—of all injuries must be recorded on a standard form. The coach should make sure that all pertinent information regarding an injury is collected and placed on file with the athletic administrator. It is advisable that a history of injuries be maintained on all athletes. In this way, coaching and medical personnel will be aware of all recent injuries a given athlete may have sustained.

7. **Attendance at in-service seminars and/or postgraduate classes.** Owing in large part to the increased concern regarding sports injury litigation, most school districts conduct periodic in-service training on the topic of the care and prevention of athletic injuries. Many times such seminars are offered by the school district, local hospitals, or a regional university. In addition, coaches are often encouraged by school administrators to enroll in postgraduate classes pertaining to the care and prevention of sports injuries. Attendance at such seminars demonstrates a willingness on the part of coaching personnel to remain informed regarding current standards of care and prevention of sports injury.

8. **Periodic inspections of facilities and/or equipment.** Such inspections must be conducted in order to ensure that any potential hazards are corrected. In addition, it is advisable to notify the athletic administrator, in writing, of any hazards that remain uncorrected.

9. **Develop and maintain effective lines of communication.** Communication with athletes, parents, athletic administrators, and medical personnel is essential to providing safe activity for sports participants.

What to Do If You Get Sued

If you are about to be sued in a tort case, it is critical that you take the appropriate steps to protect yourself. It is recommended that you first call your insurance company and contact your lawyer (Appenzeller and Appenzeller, 1980). In this way, you will be given proper advice on how to protect yourself. Furthermore, all pertinent facts related to the case can be recorded while events are still recent.

It is important to write a detailed description of all events leading up to and immediately following the injury. This should include signed statements by eyewitnesses if possible.

It is also advised that you not make statements to the media, or to other parties, without the advice of your attorney (Appenzeller and Appenzeller, 1980). In this way you will avoid compromising your position during a subsequent trial or appeal.

Ethics of Sports Injury Care

The athlete's health and safety should be the ultimate priority for all those involved in organized sports. However, society's values have changed significantly since the days of the Olympian games held in ancient Greece. More and more, sports are now seen as a business, with an increasing emphasis on winning and earning monetary rewards. Very often, a coach's livelihood and career depend upon a win-loss record. In addition, athletes (and often parents) bring pressure to ensure an opportunity to play.

More than ever before, the coach must resist the temptation to circumvent the recommendations of

WHAT IF?

You are asked to take a part-time position coaching girls' volleyball at a local junior high school. What specific steps can you take to protect yourself from a potential lawsuit if an injury occurs to one of your athletes?

medical personnel when returning an injured athlete to participation. Under no circumstance should an athlete be allowed to resume sports without the consent of a medical doctor. Remember: unethical behavior by a coach will in all probability be considered as negligence by a court of law.

Review Questions

1. Define the terms tort and negligence as discussed in the text.

2. Briefly describe the two types of negligence—commission and omission—mentioned in the chapter.

3. What are the four elements that must be present in order to prove negligence?

4. Describe briefly the five ways that a negligence suit may be defeated.

5. Does liability differ for a paid coach versus a volunteer?

6. List and describe the reasons a coach may be found negligent.

7. Outline the nine steps that can reduce a coach's chances of being sued.

8. What are the first two things a coach should do when notified of an impending law suit?

9. Elaborate on the sociologic pressures exerted on today's coach that may challenge one's sense of professional ethics.

10. *True or false:* The courts have found that a coach is responsible for giving instruction to athletes regarding the rules and regulations of participation in sports.

11. *True or false:* The first thing to do if you are sued is to phone your insurance company and your lawyer.

References

Appenzeller H. 1978. *Physical Education and the Law.* Charlottesville: The Michie Company.

Appenzeller H, Appenzeller T. 1980. *Sports and the Courts.* Charlottesville: The Michie Company.

Baley JA, Matthews DL. 1989. *Law and Liability in Athletics, Physical Education, and Recreation.* Dubuque: William C. Brown.

Berry RC. 1986. *Law and Business of the Sports Industries. Vol II: Common Issues in Amateur and Professional Sports.* Dover, Mass.: Auburn House.

Dunn LR, Ransone JW. 1996. Assessment of first aid knowledge and decision-making of high school coaches. Poster presentation at the annual meeting of the National Athletic Trainers' Association, Orlando, Fla.

Graham LS. 1985. Ten ways to dodge the malpractice bullet. *Athletic Training.* 20(2):117–119.

Ray R. 1994. *Management Strategies in Athletic Training.* Champaign: Human Kinetics.

Schubert GW, Smith RK, Trentadue JC. 1986. *Sports Law.* St. Paul: West Publishing Company.

CHAPTER 4

Sports Injury Prevention

MAJOR CONCEPTS

Prevention of sports injuries must be a priority for everyone involved in athletics, particularly coaches, officials, administrators, and sports medicine personnel. This chapter describes the critical steps that must be taken in order to reduce the likelihood of injury. First, it differentiates between two major categories of injury risk factors—intrinsic (age, gender, skill) and extrinsic (equipment, environment, sport). It then distinguishes between two essential prevention strategies: preparticipation physical evaluation (PPE) and physical conditioning with an emphasis on periodization of the training year. Finally, it concludes with a description of the major factors to be considered in order to modify the common extrinsic risk factors related to sports injuries.

Previous chapters have discussed the scope of the sports injury problem, sports medicine personnel involved in treating injuries, and the legal implications of injuries. Obviously, it would be in everyone's best interest to reduce the number of injuries through a well-planned, coordinated program of injury prevention. However, before such an endeavor can be effective, causative factors must be identified that contribute to injuries. In this way, all parties involved—coaches, officials, and athletes—can take steps to eliminate or at least reduce the risk of injury. At first, this may seem to be a simple process with regard to common sports injuries. For example, when a football running back collides with a linebacker and sustains a sprained knee ligament, the cause of the injury would seem to be the force of the collision (Figure 4.1). However, other factors may have played a role in creating the injury. The player's skill, age, hamstring/quadriceps strength ratio, shoe type, playing surface (natural turf or artificial), fatigue, and previous injuries may all have contributed.

Causative Factors in Injury

Sports scientists have collected considerable information regarding injuries, and some have conducted research to identify causative factors. Two general categories have been proposed: extrinsic factors and intrinsic factors. Extrinsic factors include equipment, environment, type of activity, and conditioning errors. Intrinsic factors include age, gender, body size, history of injury, fitness, muscle strength (especially imbalances), ligamentous laxity, skill, psychological status, and perhaps even overall intelligence (Taimela, Kujala, and Osterman, 1990). Moskwa and Nicholas (1989) have developed a list of common risk factors for musculoskeletal injuries based on anatomical region. They identified common intrinsic and extrinsic risk factors for injuries to the cervical spine, upper extremity, lumbar spine, and lower extremity. (See Table 4.1.)

It is clear that not all of these factors can be eliminated or changed. However, it is certainly possible to

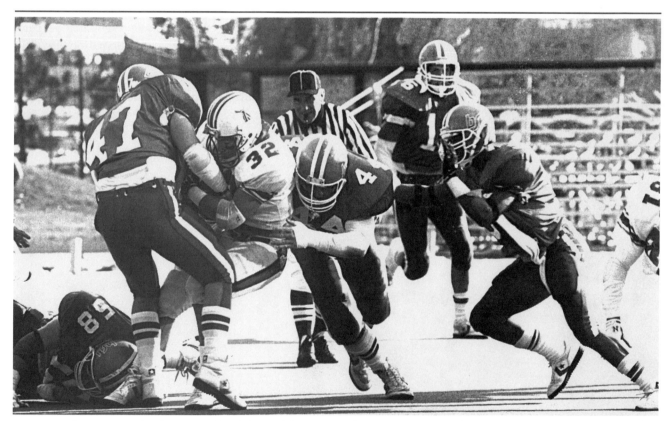

FIGURE 4.1 In some sports, the cause of an injury might seem obvious, but other factors may contribute. (Courtesy of Boise State University.)

TABLE 4.1 Musculoskeletal Injuries and Related Risk Factors

	Injury/Symptom	Risk Factor
CERVICAL	Cervical spine	Long thin neck
		Weak neck muscles
	Cervical neurapraxia	Cervical stenosis
UPPER EXTREMITY	Upper extremity neurologic/vascular symptoms, thoracic outlet syndrome	Cervical rib
	Shoulder subluxation	Generalized ligamentous laxity
		Shoulder girdle weakness
	Impingement syndrome	Tight shoulder musculature
LUMBAR	Low back pain	Tight lumbosacral fascia
		Tight hamstrings
		Weak abdominal musculature
		Tight hip flexors
		Weak paraspinal musculature
		Spondylolysis
		Spondylolisthesis
		Symptomatic disk
LOWER EXTREMITY	Iliotibial band syndrome	Tight iliotibial band
		Prominent lateral epicondyle
		Genu varum
		Internal tibial torsion
		Hyperpronated foot
	Hamstring strain	Tight and weak hamstrings
	Patellofemoral pain syndrome	Generalized ligamentous laxity
		Malalignment (hip, knee, and/or ankle)
		Weak lower extremity musculature (especially quadriceps)
		Tight lateral retinaculum
		Tight hamstrings
	Osgood-Schlatter disease	Tight and weak quadriceps
	Patellar tendinitis	Tight and weak quadriceps
	Tibial tubercle avulsion	Osgood-Schlatter disease
	Anterior tibial pain	Poor stretching and muscle conditioning
		Tight muscular compartments
	Ankle pain/sprains	Tibiofibular synostosis
		Generalized ligamentous tightness
		Weak ankle musculature (especially peroneals)
		Tarsal coalitions

Source: Moskwa CA, Nicholas JA. 1989. Muskuloskeletal risk factors in the young athlete. *Phys Sportsmed.* 17(11)51. Reprinted with permission.

reduce or eliminate problems such as poor or faulty equipment, inadequate muscle strength, poor skills, and training errors.

Intervention Strategies

It is the responsibility of all members of the sports medicine team to remain vigilant in an effort to identify causative factors before an injury occurs. Many of the extrinsic factors are quite easily recognized. For example, regular inspections of protective equipment and athletic facilities can alert personnel to potential problems. Athletes in high-risk sports can be informed of the potential hazards and prevention strategies. For example, in tackle football athletes should be taught proper blocking and tackling techniques in an effort to avoid using the helmeted head as a weapon. It has been found that the incidence of serious head and neck injuries can be greatly reduced in this way.

W H A T   I F ?

A group of parents asks you, the soccer coach at the local high school, your recommendation for the best way to provide preseason physical evaluations, required by the board of education, to the players. What would you recommend?

Both the National Collegiate Athletic Association (NCAA) and the National Federation of State High School Associations have developed and implemented guidelines regarding medical evaluations of student athletes. The NCAA Guideline 1B (Medical Evaluations, Immunizations and Records) requires that all student athletes receive a preparticipation medical evaluation at the initial entrance into the institution's athletic program. Thereafter, only an updated medical history is required unless an additional medical examination is warranted based upon the updated history (Benson, 1995). In its 1995–1996 Handbook, the National Federation of State High School Associations lists a medical examination under the section entitled "Recommended Eligibility Standards for Athletics." Specifically the document states, "Prior to the first year of participation in interscholastic athletics, a student shall undergo a medical examination and be approved for interscholastic athletic competition by the examining medical authority. Prior to each subsequent year of participation, a student shall furnish a statement, signed by a medical authority, which provides clearance for continued athletic participation."

Two factors have contributed to the development of these comprehensive guidelines regarding preparticipation medical screening. First, since the late 1970s there has been explosive growth in the number of sports participants. It has become ever more difficult for school officials to monitor the health of all of their incoming student athletes on an annual basis. Second, our society has become more litigious in recent years and, as a result, coaches, educational institutions, and sports associations have a greater fear of being sued if and when a student is injured as a result of inadequate health screening. Therefore, the preparticipation physical evaluation or PPE is an important tool for all concerned. The primary purposes of the PPE should be to identify preexisting risk factors for injury as well as to ascertain any injuries or diseases that may create problems for the student athlete later on.

Typically the PPE will be administered by a licensed physician (M.D. or D.O.), although it has been reported that not all states require a physician to conduct the PPE (Feinstein, Soileau, and Daniel, 1988). A well-administered PPE can provide a great deal of information about the athlete's readiness for participation. Commonly identified conditions include: congenital disorders such as spina bifida occulta (incomplete closure of the vertebral neural arch); absence of one of a paired set of organs (eye, kidney, testicle); postural problems such as abnormal spinal curvatures or abnormalities of the extremities; muscle imbalances; obesity; high blood pressure; cardiac defects or disorders of cardiac rhythm; respiratory conditions such as asthma; drug allergies; skin infections; and vision problems.

Historically, PPEs all too often have consisted of a simple quick check of the major physiological systems. With the increased numbers of sports participants over the past two decades, the demand on the medical community for these services has increased as well. Obviously, as the costs of health care in general have escalated, so have the costs of undergoing a PPE. As a result, many young athletes simply cannot afford to visit a personal physician (assuming they have one) each year for such an evaluation. It was recently reported that the PPE is often the *only* time healthy children come into contact with a physician during the year (Koester, 1995). In an effort to improve the overall quality nationally of PPEs, a consortium of professional medical organizations recently developed and published a comprehensive set of guidelines for PPEs (AAFP, 1992). Table 4.2 shows the primary and secondary objectives for PPEs.

Two basic PPE formats have been used successfully: the station-screening format and the office-based type. Both are highly effective tools. Schools with large numbers of athletes involved in team sports will usually employ a station-screening format. This approach is convenient because a large number of athletes can be examined in a relatively short time. Typically, a variety of personnel participate, including a physician, athletic trainer, exercise physiologist, and coach. Each must be given a comprehensive orientation as to individual responsibilities by a supervising medical doctor. Table 4.3 shows required and optional stations, along with necessary personnel for performing each phase of the PPE.

TABLE 4.2 Objectives of the PPE

PRIMARY OBJECTIVES

Detect conditions that may predispose to injury

Detect conditions that may be life-threatening or disabling

Meet legal and insurance requirements

SECONDARY OBJECTIVES

Determine general health

Counsel on health-related issues

Assess fitness level for specific sports

Source: American Academy of Family Physicians, American Academy of Pediatrics, American Medical Society for Sports Medicine, American Orthopedic Society for Sports Medicine, and the American Osteopathic Academy of Sports Medicine. 1997. *Preparticipation Physical Evaluation* (2nd ed.). Chicago: American Academy of Family Physicians. Reprinted with permission.

Advantages of the office-based PPE, especially when the exam is given by the athlete's personal physician, include familiarity with the athlete's medical history, better communication between the doctor and athlete, and improved access for subsequent evaluations in case of injury. The chief disadvantage is cost, which for many is an important factor. In addition, some physicians lack a thorough understanding of sports injuries and therefore are prone to being too conservative or liberal in their evaluation of an athlete (McKeag, 1985).

Regardless of which type of PPE is employed, the procedure can provide valuable information relative to an athlete's readiness for participation. Coaches as well as sports medicine personnel must be aware of any preexisting conditions that make the athlete vulnerable to specific medical problems. A thorough medical history, including previous injuries, represents information essential to the welfare of the athlete.

Athletes with medical conditions such as diabetes, epilepsy, and drug allergies should be identified in case of subsequent injury or other problems related to their condition. Special populations need to be evaluated on the basis of injury risk factors that may not be present in the general population. Athletes with special physical and mental problems must be assessed by physicians who are familiar with the medical implications of each specific disorder. Obviously, all information obtained during a physical examination should be handled confidentially.

Concern has been raised within the sports medicine community regarding athletes who are missing one of a paired set of organs—e.g., those who have only one eye, kidney, or testicle. The consensus is that when loss of the remaining organ can be life-threatening, as in the case of a single kidney, the athlete should not be involved in a collision sport (Dorsen, 1986).

Considerable debate exists about the appropriate frequency of the preparticipation physical evaluation. Many school districts require a PPE on an annual basis. However, as costs for such procedures increase, there is pressure to amend this requirement to a format that would require an updated physical evaluation whenever an athlete reaches a new level of competition—for example, when going from junior high to high school (McKeag, 1985). It is also advised that whenever an athlete has sustained a more serious

TABLE 4.3 Required and Optional Stations and Personnel for Station-Based Screening PPEs

REQUIRED STATIONS	PERSONNEL
Sign-in, height/weight, vital signs, vision	Ancillary personnel (coach, nurse, community volunteer)
Physical examination, history review, assessment/clearance	Physician

OPTIONAL STATIONS	PERSONNEL
Nutrition	Dietitian
Dental	Dentist
Injury evaluation	Physician
Flexibility	Athletic trainer, physical therapist
Body composition	Athletic trainer, exercise physiologist, physical therapist
Strength	Athletic trainer, coach, exercise physiologist, physical therapist
Speed, agility, power, balance, endurance	Athletic trainer, coach, exercise physiologist

Source: American Academy of Family Physicians, American Academy of Pediatrics, American Medical Society for Sports Medicine, American Orthopedic Society for Sports Medicine, and the American Osteopathic Academy of Sports Medicine. 1997. *Preparticipation Physical Evaluation* (2nd ed.). Chicago: American Academy of Family Physicians. Reprinted with permission.

Information at your fingertips

The World Wide Web—You can find more information about the American Academy of Pediatrics. Go to http://www.jbpub.com/athletictraining and click on Chapter 4.

injury, such as head or spinal trauma, he or she should receive a complete physical evaluation by a physician prior to being allowed to return to participation. The American Academy of Pediatrics (AAP) has recommended that an athlete receive a PPE biannually, with an interim history prior to any new sports season (Dyment, 1991). A sample of a preparticipation physical evaluation with a health evaluation history is included in Appendix 3.

Injury Prevention and Preseason Conditioning

Many of the intrinsic risk factors, such as fitness level and skill, can be significantly modified as a result of effective conditioning programs and coaching. An essential aspect of any injury prevention program is the optimal development of physical fitness in the athlete. The old saying "You don't play sports to get fit, you get fit to play sports" is certainly valid today. A significant body of evidence exists supporting the premise that a fit athlete is less likely to suffer an injury (Taimela, Kujala, and Osterman, 1990.)

The components of fitness include cardiorespiratory (aerobic) fitness, muscular strength and endurance, flexibility, nutrition, and body composition (Fox, Dirby, and Roberts, 1987). Athletes in any sport would be well advised to develop a total conditioning program that addresses all of these components. By so doing, the athlete will benefit in two ways—improved performance and reduction in injuries. It is important to remember that a conditioning program consists of two primary components, general conditioning and sport-specific conditioning. The general conditioning program focuses on the major fitness components as listed above while the sport-specific conditioning focuses on any aspect of a particular sport or activity that is unique to it. For example, the shoulder girdle and glenohumeral joint muscles in a tennis player need to receive special attention to avoid overuse injuries related to repetitive

overhand strokes, which are inherent to the sport. To be effective, the conditioning program should allow for general conditioning on a year-round basis. This is best accomplished by incorporating the concept of periodization in the total conditioning program.

Periodization

A conditioning program should be designed to develop all fitness components to an optimal level, while at the same time allowing adequate intervals for rest and recovery. Three major variables are continually adjusted in a well-designed training program—volume, intensity, and frequency of training. Volume is defined as the total amount of work done during a given workout. For example, volume in a weight-training program usually means the total number of sets and repetitions of a given exercise. Intensity signifies the strength of the training stimulus—i.e., the speed run or the amount of weight lifted. Frequency is generally interpreted as the number of workouts over time, usually measured in workouts per week. Adjusting these variables periodically during a training program is referred to as **periodization,** which has been defined as "the organization of training into a cyclic structure to attain the optimal development of an athlete's performance capacities" (Kontor, 1986). An important advantage to this approach is the avoidance of conditioning-related injuries. Overuse injuries, e.g., stress fractures, are a common problem, especially for athletes in endurance sports such as long-distance running. A periodized program can help prevent this problem by varying the volume, intensity, and frequency of the training program. A periodized program recognizes different segments of the training year, typically referred to as preseason, competitive season, postseason, and off-season. In between each of these seasons are transition phases. Most training programs are developed for a one-year training cycle, technically known as a macrocycle. Within a given macrocycle there will be variety of different training

Athletic Trainers Speak Out

"The athletic trainer and the strength and conditioning specialist can work as a team in order to prepare the athlete for the rigors of athletic competition. By exchanging ideas, they can formulate a plan that will maximize the athlete's program. The more successful the off-season conditioning program, the less likely that the athlete will experience a significant injury.

An off-season program that involves strength training, cardiovascular conditioning, and proper rehabilitation programs will work to the advantage of the athlete. An athletic trainer can make a significant difference as long as he or she works collaboratively to help athletes reach their full potential."

—Dan Ruiz, M.S., A.T.C.

Dan Ruiz is the assistant athletic trainer for the Carolina Panthers.

Dan Ruiz

programs, each with a specific goal. The smallest component is called a microcycle, which consists of two to four weeks of training with fluctuations in intensity, duration, and frequency (Kontor, 1986). A mesocycle consists of several successive microcycles leading to a specific conditioning goal—for example, **hypertrophy** of leg muscles. A transition phase is a period of two to four weeks that occurs between training seasons or between successive mesocycles. During a transition phase training is adjusted gradually, either to bring an athlete to peak fitness or to allow

the athlete to rest and recover after the competitive season. In short, the function of the transition phase is to give the body time to recover from the previous cycle in order to be ready for the next segment of the training season.

A typical application of periodization can be illustrated with a football lineman. During the preseason phase, he may spend the first three weeks working on muscle strength and hypertrophy (microcycle), followed by three weeks of high-intensity, low-volume strength training to develop muscle power (micro-

TABLE 4.4 Periodization Model for Football Lineman

Nov/Dec
Active Rest: Exercise, workout, and conditioning variety
Rehabilitation: Attend to any injury rehabilitation needs
Base Preparatory Phase: High volume, moderate to high intensity (8–12 RM) using primary and assistance exercises, 3 to 5 times per week. Conditioning should be enjoyable and develop a general strength/power and sports-conditioning base.

Period Length	Phase	Sets	Intensity	Frequency
Jan 2 weeks	Hypertrophy	4–6	10 RM	4–5/wk
Feb 2 weeks	Strength	3–5	4–6 RM	4–5/wk
Mar 2 weeks	Peaking	3–5	2–3 RM*	3–4/wk
Repeat cycle.				

*2–3 RM loads used to prevent injury with 1 RM loads.

Primary Exercises**	Assistance Exercises 3 to 4 Sets (8–10 RM)		
Squat	Neck exercises	**APRIL**	Spring ball Strength phase (2 × wk)
Bench press	Double- and single-leg extensions	**MAY**	Overlap
Inclines	and curls	**JUNE**	
Power clean (other	Lat pulls	**JULY**	Repeat above 6-week cycle twice
pulls)	Rows	**AUGUST**	
Deadlifts	Abdominal work		
Military press	Olympic prep lifts		
	Calf raises		
	Shrugs		
	Shoulder raises		

**Only "primary" exercises are periodized (not assistance exercises).
Source: Kontor K (ed.). 1987. Periodization: Roundtable (Part III). *NSCA Journal.* 9(1):24. Reprinted with permission.

cycle). These two microcycles would constitute a mesocycle with the goal of improving lower-extremity power. A transition phase would then be inserted just prior to the onset of the competitive season. During the season the player would reduce his weekly frequency of weight training in order to maintain the gains made during the preseason phase. Table 4.4 presents a sample of such a periodized training program.

Aerobic Fitness

It has been shown that aerobic fitness can assist in avoiding injuries related to general fatigue. This is true even in sports that do not, in themselves, require high levels of aerobic fitness in order for athletes to be successful (Taimela, Kujala, and Osterman, 1990). Fatigue can have a detrimental effect on muscle strength, reac-

Information at your fingertips

The World Wide Web—To find out more about strength and conditioning in sports, go to http://www.jbpub.com/athletictraining and click on Chapter 4.

tion time, agility, and neuromuscular coordination (Wilmore and Costill, 1988). In short, regardless of the sport, athletes who enter the season with a high level of aerobic fitness are less prone to injury. Aerobic fitness can be enhanced by regular participation in activities such as running, bicycling, swimming, cross-country skiing, roller-blading, stair-stepping, and aerobic dance. As a general rule, athletes who are not participating in an aerobic sport should include some sort of aerobic training at least three days per week.

Muscular Strength and Endurance

Improved muscle strength has also been found to be helpful in reducing the chances of injury. Several physiological and morphological changes have been attributed to strength training (Fleck and Falkel, 1986). Taken individually or as a group, these adaptations will have the effect of making the body more resistant to injury. Specifically, research has found that connective tissues (fascia, tendons, ligaments) all become stronger as a result of strength training. Furthermore, bone density increases and becomes less susceptible to both trauma and fractures related to overuse. Improving the strength of muscles that surround a joint will help the athlete protect it from injury. Improving the strength ratio between opposing muscle groups, such as hamstrings and quadriceps, continues to be a generally well-accepted technique for preventing injury. Still, debate on this topic continues (Grace, 1985). Muscular endurance has been found to increase after appropriate strength-training programs. This is particularly true of programs that incorporate a greater number of repetitions within each set of exercises.

Flexibility

Improved flexibility has been determined to reduce the incidence of musculoskeletal injuries (Shellock and Prentice, 1985). Muscles that cross two or more joints have been found to be those most commonly injured. This increase probably results, in part, because of the greater levels of stretching during activity within these muscles (Safran, Seaber, and Garrett, 1989). **Flexibility** has been defined by Jensen and Fisher (1972) as "the range of motion (ROM) in a given joint or combination of joints." They report that several factors deter-

mine the **ROM** of a given joint. These include bone structure, tissue mass surrounding the joint, and extensibility of tendons, ligaments, muscles, and skin surrounding the joint. Temperature of the tissue, which is mediated by local blood flow and external (ambient) temperature, can significantly affect tissue extensibility. Warm-up exercises have been found to be effective in increasing tissue temperatures temporarily. Both chronological age and gender have also been found to affect flexibility (Wilmore and Costill, 1988). In general, flexibility decreases with age, although maintaining an active lifestyle may greatly reduce such changes. In addition, females have been found to be more flexible than their male counterparts. This is most likely related to differences in gonadotropic hormone levels between the sexes.

Two types of flexibility have been identified: static and dynamic (Safran, Seaber, and Garrett, 1989). Static flexibility involves the ROM achieved through passive manipulation of a given joint by another person while the muscles are relaxed. Dynamic flexibility is the ROM achieved by contracting the muscles around the joint, such as the ROM of knee flexion when contracting that joint's flexor muscles. Stretching exercises have been found to be effective in improving the extensibility of muscle tissue and can serve as a preventative factor with respect to muscle strains (Safran, Seaber, and Garrett, 1989). Stretching exercises can be grouped into four different categories, based upon the method employed. **Ballistic stretching** involves powerful contractions of muscles in order to force a joint to a greater ROM. **Static stretching,** as the name implies, involves moving a joint to a position of stretch that is then sustained (held) for a period ranging from three seconds up to a minute or longer (Shellock and Prentice, 1985). **Proprioceptive neuromuscular facilitation (PNF)** involves a technique originally developed for use with patients suffering from paralysis. Essentially, PNF uses the body's proprioceptive system in order to stimulate muscles to relax. A variety of manual techniques have been developed, all using PNF principles. In order to use PNF techniques effectively, specialized training is required. Finally, **passive stretching** involves having someone, other than the athlete, move a joint through a ROM. This is commonly seen in sports such as swimming or gymnastics, in which an athlete will work with a partner to stretch the shoulders and arms behind the body.

Some research indicates that, when comparing these techniques, static stretching is probably the most effective, with effects lasting up to 90 minutes (Safran, Seaber, and Garrett, 1989). Evidence suggests

WHAT IF?

One of your cross-country runners, who suffers from chronic hamstring tightness, comes to you for advice on how to improve flexibility. What would you advise?

that the best time to use static stretching is at the end of a workout when the tissues are warmer due to increased blood flow (Weaver, Moore, and Howe, 1996). Ballistic stretching is considered the least effective method and may even result in injury. The medical evidence is overwhelming in discouraging the use of ballistic forms of stretching.

Nutrition and Body Composition

The dietary habits of any athlete, regardless of the sport, have a profound influence on overall performance and on recovery from injury. Obviously, the body will respond to a conditioning program in a more positive manner when adequate amounts of essential nutrients are consumed in the daily diet. An overemphasis on leanness—by society, parents, coaches, and athletes themselves—has resulted in abnormally high ratios of lean body weight to fat body weight among many young athletes. Specific nutritional considerations of athletes will be presented in Chapter 6.

Modification of Extrinsic Factors

Extrinsic risk factors for sports injuries include the practice/competition environments, facilities, protective equipment, and officiating and coaching. It is critical that coaching personnel, athletic program administrators, and, if on staff, NATABOC-certified athletic trainers monitor all of these factors in an effort to identify and eliminate any potential risks to the athletes.

Practice/Competition Environment

Whether outdoors or indoors, the environment must be assessed to determine if it represents a potential health risk. This is particularly true when athletes exercise in conditions of high relative heat and humidity. Specific guidelines for preventing heat-related problems are presented in Chapter 18. It is important to remember that indoor activity can pose a significant risk of thermal injury, particularly if the participant is not properly hydrated or if the indoor temperature and humidity are high.

Facilities

All sports facilities must be designed, maintained, and frequently inspected for the safety of the participants. Budgets and local building codes must be considered; however, these factors should never be allowed to supersede safety. Shared facilities are common; for example, football fields are often surrounded by an outdoor running track with field event equipment (landing pits for high jump and pole vault, shot-put ring, etc.) either on the playing field or on the ends of the field. Baseball fields may be located next to a soccer field or perhaps even share some of the same ground. Regardless of the specific situation, it is critical that care is taken that all facilities meet the minimum requirements for safe participation. These include such things as integrity of safety fences, batting cages, location of dugouts in baseball and softball, type of bases used (breakaway or fixed), soccer goals that are correctly constructed and anchored, location of water and sanitation facilities, and emergency medical services (EMS) access routes.

With respect to indoor facilities, primary concerns center on lighting, playing surfaces, and room dimensions. Poor lighting may contribute to accidents due to poor visibility. A floor that is not cleaned regularly or properly finished may become slippery and thus contribute to collisions. Budgetary constraints may mean that some gymnasiums are built that do not provide adequate space between the basketball baskets and the adjacent wall. This is especially common at the junior high and elementary school levels. In such situations it is critical that protective padding be placed on the walls behind the basketball backboards to reduce players' collisions with the wall. Locker rooms and shower facilities should be designed to enable participants to move around safely, with adequate ventilation, lighting, and nonskid floors. It is imperative that medical equipment such as whirlpool baths and other therapeutic modalities such as ultrasound or diathermy machines *not* be available for use in the locker room. Such equipment represents a significant safety risk and greatly increases the legal liability of the school.

Protective Equipment

Although a comprehensive review of protective equipment for all sports is beyond the scope of this text,

it is important to remember several important safety factors related to such equipment. First, the equipment itself should not represent a risk. Most equipment must meet specific certification standards for design and construction. For example, football helmets or shoulder pads that are improperly fitted or in a state of disrepair should not be issued to a participant. For safety helmets, the certifying agencies include the American National Standards Institute, Inc. (ANSI), the Snell Memorial Foundation, Inc., and the National Operating Committee on Standards for Athletic Equipment (NOCSAE). Many sports organizations require that safety helmets be approved by one or more of these agencies in order to be used in either practice or competition. Specific mandatory equipment requirements for sports can be obtained from either the NCAA (collegiate level only) or from your state's high school activity association.

Information at your fingertips

The World Wide Web—To learn more about both ANSI and the Snell Memorial Foundation, go to http://www.jbpub.com/athletictraining and click on Chapter 4.

Review Questions

1. Differentiate between intrinsic and extrinsic types of causative factors leading to sports injury. Provide several examples of both types.

2. List four types of intrinsic factors related to sports injury that a medical doctor might identify during a preparticipation physical examination.

3. Draw an example of an eight-station system for providing a preparticipation physical examination to a group of athletes, as shown in the chapter.

4. What are two disadvantages to using an individual format for a preparticipation physical examination?

5. List the seven components of fitness as described in the chapter.

6. Briefly describe the relationship between volume, intensity, and frequency of training as they relate to periodization.

7. Define the terms macrocycle, mesocycle, and microcycle as they relate to a sports training program.

8. *True or false:* According to the chapter, athletes, regardless of sport, can benefit from possessing a relatively high level of aerobic fitness.

9. What is the meaning of the acronym ROM?

10. Discuss the advantages and disadvantages of the four categories of stretching exercises.

References

American Academy of Family Physicians. 1992. *Preparticipation Physical Evaluation.* (1st ed.). Chicago: American Academy of Family Physicians.

Benson M (ed.). 1995. *1995–96 NCAA Sports Medicine Handbook.* (8th ed.). Overland Park: The National Collegiate Athletic Association.

Dorsen PJ. 1986. Should athletes with one eye, kidney, or testicle play contact sports? *Phys Sportsmed.* 14(7):130–138.

Dyment PG (ed.). 1991. *Sports Medicine: Health Care for Young Athletes.* (2d ed.). Elk Grove Village, Ill.: American Academy of Pediatrics.

Feinstein RA, Soileau EJ, Daniel WA. 1988. A national survey of preparticipation physical-examination requirements. *Phys Sportsmed.* 16(5):51–59.

Fleck SJ, Falkel JE. 1986. Value of resistance training for the reduction of sports injuries. *Sports Med.* 3:61–68.

Fox EL, Dirby TE, Roberts AF. 1987. *Bases of Fitness.* New York: Macmillan.

Grace T. 1985. Muscle imbalance and extremity injury: perplexing relationship. *Sports Med.* 2:77–82.

Jensen CR, Fisher AG. 1972. *Scientific Basis of Athletic Conditioning.* Philadelphia: Lea & Febiger.

Koester MC. 1995. Refocusing the adolescent preparticipation physical evaluation toward preventative health care. *J Athl Train.* 4:352–360.

Kontor K (ed.). 1986. Periodization: roundtable. *NSCA Journal.* 8(5):24.

McKeag DB. 1985. Preseason physical examination for the prevention of sports injuries. *Sports Med.* 2:413–431.

Moskwa CA, Nicholas JA. 1989. Musculoskeletal risk factors in the young athlete. *Phys Sportsmed.* 17(11):49–59.

Safran MR, Seaber AV, Garrett WE. 1989. Warm-up and muscular injury prevention: an update. *Sports Med.* 8(4):239–249.

Shellock FG, Prentice WE. 1985. Warm-up and stretching for improved physical performance and prevention of sports-related injuries. *Sports Med.* 2:267–278.

Taimela S, Kujala UM, Osterman K. 1990. Intrinsic risk factors and athletic injuries. *Sports Med.* 9(4):205–215.

Weaver J, Moore CK, Howe WB. 1996. Chapter 26, "Injury Prevention." In Caine DJ, Caine CG, Lindner KJ (eds.). *Epidemiology of Sports Injuries.* Champaign: Human Kinetics.

Wilmore JH, Costill DL. 1988. *Training for Sport and Activity: The Physiological Basis of the Conditioning Process* (3d ed.). Dubuque: William C. Brown.

PLATE 1

THE
SKELETAL
SYSTEM
(front view)

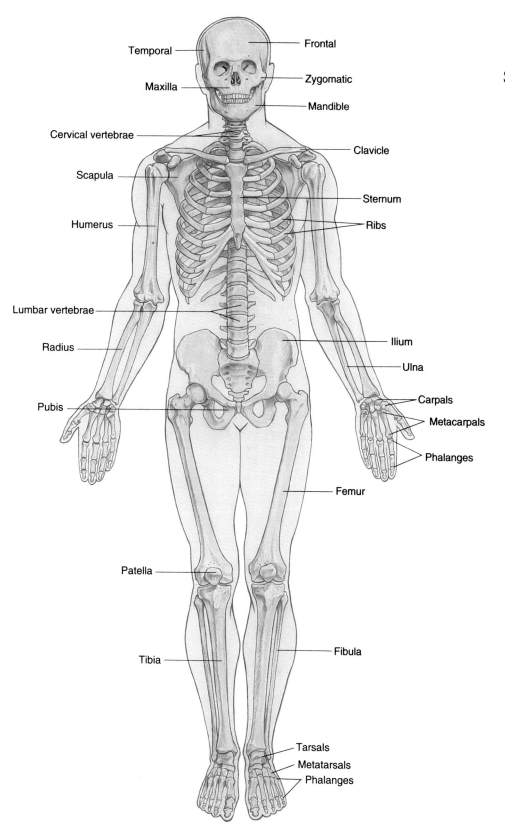

Temporal

Frontal

Maxilla

Zygomatic

Mandible

Cervical vertebrae

Clavicle

Scapula

Sternum

Humerus

Ribs

Lumbar vertebrae

Ilium

Radius

Ulna

Pubis

Carpals

Metacarpals

Phalanges

Femur

Patella

Fibula

Tibia

Tarsals
Metatarsals
Phalanges

PLATE 2

THE
SKELETAL
SYSTEM
(side and
back views)

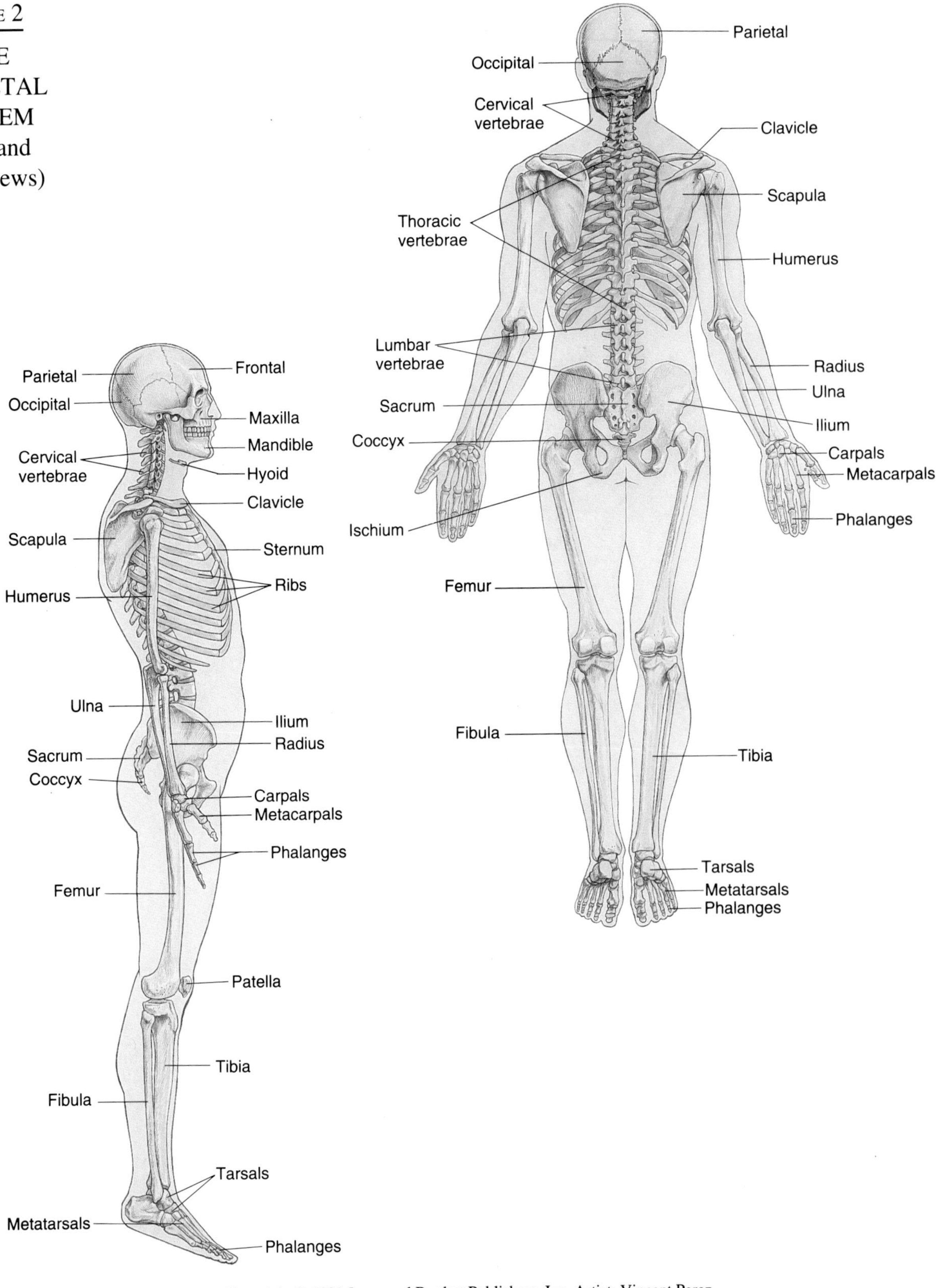

Parietal

Occipital

Cervical
vertebrae

Clavicle

Thoracic
vertebrae

Scapula

Humerus

Lumbar
vertebrae

Radius

Ulna

Sacrum

Ilium

Coccyx

Carpals

Metacarpals

Ischium

Phalanges

Femur

Fibula

Tibia

Tarsals

Metatarsals

Phalanges

Parietal

Frontal

Occipital

Maxilla

Mandible

Cervical
vertebrae

Hyoid

Clavicle

Scapula

Sternum

Humerus

Ribs

Ulna

Ilium

Radius

Sacrum

Coccyx

Carpals

Metacarpals

Phalanges

Femur

Patella

Tibia

Fibula

Tarsals

Metatarsals

Phalanges

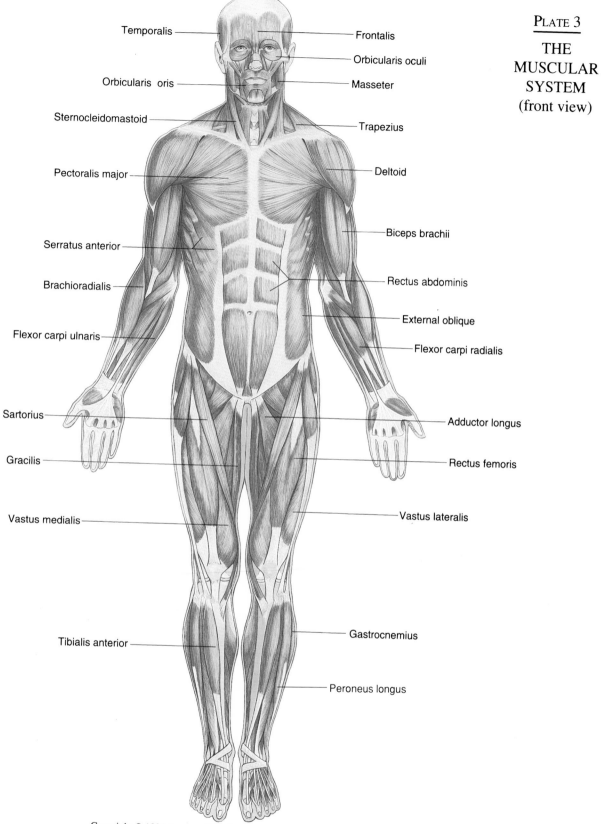

Temporalis

Orbicularis oris

Sternocleidomastoid

Pectoralis major

Serratus anterior

Brachioradialis

Flexor carpi ulnaris

Sartorius

Gracilis

Vastus medialis

Tibialis anterior

Frontalis

Orbicularis oculi

Masseter

Trapezius

Deltoid

Biceps brachii

Rectus abdominis

External oblique

Flexor carpi radialis

Adductor longus

Rectus femoris

Vastus lateralis

Gastrocnemius

Peroneus longus

PLATE 3

THE
MUSCULAR
SYSTEM
(front view)

PLATE 4

THE MUSCULAR SYSTEM
(side and back views)

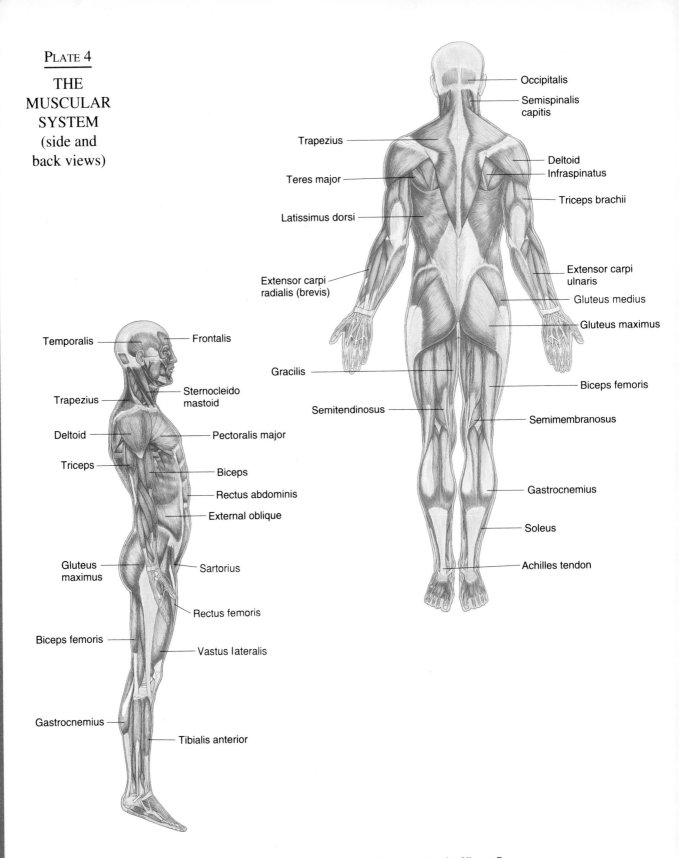

Occipitalis

Semispinalis capitis

Trapezius

Deltoid

Infraspinatus

Teres major

Triceps brachii

Latissimus dorsi

Extensor carpi ulnaris

Extensor carpi radialis (brevis)

Gluteus medius

Gluteus maximus

Temporalis

Frontalis

Gracilis

Biceps femoris

Trapezius

Sternocleido mastoid

Semitendinosus

Semimembranosus

Deltoid

Pectoralis major

Triceps

Biceps

Rectus abdominis

External oblique

Gastrocnemius

Gluteus maximus

Sartorius

Soleus

Rectus femoris

Achilles tendon

Biceps femoris

Vastus lateralis

Gastrocnemius

Tibialis anterior

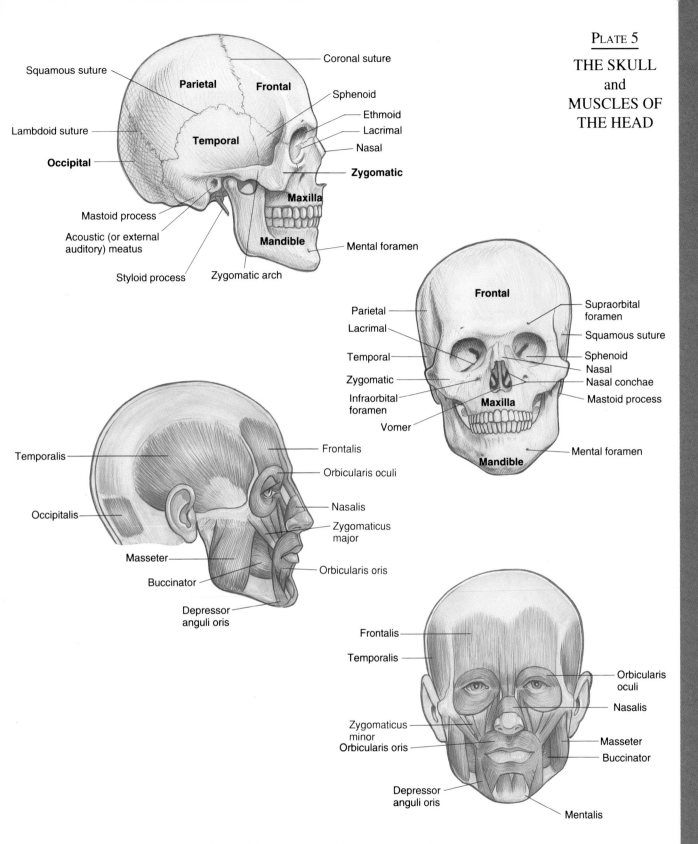

PLATE 5

THE SKULL
and
MUSCLES OF
THE HEAD

Coronal suture

Squamous suture

Parietal   **Frontal**

Sphenoid

Ethmoid

Lacrimal

Nasal

Lambdoid suture

Temporal

Zygomatic

Occipital

Maxilla

Mastoid process

Mandible

Mental foramen

Acoustic (or external
auditory) meatus

Styloid process

Zygomatic arch

Frontal

Parietal

Supraorbital
foramen

Lacrimal

Squamous suture

Temporal

Sphenoid

Zygomatic

Nasal

Nasal conchae

Infraorbital
foramen

Maxilla

Mastoid process

Vomer

Mental foramen

Mandible

Temporalis

Frontalis

Orbicularis oculi

Occipitalis

Nasalis

Zygomaticus
major

Masseter

Orbicularis oris

Buccinator

Depressor
anguli oris

Frontalis

Temporalis

Orbicularis
oculi

Nasalis

Zygomaticus
minor

Masseter

Orbicularis oris

Buccinator

Depressor
anguli oris

Mentalis

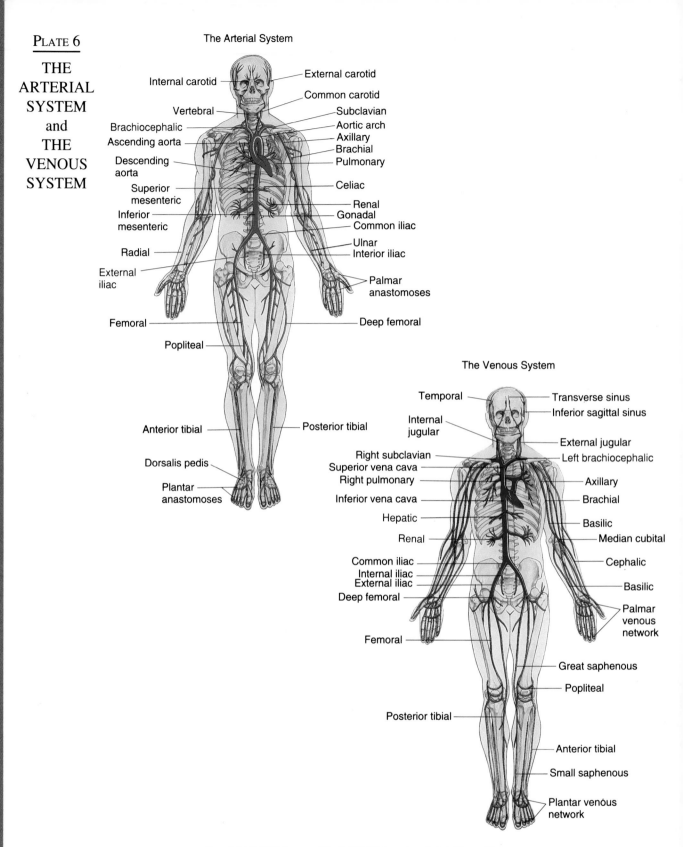

PLATE 6

THE
ARTERIAL
SYSTEM
and
THE
VENOUS
SYSTEM

The Arterial System

Internal carotid
External carotid
Common carotid
Vertebral
Subclavian
Brachiocephalic
Aortic arch
Ascending aorta
Axillary
Brachial
Descending aorta
Pulmonary
Superior mesenteric
Celiac
Inferior mesenteric
Renal
Gonadal
Common iliac
Radial
Ulnar
Interior iliac
External iliac
Palmar anastomoses
Femoral
Deep femoral
Popliteal
Anterior tibial
Posterior tibial
Dorsalis pedis
Plantar anastomoses

The Venous System

Temporal
Transverse sinus
Internal jugular
Inferior sagittal sinus
External jugular
Right subclavian
Left brachiocephalic
Superior vena cava
Right pulmonary
Axillary
Inferior vena cava
Brachial
Hepatic
Basilic
Renal
Median cubital
Common iliac
Cephalic
Internal iliac
External iliac
Basilic
Deep femoral
Palmar venous network
Femoral
Great saphenous
Popliteal
Posterior tibial
Anterior tibial
Small saphenous
Plantar venous network

Copyright © 1991 Jones and Bartlett Publishers, Inc. Artist: Vincent Perez

PLATE 7

THE
ARTERIAL-
VENOUS
SYSTEM

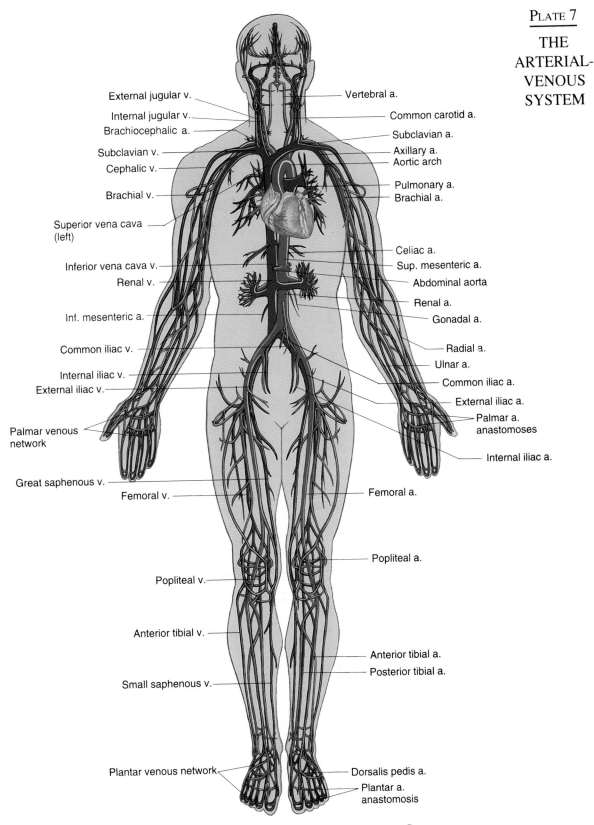

External jugular v.

Internal jugular v.

Brachiocephalic a.

Subclavian v.

Cephalic v.

Brachial v.

Superior vena cava
(left)

Inferior vena cava v.

Renal v.

Inf. mesenteric a.

Common iliac v.

Internal iliac v.

External iliac v.

Palmar venous
network

Great saphenous v.

Femoral v.

Popliteal v.

Anterior tibial v.

Small saphenous v.

Plantar venous network

Vertebral a.

Common carotid a.

Subclavian a.

Axillary a.

Aortic arch

Pulmonary a.

Brachial a.

Celiac a.

Sup. mesenteric a.

Abdominal aorta

Renal a.

Gonadal a.

Radial a.

Ulnar a.

Common iliac a.

External iliac a.

Palmar a.
anastomoses

Internal iliac a.

Femoral a.

Popliteal a.

Anterior tibial a.

Posterior tibial a.

Dorsalis pedis a.

Plantar a.
anastomosis

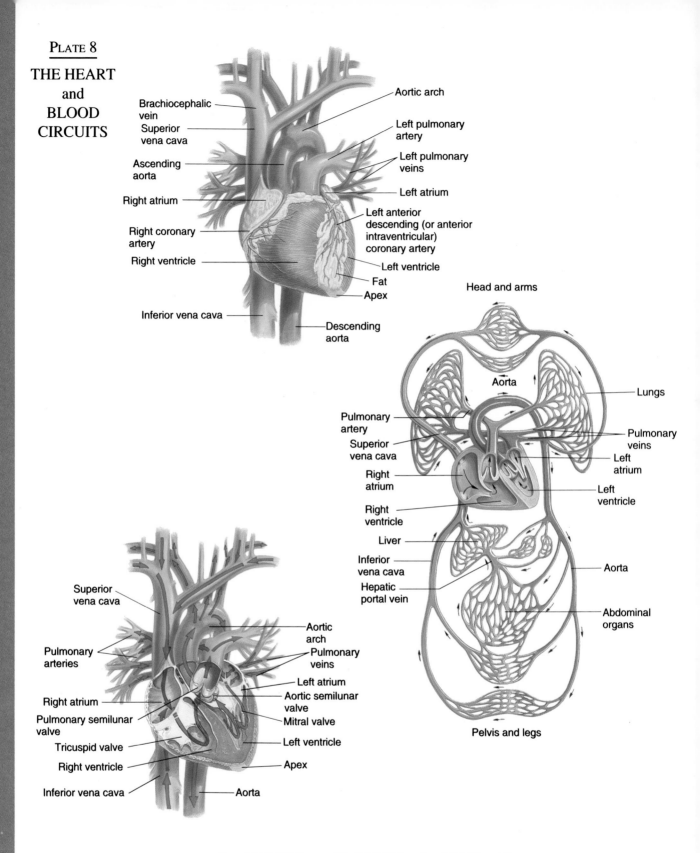

PLATE 8

THE HEART
and
BLOOD
CIRCUITS

Brachiocephalic vein
Aortic arch
Superior vena cava
Left pulmonary artery
Ascending aorta
Left pulmonary veins
Right atrium
Left atrium
Right coronary artery
Left anterior descending (or anterior intraventricular) coronary artery
Right ventricle
Left ventricle
Fat
Apex
Inferior vena cava
Descending aorta

Head and arms
Aorta
Lungs
Pulmonary artery
Pulmonary veins
Superior vena cava
Left atrium
Right atrium
Left ventricle
Right ventricle
Liver
Inferior vena cava
Aorta
Hepatic portal vein
Abdominal organs
Pelvis and legs

Superior vena cava
Aortic arch
Pulmonary arteries
Pulmonary veins
Left atrium
Right atrium
Aortic semilunar valve
Pulmonary semilunar valve
Mitral valve
Tricuspid valve
Left ventricle
Right ventricle
Apex
Inferior vena cava
Aorta

PLATE 9

THE
ENDOCRINE
SYSTEM

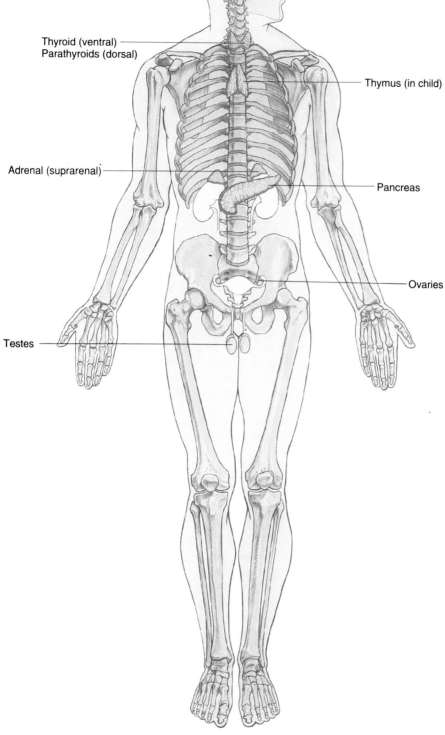
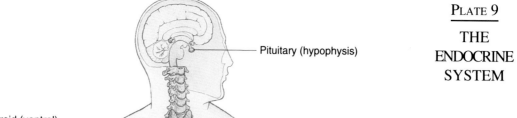

Pituitary (hypophysis)

Thyroid (ventral)
Parathyroids (dorsal)

Thymus (in child)

Adrenal (suprarenal)

Pancreas

Ovaries

Testes

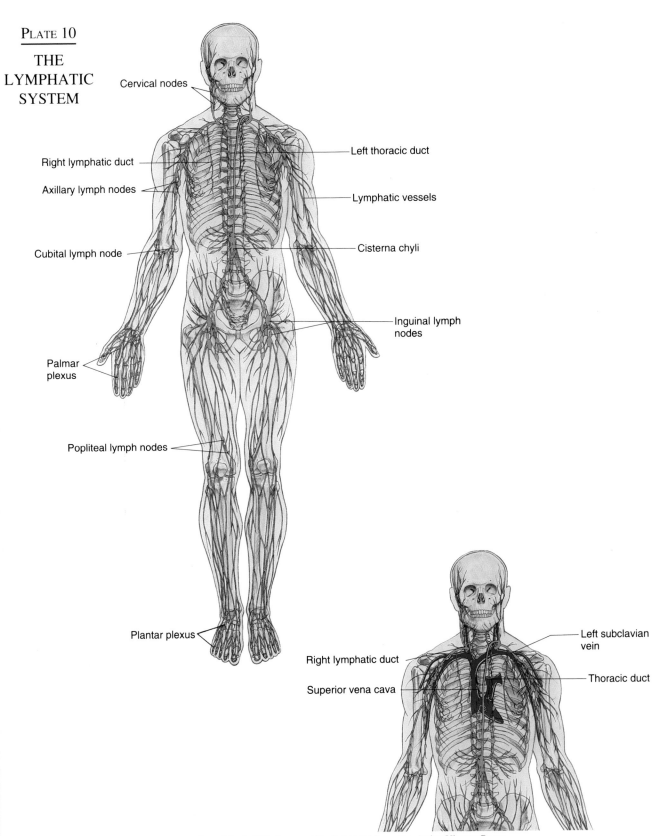

PLATE 10

THE LYMPHATIC SYSTEM

Cervical nodes

Right lymphatic duct

Axillary lymph nodes

Cubital lymph node

Palmar plexus

Popliteal lymph nodes

Plantar plexus

Left thoracic duct

Lymphatic vessels

Cisterna chyli

Inguinal lymph nodes

Right lymphatic duct

Superior vena cava

Left subclavian vein

Thoracic duct

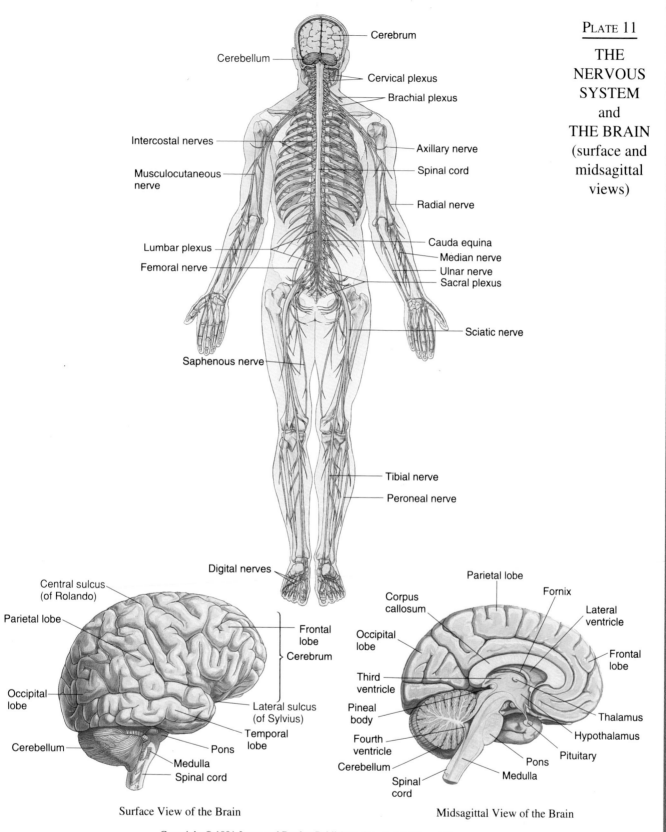

Cerebrum

Cerebellum

Cervical plexus

Brachial plexus

Intercostal nerves

Axillary nerve

Musculocutaneous nerve

Spinal cord

Radial nerve

Lumbar plexus

Cauda equina

Median nerve

Femoral nerve

Ulnar nerve

Sacral plexus

Sciatic nerve

Saphenous nerve

Tibial nerve

Peroneal nerve

Digital nerves

Central sulcus (of Rolando)

Parietal lobe

Frontal lobe

Cerebrum

Occipital lobe

Lateral sulcus (of Sylvius)

Temporal lobe

Cerebellum

Pons

Medulla

Spinal cord

Surface View of the Brain

Parietal lobe

Corpus callosum

Fornix

Lateral ventricle

Occipital lobe

Frontal lobe

Third ventricle

Pineal body

Thalamus

Fourth ventricle

Hypothalamus

Cerebellum

Pituitary

Pons

Spinal cord

Medulla

Midsagittal View of the Brain

PLATE 12

THE
VISCERA

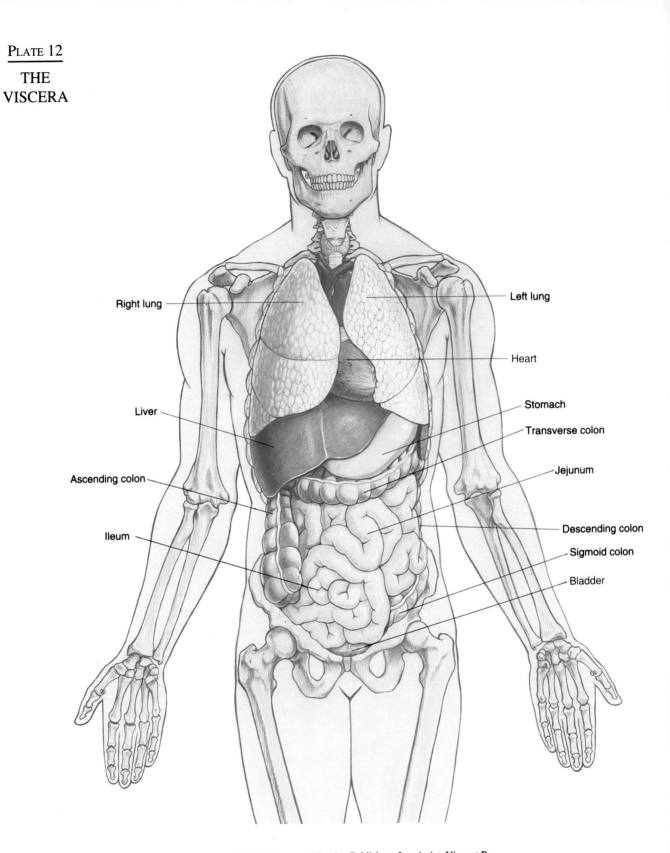

Right lung

Left lung

Heart

Liver

Stomach

Transverse colon

Ascending colon

Jejunum

Ileum

Descending colon

Sigmoid colon

Bladder

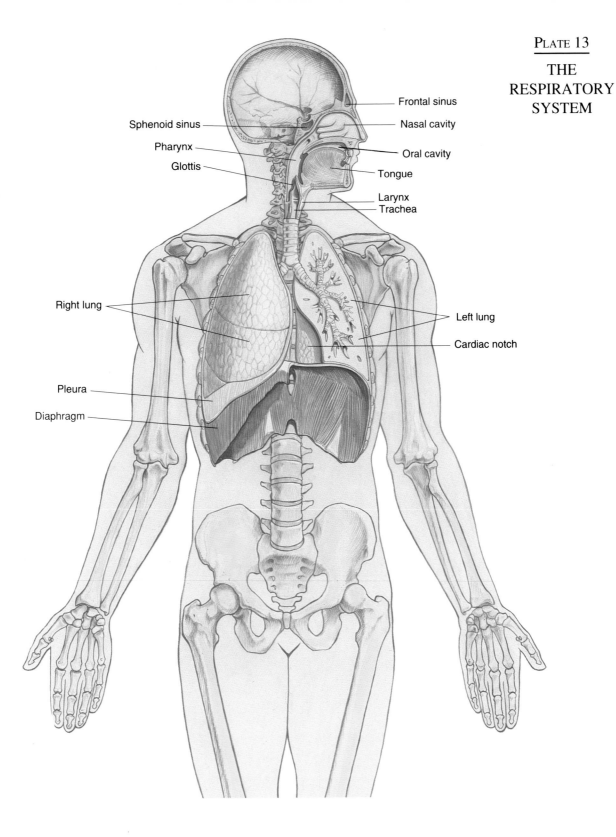

PLATE 13

THE
RESPIRATORY
SYSTEM

Frontal sinus

Sphenoid sinus

Nasal cavity

Pharynx

Oral cavity

Glottis

Tongue

Larynx

Trachea

Right lung

Left lung

Cardiac notch

Pleura

Diaphragm

PLATE 14

THE
DIGESTIVE
SYSTEM

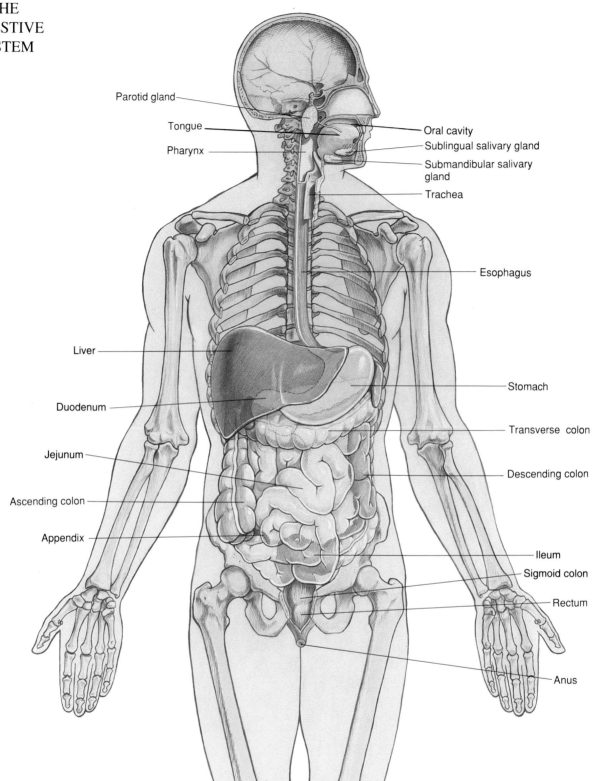

Parotid gland

Tongue

Pharynx

Oral cavity

Sublingual salivary gland

Submandibular salivary gland

Trachea

Esophagus

Liver

Stomach

Duodenum

Transverse colon

Jejunum

Descending colon

Ascending colon

Appendix

Ileum

Sigmoid colon

Rectum

Anus

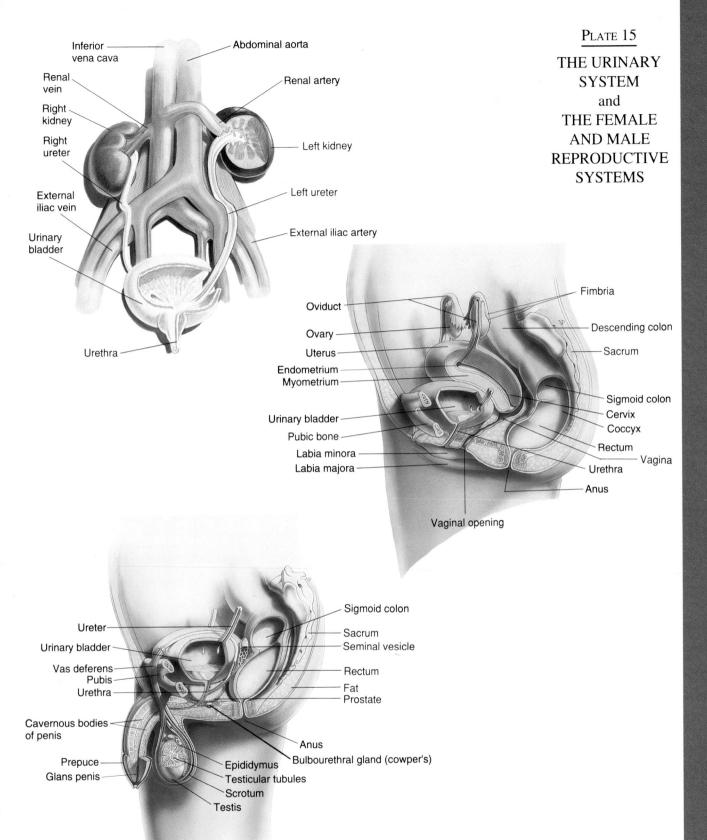

PLATE 15

THE URINARY
SYSTEM
and
THE FEMALE
AND MALE
REPRODUCTIVE
SYSTEMS

Inferior vena cava

Abdominal aorta

Renal vein

Renal artery

Right kidney

Right ureter

Left kidney

External iliac vein

Left ureter

Urinary bladder

External iliac artery

Urethra

Oviduct

Fimbria

Ovary

Descending colon

Uterus

Sacrum

Endometrium

Myometrium

Sigmoid colon

Urinary bladder

Cervix

Pubic bone

Coccyx

Labia minora

Rectum

Labia majora

Vagina

Urethra

Anus

Vaginal opening

Ureter

Sigmoid colon

Urinary bladder

Sacrum

Seminal vesicle

Vas deferens

Pubis

Rectum

Urethra

Fat

Prostate

Cavernous bodies of penis

Prepuce

Anus

Glans penis

Bulbourethral gland (cowper's)

Epididymus

Testicular tubules

Scrotum

Testis

PLATE 16

THE
SENSES

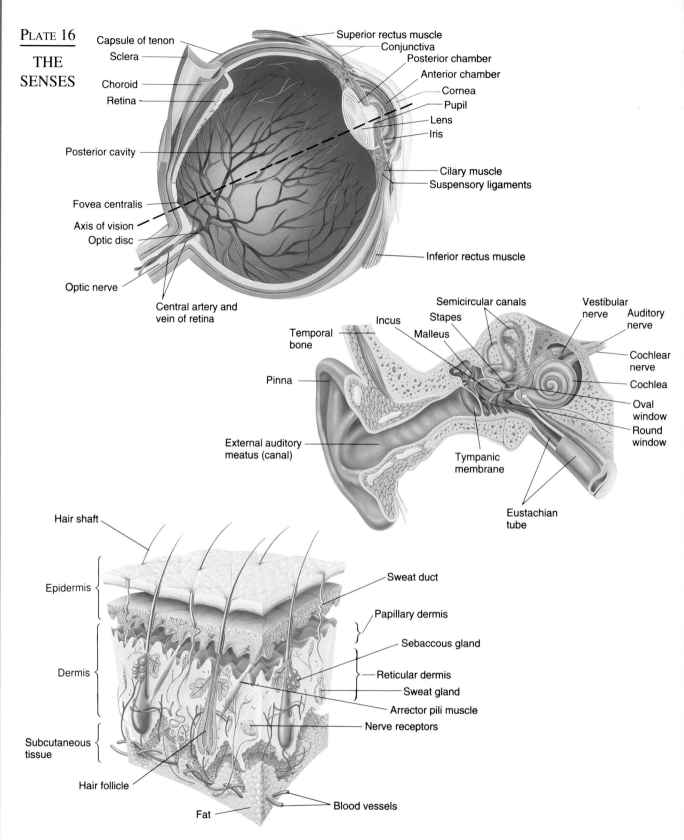

Capsule of tenon
Sclera
Choroid
Retina
Posterior cavity
Fovea centralis
Axis of vision
Optic disc
Optic nerve
Central artery and
vein of retina

Superior rectus muscle
Conjunctiva
Posterior chamber
Anterior chamber
Cornea
Pupil
Lens
Iris
Cilary muscle
Suspensory ligaments
Inferior rectus muscle

Temporal
bone
Pinna
External auditory
meatus (canal)

Incus
Malleus
Semicircular canals
Stapes
Vestibular
nerve
Auditory
nerve
Cochlear
nerve
Cochlea
Oval
window
Round
window
Tympanic
membrane
Eustachian
tube

Hair shaft
Epidermis
Dermis
Subcutaneous
tissue
Hair follicle
Fat

Sweat duct
Papillary dermis
Sebaccous gland
Reticular dermis
Sweat gland
Arrector pili muscle
Nerve receptors
Blood vessels

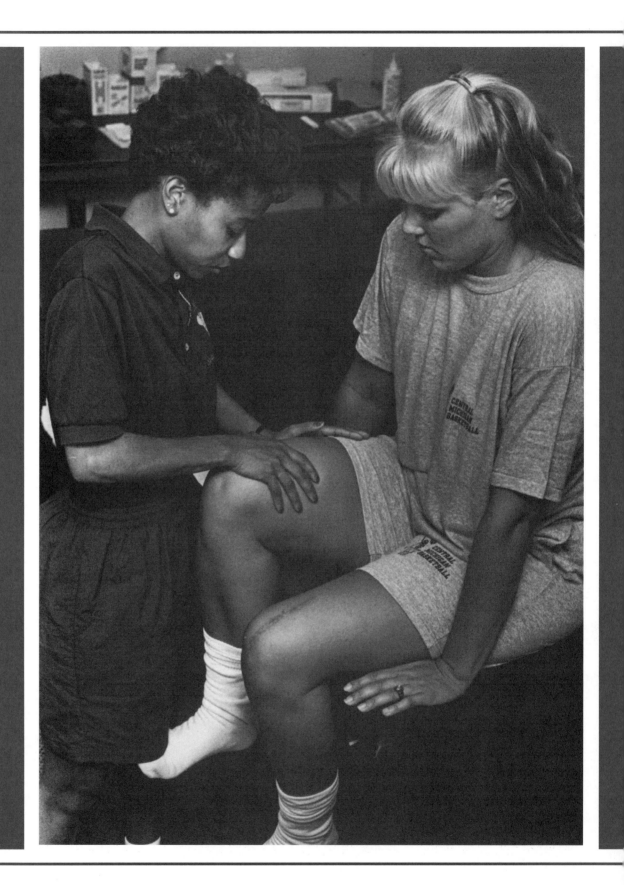

The Psychology of Injury

M A J O R   C O N C E P T S

Sports injuries involve more than damaged ligaments, tendons, and muscles; the athlete's perception of and reaction to an injury will also play a major role in the recovery process. This chapter introduces the reader to current thinking regarding the psychology of sports injuries. It begins with an examination of primary personality variables: trait anxiety, general personality, and locus of control. The chapter then examines the relationship between athlete and social environment: it is argued that social environment can induce significant stress that may predispose an athlete to injury. Recent research into the disorder known as seasonal affective disorder (SAD) is presented, along with its implications to the athletic community. This chapter also gives special attention to the effects of competitive stress on the adolescent athlete. In addition, it presents the results of recent research into the psychological effects of injury. This chapter concludes with an in-depth discussion of eating disorders as they affect today's athletes. It discusses both anorexia nervosa and bulimia nervosa in terms of early warning signs and recommended treatments.

The concept of risk factors for sports injuries was introduced and discussed in Chapters 1 and 4. Phenomena such as environmental conditions, type of playing surface, quality of protective equipment, player skill, years of experience, relative muscle strength, and type of sport were all identified as being possible contributors to an injury. Implementation of strategies designed to reduce or eliminate the impact of these risk factors represents a major responsibility of all those involved in the administration of organized sports programs. However, in spite of significant improvements in coaching and physical-conditioning techniques; rule changes; better officiating; advances in protective-equipment technology; and enhanced facilities, the overall number of participants being injured in sports has actually risen (Kerr and Fowler, 1988). Although this increase may be partly due to increased numbers of participants as well as improved systems for reporting injuries, both acute and chronic injuries continue to be a significant threat to a large percentage of young athletes.

In an effort to explain these trends, sports scientists have recently begun searching for additional risk factors. Increased attention has been given to the possible relationship between psychological variables and sports injuries (Figure 5.1). This would seem to be a logical avenue of research since it has long been hypothesized that a wide variety of psychological factors may affect both the mental and physical health of an individual. For example, early research investigating the relationship between psychological stress and disease in the general population indicated that individuals experiencing high levels of stress were more prone to illness (Holmes and Rahe, 1967). There is evidence that high levels of stress in athletes can result in physical fatigue as well as in reduced peripheral vision, either of which could conceivably increase the chances of an injury (Hanson, McCullugh, and Tonymon, 1992). As sports psychologists continued to investigate the relationship between the mind and sports injuries, the psychological attributes of athletes were divided into two general categories, personality variables and psychosocial variables. Kerr and Fowler (1988) have classified psycho-

FIGURE 5.1 Competition can create a great deal of psychological stress. (Courtesy of Boise State University.)

logical factors related to injury as either personality variables or psychosocial variables.

Personality Variables

According to Kerr and Fowler (1988), personality characteristics refer to the "stable, enduring qualities of

Information at your fingertips

The World Wide Web—Learn more about the field of sports psychology at the address of the Association for the Advancement of Applied Sports Psychology (AAASP). Go to http://www.jbpub.com/athletictraining and click on Chapter 5.

the individual." Characteristics such as general personality makeup, trait anxiety, locus of control, and self-concept have all been examined relative to their possible relationship to sports injuries. General personality makeup can be classified in a variety of ways, e.g., aggressive or passive, introverted or extroverted. **Trait anxiety** has been defined as "a general disposition or tendency to perceive certain situations as threatening and to react with an anxiety response" (Kerr and Fowler, 1988). **Locus of control** has to do with people's belief, or lack thereof, that they are in control of events occurring within their lives. Two general types of individuals have been identified—those with an external locus of control and those with an internal locus of control. The former feel they have very little control over events in their lives. These people believe factors such as destiny, luck, or fate determine life events. Individuals with an internal locus of control feel they are responsible for what happens to them— they are in charge. Research to date that has attempted to link incidence and/or severity of injury to locus of control has yielded inconclusive results. There is evidence that such connections, if they do exist, may be

rates in a group of collegiate football players. These findings support the theory that low self-concept functions as a significant risk factor for athletic injury. Apparently, athletes with a low self-concept are less able to deal effectively with the stress of competition. Their inability to cope effectively with competitive stress may even result in behavior that leads to injury. In extreme cases, being injured may become an attractive alternative to participation because it gives the athlete a legitimate excuse to avoid playing. Ironically, such injured athletes often get more attention from coaches and peers than they would otherwise have received. The prudent coach should consider the administration of a screening test such as the Tennessee Self-Concept Scale (TSCS) in order to identify athletes with low self-concept. Coaches lacking experience in the administration of these tests should seek the services of a trained professional, such as a sports psychologist, school psychologist, or guidance counselor. Athletes identified as having a low self-concept may be aided by a variety of intervention strategies. There is evidence that self-concept can be raised through a program of individualized counseling and exercise.

W H A T I F ?

You are coaching wrestling in a northern Michigan high school. It is early December and one of your athletes comes to you complaining of chronic fatigue, a craving for sweets, and a loss of interest in the sport. Could these complaints be symptoms of a psychological disorder and, if so, what would you do to help this athlete?

sport specific—i.e., locus of control may play a role in injury in certain types of sports. For example, in a study of intercollegiate football players, Petrie (1993a) found a relationship between trait anxiety and days missed owing to injury. Conversely, recent research conducted on collegiate athletes participating in track and field events failed to find statistically significant evidence of relationships between injury and locus of control or trait anxiety (Hanson, McCullugh, and Tonymon, 1992).

Self-concept may also be a risk factor with regard to injury. Athletes with low self-concept have been found to demonstrate a statistically significant relationship with sports injuries (Kerr and Fowler, 1988; Lamb, 1986). Lamb established a strong negative correlation (− .917) between self-concept and frequency of injury among a group of female collegiate field hockey players. Lamb reported similar results by Irvin in an earlier study that examined self-concept and injury

Obviously, a coach should attempt any sort of counseling with extreme caution so as not to make a bad situation worse. Once identified, athletes with low self-concept should be advised to consult a professional sports psychologist, guidance counselor, or even a clinical psychiatrist for help. The coach must exercise good judgment and tact in order to avoid labeling an athlete in a negative manner.

Seasonal Affective Disorder (SAD)

Seasonal affective disorder (SAD) is a psychiatric disorder that affects the general population, including athletes, primarily in the fall and winter seasons. SAD has been linked to a wide array of symptoms, including a loss of physical capacity and energy, increased appetite (carbohydrate craving), decreased libido, hypersomnia (excessive sleep or drowsiness), anhedonia (lack of interest in normally pleasurable activities), and impaired social activity (Rosen et al., 1996). Rosen and colleagues studied 68 NCAA Division I ice hockey players to ascertain the frequency of SAD (Rosen et al., 1996). Specifically, these players were all located in northern latitudes, with decreased daylight in the fall and winter months. The players were studied for one complete season, during which time they were given a set of questionnaires designed to identify those players exhibiting either symptomatic or subsyndromal SAD (mildly dysfunctional state, which is insufficient in intensity to meet criteria for a major depressive disorder [Kasper et al., 1989]). The findings of this research were alarming: 22 of the 68 players in the study were found to be suffering from either symptomatic SAD (N = 6 [9%]) or subsyndromal SAD (N = 16 [25%]). Considering the fact that many of the symptoms of this disorder may negatively affect performance or, worse, predispose some to injury, it seems prudent that parents, coaches, and sports medicine personnel become familiar with the signs and symptoms of SAD. While subsyndromal SAD represents a less severe form of the affliction, the potential for serious problems is high given that athletes thus affected may fail to seek medical attention. Accurate diagnostic tests are available for SAD and anyone exhibiting such symptoms as described herein should be referred to a specialist for evaluation. Regarding treatment, Rosen and colleagues have reported promising results using light therapy (Rosen et al., 1996).

Psychosocial Variables

Although overall correlations between general personality traits and injuries have been weak, more convincing findings have been produced from research examining the relationship between psychosocial factors and injury rates. Psychosocial variables develop through the interaction between the individual and a changing social environment (Kerr and Fowler, 1988). Specifically, attention has been given to studying the effects of stressful life events on athletes. Stressful life events have been defined as positive or negative episodes that usually evoke some adaptive or coping behavior or significant change in the ongoing life pattern of the individual (Holmes and Rahe, 1967). This theory holds that life events can be very stressful— even those most people would consider positive, such as getting married, taking a vacation, or even winning the lottery. Researchers have endeavored to study the effects of life events on different populations, including athletes. A variety of questionnaires have been devel-

oped, including the Social Readjustment Rating Scale (SRRS), the Social and Athletic Readjustment Rating Scale (SARRS), the Life Event Scale for Adolescents (LESA), the Life Event Questionnaire (LEQ), the Life Event Survey for Collegiate Athletes (LESCA), and the Athletic Life Experience Survey (ALES). Several studies have revealed a strong relationship between stressful life events and sports injuries (Hanson, McCullugh, and Tonymon, 1992; Kelley, 1990; Lamb, 1986; Lysens, Auweele, and Ostyn, 1986; Petrie, 1993a). Evidence suggests that when an athlete is experiencing significant personal changes, especially those seen as negative, the chances of injury increase. As was the case with determination of self-concept status, the coaching staff may find it helpful to assess the life-stress status of athletes prior to the beginning of the season as well as on a follow-up basis. In this way, athletes who are at high risk—i.e., those with high life-stress scores—can be identified and referred to a counselor in an effort to improve coping skills. There is evidence that athletes with a higher degree of such skills were less likely to be injured (Hanson, McCullugh, and Tonymon, 1992). The administration and interpretation of psychometric tests are most effectively conducted by sports psychologists and other trained professionals. Coaching personnel should avoid the temptation to play amateur psychologist with athletes as they may only make a bad situation worse.

Competitive Stress and the Adolescent

With the number of adolescents participating in sports increasing annually, serious concerns have been raised by professionals regarding the psychological impact of competition on youngsters (Nash, 1987). It is probable that the majority of children, even today, get involved in sports for recreational and social reasons. However, it is also true that the intensity of competition is being increased drastically in some sports at exceedingly early ages. Sports such as women's gymnastics, tennis, figure skating, bicycle motocross (BMX) cycling, and professional skate-boarding routinely produce regional and national champions under the age of 16. The pressure to win can come from parents, coaches, peers, sponsors, and even the media. Although the immediate effects of such pressure on children may be difficult to gauge, it is safe to assume that youngsters do not possess the psychological coping skills of adults. Consequently, the stress of competition may result in significant problems for some kids. Young athletes may be more prone to injury, psychosomatic illnesses, emotional burn-out, and other stress-related afflictions. Parents and coaches must take care not to force children beyond their ability to cope with the activity. It is a sad commentary on the values of today's society to think that some children may be driven from a sport that they love simply because they were pushed too hard, too early.

Psychology of the Injured Athlete

An injury represents a potent form of psychological stress for the athlete. For most, the possibility of being sidelined by a traumatic episode is an ever-present fear. (See Figure 5.2.) What little research is available on this topic seems to support the premise that for most athletes an injury produces a predictable psychological response. As can be seen in Figure 5.3, Weiss and Troxel (1986) reported that an injury will cause a psychophysiological reaction in the athlete that follows the classic stress-response model originally formulated by Selye.

As can be observed, in phase one the injury serves as a potent **stressor** and requires the athlete to adapt to a restriction of normal activity. Phase two involves an appraisal of the significance of the injury, both in

FIGURE 5.2 The potential for injury is an ever-present fear for most athletes.

The Stress Process

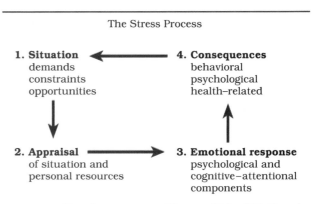

1. **Situation**
   demands
   constraints
   opportunities

4. **Consequences**
   behavioral
   psychological
   health–related

2. **Appraisal**
   of situation and
   personal resources

3. **Emotional response**
   psychological and
   cognitive–attentional
   components

FIGURE 5.3 The stress process. (Source: Weiss MR, Troxel RK. 1986. Psychology of the injured athlete. *Athletic Training.* 21(2):105. Reprinted with permission.)

a short- and long-term sense. Weiss and Troxel (1986) reported that it is during this phase that an athlete may engage in negative self-doubt ("What if I can't recover by the next game?"). Phase three of the stress model involves an emotional response, which can precipitate a host of physical and psychological reactions, ranging from severe anxiety, depression, and anger to increased muscle tension, blood pressure, and heart rate. Ermler and Thomas (1990) as well as Pedersen (1986) have developed models of injury response that fit well into this phase of the stress-response model. Ermler and Thomas theorized that an injury causes an athlete to experience feelings of alienation. Pedersen compared the effects of an injury with the grief response experienced following the death of a loved one. The fourth stage involves the long-term consequences of the emotional response in phase three. If an athlete fails to respond to an injury in a positive manner, he or she may suffer from a wide variety of problems, including sleep disorders, loss of appetite, and perhaps decreased motivation (Weiss and Troxel, 1986).

Recommendations

As a result of the development of these injury-response models, recommendations have been made regarding how best to assist the injured athlete in coping with an injury. Weiss and Troxel (1986) developed a list of guidelines for personnel to follow when working with an injured athlete. These are enumerated in Box 5.1.

Eating Disorders

With few exceptions, all sports impose an extremely narrow set of parameters for the appropriate body type

WHAT IF?

You are coaching high school girls' volleyball and one of your players keeps excusing herself from practice to go to the bathroom. Other members of the team tell you that she is vomiting each time she goes. What could such behavior imply? What would be your best course of action?

BOX 5.1   Guidelines for Working with an Injured Athlete

1. Treat the person, not just the injury.
2. Treat the athlete as an individual.
3. Keep in mind that communication skills are critical to an open coach–athlete relationship.
4. Remember the relationship between physical and psychological skills.
5. Seek the help of a sports psychologist for further ideas and strategies.

Source: Weiss MR, Troxel RK. 1986. Psychology of the injured athlete. *Athletic Training.* 21(2): 109–10. Reprinted with permission.

FIGURE 5.4 Many athletes feel compelled to conform to a certain body type.

required for success. It is difficult to imagine, for example, a world-class gymnast who is 6 feet tall and weighs 240 pounds, a long-distance runner who weighs too much, or a successful figure skater who is obese.

Reality dictates that specific sports require specific body types in order for athletes to be competitive. Some sports, such as those mentioned above, demand leanness for at least two reasons. First, the **biomechanics** of the sport may require a lean and muscular body in order to perform highly complex skills effectively. Second, the sports community and society as a whole have come to expect that successful athletes look lean and muscular. In recent years, media exposure of many top athletes has focused as much on physical appearance as on performance. This has created the need for many aspiring athletes to conform to a certain, very narrowly defined body type (Figure 5.4). This is especially true for female athletes.

Psychologists are beginning to discover that this emphasis on the ideal body has resulted in some serious negative effects on the athletic community. An increasing number of athletes are demonstrating abnormal, even pathogenic, eating behaviors that may have deeper psychological origins. **Bulimia** and **anorexia** are on the increase within the athletic community, with the former being more prevalent. The majority of athletes with eating disorders are female; likewise, the majority of people within the general U.S. population who have eating disorders are female.

Anorexia Nervosa and Bulimia Nervosa

Anorexia nervosa is characterized by a pattern of self-starvation motivated by an obsession with being thin and an overwhelming fear of being fat. Anorexic individuals typically have a grossly distorted body image: they think of themselves as being fat when they are in fact abnormally lean. **Bulimia nervosa** is characterized by repeated bouts of binge eating followed by some form

Athletic Trainers Speak Out

"It is not uncommon to see eating disorders among young athletes. Early detection of eating disordered behavior often lies in the hands of the athletic trainer. Proper recognition and intervention can be crucial to the future success of an athlete's career and, possibly, life. Certain sports emphasize weight more than others; therefore, it is vital that coaches be well educated. Properly implemented teamwork between physician, athletic trainer, and coach can reduce the risk of eating disorders."

—Jennifer Teaford, M.S., A.T.C.

Jennifer Teaford is an adjunct faculty member at Whitworth College.

Jennifer Teaford

of purging—e.g., vomiting, taking laxatives, fasting, or undertaking vigorous, excessive exercise. Both anorexia and bulimia are considered to be serious psychological problems that are most common among adolescent and young-adult females (Johnson and Tobin, 1991).

Research

Research indicates that a significant percentage of female collegiate athletes may practice dietary habits considered to be **pathogenic,** i.e., unhealthy (Grandjean, 1991). Such behavior, at the very least, may be a precursor of more serious eating disorders. When ques-

tioned, athletes report they engage in abnormal eating behaviors in an effort to improve either performance or appearance, or both. Perhaps more alarming, one study found that 70% of those reporting pathogenic eating behaviors felt such practices were harmless (Rosen et al., 1986).

Rosen and colleagues (1986) surveyed the eating habits of 182 female collegiate athletes and determined that 32% regularly practiced pathogenic eating—whether binges followed by self-induced vomiting that occurred more than twice weekly, or the regular use of laxatives, diet pills, and/or diuretics. Another more recent survey of both male and female collegiate competitors yielded similar results. Of 695 athletes questioned, 39.2% of the females and 14.3% of the males were classified as bulimic, and 4.2% of the females and 1.6% of the males were found to be anorexic (Burkes-Miller and Black, 1988). Little is known about pathogenic eating behaviors among male athletes. Historically, the sport of wrestling has received the most attention with regard to this problem. It is common knowledge that many wrestlers routinely practice a variety of strange eating and training behaviors, especially just prior to competition. These include fasting, restriction of fluids, the use of laxatives, vomiting, and sweating off weight by wearing a rubber suit in the sauna. Obviously all of these practices are to be discouraged. At best they will result in a short-term water loss; at worst they can cause severe illness and even death. More research is needed to determine if male athletes in sports other than wrestling are vulnerable to the same pressures as their female counterparts when it comes to maintaining body build and leanness.

Sport Specificity and Eating Disorders

It has been well documented that certain sports carry a high risk that participants will develop eating disorders. These include women's gymnastics, long-distance running, ballet, diving, and figure skating. All of these activities place a heavy emphasis on lean, muscular body builds. Petrie (1993b) recently surveyed 215 female gymnasts in college and determined that over 60% reported a variety of disordered eating behaviors. Not surprisingly, there is growing evidence that eating disorders may be gaining a foothold in sports historically immune to such problems. Rosen and colleagues (1986) found that significant percentages of female athletes participating in field hockey, softball, volleyball, track, and tennis reported pathogenic eating behaviors. In a survey of young (9 to 18 years old) competitive swimmers, Drummer and colleagues (1987) found that of 289 postmenarcheal females, 24.8% reported practicing some form of pathogenic eating behavior.

A variety of physical and psychological problems is associated with both anorexia and bulimia. Thornton (1990) reports that anorexic and bulimic athletes run the risk of esophageal inflammation, erosion of tooth enamel, hormone imbalances that can lead to osteoporosis and **amenorrhea,** and kidney and heart problems related to electrolyte imbalances. In addition, a variety of psychological problems, including depression and anxiety disorders, are also common.

Prevention

Prevention of eating disorders, including bulimia and anorexia nervosa, must be the goal of all those involved with organized sports. Coaches need to place less emphasis on body weight and fat when working with athletes. Referring to weight in a negative manner, requiring mandatory weigh-ins, or publicly ostracizing an athlete for being overweight are all practices to be condemned.

Coaches and parents need to be alert to the early warning signs of eating disorders. Refer to Appendix 4 for a comprehensive listing of signs and behaviors that may indicate the development of an eating disorder.

Treatment

Treatment of eating disorders ranges from simple counseling and education (when diagnosed in early stages), to hospitalization in severe cases. It must be remembered that in many cases an eating disorder may be a symptom of a psychological problem such as depression or anxiety. In spite of improved treatment programs, experts report that at least one-third of these cases will not respond to therapy. It is hoped that continued research will improve the prognosis for these individuals.

Information at your fingertips

The World Wide Web—You can learn more about eating disorders. Go to http://www.jbpub.com/athletictraining and click on Chapter 5.

Review Questions

1. Briefly define several of the personality variables described in the chapter.

2. Discuss the relationship between an athlete's self-concept and the risk of sports injury.

3. Describe briefly the relationship between psychosocial variables and the risk of sports injury.

4. List several sports in which adolescent athletes routinely achieve national-championship status. Discuss the possible relationship between this high level of competitive stress and the psychology of the adolescent athlete.

5. Discuss the psychological impact of a sports injury on an athlete in terms of the stress model shown in the chapter.

6. List the recommended guidelines for dealing with an injured athlete.

7. Define both anorexia nervosa and bulimia nervosa.

8. *True or false:* Recent research found that 70% of those reporting pathogenic eating behaviors felt such practices were harmless.

9. List several common forms of pathogenic eating behaviors found to be practiced by athletes.

10. List five common signs and/or behaviors that may indicate the development of an eating disorder.

11. Define the acronym SAD and discuss its implications for competitive athletes.

References

Burkes-Miller ME, Black DR. 1988. Male and female college athletes: prevalence of anorexia nervosa and bulimia nervosa. *Athletic Training.* 23(2):137–140.

Dummer GM, et al. 1987. Pathogenic weight-control behaviors in young competitive swimmers. *Phys Sportsmed.* 15(5):75–84.

Ermler KL, Thomas CE. 1990. Interventions for the alienating effect of injury. *Athletic Training.* 25(3):269–271.

Grandjean AC. 1991. Eating disorders: the role of the athletic trainer. *Journal of Athletic Training.* 26(2):105–112.

Hanson SJ, McCullugh P, Tonymon P. 1992. The relationship of personality characteristics, life stress, and coping resources to athletic injury. *Journal of Sport and Exercise Psychology.* 14:262–272.

Holmes H, Rahe RH. 1967. The social readjustment rating scale. *J Psycho Res.* 11:213–218.

Johnson C, Tobin DL. 1991. The diagnosis and treatment of anorexia nervosa and bulimia among athletes. *Journal of Athletic Training.* 26(2):119–128.

Kasper S, et al. 1989. Epidemiological findings of seasonal changes in mood and behavior. *Arch Gen Psychiatry.* 40:823–833.

Kelley MJ. 1990. Psychological risk factors and sports injuries. *J Sportsmed Phys Fit.* 30:202–221.

Kerr G, Fowler B. 1988. The relationship between psychological factors and sports injuries. *Sports Med.* 6:127–134.

Lamb M. 1986. Self-concept and injury frequency among female college field-hockey players. *Athletic Training.* 21(3):220–224.

Lysens R, Auweele YV, Ostyn M. 1986. The relationship between psychological factors and sports injuries. *J Sportsmed.* 26:77–84.

Nash HL. 1987. Elite child-athletes: how much does victory cost? *Phys Sportsmed.* 15(8):129–133.

Pedersen P. 1986. The grief response and injury: a special challenge for athletes and athletic trainers. *Athletic Training.* 21(4):312–314.

Petrie TA. 1993a. Coping skills, competitive trait anxiety, and playing status: moderating effects on the life stress-injury relationship. *Journal of Sports and Exercise Psychology.* 15:261–274.

Petrie TA. 1993b. Disordered eating in female collegiate gymnasts: prevalence and personality/attitudinal correlates. *Journal of Sports and Exercise Psychology.* 15:424–436.

Rosen LW, et al. 1996. Seasonal mood disturbances in collegiate hockey players. *Journal of Athletic Training.* 31(3):225–228.

Rosen LW, et al. 1986. Pathogenic weight-control behavior in female athletes. *Phys Sportsmed.* 14(1):79–86.

Thornton JS. 1990. Feast or famine: eating disorders in athletes. *Athletic Training.* 18(4):116–122.

Weiss MR, Troxel RK. 1986. Psychology of the injured athlete. *Athletic Training.* 21(2):104–105.

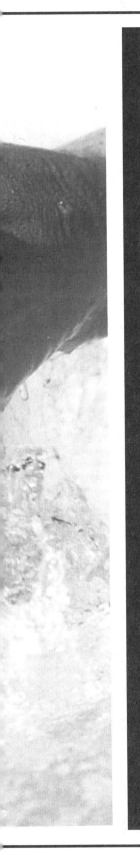

CHAPTER 6

Nutritional Considerations

MAJOR CONCEPTS

Research has shown that, regardless of the sport, an athlete's diet plays a critical if not essential role in performance. Yet misinformation and misconceptions persist among coaches and athletes regarding what constitutes an adequate diet. This chapter first examines available evidence concerning the dietary knowledge and practices of coaches and athletes. It identifies specific problems and outlines dietary recommendations pertaining to protein intake. It gives special attention to the sport of wrestling, which has been plagued with the problem of athletes attempting to lose body weight rapidly by dehydration, and provides a simple method of assessing an athlete's ability to rehydrate adequately. This chapter concludes with a brief discussion of the relationship between nutrition and recovery from injury.

An athlete's diet has a direct impact on performance, recovery from training and competition, resistance to environmental extremes, recovery from injury, and, to some extent, likelihood of injury. In essence, diet influences virtually all aspects of sports participation. Yet research demonstrates that coaches and athletes often lack adequate knowledge on the subject or incorporate unfounded nutritional practices into training programs. Parr, Porter, and Hodgson (1984) surveyed 348 coaches, 179 NATABOC-certified athletic trainers, and 2,977 athletes at the high school and college levels

The Ideal Diet vs. What Most Athletes Actually Eat and Drink

The limited amount of information available indicates that many athletes, in a variety of sports, fail to incorporate sound principles of nutrition into their training diets. Eck and colleagues (1988) surveyed 43 university football players and found that the distribution of

Information at your fingertips

The World Wide Web—For an excellent resource for current, scientifically based, sports nutrition information, go to http://www.jbpub.com/athletictraining and click on Chapter 6.

about their nutritional knowledge and practices. The majority of coaches (61%) reported they had no formal training in nutrition, and 78% reported they lacked adequate knowledge about it. However, the majority of athletes (68%) was familiar with the four food groups, and 71% reported incorporating them into their diets. Not surprisingly, certified athletic trainers were found to be the most knowledgeable regarding nutrition, with 73% reporting having had at least one college course on the subject. Perhaps what was most significant about this survey was that athletes reported that parents were their leading sources of information about nutrition—followed by TV commercials and magazines. Although the knowledge of most parents concerning nutrition cannot be measured, it is probably safe to assume that both parents and the media represent at best marginal sources of current information.

dietary nutrients for carbohydrates, protein, and fat was not in accord with current recommendations. The averages for that team were 34.7% carbohydrates, 17% protein, and 48.2% fat. These percentages conflict with recommendations by experts who advise a distribution of 45% to 70% carbohydrates, 12% to 15% protein, and 20% fat (Coyle, 1988; Nelson, 1989). It is interesting to note that in a survey of coaches involved primarily with football, the majority (51%) advocated a diet consisting of 45% carbohydrates, 45% protein, and 10% fat (Bentivegna, Kelley, and Lalenak, 1979). The findings of these studies indicate that football players as well as coaches persist in the myth that excessive dietary protein is a prerequisite to success. The elevated levels of fat consumed by players in the study by Eck and colleagues (1988) may indicate that they were consuming a high percentage of red meats and other protein sources high in fat. Such dietary practices create sev-

WHAT IF?

A female high school gymnast asks you for recommendations for her training diet. What would you suggest she consume on a daily basis in order to remain competitive?

eral cardiovascular problems, including arteriosclerosis and heart disease. It may be more than a curious coincidence that the life expectancy of an NFL football player is 52 to 55 years (Nelson, 1989).

Athletes and Dietary Habits

As more women become involved in organized sports, concerns have been raised regarding special nutritional considerations for female athletes. Perron and Endres (1985) investigated the nutritional habits of 31 female high school volleyball players. Seventy percent of them did not meet the recommended daily allowance (RDAs) for energy (total calories), calcium, and iron. It is not surprising that 81% of these athletes reported a concern about body weight; perhaps their low caloric intake was part of an attempt to lose weight. Moffatt (1984) surveyed the dietary habits of 13 female high school gymnasts who competed at advanced levels. The average body fat of these athletes was found to be 13.1%, yet 9 of the 13 girls were found to consume fewer calories than recommended. Since gymnastics is a sport that places great emphasis on being lean, it is not surprising that the majority of these girls demonstrated a deficient caloric intake. The gymnasts were also found to have diets low (below the RDA) in vitamin B-6, folic acid, iron, calcium, zinc, and magnesium. Knowledge about the nutritional habits of male and female high-school cross-country runners was examined; the results were similar to those of related studies (Upgrove and Achterberg, 1990). Ironically, in a sport in which a diet high in carbohydrates is a prerequisite to success, these young runners were found to be poorly versed in the role of this essential nutrient. In addition, they reported that coaches were their preferred source of information on nutrition. This is particularly alarming considering that many coaches are ill prepared to give sound advice on nutrition. Deuster and colleagues (1986) examined the dietary habits of a group of 51 top-level female distance runners. Their reported intake of protein, fat, and carbohydrates was 13%, 32%, and 55%, respectively. These percentages indicate a diet somewhat high in fat and low in carbohydrates. Even with the high-fat content, their diets were still too low in caloric content. In effect, these women were training and racing while adhering to diets that failed to provide adequate calories for such activity. Further analysis revealed that although many of the runners reported taking some sort of iron supplement, 43% were found to be consuming less than the adult RDA for iron, which is 18 milligrams. Current thought among sports scientists is that iron deficiency is common in athletes involved in endurance sports (Pattini and Schena, 1990). It is speculated that iron may be lost through sweating, gastrointestinal bleeding, and excessive red-cell destruction (**hemolysis**) within the blood vessels. Females are at particular risk since menstruation increases the loss of blood on a regular basis. During menstruation athletes may lose as much as 2 milligrams of iron daily. This loss may be offset by a dietary adjustment of iron-rich foods, such as organ meats, or enriched whole-grain products. A convenient method of supplementation is a daily multivitamin and mineral tablet. Numerous products are available over-the-counter that provide the adult RDA of iron.

Conclusions

Based upon the results of research pertaining to the nutritional behavior of athletes, it appears that some important conclusions can be made regarding the dietary practices of athletes:

1. Many athletes do not consume the proper proportions of protein, carbohydrates, and fat. There is growing support within the sports science community that adolescent athletes may require as much as 1.5–2 grams of protein per kilogram of body weight per day. For example, to compute the recommended one-day protein intake for an 85–pound female gymnast, make the following calculations:

   Body weight in kilograms = 38.64

   (85 pounds/2.2 pounds per kilogram)

   38.64 kilograms $\times$ 1.5 grams of protein

   = 57.95 grams daily protein requirement

   A chicken breast weighing 8 ounces will provide this amount of protein.

2. Many athletes involved in tackle football follow diets too high in fat and protein content (Figure 6.1).

3. Athletes participating in sports that stress lean builds and low body fat tend to follow diets too low in total calories.

4. Athletes tend to consume too many calories in the form of junk food (Figure 6.2).

5. Most athletes' diets are deficient in at least some important minerals, such as calcium, iron, and zinc.

FIGURE 6.1 Some red meats contain excessive amounts of fat.

FIGURE 6.2 Junk food can be convenient, but it lacks nutritional content.

Relationship Between Diet and Performance

There is no doubt that diet has a direct effect on an athlete's ability to perform. Yet most athletes, for a variety of reasons, fail to consume what most sports scientists would consider to be a balanced diet: adequate daily servings from the four basic food groups with appropriate proportions of carbohydrates, protein, and fat. For example, in endurance sports it is critical that participants consume adequate amounts of calories in order to provide the necessary energy for events. It is well known that such athletes can benefit from having large amounts of **glycogen** stored in the muscles and liver. Dietary carbohydrates (sugars and starches) provide the body with glycogen. However, equally important is the quality of the diet—i.e., the source of the carbohydrates. It is not enough to simply eat foods high in calories, such as candy and snacks. Athletes should consume foods with a large percentage of complex carbohydrates since they contain essential vitamins and minerals usually lacking in snack food and candy.

For athletes involved in sports such as tackle football, diet is also linked to performance. However, many athletes and coaches continue to adhere to antiquated dogma regarding nutrition. Many athletes follow diets that are excessively high in dietary fat and protein in a misguided attempt to boost muscle bulk and strength. Though a modest increase over the RDA of dietary protein is recommended, no reputable sports scientist advocates the megadoses of supplementary protein consumed by many competitors on a daily basis. Ironically, recent research indicates that athletes involved in sports that stress anaerobic energy systems also need to maintain high levels of muscle glycogen (Brotherhood, 1984). Football players would be well advised to include a high percentage of complex carbohydrates in their diets and place less emphasis on protein and fat.

The sport of wrestling, especially, encourages rapid, often unhealthy weight-loss procedures while still requiring that athletes perform at optimal levels. This curious paradox has evolved in response to one of the true advantages of the sport: weight categories for competitors of different sizes. Wrestling is one of only a few sports that matches participants on the basis of weight. Yet in an effort to gain an advantage, many

WHAT IF?

You are asked to make a presentation to parents of high school wrestlers on the topic of effective weight loss techniques. What specific recommendations would you make to these parents regarding their children's dietary habits?

Athletic Trainers Speak Out

"What an athlete eats or fails to eat may play a large role in how the body reacts to injury. Whether it is an acute or chronic injury, if the proper amount or type of nutrients (including water) are not readily available when an injury occurs, the recovery process will be hindered. For example, it is known that one of the predisposing factors involved with stress fractures may be a diet lacking in calcium. Knowing this, it is important for the athlete to be aware of the necessity of a properly balanced diet in order to prevent and to treat some injuries. An athletic trainer is a good resource to help find a diet specific to each athlete and the sport in which he or she participates."

—*Michelle Puetz, M.S., A.T.C.*

Michelle Puetz

Michelle Puetz is Assistant Athletic Trainer at Montana State University.

wrestlers attempt to shed pounds rapidly in order to compete in a lighter weight category. Unfortunately, the only form of rapid weight loss, short of surgical removal of tissue, is through **dehydration.** Water weighs approximately seven pounds per gallon; therefore, an athlete can significantly reduce weight by reducing the body's water content. Wrestlers have been known to use a variety of methods to rapidly lose weight, including fluid restriction, the use of laxatives and diuretics, artificially induced sweating, and even starvation. There is no definitive proof that such tactics actually present an advantage, and there are plenty of reasons not to engage in such behavior. The short-term effects of repeated bouts of extreme, rapid weight loss include strength depletion, increased blood viscosity (blood thickening), blood clots, kidney and liver problems, swelling of the pancreas (which produces insulin), and ulcers (Nelson, 1989; Williams, 1992). The long-term effects are not known at this time; however, there is speculation within the scientific community that these techniques may interfere with normal growth and development in the adolescent athlete.

In an effort to reduce the likelihood of unhealthy weight loss practices ("weight cutting") in high school wrestlers, the state of Wisconsin instituted the Wrestling Minimum Weight Project (WMWP) in 1989 (Oppliger et al., 1995). This project involved the establishment of minimum weight loss and body composition criteria that limited all participants to a body fat minimum of 7% and a maximum of 3 pounds of weight loss per week. A trained network of volunteers tested the athletes and provided an extensive offering of nutrition education for coaches around the state. Feedback regarding the program has been positive from 95% of the coaches, and wrestling participation has increased in Wisconsin as well. As a result of the WMWP, starting with the 1996–1997 season, the National Federation of State High School Associations has modified the wrestling rule #1–3–1 to include the following statement: "An ideal program would be one where a medical professional would assist in establishing a minimum weight through the use of checking body fat and hydration. The recommended minimum body fat should not be lower than 7%" (NFSHSA, 1996). In addition, the American College of Sports Medicine (ACSM) has published a position statement regarding weight loss in competitive wrestling. (See Appendix 5.)

What Can the Coach Do?

Research indicates that many athletes consider the coach to be responsible for providing guidelines on proper diet (Upgrove and Achterberg, 1990). Unfortunately, most coaches lack any sort of formal training on basic nutrition. Therefore, those planning to enter the coaching profession should incorporate at least one course in basic nutrition into their academic programs. Coaches earning either a major or minor in physical education will probably be required to take at least one class in nutrition. The same is often true for those earning a coaching endorsement or minor. Another option for coaches is attendance at in-service meetings, professional conferences, and community education programs on nutrition-related topics. Subscribing to a professional journal in the field of coaching or sports science may also provide an excellent source of current information. Furthermore, many excellent books on sports nutrition are now on the market. In addition, registered hospital dietitians are highly trained and may be more than happy to provide information on nutrition for your athletes. For assistance in locating an expert in your area, contact the American Dietetic Association, 208 S. LaSalle, Chicago, IL 60604–1003.

Another option, for coaches who live near a university, is to contact a member of the institution's sports medicine staff. Typically, this is a NATABOC-certified athletic trainer. In addition, universities often employ faculty with graduate degrees in nutrition science, and they may be willing to serve as a resource as well.

Coaches should encourage, perhaps even require, that athletes keep a daily record of what they eat and drink. This information can be combined with a training diary. Coaches should periodically review what athletes are eating and make recommendations based upon sound nutritional principles. Such a record need not be a complex, detailed document. Athletes need only record the content and approximate amount of foods and beverages consumed during each meal. Most food packages provide information regarding the nutritional content of the product. With practice, it is relatively simple to determine if an athlete is consuming the correct amount of nutrients. When working with children, coaches should discuss the nutritional needs of athletes with parents. It does little good to provide information to an athlete if his or her diet is controlled by an uninformed parent.

Dietary Guidelines for Athletes

Daily Diet

Although each sport and each athlete have specific nutritional requirements and preferences, some general recommendations can be made based upon current knowledge. It should be noted, however, that (like a conditioning program) the athlete's diet should be tailored to meet individual needs. A gymnast may need to control her body composition within a very narrow set of parameters; a football lineman may wish to gain additional lean body mass. Thus, the nutrition program must be based upon the physical characteristics of the athlete and the individual demands of the sport.

According to Brotherhood (1984), all sports nutrition programs should have three goals:

1. Nutritional maintenance and development during training to ensure adequate recovery between training sessions;

2. precompetition preparation;

3. nutrition during competition.

Athletes need to be educated about proper food selections in order to maintain the correct proportions of carbohydrates, fat, and protein. Sport scientists recommend that 10% to 15% of dietary calories be supplied by protein, 30% by fat, and the remainder in the form of carbohydrates. It may be best to keep dietary recommendations as simple as possible since most foods contain significant amounts of carbohydrates. It is important that athletes understand that many protein sources contain significant amounts of fat; therefore, these foods should be consumed less frequently than carbohydrates. Most experts agree that even highly active athletes need only 1.5 to 2 grams of protein per day for each kilogram of body weight. This means that a football player who weighs 195 pounds (88.6 kilograms) needs to consume a maximum of 177 grams of protein per day. This amount would be supplied by consuming:

4 cups of milk	32 grams
9 ounces of lean beef	72 grams
4 cups of macaroni and cheese	72 grams
Total =	176 grams

Research shows that many football players routinely consume amounts of protein far in excess of the recommended levels (Slavin, Lanners, and Engstrom, 1988). Not only are such diets expensive, but they may

of iron deficiency who complain of chronic fatigue, loss of fitness, and inability to perform—in spite of adequate diet and rest—should be referred to a physician for evaluation. A simple blood test can determine if a true iron deficiency is the problem. Researchers recommend that high-risk groups be tested periodically for iron deficiency with subsequent supplementation of iron when deemed appropriate by a physician (Magazanik et al., 1988).

Coaches should be conservative when making dietary recommendations, especially to younger athletes. Offering a few well-proven, simple guidelines probably represents the most effective approach. A good example of a nontechnical dietary guide is the food guide pyramid developed by the USDA (Figure 6.3).

The pyramid provides proportional guidelines from each of the four food groups as well as suggested foods. It may be helpful, when practical, to use a computerized dietary analysis in order to determine the nutritional content of an athlete's diet. This usually involves recording dietary intake for several days and then entering the information into the computer. The accuracy of such analysis depends on the honesty and diligence of the athlete. For this analysis to be effective, it is best to work with a person who has expertise in computerized dietary analysis, such as a registered dietitian.

Information at your fingertips

The World Wide Web—For more information on healthy diets, go to http://www.jbpub.com/athletictraining and click on Chapter 6.

be unhealthy as well. Excess protein produces metabolic waste products, especially nitrogen, which can put stress on both the kidneys and liver. Dehydration may also occur as the kidneys increase urine output.

Assuming athletes are sticking to a balanced diet, there is no need to be concerned about their getting enough vitamins and minerals. These compounds are needed in small amounts, and there is little evidence that athletes need to consume extra vitamins and minerals in order to perform. As has been discussed previously, one mineral that may prove an exception is iron. Dietary iron supplementation may be warranted in cases of identified iron deficiency. Athletes at risk

Precompetition Diets

Precompetition diets should be determined based upon the sport or activity. As a general rule, it is advised that athletes, regardless of sport, not consume a meal immediately prior to an event. The process of digestion takes time, and foods eaten just before a contest will contribute virtually nothing to performance. Experts recommend that the typical pregame diet should consist of low-fat, easily digestible foods eaten no later than three to four hours prior to the contest (Brotherhood, 1984). These guidelines are especially

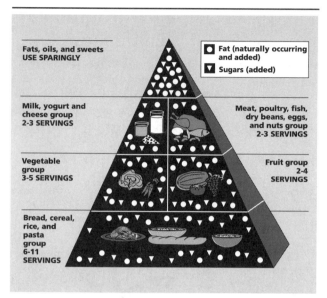

FIGURE 6.3 Food guide pyramid. (Source: U.S. Department of Agriculture/U.S. Department of Health and Human Services.)

important for the athletes participating in endurance sports. However, athletes involved in power sports such as football would also benefit from such a regimen. The traditional meal of steak and potatoes just prior to the game provides only a psychological effect; it may cause bloating and a feeling of heaviness in some athletes.

With the exception of proper water intake, nutrition during exercise is not critical unless an athlete is participating in a long-duration aerobic event. Athletes taking part in any activity involving intense exertion will perspire, thus depleting the body's water supply. This fluid must be replaced regularly; otherwise, dehydration can occur, resulting in loss of performance, heat-related illness, and even death. Brouns (1991) reports that during times of heavy exertion athletes can lose 1.5 to 2 liters of water during each hour of activity. The study recommends that athletes incorporate the following general guidelines regarding fluid replacement during exercise lasting longer than 30 minutes:

1. Urinate and defecate 30 to 45 minutes prior to the start of the event.

2. Drink 300 to 600 milliliters of fluids 3 to 5 minutes prior to the start of the event.

3. Continue drinking fluids on a regular basis during the event.

Athletes involved in team sports such as football should be encouraged to drink whenever thirsty—during both games and practice sessions. As a general

rule, these athletes should consume fluids every 10 to 15 minutes.

To determine if an athlete is consuming enough fluids during training, body weight should be recorded before and after exercise. To determine if the athlete is rehydrating properly, Broun (1991) suggests making the following calculation:

Weight loss in kilograms (2.2 pounds) − 1 kilogram = liters of fluid deficiency

As an example, assume a football player shows a weight loss of 4 pounds, or approximately 1.8 kilograms, during play. Using the above equation: 1.8 kilograms − 1 kilogram = .8 liters of fluid deficiency. In other words, this player finished practice dehydrated, with nearly a full liter less fluid than he needed. Coaches should advise their athletes to keep a training log, which includes a daily recording of body weight, both before and immediately after practice or competition.

Carbohydrate Ingestion During Exercise

Considerable attention has recently been given to the effects of carbohydrate ingestion during long-duration exercise. It is known that the body has a limited capacity for storing glycogen and that athletes may deplete glycogen supplies in the muscles and liver before completing an event. This is commonly referred to as "hitting the wall." Research supports the premise that consuming carbohydrates during long-duration exercise (1 to 3 hours at 70% to 80% VO$_2$ maximum), will allow active muscle tissue to rely upon blood glucose for energy (Coyle, 1988). The recommended dosage of carbohydrate feeding during exercise is 8 ounces of solution, containing a 5% carbohydrate mixture, taken every 15 minutes. Many commercially made carbohydrate products are now available. Coaches and athletes can also prepare their own preferred beverages.

Weight vs. Fat Management

Athletes wishing to gain or lose weight must be educated about the various ways that body weight can be changed. Body weight can be categorized as three basic forms: water, fat tissue, and lean tissue. Water makes up a substantial portion of nearly all the tissues within the body. Skeletal muscles make up the majority of lean tissue within the body. The majority of body fat is found just under the skin and is known as subcutaneous fat. The human body has devised a highly efficient method of storing excess dietary calories. When an athlete consumes more calories each day than the body requires for a given activity level, the excess calories are converted to fat. Conversely, if an athlete fails to consume enough calories to meet the daily requirement, subcutaneous fat will be metabolized to form energy. Curiously, when an athlete severely restricts caloric intake, such as in fasting, the body will consume muscle tissue in order to generate energy (Williams, 1992). Therefore, an athlete will reduce lean-tissue mass, which in most cases will result in loss of performance. It is important to note that a given volume of muscle tissue will weigh more than the same volume of fat. The ratio of fat to lean body weight is commonly referred to as body composition. From a practical standpoint, skeletal muscles make up the majority of lean-tissue weight. Determining body weight by standing on a scale is of limited value. For the vast majority of athletes, it is really a moot issue because activity and diet allow them to maintain a desirable body weight. That is the case when an athlete's caloric intake equals caloric expenditure—i.e., basic metabolic needs and exercise demands. Athletes should weigh themselves weekly, at about the same time of day, after going to the bathroom. Their body weight should not fluctuate from week to week. It is important to remember that female athletes may experience weight gains immediately preceeding their menstrual period.

There are athletes who, for a variety of reasons, desire to change their body weight. Those involved in sports that require a specific body weight, such as wrestling, may attempt to lose pounds rapidly in order to compete in a lighter weight category. These competitors need to understand that rapid weight fluctuations involve dehydration and that significant water loss can cause a number of undesirable consequences resulting in loss of performance. Wrestlers should determine their ideal body weight during the off-season and then concentrate on preparing for that weight category in the upcoming season.

▌Minimal Competitive Weight

For male athletes, it has been recommended that not less than 5% of total body composition be in the form of fat. The minimal competitive weight can then be calculated by dividing the athlete's lean body weight by 0.95 (Wilmore and Costill, 1988). In order to use this formula, the body weight and percentage of fat of the athlete must be determined. Although there are many ways of estimating body fat, the most practical method employs skin-fold measurements. However, the technique is only as good as the person administering the test. Hence, testing of body composition should be conducted by a person who has been properly trained, such as an exercise physiologist or NATA-certified athletic trainer. Once the percentage of fat has been determined, **lean body weight (LBW)** can be calculated with the following formula:

LBW = total body weight − fat weight

If an athlete weighs 135 pounds and has 14% body fat, then fat weight can be determined by multiplying percentage of fat times body weight: $.14 \times 135 = 18.9$ pounds. Thus, fat weight is approximately 20 pounds. Determining this athlete's LBW is calculated by subtracting fat weight from total body weight: $135 - 18.9 = 116.10$ pounds. To determine the minimal competitive weight for this athlete, make the following calculation:

Minimal competitive weight = 116.10/0.95
= 122.21 pounds

Thus, this athlete should not compete if weight drops below 122.21 pounds. Although no formal guidelines currently exist for female athletes, experts recommend that their levels of body fat not drop below 8% to 10% (Wilmore and Costill, 1988). Using the same equation, a 115–pound female athlete who has 12% body fat should not be allowed to compete if her weight drops below 106.53 pounds:

$115 \times .12$ (% body fat) = 13.8 pounds of fat

115 − 13.8 pounds of fat = 101.20 pounds LBW

Minimal competitive weight = 101.20/0.95
= 106.53 pounds

Athletes involved in sports such as gymnastics or diving, which tend to emphasize an ideal body type, may be faced with a dilemma when attempting to alter their appearance. First, these activities are considered to be anaerobic, deriving the required energy from glycogen supplies within working muscles. If a gymnast wishes to reduce her level of body fat, she will be required to engage in some form of aerobic exercise in addition to gymnastics training. In this way she will be able to eliminate excess body fat while at the same time sparing muscle tissue, which is needed for gymnastics.

Any athlete who demonstrates abnormal eating behaviors or exhibits unusual or unwarranted concerns about excess body fat should be referred to an expert for evaluation and dietary counseling.

Nutrition and Injury Recovery

Obviously, proper nutrition is vital to tissue healing and recovery. Although there is no evidence that supplementing vitamins and minerals will shorten recovery time, it is essential that their consumption be adequate (Wilmore and Costill, 1988).

A major concern for many injured athletes is weight gain during periods of forced inactivity. Some athletes find it difficult to adjust eating habits in order to reduce caloric intake when they are not exercising. It is important that the coach advise an injured athlete about dietary changes during recovery. It may be possible for some injured athletes to continue exercising with some form of alternate activity. Runners can often ride a stationary bicycle or run in a swimming pool, thereby maintaining aerobic fitness and burning off excess calories. Players who are suffering from infectious illnesses may be unable to exercise and should take care to reduce total caloric intake until they are healthy.

Review Questions

1. According to the chapter, a recent survey of coaches, athletes, and NATABOC-certified athletic trainers revealed that athletes depended on what sources for their information about nutrition?

2. What is the recommended level of dietary protein for adolescent athletes?

3. What is the approximate weight of a gallon of water?

4. Discuss briefly the short-term effects of repeated episodes of extreme, rapid weight loss.

5. What should be the three goals of any sports nutrition program?

6. What are the recommended percentages of protein, fat, and carbohydrates in an ideal training diet?

7. Using the equation provided in the chapter compute the protein requirement (in grams) for a football player who weighs 94 kilograms.

8. Briefly restate the five guidelines regarding a precompetition diet.

9. *True or false:* During times of heavy exertion, it is not possible to lose more than 0.5 to 1 liter of water for each hour of exercise.

10. Compute the fluid deficiency of an athlete who weighs 5.5 pounds less after practice than he did prior to practice.

11. Briefly review the effects of dietary fasting on muscle tissue.

12. *True or false:* Sports scientists recommend a training diet in which 30% to 40% of daily calories consumed are in the form of protein.

13. What is often the major nutritional concern of an injured athlete who is recovering from an injury?

References

American College of Sports Medicine. 1976. Position statement on weight loss in wrestlers. *Med Sci Sports.* 8(2):xi-xiii.

Bentivegna A, Kelley EJ, Lalenak A. 1979. Diet, fitness, and athletic performance. *Phys Sportsmed.* 7(10):99–105.

Brotherhood JR. 1984. Nutrition and sports performance. *Sports Med.* 1:350–389.

Brouns R. 1991. Heat-sweat-dehydration-rehydration: a praxis-oriented approach. *J Sports Sci.* 9:143–152.

Coyle EF. 1988. Carbohydrates and athletic performance. *Sports Science Exchange.* 1(7).

Deuster PA, et al. 1986. Nutritional survey of highly trained women runners. *Am J Clin Nut.* 44:954–962.

Eck LH, et al. 1988. Composition of training-table selections in a group of male university athletes. *Athletic Training.* 23(2):141–144.

Magazanik A, et al. 1988. Iron deficiency caused by 7 weeks of intensive physical exercise. *Eur J App Phys.* 57:198–202.

Moffatt RJ. 1984. Dietary status of elite female high-school gymnasts: inadequacy of vitamin and mineral intake. *J Am Diet Assoc.* 84(11):1361–1363.

National Federation of State High School Associations.

(1996). *Wrestling Rules Book.* Kansas City: National Federation of State High School Associations.

Nelson RA. 1989. Nutrition for the athlete. In Ryan AJ, Allman FL (eds.). *Sports Medicine.* San Diego: Academic Press. 165–181.

Oppliger RA, et al. 1995. The Wisconsin wrestling minimum weight project: a model for weight control among high school wrestlers. *Med Sci Sports.* 27(8):1220–1224.

Parr RB, Porter MA, Hodgson SC. 1984. Nutrition knowledge and practice of coaches, trainers, and athletes. *Phys Sportsmed.* 12(3):127–138.

Pattini A, Schena F. 1990. Effects of training and iron supplementation on iron status of cross-country skiers. *J Sportsmed Phys Fit.* 30:347–353.

Perron M, Endres J. 1985. Knowledge, attitudes, and dietary practices of female athletes. *J Am Diet Assoc.* 85(5):573–576.

Slavin JL, Lanners G, Engstrom MA. 1988. Amino-acid supplements: beneficial or risky? *Phys Sportsmed.* 16(3):221–224.

Upgrove NA, Achterberg CL. 1990. The conceptual relationship between training and eating in high-school distance runners. *J Nut Educ.* 23(1):18–24.

Williams MH. 1992. *Nutrition for Fitness and Sport.* Dubuque: William C. Brown.

Wilmore JH, Costill DL. 1988. *Training for Sport and Activity: The Physiological Basis of the Conditioning Process.* Dubuque: William C. Brown.

Emergency Plan and Initial Injury Evaluation

MAJOR CONCEPTS

Coaching personnel have a legal duty to develop and implement an emergency action plan to be followed in the event that an athlete is injured while participating in sports. To be effective such a plan must be carefully thought out. It must pay great attention to details, including the location of phones and keys to locks on facility entrances, and it must be tested for effectiveness via periodic rehearsal. This chapter provides a step-by-step outline of the vital components in the development of an effective emergency plan. It discusses the process of injury evaluation in the unique situations presented in the sports environment. It describes the essential steps in both the primary and secondary surveys of an injured athlete—from the ABCs of the primary survey to the history-taking and observation and palpation phases of the secondary survey.

As has been discussed in previous chapters of this book, sports injuries are an inevitable outcome of participation for tens of thousands of athletes each year. Proper planning is essential to ensure appropriate initial first aid management of an injury. There are two good reasons for developing a formal emergency plan for sports injuries. First, anything that can be done ahead of time to improve the health care of injured athletes should be a priority. Second, from a legal standpoint, failure to have an emergency plan in place has been found to constitute negligence in litigation resulting from a sports injury. According to Ball (1989), "failing to identify and properly deal with injuries in order to avoid unnecessary aggravation or complication" is a major source of liability for coaches.

In essence, an emergency plan must deal with the question: "Should someone be injured, who will be in charge, and what will be done?" It is recommended that all personnel directly involved with a particular sports program take part in the development and implementation of the emergency plan. In a school setting this could include coaches, administrators, the team physician and athletic trainer (if available), and other staff members involved with the program. The plan must be comprehensive, specifically outlining procedures for both home and out-of-town contests and practices. Furthermore, it must be written so that new staff members will be able to implement the plan when necessary (Ball, 1989). The written plan must include locations of telephones, emergency phone numbers, directions to the contest site, access points to the facility, and other critical information. Regardless of the sport, location, and personnel available, certain questions must be answered well in advance. With respect to emergency medical services (EMS), it is important that arrangements be made to have EMS personnel present at any athletic event whenever possible (Figure 7.1). Moreover, coaches and staff should know where the EMS vehicle is parked, the access route to the playing area, and the location of keys to gates and doors that may present barriers to emergency personnel. If the EMS is not present at the event, all staff members should know the EMS phone number and the location of the nearest telephone. Given the available technology, it seems prudent that all key members of the coaching staff should carry a cellular telephone, with EMS phone numbers programmed in memory, at all times during both practice and contest situations. In this way, valuable time will not be wasted finding the nearest telephone in the event of an emergency that requires EMS. A decision should be made ahead of time as to who will summon emergency personnel and who will remain with the injured athlete.

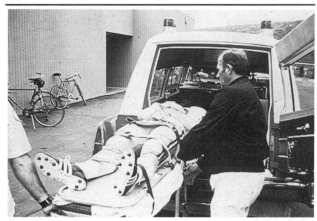

FIGURE 7.1 It is important that arrangements be made to have the EMS present at athletic events whenever possible.

On a playing field, coaches should stipulate ahead of time what type of signal will be used to alert EMS personnel to come onto the field and render care (Harris, 1988).

Important Questions and Considerations

Nowlan and colleagues recommend the following major elements of an emergency plan:

1. Phones:
   - location/access at all times
   - emergency numbers
   - who makes the call?
2. Gates/Passageways:
   - which one is to be used?
   - who has the keys?
   - will emergency vehicles have easy access?
   - who will guide emergency vehicles to the site?
3. Emergency Supplies:
   - location
   - responsible party
   - procedure for use
4. Emergency Evaluation/Care:
   - role of each individual

The emergency plan should be rehearsed periodically to ensure that it will work smoothly and effectively. Changes in staff, facilities, playing schedules, EMS services, and playing seasons can all affect the effectiveness of any plan. It is the responsibility of all those involved with organized sports programs to provide proper emergency care in the event that it is needed.

First Aid Training

It should be obvious that all personnel involved with organized sports programs must be trained in basic first aid. Such training is available through several different agencies nationwide, including the National Safety Council and the American Heart Association. It is strongly recommended that all personnel upgrade their training every three years in order to keep first aid skills current. Periodic mock emergency drills should be practiced to verify the effectiveness of the emergency plan. First aid training should include special training in cardiopulmonary resuscitation (CPR), which involves managing a victim with cardiac arrest (Figure 7.2).

Injury-Evaluation Procedures

The Coach's Responsibility

Immediate management of an acute sports injury presents the coach with a challenge unlike any other related to the profession. Immediate care is critical in determining the location and severity of the injury. It is important to remember that sports injuries generally occur amidst the confusion of a contest or practice. Therefore, it is imperative that the coach maintain a clear head and remain objective in the initial assessment of any injury. Every situation is unique, and the coach must make it clear to everyone in the immediate vicinity of the injured athlete that he or she is in charge. By law, the coach is the person most often held

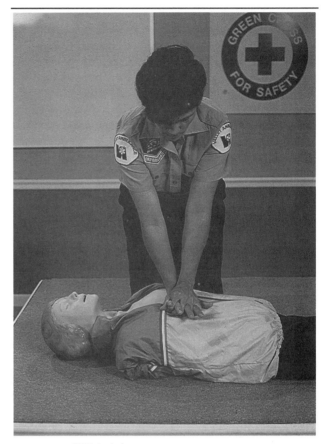

FIGURE 7.2 CPR training.

accountable for proper injury management when no athletic trainer or physician is present.

Coaching personnel should be properly trained in those first aid procedures commonly referred to as **basic life support (BLS)**. Such training is available through the National Safety Council and the American Heart Association. The primary objective of BLS is to sustain the injured athlete's life until medical assistance arrives at the scene. BLS procedures are used primarily in the case of airway obstructions and respiratory and cardiac arrest. If left unattended, any of

Information at your fingertips

The World Wide Web—For more information about the National Safety Council (NSC), go to http://www.jbpub.com/athletictraining and click on Chapter 7.

these conditions can result in death within minutes. Thus, the primary skills developed during BLS instruction focus on dealing effectively with respiratory and cardiac problems—i.e., airway assessment, techniques for opening the airway, artificial respiration, and cardiopulmonary resuscitation (CPR). All of these techniques are learned skills that require periodic practice. It is important that coaches maintain their skills in BLS through regular review sessions as well as annual recertification from agencies offering such instruction (AAOS, 1991).

As was stated earlier, each injury presents the coach with a unique set of circumstances; however, the coach's responsibilities remain the same. Coaches must have a basic knowledge of sports injuries and, more important, *the ability to differentiate minor from major injuries.* A central theme in the remainder of this book will be the development of initial assessment skills necessary to determine which injuries should be referred to medical personnel and which can be treated with simple first aid. Such determinations represent a major dilemma for many in the coaching profession. This is especially true when no athletic trainer or physician is immediately available, which more often than not is the case. Critical to the process of immediate injury management is current certification

all vital life functions and following up with a step-by-step examination to determine any and all injuries that the athlete may have sustained. In this way, tragedy can be avoided—for example, treating an unconscious athlete's head wound without first checking to see if he has an open airway and is breathing.

Primary Survey

The initial assessment of the injured athlete consists of two phases known as the primary survey and the secondary survey. The purpose of the **primary survey** (Figure 7.8) is to determine if the athlete's life is in immediate jeopardy. The primary survey must include assessments of the following:

A—Does the athlete have an open airway?

B—If so, is the athlete breathing?

C—Does the athlete have a pulse?

H—Is the athlete hemorrhaging severely?

Generally, it is best not to move an athlete unless you have a good reason. Therefore, during the primary survey make every effort to perform the assessment without moving the athlete. In some cases this may

WHAT IF?

You are coaching JV football, specifically the linebackers, when suddenly someone yells that an athlete has been hurt on the other end of the practice field. When you arrive on the scene the athlete is lying face down on the field and not moving. What should your initial actions be in this situation?

in at least basic first aid and CPR. Furthermore, the coach must be familiar with the preexisting emergency plan and be able to function effectively as a primary player on the sports medicine team.

The Evaluation Process

In order to be effective in the initial process of injury management, the person rendering first aid must have a prepared protocol to follow. The emergency treatment protocol must be generic enough to be effective, regardless of the type of injury. By following a preplanned format, the coach is assured of first evaluating

not be possible; for example, it may be necessary to roll an athlete onto her side in order to determine if she has an open airway. It is important to follow appropriate first aid procedures whenever moving an athlete.

Airway Assessment

Initial assessment can be facilitated by asking the athlete a simple question. If the athlete responds, the airway is open, and the level of consciousness is high, which indictes that circulation is adequate (Hargarten, 1993). If the victim is unconscious, assess for breathing first at the victim's head in the position she was found, if at all possible. If the victim is not breathing, either use the jaw-thrust technique (if serious head or spine injury is suspected) or the head-tilt/chin-lift method (if there appear to be no indications of serious head or spine injury. If there is any question about the possibility of serious head or spine injury, use the jaw-thrust technique (Figure 7.3). Place one hand on the athlete's forehead while gently lifting the chin with the other hand. In the case of a helmeted athlete, such as a football player, *do not remove the helmet or face mask* in order to open the airway. Opening an airway and checking for breathing can be accomplished with the helmet in place. Attempts to remove the helmet can easily aggravate an existing neck injury. (A detailed description of proper care of the injured helmeted player is presented in Chapter 9.) When there is reason to believe a neck injury may have occurred, the preferred method of opening the airway is the jaw-thrust technique (Figure 7.4). Position yourself so you are able to place your elbows at each side of the athlete's head. Place each hand at the angle of the jaw and gently push the jaw upward; this should open the airway. Remember to check for a foreign object in the airway, such as gum, a mouthpiece, chewing tobacco, a dental appliance, or other material. Remove such objects using the finger-sweep method (Figure 7.5).

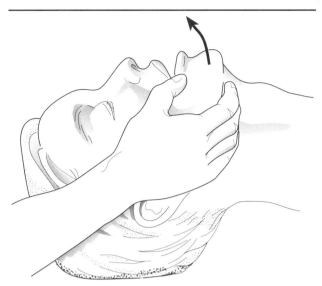

FIGURE 7.4 Jaw-thrust maneuver.

 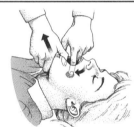

Finger sweep method
- With index finger of your hand, slide finger down along the inside of one cheek deeply into mouth and use a hooking action across to other cheek to dislodge foreign object.
- If foreign body comes within reach, grab and remove it. Do not force object deeper.

FIGURE 7.5 Finger-sweep method. (Source: National Safety Council. 1994. *First Aid and CPR* (2nd ed.). Boston: Jones and Bartlett. 35. Reprinted with permission.)

Breathing Assessment

The conscious athlete is obviously breathing; however, continue to observe for difficulty in breathing and listen for sounds that may indicate a problem. The unconscious athlete can be assessed quickly once the airway is established. Remember three words: look, listen, feel. Look for chest movements, listen for the flow of air exiting the athlete's nose and mouth, and feel for the air flow (Figure 7.6). If you determine that the athlete is not breathing, the next step is to check for a pulse.

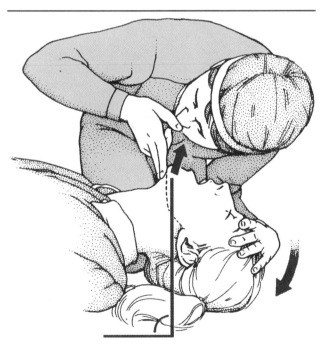

FIGURE 7.3 Head-tilt/chin-lift method. (Source: National Safety Council. 1994. *First Aid and CPR* (2nd ed.). Boston: Jones and Bartlett. 31. Reprinted with permission.)

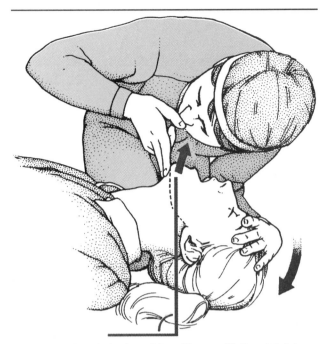

FIGURE 7.6 Check for breathing. (Source: National Safety Council. 1994. *First Aid and CPR* (2nd ed.). Boston: Jones and Bartlett. 31. Reprinted with permission.)

Pulse Assessment

A conscious athlete who is breathing has a pulse. However, remember that it is possible to have a pulse yet not be breathing. To determine if a pulse is present, the best option is to check the carotid pulse. With two fingers, press gently but firmly against the neck in the groove alongside the Adam's apple (Figure 7.7). You should feel the pressure of the blood pushing against the tissue at this point. If you detect a pulse, but the athlete is not breathing, you must begin artificial respiration immediately. If no pulse is present, begin CPR. In such a situation, the coach's primary responsibility is to keep the athlete alive and to ensure that help is summoned. There is no reason to move the athlete from the playing field or practice area. The possibility of delaying a game or practice does not justify moving someone in this situation.

Hemorrhage Assessment

Extensive external bleeding is extremely rare in athletics. Most external bleeding will be obvious and can be controlled by following appropriate first aid procedures—i.e., use of direct pressure, elevation, pressure

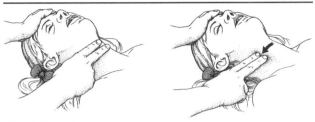

Check for pulse

- Maintain head-tilt with hand nearest head on forehead.
- Locate Adam's apple with 2 or 3 fingers of hand nearest victim's feet.
- Slide your fingers down into groove of neck on side closest to you (do not use your thumb because you may feel your own pulse).
- Feel for carotid pulse (take 5-10 seconds). Carotid artery is used because it lies close to the heart and is accessible.

FIGURE 7.7 Check for pulse. (Source: National Safety Council. 1994. *First Aid and CPR* (2nd ed.). Boston: Jones and Bartlett. 32. Reprinted with permission.)

points, and/or a pressure bandage. Any time blood or other bodily fluids are exposed, the coach should take precautions: wear eye protection and latex gloves to help prevent the possibility of bloodborne pathogen transmission.

Internal hemorrhaging is difficult if not impossible to detect during the primary survey. One of the earliest signs of severe internal bleeding will be **hypovolemic shock,** which is caused by too little blood within the vascular system. Two important signs of this condition are rapid, weak pulse and rapid, shallow breathing. Such cases represent true medical emergencies, and the primary objective must be to treat for shock and arrange for transport to a medical facility.

Remember: the purpose of the primary survey is to determine whether there is a life-threatening injury (Figure 7.8). If an airway exists, breathing and pulse appear normal, and no bleeding is detected, the next step in the evaluation process is the secondary survey. The purpose of the secondary survey is to give the injured athlete a complete evaluation for any other injuries not found during the primary survey. In order to be effective, the secondary survey must be conducted in a preplanned, sequential fashion. In cases in which injuries are obvious, it may be possible to skip certain portions of the secondary survey in order to render appropriate first aid sooner. However, even after attending to the obvious injury, the remaining portions of the survey should be completed. A good example would be a basketball player who falls to the floor immediately after having attempted to get a rebound. If you saw the accident—and noticed that she

PRIMARY SURVEY

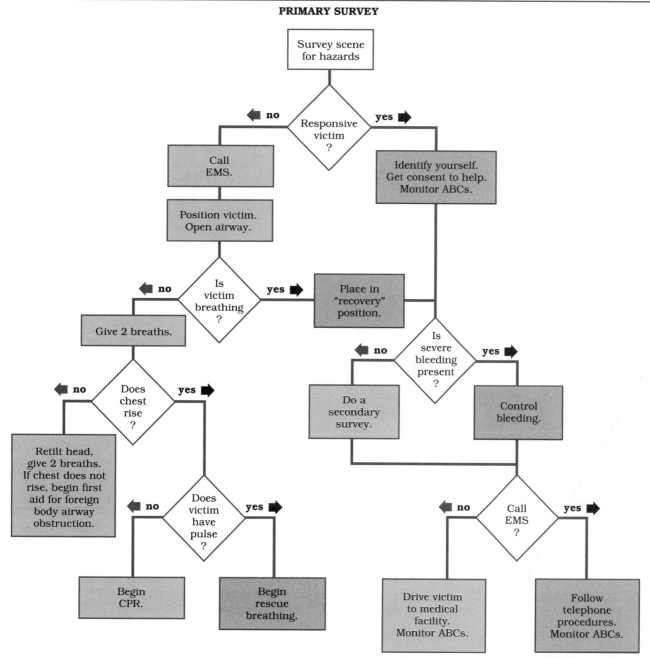

FIGURE 7.8 The purpose of the primary survey is to determine whether the athlete has sustained a life-threatening injury. (Source: National Safety Council. 1994. *First Aid and CPR* (2nd ed.). Boston: Jones and Bartlett. 16. Reprinted with permission.)

grabbed her ankle and was in obvious pain—you would be correct in performing a quick primary survey followed by the application of ice and compression as well as elevation of the injured ankle. This entire process should take no more than a few minutes, after which you should perform a more thorough secondary evaluation.

Secondary Survey

The **secondary survey** should include specific components that enable the coach to collect as much information about the injury as possible under the circumstances. The essential parts of the survey are:

History—having a discussion with either the athlete and/or onlookers

Observation—observing for obvious signs and/or symptoms related to the injury

Palpation—feeling the injured area in order to collect more information

History

Whether the athlete is conscious or unconscious, the history process is considered the single most important aspect of the secondary survey. Obviously, if the athlete is unconscious, you will need to collect information from other athletes, coaches, or bystanders who may have seen the injury occur. Regardless of the circumstances, when rendering care to an unconscious athlete always assume that there are serious head and neck injuries that require the stabilization of the athlete's head and neck. Your priorities must be basic life support, i.e., airway, cardiac function, and breathing followed by contacting the EMS. In the case of the conscious athlete, the history process begins as soon as you arrive on the scene (Figure 7.9). Its purpose is to collect information critical to identifying the body areas involved as well as the severity and mechanism(s) of injury (Booher and Thibodeau, 1989). Traumatic injuries usually present a more obvious set of complaints and possible causes than chronic, long-term ones. Although each injury is unique, your questions to the athlete should be phrased in simple, easy-to-understand terms that will elicit the desired information without leading the athlete into giving a preferred answer. Avoid using terminology too advanced for the athlete and always take

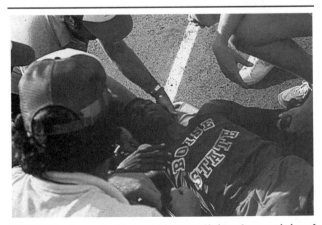

FIGURE 7.9 A coach obtains a history of injury from an injured athlete.

care not to increase the anxiety level by losing your composure. Questions should require only brief responses—preferably a yes or no. Initially attempt to gain the confidence of the athlete by letting him know what you are doing and that you are there to ensure his welfare. Ask the athlete to explain what happened and to describe his perceptions of the injury. Inquire if there is pain—and if so, where. Also ask whether the athlete heard any strange sounds during the injury and if he feels anything abnormal. The answers will provide essential information to assist you in your evaluation of both location and magnitude of the injury. Do not forget to inquire about the injury history (both long and short term) of the involved area. A good example of how such information could be useful is the case of a suspected shoulder subluxation (partial dislocation). Such an injury may be very difficult to evaluate. However, if during your history taking the athlete informs you that the shoulder has been dislocated several times in the past year, you may then focus your efforts on determining the integrity of that specific joint. Information regarding the injury history of the athlete should always be passed on to medical personnel who evaluate the athlete later.

In some cases, the medical emergency may be difficult to ascertain, as is the case with certain conditions such as diabetes, **exercise-induced asthma,** or a head injury. Clues to the problem may be given during the history process, if done correctly. In the case of the metabolic emergencies, the questions are obvious. ("Do you have diabetes—and if so, did you take your insulin today?" "Do you have epilepsy—and if so, are you on any sort of medication?") In the case of the conscious athlete with a possible head injury, behavior may be incongruent with the circumstances. Your questions should assist in determining the level of consciousness, as well as the integrity of higher thought processes. The protocols for the initial treatment of athletes with head injuries are presented in Chapter 9.

Observation

The observation phase involves noting signs and symptoms related to the injury that are relevant to your decision-making process. Critical to this is a basic understanding that a clinical **sign** involves objective findings such as bleeding, swelling, discoloration, and deformity. Symptoms are subjective in nature and may not be as reliable in determining the nature of the injury. **Symptoms** include findings such as nausea, pain, **point tenderness,** and syncope (fainting).

Athletic Trainers Speak Out

"It is every athlete's inalienable right to expect reasonable care to be provided while participating in sports. Since sports by their very nature contribute to injuries, it is reasonable to expect coaches to respond to these injuries in a reasonable manner. Therefore, CPR and basic first aid training must be in the coach's repertoire. The coach has a responsibility to prepare for injuries with the same thoroughness as if preparing for a game. A game plan for handling injuries must be executed prior to the start of any sports season and be rehearsed just like drills for practice. When the emergency does arise, the game plan is ready to be used."

—Kenneth W. Kopke, A.T.C.

Kenneth W. Kopke

Mr. Kopke is currently the president of Athletic Training Services, Inc., of Mt. Pleasant, Michigan. Prior to that he was the head athletic trainer and director of sports medicine at Central Michigan University for 18 years.

Begin observing for signs and symptoms related to the athlete even before you are near enough to render any aid. As you approach the injured athlete, note the body position and look for signs of possible significance such as odd behavior or actions. If you have seen the injury occur you will have a good idea of the mechanism of injury. This is important because you will have an idea of the forces involved and the possible type(s) of injury.

With a conscious athlete, ask him to point out the site(s) of injury. Look for the signs of injury, including swelling, deformity, and discoloration. Whenever possible, compare the injured side with the uninjured area on the opposite side of the body. In cases of possible significant injury, in which much of the body is covered with equipment and clothing, it is best to remove garments from the suspected area of injury by cutting away clothing with scissors rather than removing it in a normal fashion. In this way unnecessary movement of the athlete can be avoided. Obviously care must be taken not to cause embarrassment to the athlete. However, in the case of a potential life-or-death situation, saving the athlete's life must always take priority over modesty.

Essentially, the secondary survey should be thought of as a head-to-toe assessment of the athlete. The goal is to identify all injuries, regardless of severity, treat them appropriately, and refer the athlete for medical care if it is deemed necessary.

Palpation

The palpation phase of the evaluation can usually be included in both the primary and secondary surveys. The National Safety Council (1991) defines **palpation** as "the act of feeling with the hands for the purpose of determining the consistency of the part beneath." For example, in the unconscious athlete, initial evaluation should include careful palpation of the head and neck areas to determine if any noticeable irregularities are present that could indicate fractures, dislocations, or other types of damage. With practice, palpation skills can be refined to the point where identification of injury-related problems such as swelling, muscle spasm, localized fever, abdominal rigidity (sign of internal bleeding in abdominal cavity), deformity, crepitus (grating feeling beneath the skin surface), and skin tension can be easily detected. Palpation is a learned skill and does involve some amount of contact with the injured athlete (Figure 7.10). Consequently, it is important that great care is taken to avoid aggravation of existing injuries. Also, when evaluating a conscious athlete, an explanation of the purposes of the evaluation can be helpful in relieving anxiety. It is recommended that whenever possible the palpation process should begin in a body area away from where there are obvious injuries (Booher and Thibodeau, 1989). This allows the athlete to develop confidence in the coach's palpation skill prior to actual evaluation of the injury(ies). In the case of injury to an extremity, evaluation of the uninjured limb first is recommended as well. This provides an immediate basis for comparison when the actual injury is evaluated.

It is important that during all phases of the examination process significant findings are noted and memorized for later use. Normally the entire evaluation process should be completed in a matter of minutes, after which the appropriate first aid treatment should be initiated. If further evaluation is deemed necessary, the decision must be made to move the athlete from the playing field or practice area. If the athlete is conscious and has no obvious lower-extremity injuries that preclude walking, he may be able to leave the area under his own power (with assistance). If a lower-extremity injury exists, it is best to use some form of transport device, such as a stretcher, spine board, or even a two-person carry to remove the athlete from the site of injury. In the case of an unconscious athlete, or one who may have sustained a head or neck injury, the best policy is to stay with the athlete, monitor vital signs, treat for shock, and summon EMS personnel. Unless the athlete is in danger of being injured further, there is *no justification* for movement prior to the arrival of EMS personnel.

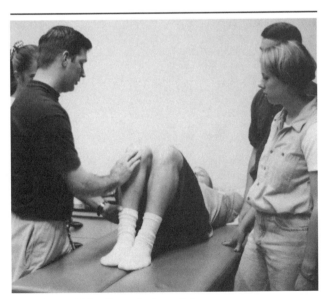

FIGURE 7.10 Palpation of a knee injury.

The Coach's Limitations

In the absence of a NATABOC-certified athletic trainer, medical doctor, or other designated health care provider, the coach will be responsible for the initial management of injuries sustained by an athlete. Yet coaches must take special care not to overstep the bounds of their training, experience, and expertise. In short, coaches should avoid the urge to assume a doctor's role. All of the procedures described so far can be classified as appropriate first aid care that should be rendered by coaching personnel at the time of an injury. *The critical point to remember, however, is that the coach should not perform procedures that are clearly the domain of medical doctors or allied health personnel such as an athletic trainer.*

Review Questions

1. List the questions that must be addressed when coaches are given the charge of providing emergency care without the services of a NATABOC-certified athletic trainer.

2. What is the meaning of the acronym BLS?

3. Who provides BLS training in most communities?

4. Briefly describe both the primary and secondary surveys as they relate to the initial assessment of an injured athlete.

5. When performing a primary survey on an injured athlete, what is the recommended procedure for opening an airway when a neck injury is suspected?

6. *True or false:* It is imperative that the helmet be removed from an injured, unconscious football player as soon as possible in order to establish an open airway.

7. What is one of the earliest clues that internal bleeding may be occurring?

8. List the essential components of the secondary survey.

9. What is considered to be the single most important step in the secondary survey?

10. When performing the observation phase of the secondary survey, what things should the coach do prior to reaching the athlete?

11. Define the term palpation.

12. Differentiate between a sign and a symptom.

13. *True or false:* When collecting a history from an injured athlete, questions should be kept brief and use a minimum of complicated terminology.

References

American Academy of Orthopaedic Surgeons. 1991. *Athletic Training and Sports Medicine* (2d ed.). Park Ridge, Ill.: American Academy of Orthopaedic Surgeons.

Ball RT. 1989. Legal responsibilities and problems. In Ryan AJ, Allman FL (eds.). *Sports Medicine.* San Diego: Academic Press. 447–489.

Booher JM, Thibodeau GA. 1989. *Athletic Injury Assessment.* St. Louis: Times Mirror/Mosby.

Hargarten KM. 1993. Rapid injury assessment. *Phys Sportsmed.* 21(2):33–40.

Harris AJ. 1988. Disaster plan—a part of the game plan? *Athletic Training.* 23(1):59.

National Safety Council. 1997. *First Aid and CPR.* Boston: Jones and Bartlett.

Nowlan WP, Davis GA, McDonald B. 1996. Preparing for sudden emergencies. *Athletic Therapy Today.* 1(1):45–47.

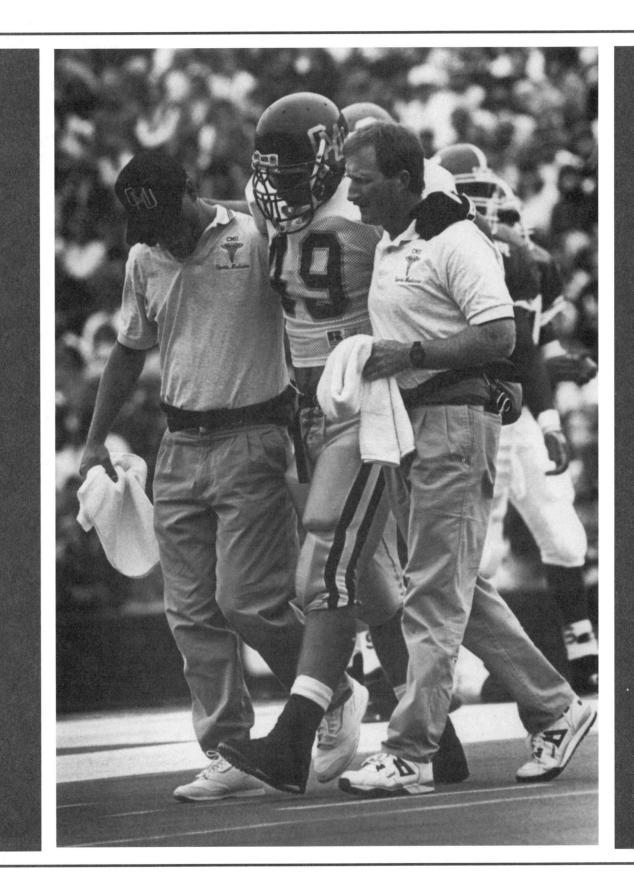

CHAPTER 8

The Injury Process

M A J O R   C O N C E P T S

This chapter examines the complex topic of the inflammatory reaction of tissues to trauma. It begins with an overview of the types of tissues involved in sports injuries, followed by a detailed, phase-by-phase description of the process of inflammation, which includes the acute, resolution, and regeneration/repair phases. It is critical that coaching personnel grasp the basic physiology of this process to better understand the recommended procedures for treating inflammation. Treatment can include ice application, compression, and elevation as well as the administration of therapeutic heat (hot packs, ultrasound) and pharmacologic agents (anti-inflammatories) if recommended by the attending physician. This chapter concludes with a discussion of the role of exercise in the rehabilitation process.

The Physics of Sports Injury

The human body consists of many different types of tissue, each serving a specific purpose. Some are highly specialized; for example, the retina of the eye contains tissue that is sensitive to light and that is not found anywhere else in the body. Other types of tissue are distributed throughout the body. **Connective tissue,** for example, is the most common type within the body (Cailliet, 1977). Included in this category are ligaments, retinaculum, joint capsules, bone, cartilage, fascia, and tendons. Cailliet (1977) classified other general categories of tissue as epithelial (used for protection, secretion, and absorption), muscular (for contraction), and nervous (for touch and conductivity). Since both connective and musculoskeletal tissue comprise a significant portion of all tissues within the body, it is no surprise that they are commonly involved in sports injuries. Existing research substantiates this: nearly 50% of all injuries in some sports are acute in nature and involve either muscle or tendon tissue (Safran, Seaber, and Garrett, 1989).

Muscles and fascia are thought to be injured when excess tension is applied while contraction is occurring. Furthermore, it is commonly held that more injuries to muscles and fascia occur during **eccentric contractions,** which have been described as "the simultaneous processes of muscle contraction and stretch of the muscle-tendon unit by an extrinsic force" (Safran, Seaber, and Garrett, 1989). Tendons are extremely strong structures able to withstand stresses ranging from 8,700 to 18,000 pounds per square inch. Yet activities such as running and jumping may generate forces in excess of these physiological limits (Curwin and Stanish, 1984). Research has demonstrated that, with respect to strains, the distal musculotendinous junction (MTJ) is usually the site of failure (Safran, Seaber, and Garrett, 1989). As of yet no scientific explanation has surfaced explaining why the majority of strains occur at this region. More research into the

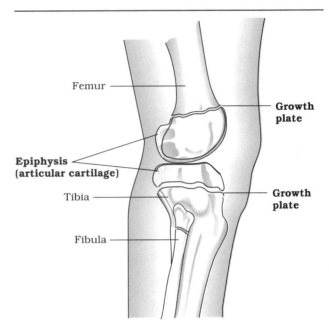

FIGURE 8.1 Growth plates in the knee.

specific causes of such injuries is warranted since it has been well documented that, of all soft-tissue injuries related to sports, musculotendinous strains are the most common (Taylor et al., 1993).

Related Injuries in the Adolescent

Although connective tissue in children reacts to traumatic forces in essentially the same manner as tissue in adults, there are some important, age-related differences. Prior to reaching adulthood, the ends of the long bones of the body comprise cartilage (**epiphysis**), commonly called growth plates (Figure 8.1). It is important for coaches and parents to realize that in a growing child the ligaments, capsules, and tendons are very often stronger than the growth plates to which

Information at your fingertips

The World Wide Web—For additional information on adolescent orthopedic injuries, go to http://www.jbpub.com/athletictraining and click on Chapter 8.

they are attached. Therefore, injuries that result in simple strains or sprains in an adult may cause a potentially serious growth-plate injury in a child. It is critical to identify these injuries should they occur: epiphyseal fractures may disrupt the normal growth mechanism in the region. A child who sustains an injury that produces extreme pain—especially one related to joint motion, swelling, or obvious deformity—should be immediately referred to a medical doctor for further evaluation. Such injuries in children can occur to any joint, but are most common in the elbow, hip, and knee.

The Mechanical Forces of Injury

Three types of forces can affect connective tissues such as tendons. They are tensile, compressive, and shear (Figure 8.2). Tendons are designed to resist ten-

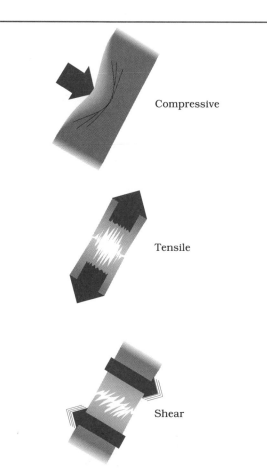

Compressive

Tensile

Shear

FIGURE 8.2 Mechanical forces of injury.

sile forces. They are less effective when subjected to shear forces and are poorly designed to deal with compressive forces. Conversely, bone tissue is designed to absorb compressive forces, but it is less effective against tensile and shear forces (Curwin and Stanish, 1984). Ligament tissue, like that of tendons, is best suited to resist tensile forces while being more vulnerable to shear and compressive mechanisms.

Regardless of tissue type, each has a limit to how much force it can withstand. This limit has been referred to as the **critical force** (Nigg and Bobbert, 1990). The critical force value varies for each type of tissue in the body. Even within the same type of tissue the critical force value may vary owing to changes in the tissue itself. For example, it has been reported that factors such as age, temperature, skeletal maturity, sex, and body weight can affect the mechanical properties of ligaments (Akeson, Amiel, and Woo, 1986).

The Physiology of Sports Injury

The Inflammatory Process

Whenever tissues are damaged as a result of an injury, the body reacts quickly with a predictable sequence of physiologic actions designed to repair the involved tissues. Regardless of what tissue has been injured, the body's initial response to **trauma** is inflammation, commonly referred to as swelling. This process begins during the first few minutes following the injury. The normal signs and symptoms of inflammation include swelling, pain, reddening of the skin (known as **erythema**), and an increase in the temperature of the area involved (AAOP, 1991).

The inflammatory process has been described as consisting of several specific stages. It begins with the acute phase, is followed by the resolution phase, and ends with the regeneration and repair phase (Lachmann, 1988). Each serves a specific purpose, and all are essential to proper repair of the structures involved.

Acute Inflammatory Phase

When tissues such as ligaments, tendons, or bones are damaged due to trauma, millions of cells are destroyed. Initially, the blood flow into the area is reduced (**vasoconstriction**); however, after only a few minutes this is followed by an increased blood flow (**vasodilation**). The mechanical force of the injury usually results in damage to a variety of soft tissues, including the blood vessels. As a result, the sudden increase in blood flow into the interstitial ("between the cells") spaces results in the formation of a hematoma. *Dorland's Pocket Medical Dictionary* (1977) defines **hematoma** as a "localized collection of extravasated blood"; it represents an important step in the inflammatory process. A hematoma can develop quickly since during the acute phase of an injury blood flow may increase 10 times over normal (Lachmann, 1988). The clotting and cessation of blood flow distal to the site of injury results in a diminished blood flow to the tissues surrounding the primary area of injury. This reduction or, in some cases, cessation of blood flow to otherwise healthy tissue results in cell death and membrane disruption due to lack of adequate oxygen supply, known as "secondary hypoxic injury" (Knight, 1976). Secondary hypoxic injury involves additional cellular breakdown and subsequent release of chemicals from within an intercellular structure known as the lysosome. Lysosomes contain powerful enzymes that, when released, hasten the breakdown of cellular structure (degradation effect). In addition, other chemicals are released that affect neighboring cells, causing changes in nearby capillaries (vasodilation and vascular permeability effect), or signaling the need for scavenger cells to migrate to the injured area (chemotactic effect).

Three specific groups of chemicals have been identified as being active during the acute phase of the inflammatory response. They are degenerative enzymes (cellular breakdown), vasoactive substances (vasodilators), and chemotactic factors (attracting other types of cells) (Fick and Johnson, 1993).

Histamine, a powerful inflammatory chemical, is released from a number of different types of cells resulting in short-term vasodilation and increased vascular permeability. An enzyme known as Hageman factor (XIIa) is carried in the blood, and under the conditions of tissue damage it becomes active. The Hageman factor induces a number of localized changes in the region of damage. The complement system is then activated; this includes a variety of chemically similar structures that play major roles in the inflammatory reaction as well as assist in attracting other cellular structures into the area. This process of attracting cells such as **leukocytes** (white blood cells) is known as chemotaxis and is essential to the process of inflammation. The Hageman factor is also responsible for the manufacture of another powerful inflammatory chemical, **bradykinin.** Bradykinin affects the vasculature by increasing vascular permeability. In addition, bradykinin triggers the release of **prostaglandins,** which are among the most powerful chemicals in the human body (Wilkerson, 1985). Prostaglandins have a number of effects within the damaged area, including vasodilation, increased vascular permeability, pain, and fever, as well as some related to the clotting mechanism (Lachmann, 1988).

Physiologically, several chemicals conspire to cause an increase in vascular permeability. This allows large structures—plasma proteins, platelets, and leukocytes (primarily neutrophils)—to pass out of capillaries and into the damaged tissue (Wilkerson, 1985). By way of **phagocytosis** (cell eating), leukocytes dispose of damaged cells and tissue debris. The number of neutrophils in the damaged area can increase greatly within the first few hours of acute inflammation—to as high as four to five times the normal levels (Guyton, 1986). Neutrophils arrive quickly to the site of injury; however, they live for only a short time period (approximately seven hours) and have no means of reproduction. When neutrophils expire they release chemicals that attract a second type of leukocyte known as a macrophage. Macrophages also consume cellular debris via the process of phagocytosis. However, unlike neutrophils, macrophages can live for months and do have the ability to reproduce (Knight, 1995).

Another important chemical mediator of the acute inflammatory process is **arachidonic acid,** which is the product of the interaction between enzymes supplied by leukocytes and phospholipids derived from the membranes of destroyed cells (AAOP, 1991). Arachidonic acid serves as the catalyst for a series of reactions that yield a variety of substances, including leukotrienes, which play a role in the inflammatory phase by attracting leukocytes to the damaged area.

In essence, the entire acute inflammatory phase results in a walling off of the damaged area from the rest of the body—along with the formation of a mass of cellular debris, enzymes, and chemicals that serves to clean up the destroyed structures while also providing the necessary components for tissue repair. The acute inflammatory phase of injury lasts up to three to four days (Arnheim, 1989), unless aggravated by additional trauma, as happens when an athlete returns to participation too soon after injury.

▌ Resolution (Healing) Phase

As stated above, in the absence of further irritation or trauma, the acute inflammatory phase usually ends

Athletic Trainers Speak Out

"The quick and correct treatment of an acute injury can help in controlling the inflammatory response. Success in this area can reduce the athlete's time lost to injury and allow better tolerance to evaluation techniques and rehabilitation exercises. Early use of ice has been found to decrease effusion that usually occurs for 4 to 6 hours following injury. It also minimizes pain and muscle spasm. Cold applied to a recent injury will lower metabolism and the tissues' demand for oxygen. This also carries over to the uninjured tissue in the surrounding area. It should be noted that prolonged application of cold can cause tissue damage, so the use of cold should be approximately 20 minutes and repeated about every 1 to 1½ hours during the waking day. This use of cold to help control the inflammatory response can hasten the recovery of the injury."

—Richard Leander, M.S./CI, A.T.C./R

Richard Leander

Richard Leander is the head athletic trainer for Moscow High School.

within three to four days after the initial injury. At this time the earliest steps in tissue repair begin to occur, with the migration into the area of specialized cells, including polymorphs and monocytes (both specialized forms of leukocytes) as well as histocytes (a type of macrophage). These cells begin the process of breaking down the cellular debris, setting the stage for generation of new tissue. The stage is then set for the final phase of the inflammatory process, regeneration and repair.

Regeneration and Repair

With the exception of bones, connective tissues of the body heal themselves by forming scar tissue, which begins to form as early as three to four days after the injury. This process begins with the migration into the area of fibroblasts. According to *Dorland's Pocket Medical Dictionary* (1977), **fibroblasts** are immature, fiber-producing cells of connective tissue that can mature into one of several different cell types. Fibroblasts become active at this time, producing collagen fibers as well as proteoglycans (large protein macromolecules), which help retain water in the tissues. This is particularly important in tissues such as articular cartilage, which act much like a sponge when exposed to fluids within joints.

The circulatory system, specifically the damaged capillaries, begin to repair themselves within just a few days after the initial injury. This process, known technically as **angiogenesis,** involves the actual formation of new capillaries, which interconnect to form new vessels.

With the formation of a new vascular supply, the new tissue is able to continue maturing, a process that may last up to four months. Scar tissue, under ideal conditions, can be 95% as strong as original tissue; it may, however, achieve considerably less strength, perhaps as much as 30% less (AAOP, 1991). A certain amount of stress is helpful to the new tissue in that it encourages the new collagen fibers to form in parallel lines, a much stronger configuration. Appropriate rehabilitative exercises are critical to this process. Figure 8.3 is a diagrammatic representation of the sequence of steps in the inflammatory process (Lachmann, 1988).

Bone injuries heal in a similar fashion to soft tissues; however, specialized cells known as osteoclasts migrate to the region of injury and remove destroyed cells as well as other debris. Specialized fibroblasts known as osteoblasts migrate to the injured area from adjacent periosteum and bone. In addition, new osteoblasts are manufactured on a large scale within the

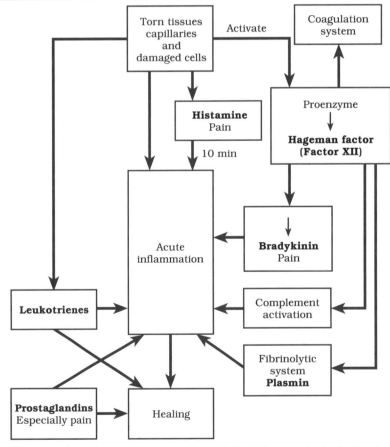

FIGURE 8.3 The process of inflammation. (Source: Lachmann S. 1988. *Soft-Tissue Injuries in Sport.* Oxford, England: Blackwell Scientific Publications. 14. Reprinted with permission.)

same region (Guyton, 1986). The function of the osteoblasts is to develop a zone of collagen and cartilage that is vascularized; this is known as a callus. A callus fills the space between the fractured bone ends and can be seen quite clearly on a standard X-ray photograph (Figure 8.4). The callus is not of sufficient strength to substitute for the original bone; however, through a process of maturation it becomes fully functional bone. With the majority of fractures some type of immobilization will be required, usually in the form of a splint or a plaster or synthetic cast. In severe fractures, surgical placement of appliances such as plates and screws may be necessary.

Pain and Acute Injury

While inflammation is often the most visible aspect of an acute injury, from the athlete's perspective, pain is often the biggest immediate problem. It is important to remember that while everyone has experienced pain associated with injury, everyone copes with pain differently, and further, pain is as much psychological (emotional) as it is physiological (tissue damage) (Thomas, 1997). As a physiological phenomenon, pain is essentially the result of sensory input received through the nervous system that indicates the location of the damage.

When damage occurs to tissues the result is an alteration of the normal homeostasis of the structures involved. It is the process of altered homeostasis that triggers the pain response resulting in sensory nerve receptors (afferents) transmitting impulses to the cen-

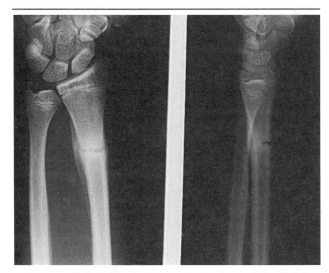

FIGURE 8.4 Callus forming around a fracture of the distal radius.

tral nervous system (CNS). When pain is the result of external forces, impulses travel on relatively slow nerve fibers known as nocioceptive C fibers. These fibers are labeled as slow because their conducting velocity is comparably slower than other afferent nerve fibers, such as those for the sense of touch and temperature. The nocioceptive fibers are slower because of two primary factors: first, they are smaller in diameter than other afferent nerves, thus limiting the volume of information they can carry at any given time. Second, unlike most nerve cells, they have little or no fat in their bodies. It is the fat, known as mylination, that is responsible for substantially increasing conduction velocities of the impulses traveling from the periphery to the CNS. Mylination acts as an insulator that tends to help maintain high velocities of resultant stimuli.

The speed of nerve conduction is important and plays a primary role in the effective treatment of pain. As afferent messages are sent to the CNS they are "ranked" based on the number of impulses received per unit of time. As such, messages with the highest velocities receive priority status by the CNS. For example, if a pain message (relatively slow) and a touch message (relatively fast) reach the CNS simultaneously, the touch message is given higher priority. As a result, the CNS first recognized the touch message, with the pain message being given a lower priority. This can be demonstrated by noting that more often than not, when a person suffers a blow, such as hitting one's head on something, the first reaction is to rub the area. The process of rubbing the injured area stimulates the fast velocity touch receptors, thus blocking the pain signals. This explanation of pain is based on the gate control theory of pain, which was first developed in the 1960s and published in the journal *Science* (Melzack and Wall, 1965). The gate control theory of pain is only one possible explanation of the pain process and it should be noted that research continues regarding our understanding of pain.

Sports medicine personnel can use a variety of **modalities** to treat pain associated with injury. Shown in Table 8–1 are the commonly used modalities that take advantage of the gate control theory to control pain.

Perhaps as important as understanding the precise mechanisms of pain is understanding how each athlete responds to pain. Pain has been defined as "the perception of an uncomfortable stimulus or is the presentation or response to that stimulus by the individual" (Thomas, 1997). As such, it must be remembered that each individual responds to pain differently. It is essential to the process of the initial evaluation of an injury to be familiar with the athlete's typical response to pain. An athlete with an extremely high pain tolerance may underestimate the severity of an injury and, con-

TABLE 8.1	Common Modalities Used to Treat Pain
Modality	**Afferent Nerve Stimulated**
Ice	Temperature receptors
Heat	Temperature receptors
Electrical stimulation	Touch receptors
Massage	Touch receptor
Prophylactic wrapping	Touch and proprioceptive receptors

versely, an athlete with low pain tolerance may grossly exaggerate the severity of an injury. In essence, pain may not be a useful indicator of the severity of an injury. When a coach must make a decision about the significance of an injury, it is best to err on the conservative side and, when in doubt, refer the athlete to medical personnel. Pain may also be thought of as the athlete's friend, in that it serves as a mechanism to reduce the athlete's activity level until adequate tissue healing has occurred. It is critical to remember that the treatment of pain should be the domain of sports medicine personnel. Coaches, athletes, and parents should not treat the pain associated with an injury to enable an athlete to return to participation.

Intervention Procedures

Although it is clear that the acute inflammatory process is a necessary component of healing, athletes, coaches, and even many sports medicine personnel typically think of inflammation as something to be avoided at all cost. This sentiment is so common within the sports community that the variety of suggested first aid treatments for acute injuries is overwhelming. Curiously, even today, no clear, concise set of criteria has been universally accepted within the sports medicine community regarding first aid treatment of acute soft-tissue injury. Suggested treatments of inflammation include the application of **cryotherapy** (therapeutic use of cold), such as crushed-ice packs, ice cups applied via massage, ice-water baths, commercially available chemical cold packs, and aerosol coolants (ethyl chloride). After the acute inflammatory phase has passed, usually 48 to 120 hours following injury, **thermotherapy** (therapeutic use of heat)—including commercially available hydrocollator packs, warm moist towels, and ultrasound diathermy—may be appropriate. It should be noted, however, that use of modalities such as ultrasound should always be done under the direct supervision of trained, allied health personnel such as an athletic trainer, physical therapist, or physician.

In addition to cold and heat therapy, pharmacologic agents—drugs designed to prevent swelling (**anti-inflammatories**) or drugs designed to prevent pain (**analgesics**)—are often used to treat the inflammatory response. The majority of these drugs must be prescribed by a medical doctor and represent treatment beyond the training of coaching personnel. However, there are anti-inflammatory drugs, such as aspirin, which are available over the counter (OTC) and are often effective for minor acute injuries. Caution should be exercised, however, particularly when the coach is dealing with athletes under the age of 18: he or she should consult with parents prior to recommending any sort of pharmacologic agent.

Most experts agree that some sort of treatment, beyond simple rest, be applied during both the acute inflammatory phase as well as later stages of healing. However, little agreement exists regarding what approach is most effective. This confusion is partly the result of the conflicting conclusions from the available research regarding the use of modalities such as ice, compression, and elevation as well as pharmacologic agents such as anti-inflammatory drugs (Dupont, Beliveau, and Theriault, 1987; Knight, 1985). Obviously, more research is needed in order to determine the most effective first aid procedures as well as long-term treatments.

Cryotherapy and Thermotherapy

It has been found that changing the temperature of injured tissues can have dramatic effects on the physiologic activities of inflammation and healing. During the first few minutes of the acute inflammatory phase, direct application of cold (generally in the form of crushed ice) may reduce vasodilation, thereby reducing the amount of initial swelling. Additionally, in the case of an injury to an extremity, elevation and compression are also useful. The application of ice, compression, and elevation (**ICE**) is a standard first aid procedure for injuries such as sprains, strains, dislocations, contusions, and fractures. Though many variations on application exist, experts recommend that the most effective way of applying cold to the body is a plastic bag filled with crushed ice (Figure 8.5). Nothing exotic need be used—just a simple sandwich bag with some type of closure is most effective. Crushed ice is made relatively inexpensively by ice machines, which are a good investment for a school athletic department. Crushed ice can even be purchased prior to a game or

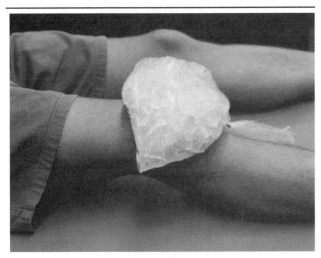

FIGURE 8.5 Bags filled with crushed ice are the most convenient way of applying cold to an injury.

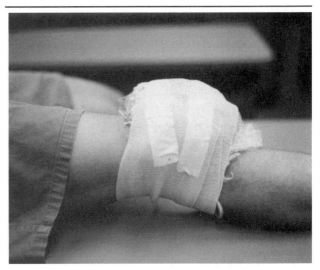

FIGURE 8.6 Elastic wrap provides a convenient method of compression.

practice session and stored in a cooler for later use. Commercially available chemical cold packs and aerosol sprays (ethyl chloride) are less effective than crushed ice and can even be dangerous in some situations. Research has shown that the risk of **frostbite** during the application of a bag of crushed ice is minimal. Human tissues freeze at around 25° F; a bag of crushed ice reaches a low temperature of only 32° F. It is recommended that the ice bag be left in place for 30 minutes, then removed. If medical help is delayed for more than 30 minutes, allow the injury to rewarm for a period of 2 hours; then follow up with another 30–minute application of cold if needed (Knight, 1985). Compression is best achieved by using a commercially available elastic wrap (Figure 8.6). They come in a variety of sizes, ranging in widths that will accommodate almost any anatomic site and body size. It is best to place the ice bag directly against the skin with the elastic wrap secured over the bag. Wrap in a closed spiral fashion, starting distally and finishing proximally. Care must be taken not to make the wrap excessively tight as this could compromise circulation. Always check the pulse distal to the wrap once it is in place. You should be able to easily slip two fingers under the elastic once it is secured. Leave the wrap in place until the injury is seen by medical personnel.

Elevation of the injury is self-explanatory; however, some precautions are necessary. When elevating an injury to the lower extremity, make sure adjacent joints are supported with padding. Elevation during sleep can be accomplished simply by raising the foot end of the bed a few inches off the floor.

Generally there is some sort of delay—e.g., transporting the participant from the playing field to the sideline or perhaps to a treatment area a considerable distance from the site of injury. The period immediately after the injury has occurred is generally considered to be the best time to evaluate the extent of injury. Coaching personnel should avoid the temptation, however, to perform medical tests, such as ligament laxity assessments. Such testing should be performed only by properly trained medical personnel such as a physician, athletic trainer, or sports physical therapist. When such tests are performed improperly the injury may be aggravated.

Knight (1985) has reported that the application of ice to an injury during the acute inflammatory phase helps decrease the recovery time. This occurs because tissue cooling reduces the metabolic activity of the cells in the injured area, thereby reducing their need for oxygen. Consequently, the cells are better able to survive the initial period of inflammation when oxygen is in short supply. This sparing of cells contributes to a smaller collection of debris in the region of the injury, thereby promoting an earlier repair phase. In essence, the immediate application of ice helps reduce the severity of the secondary hypoxic injury, as described earlier in this chapter. Finally, application of cold provides an analgesic effect and reduces muscle spasm. These two effects allow the athlete to engage in therapeutic activities more effectively.

Thermotherapeutic agents such as moist heat packs or ultrasound may also have a beneficial effect on soft-tissue injury. However, available research is unanimous that such treatments should never be applied during the acute inflammatory phase. By heating the tissue during the early phases of the injury, the metabolic activity of the inflammatory agents will be increased, thereby resulting in an increase in inflammation (Wilkerson, 1985).

Thermotherapies may be useful during the final phases of injury repair by increasing available oxygen and stimulating vasodilation in the region of the injured tissues. In addition, heat increases local metabolic activities, including those resulting in regeneration of tissues.

Pharmacologic Agents

A wide variety of pharmacologic agents are currently available for the treatment of inflammation. Based upon fundamental chemical configuration, they can be

volve the negative effects they have on the process of collagen formation. In essence, steroids can decrease the overall strength of the connective tissue structures within an injured region. Great care must be taken when using these powerful drugs. Discuss both the risks and benefits with the athlete prior to treatment.

■ Nonsteroidal Anti-inflammatory Drugs
Nonsteroidal anti-inflammatory drugs (**NSAIDs**) block specific reactions in the inflammatory process; however, they do not negatively affect collagen formation. These drugs have become extremely popular within the medical community. A reported 1.3 million prescriptions were written in 1991 (Fick and Johnson, 1993). According to Wilkerson (1985), some of the more commonly used NSAIDs include:

WHAT IF?

A parent asks you for advice on what over-the-counter drug would be best to give his daughter to help her recover from a second-degree ankle sprain. What would you suggest?

classified into two groups: steroidal and nonsteroidal anti-inflammatory drugs (NSAIDs). Both groups seem to interfere with some aspect of the inflammatory process, thereby reducing either the amount of swelling (anti-inflammatory) or pain (analgesic).

■ Steroidal Anti-inflammatory Drugs
Steroidal drugs are manufactured in such a way as to resemble a group of naturally occurring chemicals in the body known collectively as glucocorticoids, which are active within the body relative to the metabolism of carbohydrates, fats, and proteins. Curiously, the exact mechanism of steroidal drugs on the inflammatory process is not clearly understood. There is evidence that steroids lower the amount of chemicals released from intracellular lysosomes, decrease the permeability of capillaries, diminish the ability of white blood cells to phagocytize tissues, and reduce local fever (Guyton, 1986). Probably the best known of the steroidal preparations is cortisone; however, others commonly used include hydrocortisone, prednisone, prednisolone, triamcinolone, and dexamethasone. Steroidal preparations are generally either orally ingested or injected. They may even be introduced through the skin via **phonophoresis** (using ultrasound energy) or **iontophoresis** (using electrical current) (Fick and Johnson, 1993). Problems with steroidal chemicals in-

1. acetylsalicylic acid (aspirin)
2. ibuprofen (Motrin, Rufen, Advil, Nuprin)
3. naproxen (Naprosyn)
4. naproxen sodium (Aleve)
5. indomethacin (Indocin)
6. piroxicam (Feldene)
7. sulindac (Clinoril)
8. fenoprofen calcium (Nalfon)
9. tolmetin sodium (Tolectin)
10. meclofenamate sodium (Meclomen)
11. phenylbutazone (Butazolidin).

As a group these drugs appear to block the breakdown of arachidonic acid to prostaglandin, which in turn decreases the inflammatory response to injury (AAOP, 1991). Aspirin, known chemically as acetylsalicylic acid, produces several effects—anti-inflammatory, analgesic, and **antipyretic** (reducing fever).

Though the physiological effects of NSAIDs on inflammation are quite clear, what remains to be clarified is their effect, if any, on the healing process itself. Does using a particular drug in any way enhance the healing process by decreasing the healing time or by increasing the strength of the new tissue? Research to date is inconclusive; however, two recent studies have shed some light on both questions. Dupont, Beliveau, and Theriault (1987) reported the effects of a commonly used NSAID on the treatment of acute ankle sprains. They compared the effects of the NSAID with treatment that used ice, elevation, and taping only. The duration of the study was 28 days, and effects were evaluated on the basis of a variety of subjective criteria, including pain and the number of painful ligaments upon palpation. The results indicated that a positive trend occurred in favor of the NSAID group; however, none of the trends were found to be statistically significant.

Dahners and colleagues (1988) aspired to determine if a commonly used NSAID would in any way affect the healing process of damaged ligaments. They studied damaged medial collateral ligaments in rats and compared the drug-treated group with a nondrug group. Their conclusion was that the drug did not increase the strength of the ligament after the normal time for

seen by medical personnel before further treatment (in any form) is given.

The Role of Exercise Rehabilitation

It may seem paradoxical, but the most effective treatment for many sports injuries, especially those involving soft tissues, is physical activity. Obviously, asking an athlete to run on a sprained ankle is incorrect, but properly constructed and supervised exercise can have a dramatic impact on the healing process (Figure 8.7). Research indicates that rehabilitative exercise can exert a variety of positive effects on collagen formation (AAOP, 1991). Since **collagen** is a major constituent of tendon and ligament tissues, exercise is a logical

Information at your fingertips

World Wide Web—You can find additional information on pharmaceutical drugs. Go to http://www.jbpub.com/athletictraining and click on Chapter 8.

complete healing, which was 21 days. Curiously, it was found that the drug did seem to decrease the time required for the healing ligaments to get stronger when compared with subjects not receiving the drug. This finding could have significant implications for athletes, particularly those who feel the need to decrease injury recovery time. However, it is important to remember that this study involved nonhuman subjects; consequently, implications for athletes must be evaluated in that context.

Until more conclusive research is available, it would appear that the best approach to treating the majority of soft-tissue injuries involves the application of ICE during the acute inflammatory phase, followed by a combination of ICE, prescribed pharmacologic agent(s), and prescribed and properly supervised rehabilitative exercises. From a legal and ethical standpoint, the coach or physical educator should provide only initial first aid to any soft-tissue injury and then refer the athlete to the appropriate medical authority. Nonmedical personnel should avoid prescribing any type of medication, even an over-the-counter (OTC) drug such as aspirin. It is always best to have any injury

FIGURE 8.7 Exercise can be the most effective treatment for many athletes who have sustained sports injuries.

form of treatment. According to Knight, exercise is essential during the healing process for two reasons. First, exercise results in increased circulation with a concomitant increase in oxygen supply to the healing tissue. Second, exercise stresses the healing tissue and in essence "guides" the proper structuring of the collagen cells (Knight, 1995). It is important to remember, however, that while exercise is essential to proper tissue healing, the old saying "too much too soon" is worth remembering during the rehabilitation process. At the very least, the process of collagen formation and tissue regeneration will require two to three weeks (Page, 1995). Further, after the final phase of healing the athlete should, when appropriate, have the area properly protected with adhesive taping, wrapping, or bracing. Decisions concerning any return to participation should be made by a medical professional with experience in sports injuries. Coaches should avoid returning an athlete to participation too early because he or she may be critical to the team's success.

Any injury severe enough to warrant a medical diagnosis should be treated with a comprehensive program of exercise rehabilitation. Such a program must consist of essential components and must be planned by professionals with the appropriate training—either a NATABOC-certified athletic trainer or a physical therapist who has sports medicine training. Responsibility for implementation and supervision of the exercise program usually falls upon the coach or physical educator. Thus, communication between the athlete, coach, and medical personnel is essential for any program to be effective.

Rehabilitative exercise, often called therapeutic exercise, is a four-phase process consisting of categories of exercise based upon a continuum of severity and recovery. If the athlete's injury is severe, the initial exercise protocol may make the athlete a passive participant; a therapist actually moves the injured extremity through a series of passive exercises. The benefits of that are the reestablishment of a normal range of motion (ROM) as well as reduction of swelling and muscle spasm. As the injury improves, the next phase of exercise becomes active assisted. During this phase the athlete becomes a working partner in the exercise process, making a voluntary effort to move the injured joint while being assisted by a therapist. The benefits of this phase are improved ROM and increased muscle strength. The next phase in the rehabilitation process is active exercise. At this point the athlete continues moving the joint through a full ROM, using gravity as resistance in order to stimulate development of muscle strength. The important aspect of this phase is that the therapist merely supervises the activity; no physical assistance is given to the athlete. The final phase of the recovery program is known as resistive: external resistance is applied to the joint movements. This can be done via manual resistance provided by the therapist, through the use of resistive exercise machines, or even with free weights. The primary objective of this phase is to improve the strength of the muscles surrounding the injured area in order to protect it from future injury.

Injury rehabilitation should be considered an ongoing process: injury-specific exercise should be a permanent component in the total training and conditioning program of the athlete. Without such an approach the likelihood of reinjury is high in many cases. The coach must communicate with the appropriate members of the sports-medicine team—athletic trainer, physical therapist, and/or physician—in order to plan and implement an effective program of therapeutic exercise. (For more information see Appendix 8.)

Review Questions

1. During what type of muscular contraction do the majority of muscle and/or fascia injuries occur?

2. *True or false:* The proximal musculotendinous junction has been found to be the most common site for injuries.

3. List the three types of mechanical forces that can cause soft-tissue injury.

4. Define critical force.

5. Describe the major steps that occur during the acute inflammatory phase of an injury—with particular emphasis on vasoconstriction, vasodilation, and subsequent hematoma formation.

6. Define chemotaxis.

7. Describe briefly the group of chemicals known as prostaglandins and discuss some of their known physiological effects during the acute phase of an injury.

8. Briefly describe the overall purpose of the acute inflammatory phase of an injury.

9. What is the typical duration in hours of the acute inflammatory phase?

10. List the types of cells that migrate into the injured area during the early part of the resolution phase.

11. What type of tissue does not heal itself with scar tissue?

12. What are fibroblasts?

13. What is angiogenesis?

14. What is the relationship between a bony formation known as a callus and the healing of a fracture?

15. Describe the mechanism for the secondary hypoxic effect as described by Knight.

16. What is the effect of ice application on the secondary hypoxic effect?

17. What is the normal duration for the acute inflammatory phase, assuming no additional trauma occurs?

18. *True or false:* Nerve messages sent to the CNS are ranked based on the number of impulses received per unit of time.

19. Explain how rubbing an injured area reduces the pain perception.

20. Explain the gate control theory of pain.

21. Explain briefly the physiological effects of the application of ice, compression, and elevation on acute inflammation.

22. What is an easy and effective way of applying cold and compression to an injury simultaneously?

23. What is the recommended duration of ice application for the treatment of acute inflammation?

24. At what temperature do human tissues freeze?

25. At what point during the process of injury repair can thermotherapies be useful?

26. Differentiate between steroidal and nonsteroidal anti-inflammatory pharmacologic agents.

27. What is the mode of action of NSAIDs with respect to the acute inflammatory phase of an injury?

28. Give a definition of the acronym OTC.

29. Give a brief explanation of the four types of therapeutic exercise outlined in the chapter—passive, active assisted, active, and resistive.

References

Akeson WH, Amiel D, Woo SL-Y. 1986. Cartilage and ligament: physiology and repair processes. In Nicholas JA, Hershman EB (eds.). *The Lower Extremity and Spine in Sports Medicine.* St. Louis, Mo.: Mosby. 3–41.

American Academy of Orthopaedic Surgeons. 1991. *Athletic Training and Sports Medicine* (2d ed.). Park Ridge, Ill.: American Academy of Orthopaedic Surgeons.

Arnheim DD. (1989). *Modern Principles of Athletic Training* (7th ed.). St. Louis, Mo.: Times Mirror/ Mosby. 198–231.

Cailliet R. 1977. *Soft-Tissue Pain and Disability.* Philadelphia: F. A. Davis.

Curwin S, Stanish WD. 1984. *Tendinitis: Its Etiology and Treatment.* Lexington, Mass.: D. C. Heath and Company.

Dahners LE, et al. 1988. The effect of a nonsteroidal anti-inflammatory drug on healing of ligaments. *Am J Sports Med.* 16:641–646.

Dorland's Pocket Medical Dictionary. 1977. Philadelphia: W. B. Saunders.

Dupont M, Beliveau P, Theriault G. 1987. The efficacy of anti-inflammatory medication in the treatment of the acutely sprained ankle. *Am J Sports Med.* 15:41–45.

Fick DS, Johnson JS. 1993. Resolving inflammation in active patients. *Phys Sportsmed.* 21:55–63.

Guyton AC. 1986. *Textbook of Medical Physiology.* Philadelphia: W. B. Saunders.

Knight KL. 1995. *Cryotherapy in Sport Injury Management.* Champaign: Human Kinetics.

Knight KL. 1985. *Cryotherapy: Theory, Technique, and Physiology.* Chattanooga: Chattanooga Corp.

Knight KL. 1976. Effects of hypothermia on inflammation and swelling. *Athletic Training.* 11:7–10.

Lachmann S. 1988. *Soft-Tissue Injuries in Sport.* Oxford, England: Blackwell Scientific Publications.

Melzack R, Wall PD. 1965. Pain mechanisms, a new theory. *Science.* 150: 971–979.

Nigg BM, Bobbert M. 1990. On the potential of various approaches in load analysis to reduce the frequency of sports injuries. *J Biomech.* 23:3–12.

Page P. 1995. Pathophysiology of acute exercise-induced muscular injury: clinical implications. *Journal of Athletic Training.* 30:29–34.

Safran MR, Seaber AV, Garrett WE. 1989. Warm-up and muscular injury prevention—an update. *Sports Med.* 8:239–249.

Taylor DC, et al. 1993. Experimental muscle-strain injury—early functional deficits and the increased risk of reinjury. *Am J Sports Med.* 21:190–193.

Thomas CL (ed.). 1997. *Taber's Cyclopedic Medical Dictionary.* (18th ed.). Philadelphia: F. A. Davis.

Wilkerson GB. 1985. Inflammation in connective tissue: etiology and management. *Athletic Training.* 20:298–301.

CHAPTER 9

Injuries to the Head, Neck, and Face

MAJOR CONCEPTS

Injuries to the head, neck, and face present some of the most perplexing problems associated with sports injury. The chapter begins with a review of the gross anatomy of the head, neck, and face. It goes on to describe the central nervous system, giving special attention to the structures often involved in head and neck injuries, along with data on the incidence and severity of such injuries in a variety of sports. It provides a classification system for cerebral concussion that lists clear, concise signs and symptoms for each category and also discusses more severe forms of head injury, including intracranial injuries. The latest information on second impact syndrome is presented, along with recommendations on how to best avoid this potentially lethal problem. In addition, this chapter contains a special section on the helmeted football player, plus guidelines and a decision flow chart with instructions on the initial treatment of suspected head injuries.

Next, the chapter outlines major mechanisms of cervical spine injuries, followed by a discussion of the various types of injuries that can occur, including simple sprains and strains as well as more severe forms such as disk herniations and vertebral fractures. In addition, it presents information regarding the mechanisms and signs and symptoms of brachial plexus compression or stretching injuries. As with head injuries, it features guidelines for the initial treatment of suspected injuries to the cervical spine in an easy-to-use format.

The remainder of the chapter deals with recognition and care of injuries to the face, teeth, eyes, nose, and ears.

Anatomy Review of the Region

In a practical sense, the head may be considered as a single structure with a variety of functions. These include housing the brain, providing sockets for the eyes, openings for the ears, nose, and mouth, and a site of attachment for the vertebral column. The neck serves as the mechanism for attachment of the head to the body. Though this arrangement works well for the day-to-day functions of our species, in the context of sports such an anatomical arrangement provides significant potential for a multitude of injuries. The brain, consisting of neural tissues that are easily damaged, must be protected, especially when one considers the potential forces involved in many different sports and activities.

Skull

The skull, which consists of 8 cranial bones and 14 facial bones, is a complex structure. The brain (encephalon) is housed within the cranium and is afforded considerable protection via an ingenious system of bony and soft-tissue structures.

The bones of the cranium (Figure 9.1) form a rigid housing for the brain and are held together by specialized articulations known as suture joints.

Curiously, the suture joints of the cranium are not rigid at birth; in fact, they do not complete their ossification process until human beings are between 20 and 30 years old (Gray, 1985). However, the anatomical arrangement of the cranial bones and their respective

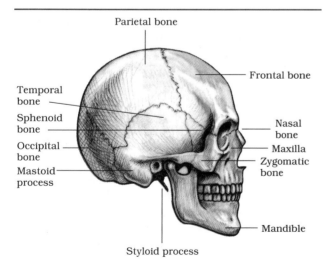

FIGURE 9.1 The bones of the human cranium.

joints provides a protective outer structure for the brain.

The soft-tissue structures that serve a protective function include the five layers of tissues of the scalp. These are illustrated in Figure 9.2; they include the skin, a layer of dense connective tissue, the Galea aponeurotica (essentially a broad, flat tendon), loose connective tissue, and the periosteum of the cranial bone.

The Meninges

Below the cranial bones another group of soft-tissue structures can be found that protect the brain as well. These are collectively referred to as the cerebral meninges (Figure 9.3). They consist of three distinct layers of tissues located between the underside of the cranium and the surface of the brain. The outermost layer is known as the *dura mater*. It consists of tough, fibrous connective tissue that functions as periosteum to the inside surfaces of the cranial bones as well as a protective membrane to the brain (Gray, 1985). The dura mater is highly vascular, containing both arteries and veins that transport blood to and from the cranial bones. The middle meningeal layer is the *arachnoid;* compared with the dura mater it has significantly less strength and contains no blood supply. The arachnoid is separated from the dura mater by a small amount of fluid. Below the arachnoid is the subarachnoid space containing **cerebrospinal fluid (CSF).** The purpose of CSF is to cushion the brain and spinal cord from external forces such as those encountered in collision and contact sports. The innermost meningeal layer is the *pia mater,* which is physically attached to the brain tissue and serves to provide a framework for an extensive vasculature that supplies the brain. The pia mater is a very thin, delicate membrane; like the arachnoid it is more susceptible to trauma than the dura mater.

The Central Nervous System (CNS)

The brain (encephalon) along with the spinal cord comprise the **central nervous system (CNS).** Both the brain and spinal cord are protected by the meninges as well as the bony structure of the cranium and vertebrae. The CNS tissue consists of both gray and white matter that represent two distinct types of neural tissues. The brain of an adult weighs 3 to 3.5 pounds and contains approximately 100 billion neurons (VanDe-Graaff, 1984). The brain consists of three basic parts: cerebrum, cerebellum, and brain stem. The cerebrum is the largest of the three and is involved in complex

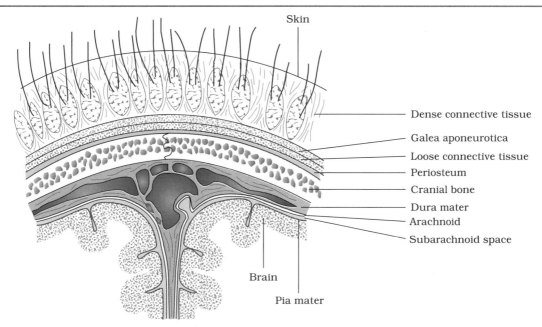

FIGURE 9.2 The human scalp: a cross section.

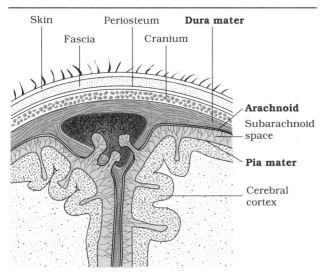

FIGURE 9.3 The cerebral menenges.

functions such as cognition, reasoning, and intellectual functioning. The cerebellum, located in the lower posterior portion of the cranial area, performs functions related to complex motor skills. The brain stem is located at the base of the brain and serves to connect the brain to the spinal cord. Neural impulses travel to and from the CNS via the cranial nerves (directly from the brain) or by way of the spinal nerves exiting the spinal cord. There are 12 pairs of cranial nerves that are directly attached to the base of the brain and exit the CNS through openings (foramina) in the base of the skull. The spinal nerves are attached to either side of the spinal cord and exit the CNS at precise intervals through the intervertebral foramina of the spinal column. There are 31 pairs of spinal nerves: 8 cervical, 12 thoracic, 5 lumbar, 5 sacral, and 1 coccygeal. The cranial, spinal, and autonomic nerves comprise that portion of the nervous system known as the peripheral nervous system.

Information at your fingertips

The World Wide Web—Learn more about the anatomy of the central nervous system. Go to http://www.jbpub.com/athletictraining and click on Chapter 9.

The CNS receives an extensive blood supply that must remain constant in order to function. Even brief interruptions of blood flow lasting only seconds may result in loss of consciousness. Neural tissue may be destroyed when deprived of blood for only a few minutes.

The Face

The human face is composed of an outer layer of skin placed loosely over underlying bones. There are some subcutaneous muscles, cartilage, and fat deposits offering minimal protection from trauma. The facial bones consist of the maxilla (upper jaw), the right and left palatine, the right and left zygomatic, the right and left lacrimal, the right and left nasal, the right and left inferior nasal concha, the vomer, the mandible (lower jaw), and the hyoid.

Several areas around the face are especially prominent and thus prone to injury. The orbits for the eyes, particularly the supraorbital regions, are vulnerable to contusions. The nasal bones are located centrally on the face and can also receive direct blows, often resulting in fractures. The lower jaw (mandible) is subject to excessive external forces as well.

The Neck (Cervical Spine)

The bones of the neck are the seven cervical vertebrae (Figure 9.4) that provide support for the head as well as protection for the upper portion of the spinal cord. The first cervical (C-1) vertebra (atlas) articulates directly with the occipital bone to form the right and left atlanto-occipital joints. The skull and C-1 articulate as a unit with the second cervical (C-2) vertebra (axis) to form the atlantoaxial joint, which allows for rotation of the head on the neck. The remaining five cervical vertebrae become progressively larger as they approach the thoracic spine.

Head Injuries in Sports

Although the majority of contusions to most parts of the body result in injuries that are self-correcting and without serious consequence, even relatively minor trauma to the head can result in severe, sometimes life-threatening injury. Because of the inability of brain

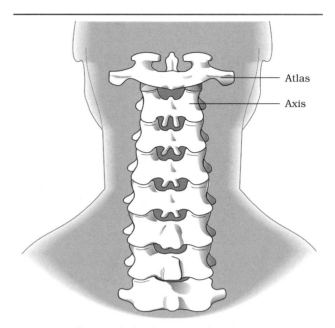

FIGURE 9.4 The cervical spine (posterior view).

tissue to repair itself, any loss of tissue results in some level of permanent disability. If the injury is severe enough, death can result. The possible mechanisms, types, and severity of head injuries in sports are nearly infinite. However, significant advances in our understanding regarding head injuries in sports have been made in recent years. As a result, with appropriate education coaches can learn to recognize head injuries and render effective first aid when necessary. Although head injuries can occur in almost any sport or activity, scientific surveys have provided additional insight into which sports appear to carry a higher risk. High school and junior high school football for the period 1982 to 1991 averaged 1.5 million participants, and these players accounted for the greatest number of directly related catastrophic injuries of sports studied (Mueller and Cantu, 1993). Conversely, studies of college athletics found that soccer and women's softball produced the fewest concussions per participant (Clarke, 1982). Research indicates that in tackle football as many as 20% (1 in 5) high school players are reported to have sustained a concussion annually (Cantu, 1986). Assuming these numbers are valid, the implications are rather alarming; perhaps as many as 250,000 high school football players each year sustain some level of cerebral concussion! There is a multitude of descriptive classifications for head injuries. However, all can be placed into three general categories: cranial injury, concussion, and intracranial injury (McWhorter, 1990).

Cranial Injury

Cranial injuries involve those to the bones of the skull. In the majority of cases, the force injuring the bones is of sufficient magnitude to also cause damage to the tissues of the scalp. Thus, along with cranial injury there may also be some bleeding and soft-tissue damage. Skull fractures can be simple, linear fractures with no damage to underlying tissue. In many cases these injuries produce few neurological problems. The more severe forms of cranial injuries involve what are known as depressed skull fractures. These are potentially much more serious since bone fragments have

absence thereof. Any such system can be problematic when used in a crisis situation since it is often extremely difficult to gauge the length of time a person is unconscious. In an effort to simplify this process, the Sports Medicine Committee of the Colorado Medical Society (CMS, 1991) recently published *Guidelines for the Management of Concussion in Sports.* Unlike most other classification systems, the CMS guidelines identify three levels (grades) of concussion. Perhaps the most innovative aspect of these new guidelines is that they greatly simplify deciding whether to allow an athlete to return to participation after such an injury. Given the potential implications of a bad decision in such situations, these guidelines can help the coach-

---

WHAT IF?

You are coaching soccer practice when suddenly a wing player collides with the goalie while attempting to kick a goal. Upon your arrival at the scene, the goalie appears to be all right; however, the other player is conscious but unable to remember the score or the team she is playing against. What type of injury is probable given this history and these symptoms?

---

been pushed into the cranial region. Obviously this type of injury is more likely to produce serious, perhaps life-threatening, neurological damage. A variety of signs and symptoms of cranial injuries may be present. These will be discussed in some detail later in this chapter.

Cerebral Concussion

Cerebral concussion has been defined by Jordan (1989) as "a clinical syndrome characterized by immediate and transient impairment of neurologic function secondary to mechanical forces. The clinical manifestations of concussion can include unconsciousness or other neurologic symptoms such as disorientation, amnesia, dizziness, or disequilibrium." In essence this implies that any sort of external blow of sufficient magnitude can cause temporary disruption of normal neurologic function without any significant amount of neurologic damage. The precise mechanism of neurologic disruption is poorly understood; however, it appears to be related to a temporary disruption of blood supply. A variety of classification systems for cerebral concussion are currently in use; the majority base the level of severity on duration of unconsciousness or the

ing staff avoid errors in judgment. The CMS system is shown in Table 9.1.

Grade-1 concussions are by far the most common seen in sports; ironically they are the most difficult to identify. The major distinction between grades 1 and 2 is the presence of amnesia. Two types of amnesia resulting from head injury have been identified: posttraumatic and retrograde. **Posttraumatic amnesia** has been defined as an inability to recall events that have

---

TABLE 9.1   CMS Guidelines for Determining the Severity of Concussions

GRADE 1	Confusion without amnesia No loss of consciousness Remove from event pending on-site evaluation prior to return
GRADE 2	Confusion with amnesia No loss of consciousness Remove from event and disallow return
GRADE 3	Loss of consciousness Remove from event and transport to appropriate medical facility

Source: Colorado Medical Society. 1991. *Guidelines for the Management of Concussion in Sports.* Denver: Colorado Medical Society.

occurred from the moment of injury (Vegso, Bryant, and Torg, 1982). **Retrograde amnesia** is present when the athlete is unable to recall events that occurred just prior to the injury. It is generally thought that retrograde amnesia is indicative of more severe forms of head injury. When evaluating an athlete the coach should ask several specific questions designed to elicit the presence of such forms of amnesia.

Grade-3 concussions are unique from the other two categories; the key difference is loss of consciousness. Level of consciousness is a qualitative phenomenon to be determined as soon as possible after a head injury is suspected. This is generally accomplished by first determining if the athlete is alert and will respond to simple questions. Though almost any sort of questioning will yield some useful information, the best approach is to keep questions simple in order to evaluate the athlete's perspective of time and place. Unconsciousness is usually identified when the athlete fails to respond to verbal stimuli or is obviously knocked out. Generally, consciousness is considered a positive sign; however, consciousness does not guarantee the absence of a potentially serious head injury.

Second Impact Syndrome

Recent research related to the phenomenon known as second impact syndrome (SIS) has raised concern within the sports medicine community that there needs to be a more cautious approach to the care and management of athletes who sustain minor concussions. SIS, according to medical experts, "occurs when an athlete who has sustained an initial head injury, most often a concussion, sustains a second head injury before symptoms associated with the first have fully cleared" (Cantu and Voy, 1995). Essentially SIS involves the rapid development of catastrophic swelling of the brain, specifically a region known as the uncus of the temporal lobes, which puts pressure directly against the brain stem (Figure 9.5a, b.)

A typical scenario involves an athlete receiving a minor concussion with associated symptoms that include headache, nausea, and tinnitus (ringing in the ears). Several days later the same athlete, while engaging in the same activity, receives a relatively minor blow to the head. Shortly thereafter the athlete collapses, becomes unresponsive, and is taken to a health care facility. While there, the athlete dies in a deep coma. Upon autopsy the cause of death is confirmed as massive cerebral edema resulting from uncontrolled vascular engorgement of brain tissue, i.e., SIS. It is crucial to realize that any athlete who sustains what appears to

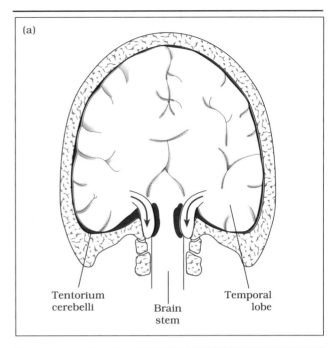

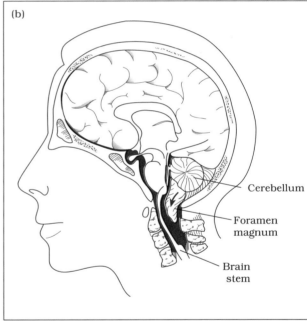

FIGURE 9.5 In second impact syndrome, vascular engorgement within the cranium increases intracranial pressure, leading to herniation of the uncus of the temporal lobes (arrows) below the tentorium in this frontal section (a), or to herniation of the cerebellar tonsils (arrows) through the foramen magnum in this midsaggital section (b). These changes compromise the brain stem, and coma and respiratory failure rapidly develop. The shaded areas of the brain stem represent the areas of compression. (Source: Robert Cantu, MD, FACSM, Neurological Surgery, Inc., Concord, MA. Reprinted with permission.)

be even a minor concussion should be examined carefully by a physician before being allowed to return to participation. This concern is especially acute in the case of an athlete with a recent history of concussion. It is important to remember that symptoms related to a concussion may take days or even weeks to be resolved. As such, it seems prudent that medical personnel, athletes, coaches, and parents need to apply extreme caution when making decisions regarding return to play for an athlete with a history of head injury.

Intracranial Injury

Intracranial injury in sports represents a potentially life-threatening situation. These injuries can be the result of a variety of mechanisms, including direct blows, rapid deceleration, and even rapid rotational motions of the head. By far the majority of intracranial injuries result from blunt trauma to the head. The injury is characterized by disruption of blood vessels, either veins or arteries, resulting in the development of a hematoma or swelling within the confines of the cranium. Such a condition places the brain tissues in jeopardy since these structures are extremely sensitive to pressure.

Jordan (1989) has identified the major forms of **intracranial injury** as **epidural hematoma** (bleeding between the dura and the cranial bones), **subdural hematoma** (bleeding below the dura mater), **intracerebral hematoma** (bleeding within the brain tissues), and **cerebral contusion** (bruising of the brain tissue). It is important to note that an epidural hematoma involves arterial bleeding; therefore, the signs and symptoms of injury will usually develop rather quickly. The subdural hematoma, however, involves arterial or equalize venous bleeding and may develop in a more insidious manner, perhaps over a period of hours. Any of these conditions can result in some degree of permanent neurological damage and even death.

Initial Treatment of a Suspected Head Injury—Guidelines

Though the numbers of head and neck injuries in all sports including tackle football are low **when compared to the total number of participants,** those that do occur are significant when one considers the potential seriousness of either type of injury. As a general rule, any athlete who sustains an apparent head injury should be treated as if a neck injury is also present; conversely, any athlete sustaining a neck injury should be treated as if there is also a head injury. The mechanism of injury for both is similar; consequently, it is possible that both could occur simultaneously.

Primary Survey

The first step in the management of these injuries is based upon basic first aid procedures: determine if the athlete is in either respiratory or cardiac arrest. This is accomplished by executing the primary survey. Any problems, such as an obstructed airway or cardiac arrest, must be attended to before continuing with any further evaluation of injuries. The first few seconds of the primary survey should provide important information about the injured player. Upon reaching the athlete note body position, movement or lack thereof, unusual limb positions, and (if present) the position of helmet, face mask, and mouth guard. If the athlete appears to be unconscious, attempt to arouse him or her by placing your hands on the shoulders, chest, or upper back and speaking loudly. If the athlete is conscious, the airway in all probability is open. If the athlete appears to be unconscious, make a mental note of the time; this will be of great value when the athlete arrives later at a health care facility. It is critical that the coaching staff be trained and well rehearsed in dealing with such situations, since immobilization of the head and neck should also take place at this time. This is accomplished quickly by having a person stationed at the athlete's head stabilize it with both hands (Figure 9.6).

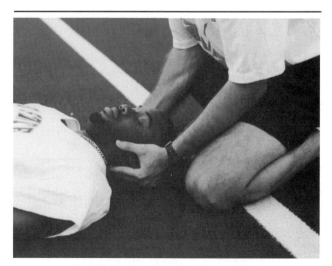

FIGURE 9.6 Stabilizing an athlete's head and neck.

In the case of a helmeted football player, it is not necessary to remove the helmet in order to determine if the athlete is breathing. (Refer to the guidelines later in this section regarding removal of a face mask from a football player with a head and/or neck injury.) Breathing can usually be detected by placing your ear near the athlete's face and listening for the typical sounds of respiration. By doing this you may also detect sounds indicating airway obstruction, such as gagging, wheezing, or choking. You may also note movements of the thorax or abdomen, both of which can confirm normal respiration.

Circulation is best assessed on the field by palpating for the carotid pulse. Place two fingertips (not your thumb) in the groove directly adjacent to the player's Adam's apple. Do not monitor the pulse on both sides of the neck simultaneously and do not push too hard. Monitor for 30 seconds in order to determine if a pulse is present and if the heart rhythm seems normal. Remember that an excited, anxious player will have an elevated pulse, probably well in excess of 100 beats per minute. If no pulse is detected, then your emergency plan should include two critical steps: summon EMS personnel and begin CPR immediately.

▌Secondary Survey

Obviously, an athlete who is conscious and alert represents a less complicated case than does a player who appears to be unconscious and not breathing. Once the primary survey has been completed, *which can be accomplished with practice in around 30 seconds*, and the athlete's vital signs have been ascertained, proceed to the secondary survey, in which the coach collects as much information about the suspected head injury as possible. The secondary survey must include assessments of the following:

C—Conscious or unconscious

E—Extremity strength (if conscious) (Test without moving neck)

M—Mental function (if conscious)

E—Eye signs and movements

P—Pain specific to the neck

S—Spasm of neck musculature.

It is important for the coaching staff to remember that there are certain procedures **not** to be followed when evaluating an athlete with a suspected head injury:

- **Don't** remove the helmet of a football player.
- **Don't** move the athlete.
- **Don't** use ammonia capsules.
- **Don't** rush through the secondary evaluation.

Determining whether an athlete is conscious is not always an easy process. Obviously, an athlete who cannot be aroused by loud talking and is not moving presents an easy assessment of unconsciousness. However, head injuries result in many variations of signs and symptoms. If the athlete appears to be conscious, attempt to communicate by asking simple questions requiring the use of short-term memory. For example, ask the name of the opposing team, what day it is, the location of the contest, or the score of last week's game. Loss of short-term memory is indicative of a concussion and possibly a serious head or neck injury. Do not attempt to revive an unconscious athlete by using a commercially made inhalant such as ammonia capsules. An athlete may attempt to jerk his head away from the inhalant, resulting in aggravation of an existing neck injury.

If the athlete is conscious, a series of quick, simple tests can be conducted in order to determine if any significant neurological damage has occurred. Place two of your fingers in one of the athlete's hands and ask him to squeeze as hard as possible. Then perform the test on the opposite hand and compare grip strength. You can also place your hands on the tops of the athlete's feet and ask the player to dorsiflex in order to compare bilateral strength. Check sensation on both sides of the body by pinching the skin on the insides of the arms, thorax, and legs.

To determine possible brain injury, monitor the athlete's eyes by noting the size of the pupils. Place your hand over one eye and remove it quickly to determine if the pupil reacts to light. Perform the same test on the

WHAT IF?

You are confronted with a situation during a tackle football game in which a player is apparently knocked unconscious during a play. When you arrive at the scene, the player is lying face down and is not moving. What would you do to ascertain this athlete's level of injury? What would you NOT do, and why?

Athletic Trainers Speak Out

"I recently had a player hit in the face with a line drive that knocked him face down on the mound. The player remained conscious but was incoherent. He gathered his senses and after having passed a neurological review was allowed to sit up by the attending physician. At this time there was immediate bloody drainage from both nostrils. He was once again placed lying down, a stretcher was asked for, and the player was taken by ambulance to the hospital, where a CAT scan revealed a bilateral fractured sinus."

—Rick Griffin

Rick Griffin is the head trainer for the Seattle Mariners.

Rick Griffin

other eye. Pupils are generally the same size; however, some people normally have pupils of unequal size. Hold a finger or pen directly in front of the athlete's face and move it from side to side slowly. Ask the player to tell you when it is no longer visible. Note any difference in peripheral vision and also any jerking movements of the eyeballs, especially when the athlete is looking to the side. Loss of peripheral vision or jerking of the eyes is indicative of possible brain injury.

Gently palpate the athlete's neck, beginning at the base of the skull and working slowly down to the bottom of the neck. Note any deformity, such as cervical protrusions or muscle spasms. Ask the athlete if pain occurs at any specific area during your evaluation.

Emergency Procedures for the Treatment of Head and Neck Injuries in Football

Though head and neck injuries carry the potential of catastrophic results regardless of the sport, football players who sustain such injuries present special problems because of their equipment. The standard equipment protecting the player's head and neck is a helmet with an attached face mask, chin strap, and some type of mouth guard. This apparatus can make dealing with airway problems very difficult. Management procedures for the helmeted athlete have become a major issue within the sports medicine community—with strong opinions on how best to handle such an athlete (Feld, 1993; Putman, 1992; Segan, Cassidy, and Bentkowski, 1993). The National Athletic Trainers' Association (NATA) has developed guidelines regarding the removal of helmets from injured athletes. According to these guidelines, attempts at removing the helmet from an athlete with cervical spine injury may worsen existing injuries or create new injuries (NATA, 1996) (Box 9.1). Coaching personnel are advised to exercise extreme caution when making decisions on immediate care of a helmeted athlete with possible head and/or neck injury. Removal of the helmet, unless exe-

cuted by a physician or other emergency care provider such as an athletic trainer or paramedic, should be avoided unless absolutely necessary.

In situations in which an airway must be established, careful and properly executed removal of the face mask is the most prudent approach. Depending on the age and design of the helmet, removal of the face mask can be accomplished in a variety of ways. While intense research into the most effective method of face mask removal is ongoing, the best technique to date appears to be cutting all the plastic clips (typically four: two upper and two lower) that hold the face mask to the helmet. Recently published data reveal that it may be better to cut all the retaining clips and remove the face mask completely rather than cutting only the lower two clips and rotating the face mask up (Kleiner, 1996). It is critical to remember that the *head and neck must be stabilized at all times*, including during removal of the face mask. The majority of current designs secure the face mask to the helmet with small plastic clips attached to the helmet with screws (Figure 9.7). Cutting the plastic straps on each side of the face mask—using devices such as a Trainer's Angel (Figure 9.8), anvil pruner, wire cutters, or tin snips—while the head and neck are stabilized will allow the mask to be rotated up and away from the face (Figure 9.9). Another option involves removal of the screws holding the plastic clips using a screwdriver (Putman, 1992). It was recently reported that new materials are now being used on some helmets that may make the procedures just described more difficult. The Ridell company is currently manufacturing a new face mask called the Cra-lite that is fastened to the helmet using clips made of a dense, polycarbonate material (Segan, Cassidy, and Bentkowski, 1993). It is imperative that coaching

---

BOX 9.1   NATA—Athletic Helmet Removal Guidelines

The National Athletic Trainers' Association has adopted the following guidelines with regard to the on-site removal of the athletic helmet.

Removing helmets from athletes with potential cervical spine injuries may worsen existing injuries or cause new ones. Removal of athletic helmets should, therefore, be avoided unless individual circumstances dictate otherwise.

Before removing the helmet from an injured athlete, appropriate alternatives such as the following should be considered:

- Most injuries can be visualized with the helmet in place.

- Neurological tests can be performed with the helmet in place. The eyes may be examined for reactivity, the nose and ears checked for fluid and the level of consciousness determined.

- The athlete can be immobilized on a spine board with the helmet in place.

- The helmet and shoulder pads elevate the supine athlete. Removal of helmet and shoulder pads, if required, should be coordinated to avoid cervical hyperextension.

- Removal of the facemask allows full airway access to be achieved. Plastic clips securing the facemask can be cut using special tools, permitting rapid removal.

In all cases, individual circumstances must dictate appropriate actions.

Source: National Athletic Trainers' Association, Dallas, TX. Reprinted with permission.

FIGURE 9.7 Plastic straps and screws secure the face mask to most football helmets.

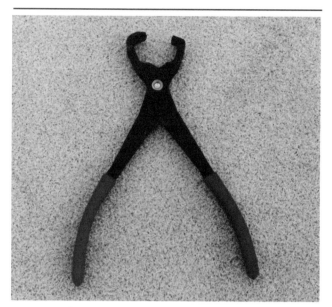

FIGURE 9.8 In the event of an injury, qualified personnel can use a Trainer's Angel to cut the straps on each side of a player's face mask.

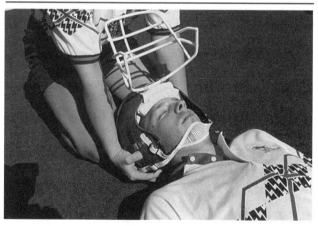

FIGURE 9.9 Once the straps are cut, the face mask can be rotated up and away from the player's face, or as recently recommended, completely removed.

personnel be aware of the specific types of equipment their athletes are wearing in the event that such an emergency arises.

Do not attempt to move the player until the secondary survey is completed and your evaluation determines that he or she is not injured. An athlete who appears to have recovered fully during the primary or secondary evaluation should be escorted from the playing field, taken to the bench, and observed for a few minutes to determine if he or she is developing any signs or symptoms of head injury. Any player who was unconscious qualifies as having a grade-3 concussion and should be taken to a medical facility for evaluation.

If on the other hand your evaluation yields some suspicious signs and symptoms or the player is unconscious, stabilize the head and neck, summon EMS personnel, and monitor the athlete's vital signs. As can be seen in Figure 9.10, the helmet provides an excellent adjunct to cervical immobilization in the case of possible neck injury (Fourre, 1991). In most instances, there is no reason to move an injured player from the field before EMS personnel arrive. No game or practice is so important that it cannot be delayed to ensure proper first aid for an injured player. The appropriate steps in the management of a player with a possible head or neck injury are shown in Table 9.2.

In the vast majority of head injuries related to football, the best course of action is typically unclear; in many cases the injury itself may be difficult to identify. It is not uncommon for athletes with varying degrees of concussion to appear normal, at least for brief periods of time following the initial trauma. Therefore, the football coach, officials, and fellow players may be totally unaware that anything is wrong with the athlete. *In general, when in doubt regarding the athlete's head injury, it is best to err on the conservative side; pull the player out of the game until he or she has been properly evaluated.*

General Guidelines

The concussion classification systems described earlier in this chapter provide guidelines for recognizing signs and symptoms of the most common forms of cerebral concussion. It has been said that "the single

FIGURE 9.10 In the event of a neck injury, the helmet provides an excellent means of cervical immobilization.

TABLE 9.2   Field Decision-Making—Head and Neck Injuries (Unconscious Athlete)

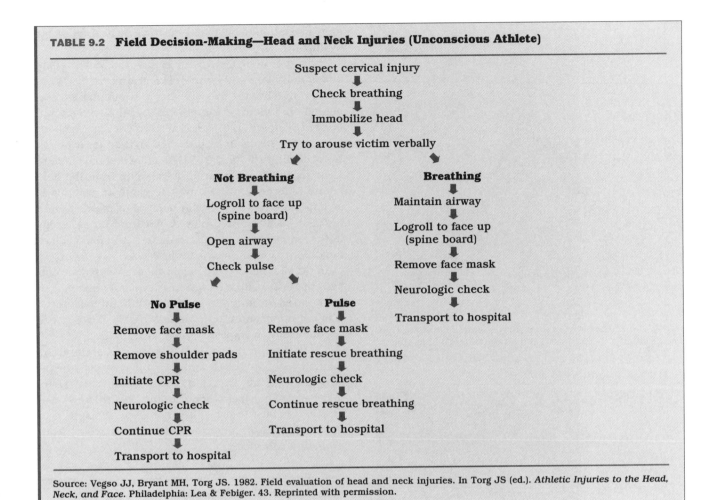

Source: Vegso JJ, Bryant MH, Torg JS. 1982. Field evaluation of head and neck injuries. In Torg JS (ed.). *Athletic Injuries to the Head, Neck, and Face*. Philadelphia: Lea & Febiger. 43. Reprinted with permission.

most important indicator of the severity of brain injury is the level of consciousness" (Jordan, 1989). However, in the majority of sports-related head injuries, the athlete never loses consciousness. The CMS guidelines make it quite easy to differentiate between the three categories of concussion—based upon the presence of amnesia and/or unconsciousness. Typically, the athlete will appear dazed, confused, and may demonstrate dizziness along with an unstable gait. These signs may be accompanied by complaints of **tinnitus** (ringing in the ears) as well as some loss of memory, either posttraumatic or retrograde. Common sense dictates that any athlete who demonstrates these characteristics should be removed from play or practice for further observation. It is also important to remember that a skull fracture can be present even if the athlete is conscious. The CMS (1991) recommends that an athlete who sustains a grade-1 concussion be pulled from participation for a minimum of 20 minutes for observa-

tion. The athlete should be checked for dizziness, tinnitus, amnesia—both at rest and after some form of exertion—before being allowed to return to play. If there is any question about the athlete's status, remove the athlete from play and refer to a medical doctor. The CMS guidelines as well as those of Vegso, Bryant, and Torg (1982) recommend that any athlete demonstrating posttraumatic amnesia should be disqualified from play for the remainder of the day and referred for a medical evaluation before being allowed to return.

It is always wise to administer some sort of quick test for neurological integrity prior to allowing an athlete to return to play. The finger-to-nose test (Figure 9.11) is administered by asking the athlete to stand with feet together, arms extended away from both sides of the body with elbows straight, and eyes closed. The athlete is then asked to touch the nose with an index finger—first with one arm, then the other. If the athlete

FIGURE 9.11 The finger-to-nose test.

is unable to touch the nose easily with either finger, return to play should not be allowed. The Romberg's test (Figure 9.12) involves asking the athlete to stand with feet together, arms at sides, and eyes closed. If the athlete is unable to maintain an erect posture and begins to sway, losing balance, the test is positive for a serious head injury. When administering such a test, be sure to position yourself to catch the athlete in case he or she loses balance and begins to fall.

The decision-making process for determining a grade-3 concussion is clear-cut. Render the appropriate first aid procedures and arrange for transportation to a medical facility.

FIGURE 9.12 The Romberg's test.

Background Information on Cervical Spine Injuries

Injuries involving the cervical spine occur in a variety of sports but most often in football, rugby, ice hockey, soccer, diving, and gymnastics. While any injury to this region of the body is potentially extremely serious, it is interesting to note that those which meet the criteria for the catastrophic category are quite rare: 2 in 100,000 of all neck injuries reported (Wiesenfarth and Briner. Howe WB [ed.], 1996). The annual incidence of cervical spine injuries among high school tackle football players ranges from 1 in 7,000 to 1 in 58,000 players, depending on the survey (Fourre, 1991). It was recently reported that within the United States less than 10 football players per year have suffered permanent spine injury since 1977 (Wiesenfarth and Briner. Howe WB [ed.], 1996). With the possible exception of a severe head injury, neck injuries are considered to be potentially the most serious category of sports injury. Many in the sports medicine community refer to the more severe forms of these injuries as catastrophic, which seems to be an appropriate term considering the potential outcome of trauma to this area. Neck (cervical) injuries occur in almost any sport and can involve a variety of tissues in the region, including bones, ligaments, intervertebral disks, spinal cord, spinal nerve roots, and/or the spinal nerves themselves (Torg, 1989).

Historically, the mechanism of injury considered to be potentially the most common and serious was excessive forced flexion (hyperflexion) of the cervical spine. However, extensive film analysis and objective research have disputed this long-held belief. Most experts now agree that the mechanism known technically as axial load produces the majority of serious cervical spine injuries. This is especially true in tackle football; prior to the mid-1970s tackling with the crown of the helmet (spearing) was a common practice. Axial loading of the cervical spine occurs when the head is lowered (flexed slightly) just prior to impact—the net effect being a straightening of the normal vertebral curve (extension) (Burstein, Otis, and Torg, 1982). In this position, forces applied to the top of the head are absorbed directly by the bones of the vertebral column without the protective assistance of surrounding ligaments and muscles. In 1976 the National Collegiate Athletic Association (NCAA) enacted a rule change that prohibited spearing or leading with the head for contact. The results were impressive: there was a significant drop in the number of cervical cord injuries the following year. (See Table 9.3.)

While the data in Table 9.3 show graphically an obvious decrease in the incidence of high school and collegiate football permanent cervical cord injuries, a recent publication calls into question the effectiveness of the rule change mentioned above. Bishop (1996) examined available data on the frequency of quadriplegia in both high school and collegiate football from 1976 to 1993. As can be seen in Figure 9.13, the annual incidence of this injury has remained below that reported in 1976, with periodic fluctuations as can be seen between the years 1980 and 1993.

In an effort to determine if rule changes had been effective in decreasing the incidence of spearing, Heck (1996) examined game films from a New Jersey high school for two seasons, 1975 and 1990, to determine if the incidence of spearing, by position, had been reduced. Curiously, the overall rate of spearing differed very little, that is, the incidence was 1/2.5 plays in 1975 compared with 1/2.4 plays in 1990. Spearing by running backs actually increased in 1990 when compared with 1975, and it was noted that tacklers were more likely to spear if the running back was spearing. The only decrease in spearing was noted among defensive linemen and independent tacklers. Heck determined that the majority of spearing involved defensive backs and linebackers.

Assuming Heck's research is representative of high school football participants nationally, compliance or, rather, noncompliance with the no-spearing rule makes it seem that more emphasis needs to be given to teaching these young athletes not to practice this extremely dangerous maneuver. Coaches, officials, parents, and sports medicine personnel all share some

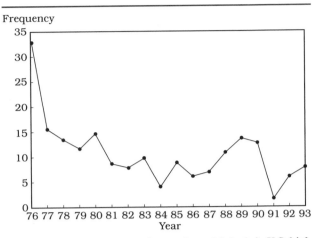

FIGURE 9.13 The frequency of annual quadriplegia in U.S. high school and college football from 1976 to 1993. (Source: Bishop PJ. 1996. Factors related to quadriplegia in football and the implications for intervention strategies. *Am J Sports Med.* 24(2):235–239. Reprinted with permission.)

responsibility in monitoring these young athletes during both games and practice.

While spearing has been identified as a continuing problem and an extremely hazardous practice among football players, it is also true that any forced movement of the cervical spine can result in injury. These mechanisms can be grouped into the categories listed below:

- Hyperflexion
- Hyperextension
- Rotation
- Lateral flexion
- Axial loading.

The types and severity of injury to the cervical spine are extensive; however, they can be classified according to the tissues involved and the extent of the damage. In order of severity, these range from simple compressions of the brachial plexus, which are self-correcting within minutes of the injury, to more severe problems involving ruptures of the intervertebral disks and fractures of the vertebrae. Sprains of the cervical spine are common in some sports and generally involve portions of the major ligaments that serve to stabilize the vertebrae. Such injuries are usually self-correcting and resolve themselves over a period of days. Occasionally, however, the mechanism of a sprain is severe enough to result in an actual displacement of vertebrae, which can result in more serious neurologic problems.

Strains can involve the muscles and tendons of the

TABLE 9.3	**U.S. Nonfatal Permanent Neurotrauma in High School and College Football, 1975–1980**					
	1975	1976	1977	1978	1979	1980
Cerebral						
High school	6	3	3	5	5	2
College	2	1	1	1	0	0
Cervical cord						
High school	23	25	10	11	7	8
College	4	7	2	0	3	2

Source: Clarke KS. 1982. An epidemiologic view. In Torg JS (ed.). *Athletic Injuries to the Head, Neck, and Face.* Philadelphia: Lea & Febiger. 20. Reprinted with permission.

neck region and are normally more painful than serious. Exceptions to this are injuries such as a whiplash, which consists of a combination of joint sprain and musculotendinous strain to the region.

The most extreme forms of cervical injury occur when the damage involves fractures or dislocations resulting in pressure being placed directly on the spinal cord. The spinal cord is extremely sensitive to such trauma, and permanent neurologic damage and even death can occur depending upon the specific location of the injury. The spinal cord may also suffer damage secondary to the initial trauma as a result of circulatory problems related to blood supply. When the spinal cord is bruised, bleeding and swelling may ensue, resulting in neurologic problems (Bailes, 1990).

The extent and severity of neurologic damage that occur in a neck injury depend upon the magnitude of the mechanism of injury, the resulting movement of the neck, and the extent of tissue damage. In the case of simple neck strains, neurologic involvement is extremely rare. An injury to the brachial plexus typically results in significant but transient symptoms ranging from an intense burning sensation in the shoulder, arm, and hand to loss of sensation in the same areas. As can be seen in Figure 9.14, injury to the brachial plexus involves an abnormal traction or compression of one or more of the large nerves that comprise the entire plexus (Sallis, Jones, and Knopp, 1992).

Cervical injuries are expressly more serious when displacement of an intact vertebra occurs, when fragments of a vertebral fracture are displaced, or when an intervertebral disk ruptures placing pressure directly on the spinal cord or nerve roots. In these situations the potential for permanent neurologic damage is high. Curiously, significant neurologic symptoms may be totally absent even when significant damage has occurred to tissues surrounding the spinal cord. Therefore, it is critical that the coach be objective and complete during the initial assessment process in order to avoid converting a treatable injury into a permanent one. Although it is not expected that the coach conduct a complete neurologic evaluation that would be expected of a physician, a few simple field tests will often yield sufficient information to make an informed decision regarding initial management of the athlete.

Initial Treatment of a Suspected Neck Injury—Guidelines

When considering specific actions in treating an athlete with a suspected neck injury, an immediate distinction must be made. Is the athlete conscious or unconscious? The answer to this question determines the initial treatment approach. With the unconscious athlete, it must be assumed that both head and neck injuries are present. The primary objective is to determine if the athlete's life is in immediate jeopardy. Does the athlete have an open airway? Is the athlete breath-

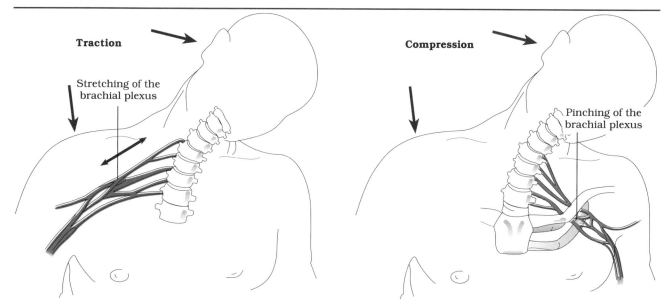

Traction

Stretching of the brachial plexus

Compression

Pinching of the brachial plexus

FIGURE 9.14 Common mechanism of injury to the brachial plexus.

ing? Does the athlete have a pulse? These questions are answered during the primary survey discussed earlier. If the answer to any of the above questions is no, then basic life support must be initiated and continued until the condition is resolved. The coaching staff should have a preplanned emergency protocol for handling athletes with head and neck injuries. One staff member must be designated as the emergency team leader whose primary responsibility is the supervision of the entire management process. In addition, the team leader must monitor the position of the athlete's head and neck, making sure that the injured player is not moved unnecessarily. Although sports medicine literature is replete with explanations of how to effectively and safely transport athletes with head and neck injuries, there does not seem to be much practice of these measures when actual cases are examined in retrospect. In the vast majority of school sports situations, which are normally located in population centers, emergency medical services should be readily available. Even in rural settings, EMS services are normally only minutes away. Although it is important that coaching personnel be trained in proper transportation techniques, it should be remembered that training does not mandate implementation. This is especially true when considering the potential for catastrophic injury if a head or neck injury is improperly handled. As was discussed earlier in this section, special consideration must be given to the care and handling of the helmeted football player.

In general, when dealing with an unconscious athlete the most important criteria should be prevention of further injury (Vegso, Bryant, and Torg, 1982). The team leader or designate should immediately stabilize the head and neck manually and continue doing so throughout the evaluation. The next step involves checking airway, breathing, and pulse. If the athlete is breathing and has a pulse, the next step is to summon the EMS while maintaining support to the athlete's head and neck as well as continuously monitoring the ABCs. If any delay of EMS is anticipated, it is prudent to place the athlete on a spine board to ensure adequate immobilization. This procedure requires a properly constructed spine board (Figure 9.15) and a trained staff of a minimum of five people, including the team leader. The team leader is charged with maintaining the head and neck in a neutral position as well as in directing the actions of the other team members. As shown in Figures 9.16 through 9.19, team members should be positioned at the athlete's shoulders, hips, and legs in order to properly roll the athlete onto the spine board. A fifth team member is required to slide the spine board under the athlete once he or she has

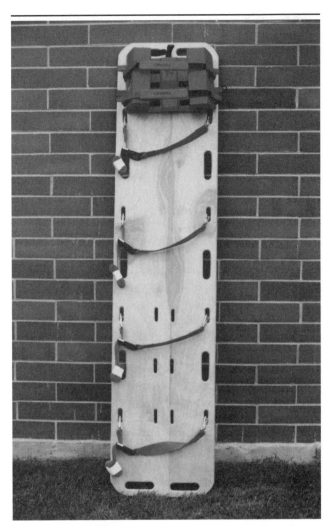

FIGURE 9.15 A full-length spine board ensures adequate immobilization for an injured athlete.

been rolled onto the side by the other team members. The athlete should then be secured to the board, the head and neck supported by sandbags or towels, with straps properly placed to immobilize not only the head and neck, but also the entire body. Adhesive tape works well to provide additional immobilization to the head; place a strip across the athlete's forehead and chin. It is important to remember that placing an injured athlete on a spine board should be done only if absolutely necessary and, further, that the procedures for placing an athlete on this device be rehearsed frequently according to the recommendations of the emergency plan.

With the conscious athlete, the initial treatment procedures differ from those employed with the unconscious athlete. With the conscious athlete the coach can obtain immediate feedback regarding the player's

FIGURE 9.16 Members of the rescue team stationed at the legs, hips, and shoulders with the team leader providing stabilization to the head and neck.

FIGURE 9.18 A fifth team member slides the spine board under the athlete. Note how the straps are placed to facilitate ease of securing the athlete to the board.

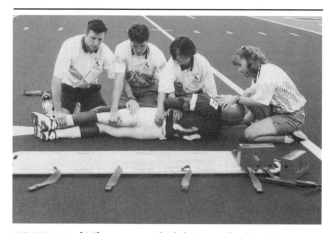

FIGURE 9.17 At the command of the team leader, the team rotates the athlete, as a unit, to enable movement of the spine board.

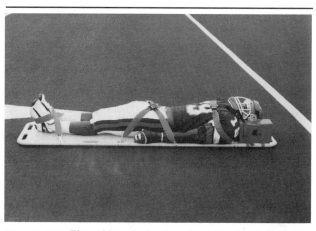

FIGURE 9.19 The athlete is firmly secured to the board with straps holding the ankles/feet, thighs/pelvis/arms, shoulders and head and neck.

condition. The athlete should be questioned regarding numbness of extremities, **dysesthesia** (impairment of the sense of touch), weakness, or neck pain (Bailes, 1990). In addition, if the athlete reports a loss of ability to move a limb or limbs or significant strength deficit (involving grip strength, or plantar or dorsiflexion), arrangements must be made to stabilize the head and neck, and the EMS must be summoned.

Injuries to the Maxillofacial Region

A variety of injuries can occur to the maxillofacial region of the body, which includes the jaw and teeth, eyes, ears, nose, throat, facial bones, and facial skin. With the increased participation in sports, the inci-

WHAT IF?

You are asked to provide first aid care to a high school basketball player who just received a blow to his mouth from an opponent's elbow. Upon examination you note that two teeth appear to have been completely knocked out of their sockets. The teeth are still in the athlete's mouth. What would you do for this athlete?

dence of injuries to the maxillofacial area appears to be rising. The National Electronic Injury Surveillance System (NEISS) recorded 170,000 sports-related facial injuries in the United States in 1984 (Kerr, 1986). Fortunately, with the advent of modern technology, protective equipment has been developed for use in high-risk sports (Matthews, 1990). These devices have significantly reduced the overall numbers of injuries to this region.

Dental Injuries

There are 32 teeth in the adult human jaws, the majority of which are located just inside the front and sides of the mouth, where they are vulnerable to external blows common in both collision and contact sports. Teeth are firmly secured into either the maxilla (upper jaw) or mandible (lower jaw) by way of the root, which is cemented into the sockets of the jaws with a specialized form of bone known as cementum. In addition, the sockets are lined with periosteum that aids in securing the teeth to the jaw.

■ Specific Injuries

The majority of dental injuries in sports result from direct blows resulting in tooth displacement, a fracture or avulsion, and, in extreme cases, fracture of the jaw or other facial bones. Signs and symptoms of dental injury are listed in Box 9.2 along with the most likely injury.

■ Initial Evaluation and Treatment—Guidelines

Whenever rendering first aid to someone suffering a dental injury it is important to avoid exposure to any injury-related blood. As such, bloodborne pathogen prevention steps should be taken, which include protective gloves (latex) and, if possible, eye protection, such as goggles. (See Appendix 2.) Collect the history of the accident; this is an important component of the secondary survey. Check to see if the athlete can open and close the mouth without pain or difficulty. Assess the general symmetry of the teeth, that is, look for irregularities visible in adjacent teeth. Examine the upper and lower teeth separately and carefully note any bleeding around the gumline or teeth, or obvious chips or fractures.

Treatment for dental injuries includes direct finger pressure with a sterile gauze over the area of bleeding, if any. For loose teeth, gently push them back into their normal position. In the case of avulsions, make every effort to locate the tooth and protect it by placing it into either a commercially prepared solution or ster-

BOX 9.2 Dental Injuries	
Type of Injury	**Signs and Symptoms**
Tooth displacement	A single tooth or several teeth pushed either forward or backward, with bleeding along the gumline.
Tooth fracture	Obvious defects (missing fragments) along the crown of the tooth or visible fracture line vertically placed within the tooth. Less severe fractures are not painful when breathing through the mouth, while more severe fractures (at or below gumline) are extremely painful and are often loose.
Fractures of jaw or other bones	Fractures of the jaw, either mandible or maxilla, will result in loosening of adjacent teeth, along with bleeding gums and numbness. In the case of the mandible, obvious deformity and an inability to open or close the mouth are apparent.
Tooth avulsion	Missing tooth with bleeding from the exposed socket.

ile saline (Matthews, 1990). Send the athlete to a dentist or physician immediately in order to have the tooth put back in place. Time is of the essence in these situations and the prognosis for the tooth is poor if more than two hours elapse between the time of the injury and time of replantation (Godwin, 1996).

■ Protection Against Injury

The most common method of dental protection in sports is the mouth guard, and many varieties are currently available. All mouth guards fall into one of three groups: stock, mouth-formed, and custom (Godwin, 1996). Stock versions are the least expensive; however, they are generally thought to be the least effective as well. The most commonly used are the mouth-formed type and, short of visiting the dentist to get a custom fit, are probably the most cost effective for junior and senior high school athletes. The custom mouth guard provides the best possible fit and protection; however, the costs can be prohibitive for many athletes. Obviously, in high-risk sports such as tackle football, a well-fitted mouth guard should be utilized to protect the athlete from such injuries. In the United States the use of mouth guards has been required in high school football since 1966. In 1974 the NCAA mandated their use in tackle football as well. The use of either stock

Information at your fingertips

The World Wide Web—For more details on the incidence of dental injuries, go to http://www.jbpub.com/athletictraining and click on Chapter 9.

or custom-made mouth guards is strongly recommended—by both the American Association of Oral and Maxillofacial Surgeons and the U.S. Olympic Committee—for protection in a variety of sports, including ice hockey, field hockey, rugby, wrestling, boxing, basketball, lacrosse, skiing, weight lifting, shot-putting, discus throwing, and even horseback riding (Kerr, 1986).

Eye Injuries

The human eye is an incredibly complex structure located within the orbit of the skull (Figure 9.20). The front of the eye consists of clear tissue known as the cornea, behind which the iris (pupil) and lens are situated. Located within the eyeball is the vitreous body, consisting of transparent, semigelatinous material that essentially fills the globe of the eye. The posterior surface of the inside of the eye is covered by retina, which contains the specialized neural cells of vision known as rods and cones. With the exception of the clear tissue on the anterior surface of the eye, the majority of the eyeball is encased in a tough tissue known as the sclera.

Eye injuries in some sports, such as track, are quite rare; yet when all sports are examined together these injuries appear to be on the increase. It was reported recently that sports were responsible for 25% of severe injuries to the eye (Jones, 1989). Within the United States the leading sport producing eye injuries is baseball, followed by basketball and bicycling. (See Table 9.4.)

With their increasing popularity, sports such as racquetball, squash, and badminton have produced an increase in eye trauma as well. Problems related to these sports include the small size of the striking objects (balls and shuttlecocks) as well as their velocity (Table 9.5) and the confined areas in which the games are played. Together, these factors greatly increase the probability of injury.

▪ Specific Injuries

Jones (1989) groups eye injuries into two different categories: contusional and penetrating. A contusional

FIGURE 9.20 Anatomy of the eye.

TABLE 9.4 U.S. Eye Injuries by Sport	
United States	
Baseball	30.0
Basketball	24.5
Bicycling	10.0
Football	7.5
Squash & racquetball	7.0
Tennis & badminton	5.5
Soccer	5.5

Source: Jones NP. 1989. Eye injury in sport. *Sports Med.* 7(3):165. Reprinted with permission.

TABLE 9.5	Potential Speed* of Objects in Racquet Sports
Squash ball	62 [140]
Badminton shuttlecock	57 [130]
Racquetball	48 [110]
Tennis ball	48 [110]

*Velocity is measured first in meters per second, then in miles per hour.
Source: Jones NP. 1989. Eye injury in sport. *Sports Med.* 7(3):168. Reprinted with permission.

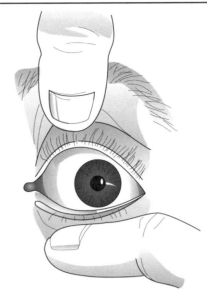

FIGURE 9.21 Proper positioning of fingers when initially examining the eye.

injury is the result of a blow from a blunt object such as a squash or tennis ball. Contusional injuries vary greatly in severity, ranging from simple corneal abrasions to major distortions of the eyeball resulting in rupture of the eye, fracture of the inner orbit, or a combination of the two. Additionally, the retina may be torn away from the inside of the eye, resulting in an injury commonly known as a detached retina. Penetrating injuries of the eye are less common, but can occur in shooting sports or even as the result of protective eye equipment that is defective.

■ Initial Evaluation and Treatment—Guidelines

The majority of sports-related eye problems will involve either simple corneal abrasions or a small foreign object in the eye. The symptoms for each are often nearly identical: pain, irritation, and excessive tearing. A quick examination of the eye can be conducted by gently holding the upper eyelid up and away from the eye while checking the anterior of the eyeball for any problems (Figure 9.21). Small foreign bodies are usually washed away from the center of the eye by tears. Therefore, the particle may be located below the lower eyelid or on the side of the eyeball at a site known as the medial canthus.

If the foreign object can be seen, it can usually be carefully removed with a moist cotton swab or Q-tip. If the object appears to be imbedded in the eye tissue, cover *both* eyes carefully with clean gauze and immediately arrange for transport of the athlete to a medical facility.

If no object can be seen in the eye, the injury is most likely a corneal abrasion. Do not allow the athlete to continue participation until the symptoms abate. If they persist or vision is severely disturbed, the athlete should be referred to the appropriate medical specialist for further evaluation.

When the eye receives a significant blow or contusion—from being hit by an elbow in a game of basket-

ball or by a racquetball, for example—vision is usually at least temporarily disturbed. In most cases this causes a black eye resulting from hemorrhaging of tissue surrounding the eye. The immediate care of this injury is periodic application of cold for 24 hours after the injury. In the case of severe contusions, bleeding into the anterior portion of the eye (**hyphema**) may occur quickly. This is a potentially serious sign as it may indicate vascular damage within the eyeball. In addition, the eyeball itself may have been ruptured, or the socket (orbit) may be fractured, an injury known as orbital blowout. Symptoms of such an injury include pain (especially when attempting to move the eye), double vision (**diplopia**), and obvious hemorrhaging within the eye. An athlete with any of these signs and/or symptoms should be immediately referred for further medical evaluation.

Injuries resulting in a detached retina can be caused by the mechanisms described above; however, the symptoms may not be immediately apparent. An insidious aspect of this injury is that the retina may slowly fall away from the posterior section of the eye over a period of days, weeks, or even months in some cases. Early symptoms include seeing particles floating inside the eye, distorted vision, and abrupt changes in the amount of light seen. Any athlete with a history of blunt trauma to the eye who later complains of any of these symptoms should be referred to a medical specialist.

■ Contact-Lens Problems

Many athletes are fitted with contact lenses (both hard and soft). Few difficulties occur with these appliances; however, as a rule, more problems arise with hard lenses. Most result from the lens slipping out of place or dust that gets trapped between the lens and the eye. The coach should have the necessary materials handy in the first aid kit—including commercially prepared wetting solution, a small mirror, and perhaps even a contact-lens case—to deal with problems involving contact lenses.

Nose Injuries

The human nose is, by nature of its location, often subjected to trauma in sports. The classic nosebleed (**epistaxis**) may well be one of the most common facial injuries in sports. Anatomically, the nose consists of a combination bone-cartilage framework over which the skin is attached. The nose consists mostly of soft tissue (cartilage and skin) and can absorb significant amounts of force. The bones of the nose include the right and left nasal bones and the frontal processes of the maxilla (Gray, 1985). The superior portions of the nasal bones meet with the frontal bone between the orbits. The nose has two openings, commonly called nostrils (nares), which are separated in the middle by the cartilaginous septum. The areas immediately inside the nares contain hairs that trap large particles during respiration. Further up, the nares tissue is covered with mucous membrane.

■ Initial Evaluation and Treatment—Guidelines

When an athlete receives a blow to the nose that results in bleeding, the nose should immediately be examined for the possibility of fracture. The signs of such a fracture include an obvious deformity of the bridge of the nose, which usually swells quickly. Fractures of the nasal bones constitute the most frequent fractures of the facial region (Booher and Thibodeau, 1989). If one is suspected, first control the nosebleed and then immediately refer the athlete for medical evaluation. Generally, uncomplicated nasal fractures are easily corrected by a physician.

Care of a simple nosebleed should include application of finger pressure directly against the nostril that is bleeding. The person rendering first aid should wear a latex glove for protection against exposure to blood. If the bleeding persists, application of a cold compress against the nasal region is usually effective in causing immediate vasoconstriction of the affected vessels. In addition, the athlete should be instructed to lie on one side (the same side as the bleeding nostril). If the athlete needs to continue participation, the nose can be packed with gauze, which should be allowed to protrude slightly from the nose in order to aid with extraction later.

Septal injuries present unique problems and the possibility of later complications. As a result of external blows the septum can be bruised; bleeding can occur between the septum and the mucous membrane covering it. This injury is referred to as a septal hematoma and can lead to serious septal erosion if not corrected. The signs of a septal hematoma are swelling that is usually visible both inside and outside the nose. In addition, the nose may appear red and infected externally, and the athlete will complain of pain, especially when the nose is gently palpated. This injury should be referred to the appropriate medical specialist for diagnosis and correction. The coach or athlete should not attempt to drain a septal hematoma since the likelihood of infection and permanent damage is high.

Ear Injuries

Anatomically, the human ear shares some common characteristics with the nose. Externally it appears as a cartilaginous framework covered with a layer of skin, but it has an extensive internal structure as well. Specifically, the ear can be divided into several anatomical components. The external ear consists of the large expanded portion called the auricula and the opening into the ear canal known as the external acoustic meatus. The middle ear, which is a small space within the temporal bone, contains a small group of bones that transmit vibrations to the tympanic membrane (ear drum). The inner ear comprises the complex structure known as the labyrinth or specialized bones (vestibule, semicircular canals, and cochlea) that are directly attached with the vestibulocochlear nerve (Gray, 1985). The structures of the inner ear also play a major role in the maintenance of equilibrium (VanDeGraaff, 1984). Thus injuries to this area often affect not only hearing but balance as well.

With the exception of aquatic sports, the majority of sports-related medical problems with the ear affect its external parts. Sports such as wrestling, which involves a great deal of body contact between opponents and the playing surface, result in a large number of abrasions and contusions to the auricula. Although the use of protective equipment has reduced the overall numbers of such injuries, they do still occur. Since the tissues of the auricula have some degree of vascu-

via aspiration. The ear will then be packed with a special material to prevent swelling from returning. Athletes with a history of this injury, or those involved in high-risk sports such as wrestling, should be required to wear properly fitted protection.

Anytime an athlete receives a blow to the ear region that is immediately followed by a sudden reduction in hearing and/or dizziness, immediate referral to a physician is required. Blows to the outer ear can produce dramatic increases in pressure within the ear, resulting in ruptures of either the ear drum or a specialized structure known as the round window. When such an injury occurs, the immediate effects are significant reduction in hearing as well as transient loss of equilibrium. Other signs and symptoms may include bleeding from the ear as well as persistent and intense ringing in the ear. Damage to the round window may require surgical intervention to correct the problem (Matthews, 1990). Athletes with ear infections should be advised not to participate in aquatic sports until the problem has resolved itself. This is particularly true in diving since infection and subsequent inflammation within the ear may make it impossible for the athlete to clear the ears while underwater, often resulting in injury to the ear drum.

Information at your fingertips

The World Wide Web—Check out outstanding ear anatomy sites; go to http://www.jbpub.com/athletictraining and click on Chapter 9.

larity, trauma can lead to the development of a hematoma between the skin and underlying cartilage, known technically as an auricular hematoma (Matthews, 1990). If this condition is not treated properly or is repeatedly irritated prior to treatment, a serious cosmetic problem known as cauliflower ear can occur. In extreme cases the cartilage of the auricula may even begin to break down, thereby complicating the problem. Signs and symptoms of auricular hematoma include skin redness, local increase in tissue temperature, pain, and/or a burning sensation. This condition should be treated immediately with a cold pack. If swelling within the auricula occurs, the athlete should be referred to a physician so the fluid can be removed

Fractures of the Face (Non-nasal)

Though fractures can occur almost anywhere on the face, certain sites are more often involved in sports. A relatively common form of facial fracture involves the mandible (lower jaw) and occurs in boxing and other collision sports. The signs and symptoms of such an injury include obvious pain and swelling at the site of the fracture, observable deformity, and malocclusion (misalignment of the maxillary and mandibular teeth). Treatment entails gentle application of a cold pack and immediate referral to a physician. If a fracture has occurred, the jaw will be treated by wiring the mouth closed; in severe cases, surgical fixation may be required until the fracture is healed (Matthews, 1990).

A related injury is dislocation of the jaw, which can result from the same type of mechanism. Here the joint involved is the **temporomandibular joint (TMJ),** which is classified as ellipsoid and is formed by the union of the mandibular condyle and the mandibular fossa of the temporal bone (Figure 9.22). The TMJ is held together by numerous ligaments and joint capsules. Due to its bony configuration this joint tends to dislocate relatively easily. The signs and symptoms of this injury include extreme pain and deformity in the region of the TMJ and inability to move the lower jaw; in some cases the mouth may be locked in an open position. Treatment for this injury is essentially the same as for a fracture. It is important that on-site reductions (putting the joint back in place) not be attempted.

Other bones of the face may be fractured, including the zygomatic bone. Generally, the signs and symptoms will include pain and swelling at the site of injury. In the case of the zygomatic bone, swelling and discoloration may spread to the orbit of the eye as well. Any athlete with a history of a blow to the face who has some or all of the above signs and symptoms should be referred immediately to a physician for diagnosis and treatment.

Wounds of the Facial Region

Wounds to the face may take many forms; in general, their treatment should be based upon basic first aid guidelines. Carefully clean the wound with mild soap and warm water, apply a sterile, commercially prepared dressing (not loose cotton), and refer the athlete to a physician. Facial wounds take on greater significance

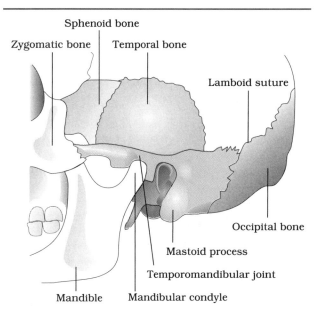

FIGURE 9.22 The temporomandibular joint.

than injuries to other parts of the body primarily because of cosmetic reasons. Thus, any wound to the face, whether it is a simple **abrasion** (scraped skin), a more serious incision (smoothed edged, bleeds freely), or laceration (skin cut with jagged, irregular edges), should be evaluated relative to the potential long-term cosmetic effects. As a general rule, any incision or laceration resulting in an observable space between the margins of the skin should be seen by a physician for suturing (Matthews, 1990). Normally, athletes can return to participation once the wound has been treated and (when necessary) sutured. The decision to release such an athlete to return to activity is best determined by the attending physician, especially in the case of a minor (Crow, 1993).

Review Questions

1. List the names of the cranial bones and give a description of their anatomic relationship.

2. What are the correct names of specialized tissues known collectively as the cerebral meninges?

3. What is located within the subarachnoid space?

4. What is the approximate weight in pounds of an adult human's brain?

5. What are the three basic components of the human brain?

6. List the correct number of cervical, thoracic, lumbar, sacral, and coccygeal nerves.

7. According to the chapter, what is a cerebral concussion?

8. What is the major difference between a grade-2 and grade-3 concussion as described in the chapter?

9. Describe the condition known as diffuse brain injury.

10. What is posttraumatic amnesia as it relates to a head injury?

11. Define subdural, epidural, and intracerebral hematomas; also define cerebral contusion.

12. When rendering first aid to an athlete with a suspected head injury, what are the top three objectives?

13. *True or false:* The single most important indicator of the severity of head injury is the level of consciousness.

14. Describe the administration of the finger-to-nose test and the Romberg's test.

15. What is the most likely mechanism of a sports-related injury to the cervical spine?

16. What conditions must be assumed present whenever treating an unconscious athlete?

17. What types of information should be obtained when treating a conscious athlete with a suspected head and/or neck injury?

18. Give a definition of the acronym NEISS.

19. What is the cause of the majority of dental injuries?

20. What is a simple, practical form of dental protection in sports?

21. *True or false:* The majority of sports-related eye injuries occur in basketball.

22. What is the recommended method of removing a small, nonimbedded object from an athlete's eye?

23. What is an orbital blowout?

24. What materials should the coach have available in a first aid kit for treating problems related to athletes' wearing contact lenses?

25. Define the term epistaxis.

26. Describe the appropriate method for controlling a nosebleed.

27. *True or false:* With the exception of aquatic sports, the majority of sports-related medical problems with the ear involve the auricula.

28. Briefly describe the process leading to the condition known as cauliflower ear.

29. Why are facial wounds of greater significance than wounds on other areas of the body?

References

Bailes JE. 1990. Management of cervical spine sports injuries. *Athletic Training.* 25:156–159.

Bishop PJ. 1996. Factors related to quadriplegia in football and the implications for intervention strategies. *Am J Sports Med.* 24(2):235–239.

Booher JM, Thibodeau GA. 1989. *Athletic Injury Assessment.* St. Louis: Times Mirror/Mosby.

Burstein AH, Otis JC, Torg JS. 1982. Mechanisms and pathomechanics of athletic injuries to the cervical spine. In Torg JS (ed.). *Athletic Injuries to the Head, Neck, and Face.* Philadelphia: Lea & Febiger. 139–154.

Cantu RC. 1986. Guidelines for return to contact sports after cerebral concussion. *Phys Sportsmed.* 14(10):75–83.

Cantu RC, Voy R. 1995. Second impact syndrome—a risk in any contact sport. *Phys Sportsmed.* 23(6):27–34.

Clarke KS. 1982. An epidemiologic view. In Torg JS (ed.). *Athletic Injuries to the Head, Neck, and Face.* Philadelphia: Lea & Febiger. 15–25.

Colorado Medical Society. 1991. *Guidelines for the Management of Concussion in Sports.* Denver: Colorado Medical Society.

Crow RW. 1993. Sports-related lacerations—promoting healing and limiting scarring. *Phys Sportsmed.* 21:143–147.

Feld F. 1993. Management of the critically injured football player. *Journal of Athletic Training.* 28(3):206–212.

Fourre M. 1991. On-site management of cervical spine injuries. *Phys Sportsmed.* 19(4):53–56.

Godwin WC. 1996. A tale of two teeth. *Training & Conditioning.* IV(3):39–42.

Gray H. 1985. *Anatomy of the Human Body.* Philadelphia: Lea & Febiger.

Heck JF. 1996. The incidence of spearing during a high school's 1975 and 1990 football seasons. *Journal of Athletic Training.* 31:31–37.

Jones NP. 1989. Eye injury in sport. *Sports Med.* 7(3):163–181.

Jordan BD. 1989. Head injury in sports. In Jordan BD, Tsairis P, Warren RR (eds.). *Sports Neurology.* New York: Aspen Publishers. 75–83.

Kerr IL. 1986. Mouth guards for the prevention of injuries in contact sports. *Sports Med.* 3:415–427.

Kleiner DM. 1996. Football helmet face mask removal. *Athletic Therapy Today.* 1:11–13.

Matthews B. 1990. Maxillofacial trauma from athletic endeavors. *Athletic Training.* 25:132–137.

McWhorter JM. 1990. Concussions and intracranial injuries in athletics. *Athletic Training.* 25:129–131.

Mueller FO, Cantu RC. 1993. *National center for catastrophic sports injury research—tenth annual report—fall-spring 1992.* Unpublished monograph. Chapel Hill: University of North Carolina, Department of Physical Education.

National Athletic Trainers' Association. 1996. Athletic helmet removal guidelines.

Putman LA. 1992. Alternative methods for football-helmet face-mask removal. *Journal of Athletic Training.* 27(2):170–172.

Sallis RE, Jones K, Knopp W. 1992. Burners—offensive strategy for an underreported injury. *Phys Sportsmed.* 20:47–55.

Segan RD, Cassidy C, Bentkowski J. 1993. A discussion of the issue of football-helmet removal in suspected cervical spine injuries. *Journal of Athletic Training.* 28(4):294–305.

Torg JS. 1989. Athletic injuries to the cervical spine. In Jordan BD, Tsairis P, Warren RR (eds.). *Sports Neurology.* New York: Aspen Publishers. 133–158.

VanDeGraaff KM. 1984. *Human Anatomy.* Dubuque: William C. Brown.

Vegso JJ, Bryant MH, Torg JS. 1982. Field evaluation of head and neck injuries. In Torg JS (ed.). *Athletic Injuries to the Head, Neck, and Face.* Philadelphia: Lea & Febiger. 39–52.

Wiesenfarth J, Briner W. Howe WB (ed.). 1996. Neck injuries—urgent decisions and actions. *Phy Sportsmed.* 24:35–41.

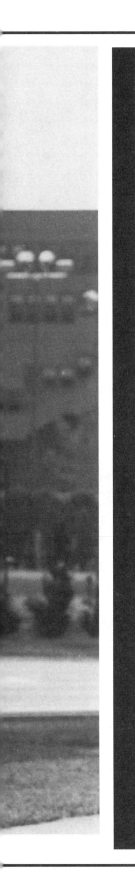

Injuries to the Thoracic Through Coccygeal Spine

M A J O R   C O N C E P T S

This chapter presents a brief review of the gross anatomy of the thoracic spine and thoracic cage along with a discussion of possible injuries to the region. Although relatively uncommon in sports, injuries to the thoracic spine do occasionally occur. These injuries are usually sprains; much less frequently they involve fractures. The chapter covers typical mechanisms of injury as well as common signs and symptoms and recommended initial treatment for both sprains and fractures.

Injuries to the lumbar spine in sports are quite common: the vast majority are related to an anatomical defect known as spondylolysis. This chapter provides descriptions of the common problems associated with this part of the spinal column along with information regarding the signs and symptoms of related lumbar spinal disorders. It also discusses traumatic sprains, strains, and intervertebral disk injuries with a focus on recognition and initial management.

Anatomy Review of the Thoracic Spine

The portion of the human vertebral column known as the thoracic spine consists of 12 vertebrae that articulate at the top with the cervical spine and with the lumbar spine at the bottom. The thoracic vertebrae are commonly numbered 1 through 12 beginning with the uppermost vertebra and ending with the 12th at the junction with the lumbar spine. An intervertebral disk is located between each thoracic vertebra. A unique aspect of the thoracic vertebrae is their relationship with the 12 pairs of ribs in the human skeleton. The thoracic vertebrae, their corresponding ribs, and the sternum form a strong **thoracic cage** (Figure 10.1), which among other things serves to protect the internal organs of the region including the heart and lungs (Gray, 1985).

Because of the bony union of the ribs and adjacent vertebrae, the thoracic spine is much less mobile than either the cervical or lumbar sections of the spine. The majority of movements within the thoracic region of the spine result from the process of respiration (Rasch, 1989). The limited movements of the thoracic vertebrae themselves help to make injuries to this part of the body uncommon.

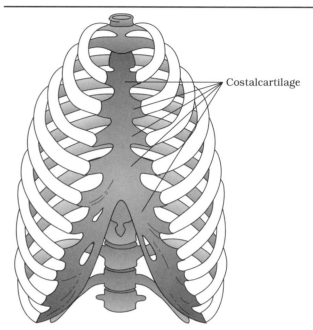

FIGURE 10.1 The thoracic cage (anterior view).

(O'Leary and Boiardo, 1986). This injury occurs near the junction of the thoracic and lumbar spines and is usually related to violent, ballistic movements that are unique to sports involving high velocities. An athlete

Information at your fingertips

The World Wide Web—For an excellent review of entire vertebral column, go to http://www.jbpub.com/athletictraining and click on Chapter 10.

Common Sports Injuries

As stated, sports injuries to the thoracic spine are rare. Those sports-related injuries that do occur can be divided into two groups: skeletal and soft tissue (ligaments, muscles and tendons, and intervertebral disks). Available data demonstrate that bone-related injuries in this region are more common than those involving soft tissues (AAOS, 1991).

■ Skeletal Injuries

The most common injury to the thoracic spine involves a compression type of fracture to the vertebral body

with a history of recent trauma to the thoracic spine who complains of severe pain in the region or perhaps even neurologic signs (pain or numbness of the extremities) should be referred to a medical doctor immediately for evaluation. Another problem related to the vertebrae of the thoracic spine is Scheuermann's disease, which is sometimes seen in adolescents and is characterized by **kyphosis** (an abnormal amount of convexity of the spine). Children involved in activities that subject the spine to severe bending, such as gymnastics, may develop this condition. A child who complains of recurrent pain in the region of the thoracic spine that is associated with activity should be evaluated. A quick visual examination may confirm an ab-

Athletic Trainers Speak Out

"To be in this field [one] definitely has to be a people person. Good communication skills are a necessity for [being effective] because you deal with so many individuals and groups as part of your responsibilities. Organizing the care of the athlete, from prevention to total rehabilitation, involves a number of people with [you] at the core."

—**Doris E. Flores, A.T.C.**

Mrs. Flores is the program director of the athletic-training curriculum at California State University at Sacramento.

Doris E. Flores

normal amount of spinal curvature, which is made worse when the child bends forward as if to touch the toes. In some cases, related spinal problems such as **scoliosis** (lateral curvature) and lumbar **lordosis** (swayback) may also be present. Children with either of these disorders need to be referred to a doctor for extensive evaluation. If a diagnosis of Scheuermann's disease is made, treatment will involve both prescribed exercises and spinal bracing.

Fractures caused by direct blows to the thoracic spine are extremely rare; however, significant soft-tissue damage can occur to the skin and underlying muscles. The signs and symptoms of such injuries include pain, dysfunction, swelling, and discoloration. Initial treatment should include the immediate application of ice and compression with a follow-up evaluation 24 hours later. If symptoms persist referral to a

physician is necessary to rule out more serious injuries such as fractures or disk problems.

Another type of fracture that may occur in this region involves the ribs and is known as a posterior rib fracture (AAOS, 1991). The mechanism for this injury is typically a direct blow to the lateral or posterior thorax. Fractures may occur anywhere along the rib; however, most commonly they occur near an angle of the rib, which is anatomically the weakest point (Booher and Thibodeau, 1989). The signs and symptoms of rib fractures, regardless of specific location, are relatively generic. Following a direct blow or compression to the thorax, painful respiration, swelling, discoloration in the region of injury, and possibly even some noticeable displacement of the rib may be observed. Complications of these injuries are rare; however, when they do occur they can be quite dangerous.

Displaced rib fractures may damage internal thoracic structures, particularly the lungs, resulting in either a traumatic **pneumothorax** (Figure 10.2) or hemopneumothorax (blood and air in the thorax). Such injuries will result in significant changes in breathing and may also induce shock.

First aid for an athlete with a suspected rib fracture includes application of ice and compression, which is generally best accomplished by using a 6 or 8-inch-wide elastic wrap and a bag of crushed ice. In addition, the athlete should be treated for shock and referred immediately to a physician for further evaluation. For more detailed information on the care and management of these injuries refer to Chapter 13.

■ Sprains

Sprains occur whenever a joint is forced through an abnormal range of motion (ROM) that results in damage to supporting structures such as ligaments and joint capsules. Since the thoracic spine is well supported, limited movement is allowed, thereby reducing the incidence of sprains. Evaluation of a sprain to the thoracic spine is difficult and must be based upon a detailed history of the injury. An athlete with such an injury will usually report having sustained an unusual movement of the thoracic spine that is associated with localized pain, a feeling of popping or snapping, and in some cases swelling. A consistent symptom of injury to the thoracic area is painful respiration, which is associated with many different injuries to the region, including rib fractures and contusions. First aid for

sprains to the thoracic spine includes the application of ice and compression. If significant symptoms such as **dyspnea** (difficult breathing) persist for more than 24 hours, the athlete should be referred to a medical doctor.

■ Strains

Strains involve primarily contractile tissues and their support structures—muscles, fascia, and tendons. The muscles of the thoracic spine region include the erector spinae and the intercostals. Strains may occur related to maximum exertion in sports requiring large amounts of force, such as tackle football, wrestling, or ice hockey. Signs and symptoms of strains may be very difficult to differentiate from sprains. Often the injury mechanism will be identical to that of a sprain. Muscle spasms of erector spinae in the region may be noticeable. These muscles may also be sensitive to touch (palpation) and should be inspected for this symptom. First aid for suspected strains of this region is the same as for sprains: application of ice and compression.

■ Intervertebral Disk Injuries

Although extremely rare in the thoracic region of the spine, injuries can occur to the intervertebral disks located between each of the vertebrae. Disk problems may be secondary to a compression fracture of thoracic vertebrae. Any athlete who complains of persistent neurologic symptoms, such as numbness or pain radiating around the thoracic region or into one or more of the extremities, should be referred immediately to a medical doctor for more detailed evaluation.

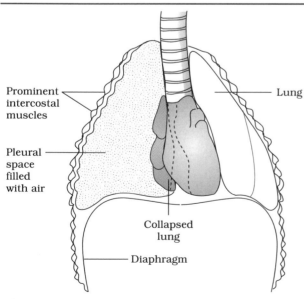

Prominent intercostal muscles

Pleural space filled with air

Lung

Collapsed lung

Diaphragm

FIGURE 10.2 Pneumothorax.

Anatomy Review of the Lumbar Spine Distally to the Coccyx

The lumbar spine consists of five vertebrae that articulate superiorly with the thoracic vertebral column and inferiorly with the sacrum. The lumbar vertebrae are the largest vertebrae of all those that move—i.e., cervical, thoracic, and lumbar (Gray, 1985). The lumbar vertebrae are numbered L-1 to L-5, from proximal to distal. As is the case with the thoracic and cervical sections of the spine, intervertebral disks are located between each of the lumbar vertebrae, as well as between T-12 and L-1 and between L-5 and S-1 (the first sacral vertebra). Additionally, large, strong ligaments assist in stabilization of the lumbar vertebrae (Figure 10.3),

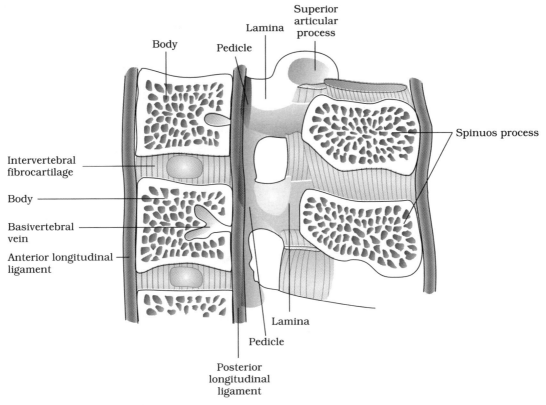

FIGURE 10.3 The lumbar vertebrae (sagittal view).

along with the thoracic spine and the sacrum. The anterior and posterior longitudinal ligaments are located on the anterior and posterior surfaces of the vertebral bodies (within the spinal cord canal), respectively. Both of these important ligaments span the vertebral column from the level of C-2 (axis) distal to the sacrum.

The sacrum, consisting of five fused vertebrae, is located between the two pelvic bones posteriorly. In essence, the sacrum serves to connect the spinal column to the pelvis (Figure 10.4). Two articulations, the right and left sacroiliac joints, are formed by the union of the sacrum and the pelvis.

The most distal portion of the vertebral column is a small, arrowhead-shaped structure called the coccyx.

Common Sports Injuries

Injuries are more common to the lumbar spine than to the thoracic. Of all the injuries that can affect the bony portion of the lumbar spine, the most common is spondylolysis.

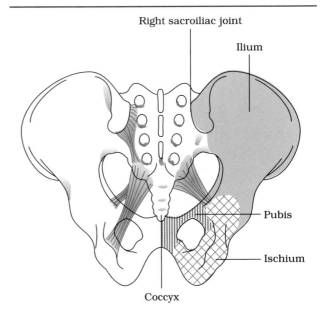

FIGURE 10.4 The pelvis (posterior view).

■ Spondylolysis and Spondylolisthesis

Spondylolysis (Figure 10.5) is a defect in that part of a vertebra that forms the bony ring around the spinal cord (neural arch). Spondylolysis involves that portion of the neural arch known as the pars interarticularis (there are two on each vertebra, one on the right side and one on the left). The significance of bony defects in this region relates to superior articulations with adjacent vertebrae. Thus, any defect of the neural arch in this area can compromise the integrity of the articulation between any two vertebrae.

In cases in which both the right and left neural arches are affected, the involved vertebra has the potential to slide forward, thus producing a condition known as **spondylolisthesis.** As can be seen in Figure 10.6, the most common site for this condition is between L-5 and the sacrum (O'Leary and Boiardo, 1986). Given the normal slope of the sacrum, bony instability of the last lumbar vertebra makes anterior displacement possible, especially when the lumbar region is subjected to abnormal amounts of stress, such as occurs in gymnastics, tackle football, or competitive weight lifting.

The exact **etiology** of spondylolysis is not clear; however, evidence suggests that the bony defects may be either congenital (present at birth) or related to excessive stress to the bones during childhood. The symptoms of spondylolysis include lower back pain, which becomes particularly acute when the lumbar spine is placed into **hyperextension.** When the defect is unilateral (one side only), standing on one leg in

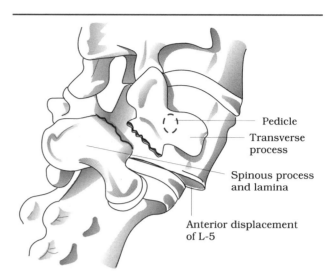

FIGURE 10.6 Anterior displacement of the L-5 vertebra that induces spondylolisthesis.

conjunction with lumbar hyperextension will elicit pain only on the side of the defect (Halpern and Smith, 1991). If spondylolysis progresses to spondylolisthesis, symptoms may become more severe. Pain in the lumbar region may increase during activity, and in some cases radiating pain may occur in the buttocks and upper thighs (Booher and Thibodeau, 1989).

Any athlete complaining of symptoms of this type, particularly those involved in high-risk sports for lumbar injuries (gymnastics, tackle football, and weight lifting), should be referred to a medical doctor for further evaluation. Treatment for spondylolysis and spondylolisthesis may include rest, drug therapy, lumbar bracing, exclusion from certain sports, and in severe cases surgical spinal fusion.

■ Traumatic Fractures

Traumatic fractures of the lumbar vertebrae are infrequent in sports. Such injuries will normally be associated with a history of a severe blow to the lumbar region. Depending on the specific location and type of fracture, neurologic symptoms, such as radiating pain into the buttocks or legs, may be present. Such injuries need to be treated initially with great care via immobilization on a spine board and transport to a medical facility, where complete evaluation by a physician can take place. It must be remembered that an external blow to the lumbar region may also cause injury to internal organs, specifically the kidneys. Thus, it is important that the athlete be evaluated for such an injury. Special attention should be given to the signs

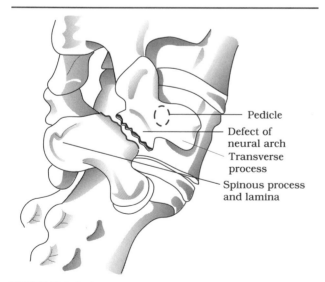

FIGURE 10.5 Defect of the neural arch that causes spondylolysis.

and symptoms of internal injury such as deep abdominal pain, **hematuria,** or shock.

Injuries to the sacrum or coccyx are generally limited to those caused by direct blows. Such injuries are normally self-limited and require only protection from future trauma. One notable exception is a severe blow to the coccyx, which may result in a fracture or severe bruise. Such an injury can occur when an athlete falls backwards, landing hard on the buttocks and impacting the coccygeal region. The signs and symptoms of this injury involve an observable bruise in the coccygeal region, severe point tenderness, and swelling. This injury needs to be evaluated by a medical doctor since a fracture may be present.

■ Sprains and Strains

By far the most common soft-tissue injuries to the lumbar region are strains and sprains (O'Leary and Boiardo, 1986). Strains involve the contractile tissues of the region, i.e., the erector spinae muscles (Figure 10.7).

Sprains involve the many ligaments and joint capsules of the region. As previously mentioned, there are large ligaments (the anterior and posterior longitudinal ligaments) that bind the vertebral bodies together. In addition, there are ligaments and capsules binding the joints between adjacent neural arches (facet joints). Major joints in the region include the lumbosacral, sacroiliac, and the sacrococcygeal. Generally, injuries to the joints are rare in this region. However, muscle strains occur frequently, particularly in sports that place significant stress on the lumbar spine. Activities such as gymnastics, tackle football, and weight lifting can place the athlete in situations in which abnormal loads are exerted on the lumbar region of the spine. The signs and symptoms of lumbar strain include local muscle spasm, pain, and acute postural abnormalities in association with a history of recent trauma. Often the athlete will be able to relate a specific incident to the onset of symptoms. It is important to remember that an injury mechanism of sufficient magnitude to cause a strain may have also caused more severe injury. It is always best to refer such athletes for further evaluation by a medical doctor (Shankman, 1991). This is especially important in cases in which the athlete complains of pain radiating into one or both legs. Such symptoms can indicate a significant injury such as a herniated disk (O'Leary and Boiardo, 1986).

The immediate treatment of a suspected lumbar strain or sprain includes the application of ice and compression. In cases involving severe pain, it may be difficult for the athlete to find a body position that is tolerable. Although each situation is unique, a position that often helps is lying supine, with legs parallel and both knees drawn up so that both the hips and knees are flexed (Figure 10.8). Some type of padding should be placed under the lumbar region for support, leaving enough room for a bag of crushed ice.

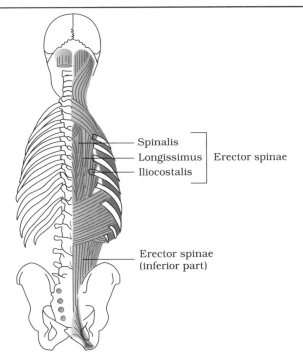

Spinalis
Longissimus | Erector spinae
Iliocostalis

Erector spinae
(inferior part)

FIGURE 10.7 The erector spinae muscles of the upper and lower back.

FIGURE 10.8 Recommended position for an athlete with acute lower back pain.

WHAT IF?

You are coaching gymnastics. One of your athletes just over-rotated on a double-back on floor. As soon as she hit the mat, she collapsed to the floor, complaining of severe pain in her lumbar region. In addition, she complains of a burning sensation in the back of her thigh and lower leg. What type of injury might she have? What type of first aid care would you provide?

■ Lumbar Disk Injuries

A more serious form of soft-tissue injury to the lumbar region involves damage within an intervertebral disk, commonly known as a **herniated disk.** Though such injuries can occur to any of the disks of the spine, the most commonly injured in the lumbar region are L-4 and L-5 (Keim and Kirkaldy-Willis, 1980). Most often these injuries occur when an athlete is subjected to a great deal of force while in an awkward position. The anatomy of a typical intervertebral disk consists of an outer ring called the annulus fibrosus and a softer, inner portion known as the nucleus pulposus (Gray, 1985). In the case of a herniation, a weakness develops within the annulus, which then allows the nucleus pulposus to cause a protrusion through the wall of the annulus. Depending upon the exact location of the herniation, pressure may be placed directly on the large spinal nerves passing through the region (Figure 10.9).

The symptoms of disk herniation include intense local pain in the region of the injury as well as radiating pain anywhere throughout the distribution of the sciatic nerve. Thus, the athlete may complain of pain in the buttock, posterior thigh, leg, ankle, or foot. In addition, symptoms might include loss of skin sensation and even noticeable loss of muscle strength unilaterally. Any athlete with such symptoms should be placed in the most comfortable position possible and transported immediately for detailed medical evaluation. If

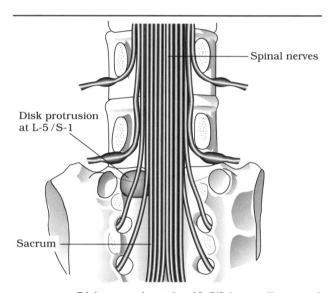

FIGURE 10.9 Disk protrusion at level L-5/S-1 may affect sacral nerves.

possible, apply a bag of crushed ice to the lumbar region. This may help reduce the lumbar pain and muscle spasm that usually accompany these injuries. Although little can be done in the field for such injuries, much can be done to alleviate long-term symptoms with a combination of physical therapy and drug therapy. The major goal of such a strategy is to return the athlete to participation and avoid the need for surgery.

Review Questions

1. *True or false:* Because of the bony relationship between the ribs and adjacent vertebrae, the thoracic spine is much less mobile than either the cervical or lumbar regions of the spine.

2. *True or false:* Available data indicate that soft-tissue injuries of the thoracic spine are more frequent than bone-related injuries.

3. Describe briefly the condition known as Scheuermann's disease along with its signs and symptoms.

4. Define scoliosis, kyphosis, and lordosis.

5. What is a posterior rib fracture, and what are its common signs and symptoms?

6. What is a consistent symptom related to sprains within the thoracic spine?

7. *True or false:* Intervertebral disk injuries are extremely common to the thoracic spine.

8. Anatomically, the sacrum consists of how many fused vertebrae?

9. Describe the condition known as spondylolysis.

10. Describe briefly the condition known as spondylolisthesis, including both the signs and symptoms as well as recommended treatment.

11. What is the recommended immediate treatment for a suspected strain or sprain of the lumbar spine?

12. Describe briefly the normal anatomy of a typical lumbar intervertebral disk as well as the process of disk herniation.

13. What are the signs and symptoms of lumbar disk herniation?

References

American Academy of Orthopaedic Surgeons. 1991. *Athletic Training and Sports Medicine* (2d ed.). Park Ridge, Ill.: American Academy of Orthopaedic Surgeons.

Booher JM, Thibodeau GA. 1989. *Athletic Injury Assessment.* St. Louis: Times Mirror/Mosby.

Gray H. 1985. *Anatomy of the Human Body.* Philadelphia: Lea & Febiger.

Halpern BC, Smith AD. 1991. Catching the cause of low-back pain. *Phys Sportsmed.* 19:71–79.

Keim HA, Kirkaldy-Willis WH. 1980. *Low Back Pain.* Summit, N.J.: CIBA Pharmaceutical Company. 32:17.

O'Leary P, Boiardo R. 1986. The diagnosis and treatment of injuries of the spine in athletes. In Nicholas JA, Hershman EB (eds.). *The Lower Extremity and Spine in Sports Medicine.* St. Louis: Mosby. 1171–1229.

Rasch PJ. 1989. *Kinesiology and Applied Anatomy.* Philadelphia: Lea & Febiger.

Shankman G. 1991. *Athletic Injury Care and Sports Conditioning.* Woodstock, Ga.: Sports Health Education.

CHAPTER 11

Injuries to the Shoulder Region

MAJOR CONCEPTS

The initial sections of this chapter review the gross anatomy and arthrology of the articulations of the shoulder, followed by a brief discussion of acute and chronic injuries common to the shoulder region. It describes clavicular fractures with respect to the common mechanisms of injury, signs and symptoms, and recommended first aid care. It also covers injuries to the acromioclavicular, sternoclavicular, and glenohumeral joints, outlining the common mechanisms of injury, signs and symptoms, and recommended first aid care.

Next the chapter reviews musculotendinous injuries of the shoulder region related to common mechanisms of injury such as throwing and swinging; it summarizes the basic kinesiology with identification of the various types of muscle contractions during each phase of movement. This is followed by specific information regarding strains to the rotator cuff, with special attention given to the signs and symptoms of this debilitating injury. It then discusses a related injury known as impingement syndrome with respect to its anatomy, signs and symptoms, and recommended treatment.

The concluding portions of the chapter contain information regarding two groups of injuries—problems with biceps tendons and contusions of the shoulder region. It presents practical information about the signs and symptoms of these injuries along with the suggested first aid.

Anatomy Review

The shoulder allows for a great deal of movement while at the same time providing a point of attachment for the arm to the thorax. The skeleton of the shoulder (Figure 11.1) consists of the bones of the shoulder girdle and the upper arm bone (humerus). The *clavicle* and the *scapula* make up the shoulder girdle, so named because these two bones surround (girdle) the upper thorax. The head of the *humerus* combines with the shallow glenoid fossa of the scapula to form the highly mobile **glenohumeral (GH) joint,** commonly known as the shoulder joint (Figure 11.2). The GH joint is given additional stability by a fibrocartilaginous cuplike structure known as the glenoid labrum, which is directly attached to the glenoid fossa (Gray, 1985). The shoulder region also includes the **acromioclavicular (AC) joint,** located between the distal end of the clavicle and the acromion of the scapula (Figure 11.2) and the **sternoclavicular (SC) joint,** located between the proximal end of the clavicle and the manubrium of the sternum (Figure 11.3). Each of these joints is held together with ligaments and joint capsules that provide stability while also allowing for necessary movement, which is quite limited.

Many muscles move both the shoulder girdle and the GH joint in a multitude of directions. In nearly all motions the shoulder girdle and the GH joint work together to move the arm. Consequently, any limita-

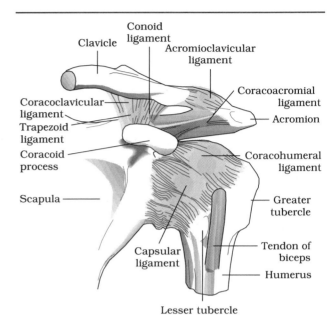

FIGURE 11.2 Ligaments of the acromioclavicular and glenohumeral joints.

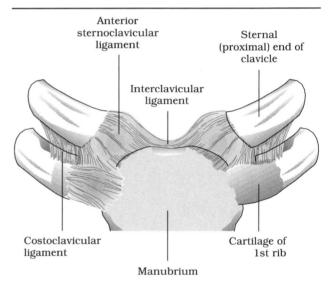

FIGURE 11.3 Ligaments of the sternoclavicular joint.

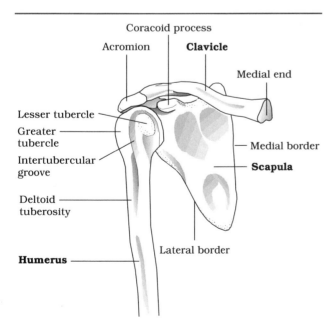

FIGURE 11.1 Skeleton of the shoulder region.

tion from injury to the shoulder girdle will indirectly affect the GH joint. In athletes a large amount of soft tissue covers both the shoulder girdle and the GH joint; as a result they are somewhat protected from external blows. However, even in extremely muscular athletes both the AC and SC joints lie just under the skin and are therefore more exposed to injury.

The blood supply to the entire upper extremity, including the shoulder, originates from branches of the

Information at your fingertips

The World Wide Web—For additional information on the anatomy of the human shoulder, go to http://www.jbpub.com/athletictraining and click on Chapter 11.

subclavian artery. As this artery passes into the axillary region it becomes the axillary artery; it continues into the upper arm becoming the brachial artery and splits just distal to the elbow into the radial and ulnar arteries that extend into the forearm and hand (Figure 11.4).

The major nerves of the shoulder and upper extremity originate from that group known collectively as the brachial plexus (Figure 11.5). The brachial plexus originates from the ventral primary divisions of the fifth through the eighth cervical nerves and the first thoracic nerve (Gray, 1985). Through a complex series of

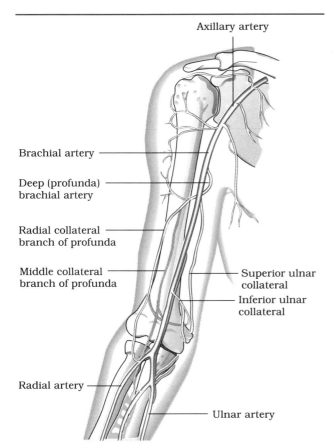

FIGURE 11.4 Major arteries of the arm.

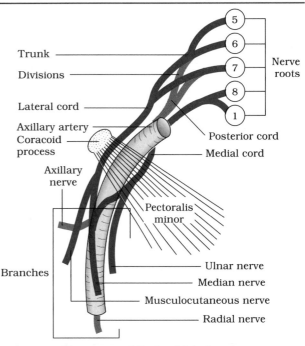

FIGURE 11.5 The nerves of the brachial plexus.

divisions the brachial plexus provides all the major nerves to the entire upper extremity.

Common Sports Injuries

Injuries to the shoulder region are common in many sports and in some cases are highly sport specific. For example, injuries to both the GH and AC joints are quite common in wrestling. Sports that emphasize a throwing or swinging action often produce injuries caused by overuse to the muscles of the rotator cuff (infraspinatus, supraspinatus, teres minor, subscapularis), which act on the GH joint. The rotator cuff muscles are extremely important to the stability of the GH joint since this large ball-and-socket structure lacks inherent strength. Sports such as cycling and skating produce a large number of fractures of the clavicle brought about by falls.

Injuries of the shoulder region can be classified as either acute (of sudden onset) or chronic (resulting from overuse). Sports involving heavy contact or collisions yield more acute injuries; those necessitating repeated movements tend to produce more chronic injuries.

Skeletal Injuries

■ Fractured Clavicle

The most common fracture of the shoulder region is a fracture of the clavicle. Such fractures can result from direct blows to the bone; however, the majority occur as a result of falls that transmit the force to the clavicle either through the arm or shoulder. The majority of clavicular fractures occur about midshaft; the remainder involve either the proximal or distal end of the bone (AAOS, 1991). In the adolescent athlete another type of clavicular fracture, commonly known as a greenstick fracture, can occur. This fracture occurs in immature bone and involves a cracking, splintering type of injury.

Although a fractured clavicle is potentially dangerous, given the close proximity of the bone to major blood vessels and nerves, the vast majority of these injuries cause few complications. It is critical that appropriate first aid be applied to prevent unnecessary movement of the fracture that can result in additional soft-tissue damage.

Signs and symptoms of a fractured clavicle include:

1. Swelling and/or deformity of the clavicle.
2. Discoloration at the site of the fracture.
3. Possible broken bone end projecting through the skin.
4. Athlete reporting that a snap or pop was felt or heard.
5. Athlete holding the arm on the affected side in order to relieve pressure on the shoulder girdle.

First aid care for a fractured clavicle includes:

1. Treat for possible shock.
2. Carefully apply a sling-and-swathe bandage as seen in Figure 11.6 (National Safety Council, 1991).
3. Apply sterile dressings to any related wounds.
4. Arrange for transport to a medical facility.

■ Fractured Scapula

A much less common type of fracture in the shoulder region involves the scapula. A unique group of scapular

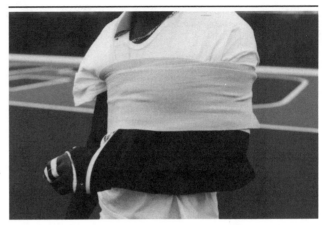

FIGURE 11.6 A sling-and-swathe bandage is effective for a variety of injuries to the upper extremity.

fractures among professional football players was recently described by Cain and Hamilton (1992) in the *American Journal of Sports Medicine*. In all cases these fractures resulted from direct blows to the shoulder region. The symptoms of this type of fracture are less clear than those related to fractures of the clavicle. An athlete with a history of a severe blow to the shoulder region, followed immediately by considerable pain and loss of function, should be referred to a physician for further evaluation. This injury can be identified only by X-ray analysis. Treatment is determined by the specific location and extent of the fracture(s). Typically the athlete's arm will be placed in a sling, and the player removed from sports participation for a period of six weeks.

Soft-Tissue Injuries

A variety of sprains and strains involving any number of specific ligaments and tendons occurs in this region of the body. Although any joint can sustain a sprain, the GH and AC joints are the most commonly injured in the shoulder region in sports.

■ Acromioclavicular Joint Injuries

Located just under the skin on the lateral superior surface of the shoulder is the AC joint. This synoviated articulation is supported by the superior and inferior AC ligaments and contains an intra-articular cartilaginous disk as well (Dias and Gregg, 1991). Additional support to the AC joint is provided by the coracoclavicular (CC) ligament (see Figure 11.2), which comprises the trapezoid and conoid ligaments. The CC ligament is attached between the superior coracoid process and the inferior lateral surface of the clavicle.

The typical mechanism of injury for the AC joint is a downward blow to the outer end of the clavicle, which results in the acromion process being driven inferiorly while the distal clavicle remains in place. Another possible mechanism is a fall forward on an outstretched arm, which then transmits the force up the extremity and results in the humeral head driving the acromion superiorly and posteriorly while the clavicle remains in place (O'Donoghue, 1976). Either of these two mechanisms can result in varying degrees of ligament damage. According to O'Donoghue (1976), the severity of the injury is graded based upon the amount of damage to specific ligaments; however, any injury can be placed into one of the three following categories:

1. **First degree:** no significant damage, all ligaments intact.

2. **Second degree:** relatively severe damage (tearing) of the ligaments. There will be no abnormal movement, and the clavicle will be in the normal position.

3. **Third degree:**
   a. Complete rupture of the AC ligament with an intact CC ligament (Figure 11.7).
   b. Complete rupture of the AC and CC ligaments (Figure 11.8).

Signs and symptoms of AC joint sprains include:

1. With first- and second-degree sprains there will be mild swelling with point tenderness and discoloration around the AC joint.

2. Any movement of the shoulder region will elicit pain.

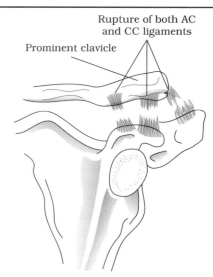

FIGURE 11.8 Complete rupture of both the acromioclavicular and coracoclavicular ligaments.

3. With a third-degree sprain there will be significant deformity in the region of the AC ligament. In the case of ruptures of both the AC and CC ligaments there will be total displacement of the clavicle.

4. The athlete may report having felt a snap or heard a pop.

First aid care of AC joint sprains includes:

1. Immediate application of ice and compression. This is best accomplished by placing a bag of crushed ice over the AC joint and securing it with an elastic wrap tied in a figure-8 configuration.

2. Once the ice and compression are in place, apply a standard sling-and-swathe bandage as described by the National Safety Council (1991).

3. Immediately refer the athlete to a medical facility for further evaluation. In the event of severe injury, arrange for transport and treat for shock.

Long-term treatment for AC separations is dependent upon the level of severity of the injury. In the case of first- and relatively minor second-degree sprains, rest and immobilization are normally effective. Considerable debate exists regarding the appropriate care for severe second- and third-degree AC injuries. Several surgical procedures have been employed; however, research indicates that more conservative, nonsurgical approaches may be just as effective (Bach, VanFleet, and Novak, 1992; Dias and Gregg, 1991).

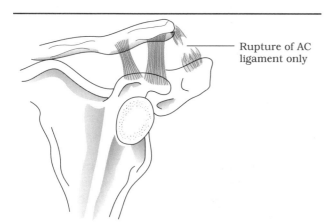

FIGURE 11.7 Complete rupture of the acromioclavicular ligament with an intact coracoclavicular ligament.

WHAT IF?

You are at a high school wrestling tournament examining an athlete who just sustained a shoulder injury. You notice a large mass in the armpit area as well as a definite sloping of the shoulder's contour. The athlete is holding his arm in slight abduction and states that he felt his shoulder "pop out." What would you conclude based upon all of this information? How would you manage this injury?

▪ Glenohumeral Joint Injuries

This articulation consists of the relatively large humeral head opposing the rather shallow glenoid fossa of the scapula. This bony arrangement is effective in giving the joint a great deal of mobility. The GH joint is classified as a spheroidal articulation that moves within all three planes of motion: frontal, sagittal, and transverse. However, this mobility makes the GH joint very unstable (Grabiner, 1989). According to Gray (1985), the major soft-tissue structures of the GH joint (Figure 11.2) include the capsular ligament and the coracohumeral ligament.

The typical mechanism of injury for the GH joint involves having the arm abducted and externally rotated. In this position the anterior portion of the joint capsule, specifically the GH ligament, can be stressed beyond its capacity. If the ligament fails, the head of the humerus can move forward and out of place, resulting in the most common type of GH joint dislocation, an anterior dislocation. Depending upon the severity, this injury may be either a subluxation or a complete dislocation.

Signs and symptoms of an anterior GH dislocation include:

1. Deformity of the shoulder joint: the normal contour of the shoulder is lost, and it appears to slope down abnormally.

2. The arm of the affected side will appear longer than normal.

3. The head of the humerus will be palpable with the axilla.

4. The athlete will be supporting the arm on the affected side with the opposite arm; the affected arm will be slightly abducted at the shoulder and flexed at the elbow.

5. The athlete will resist all efforts passively or actively to move the GH joint.

6. SPECIAL NOTE. In cases of subluxations of the GH, the shoulder may appear normal. However, it will be extremely painful for the athlete to attempt any movement. In addition, the joint may be point tender.

First aid care of GH joint sprains includes:

1. Immediate application of ice and compression. Put a rolled towel in the axilla. Place a bag of crushed ice on the front and back of the shoulder joint and secure with an elastic wrap tied in a figure-8 configuration.

2. Once the ice and compression are in place, apply a standard sling-and-swathe bandage as described by the National Safety Council (1991).

3. Immediately refer the athlete to a medical facility for further evaluation.

4. Since soft-tissue injury may be extensive, treat for shock.

A common complication of GH joint sprains is chronic GH subluxation. It has been reported that, once sustained, up to 85% to 90% of all GH joint dislocations recur (Arnheim, 1987). The joint capsule, ligaments, and supporting musculature are often stretched; therefore, as the athlete continues to participate in stressful activity the joint becomes progressively less stable. The athlete typically will report that during certain movements, often those placing the GH joint in abduction and external rotation, the joint will pop out and then return to its normal position.

Such cases are usually treated conservatively with rest and exercises that specifically focus on the muscles surrounding the joint, including those of the rotator cuff. In severe cases surgical reconstructive procedures may be prescribed.

▪ Sternoclavicular Joint Injuries

The SC joint is formed by the union of the proximal end of the clavicle and the manubrium of the sternum. This synoviated articulation is strengthened by several ligaments (Figure 11.3). These include the joint capsule, the anterior and posterior SC ligaments, the interclavicular and costoclavicular ligaments, and an articular disk located within the joint (Gray, 1985).

Although there are fewer injuries to the SC joint than to either the AC or GH joints, the coach should be prepared to recognize and treat them correctly. The mechanism of injury for the SC joint involves an external blow to the shoulder region that results in a dislocation of the proximal clavicle, most commonly with the bone moving anteriorly and superiorly. A sprain to the SC joint can range in severity from minor stretching, with no actual tearing of tissues, to a complete rupture of ligaments and extensive soft-tissue damage. Fortunately, anterior/superior dislocations cause few additional problems and are easily treated. Occurring much less frequently, but potentially more dangerous, is a posterior SC dislocation. In this instance the proximal end of the clavicle is displaced posteriorly, with the possibility of placing direct pressure on soft-tissue structures in the region, such as blood vessels or even the esophagus and trachea (AAOS, 1991).

Signs and symptoms of SC joint injuries include:

1. In most cases (second- and third-degree sprains) there will be gross deformity present at the SC joint.

2. In all but the least severe cases swelling will be immediate.

3. Movement of the entire shoulder girdle will be limited owing to pain within the SC joint.

4. The athlete will typically report having heard a snapping sound or may have experienced a tearing sensation at the SC joint.

5. Note the body position of the athlete because in this injury the arm may be held close to the body and the head/neck may be tilted/flexed toward the injured shoulder (Wroble, 1995).

First aid care of SC joint injuries includes:

1. Application of ice and compression, which is best accomplished using a plastic bag filled with crushed ice that is secured with an elastic wrap tied in a figure-8 configuration. Take care not to put pressure over the airway when wrapping the shoulder for compression of the SC joint.

2. Place the arm of the affected shoulder in a standard sling-and-swathe bandage as described by the National Safety Council (1991).

3. In cases of severe soft-tissue damage, treat the athlete for shock.

Medical treatment for the majority of SC joint sprains is conservative, that is, reduction of the dislocation if present followed by two to three weeks of support with a sling-and-swathe bandage. It is very rare that any sort of surgical correction is attempted, especially in the case of anterior dislocations. Obviously a sound program of rehabilitation exercises prescribed by a competent sports medicine professional will be helpful in getting the athlete back into action.

▪ Strains of the Shoulder Region

A large number of muscles attach to the bones of the shoulder girdle, any one of which can suffer a strain. As was mentioned earlier, certain sports produce very specific injuries to the shoulder. Perhaps the most common strain involves the muscles of the rotator cuff.

Rotator Cuff The muscles of the **rotator cuff** (Figures 11.9 and 11.10) serve a variety of purposes, including stabilization of the humeral head in the glenoid fossa as well as abduction and internal and external rotation of the GH joint.

In order to better understand the mechanism of injuries involving the rotator cuff, it is necessary to re-

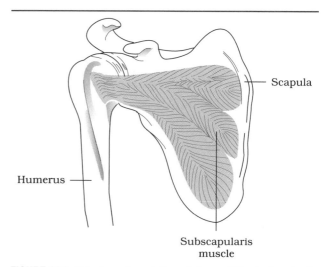

FIGURE 11.9 The muscles of the rotator cuff (anterior view).

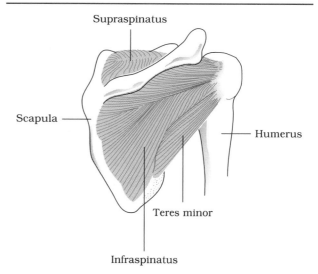

FIGURE 11.10 The muscles of the rotator cuff (posterior view).

WHAT IF?

You are examining a baseball player (center fielder) who is complaining of chronic pain in the back of his shoulder. He notices the pain especially after he throws a ball and he is point tender in the region of the posterior scapula. What structure could be involved in this case?

view the kinesiology of the overhand throw and/or swing. Throwing has been described as a five-phase process involving wind-up, cocking, acceleration, release, and follow-through (AAOS, 1991). Essentially, the wind-up phase requires putting the entire body into the best position to generate throwing forces. The cocking stage involves pulling the throwing arm into an abducted and externally rotated position at the GH joint; this incorporates a **concentric contraction** of several of the rotator cuff muscles, as well as other muscles of the shoulder region. The acceleration phase involves a sudden reversal of cocking: the arm is moved rapidly into internal rotation, horizontal flexion, and adduction of the GH joint via concentric contractions of muscles such as the pectoralis major, anterior deltoid, teres major, latissimus dorsi, and triceps. Depending upon the skill and strength of the athlete, the forces generated during the acceleration phase can be substantial and must be dealt with effectively during follow-through. The release phase is the shortest in the throwing cycle and involves timing the release at the point of maximum velocity. The follow-through phase requires that the entire upper extremity be decelerated immediately after the release. It is critical to note that several muscles of the rotator cuff are actively contracting eccentrically in an effort to slow the arm down.

The vast majority of strains to the rotator cuff occur during the follow-through phase, specifically during the eccentric phase of the contraction. This problem is made worse when the muscles of the rotator cuff are significantly weaker than those muscles involved in the acceleration phase. This problem can best be addressed with a properly designed conditioning program aimed at strengthening the muscles of the rotator cuff.

Strains to the rotator cuff are normally the result of overuse: they develop slowly over many weeks or months. Athletes who are involved in sports that require throwing and swinging are at risk for this type of injury, especially athletes with weak rotator cuffs or those who are older. Proper warm-up of the throwing

and/or swinging arm can also help reduce the stress on the musculature of the shoulder girdle. Often errors in execcution of the throw or swing can contribute to overuse injury. Therefore, it is critical that athletes learn correct techniques to reduce the chances of developing an injury.

Signs and symptoms of rotator cuff injuries include:

1. Pain within the shoulder, especially during the follow-through phase of a throw or swing.

2. Difficulty in bringing the arm up and back during the cocking phase of a throw or swing.

3. Pain and stiffness within the shoulder region 12 to 24 hours after a practice or competition that involved throwing or swinging.

4. Point tenderness around the region of the humeral head that appears to be deep within the deltoid muscle. (It should be noted that rotator cuff injuries can mimic many others common to the shoulder region including **bursitis** and **tendinitis.**)

First aid care of rotator cuff strains must take the following into consideration.

1. Overuse injuries are difficult to treat effectively without a thorough medical evaluation. When symptoms occur, the application of ice and compression may prove helpful in reducing the pain and loss of function associated with the injury.

2. In the majority of cases the athlete will report repeated episodes of symptoms spanning many weeks or even months. Therefore, medical referral for a complete evaluation is essential.

Glenohumeral Joint-Related Impingement Syndrome To impinge means to be forced "upon or against something" (Guralnik and Friend, 1966). A **syndrome** is defined as "a number of symptoms occurring together and characterizing a specific disease" (Guralnik and Friend, 1966). Hence, an impingement syndrome of the shoulder occurs when a soft-tissue structure such as a bursa or tendon is squeezed between moving joint structures, resulting in irritation

Athletic Trainers Speak Out

Andrew Pruitt

"The quick and correct treatment of an acute athletic injury may truly lessen the severity and hasten the recovery of that injury, which is important to the athlete. Properly trained coaches can help assure that quick and correct treatment is initiated. A seemingly minor head injury can turn into a catastrophe if not treated appropriately. The ideal situation would employ a full-time certified athletic trainer with physician support; in the absence of that, well-informed coaches must take on the role. Therefore, the availability of cutting-edge information on sports medicine and athletic training is of utmost importance."

—*Andrew Pruitt, A.T.C., Ed.D.*

Dr. Pruitt is the director of Western Orthopedic Sports Medicine and Rehabilitation in Denver, Colorado, and the sports-medicine coordinator for the U.S. cycling team.

and pain. In the case of the GH joint, the most common impingement occurs to the tendon of the supraspinatus muscle as it passes across the top of the joint en route to its insertion (Lo, Hsu, and Chan, 1990). The normal anatomy of the GH joint is a tight fit relative to the amount of available space for structures above the joint capsule. This region, located directly beneath the acromion process, is known as the subacromial space. The floor of the subacromial space is the GH joint capsule. The ceiling comprises the acromion process and the coracoacromial ligament, which form an arch across the top of the GH joint known as the coracoacromial arch (Figure 11.11).

Any condition, whether related to sports or congenital, that decreases the size of the subacromial space may result in the development of an impingement syndrome. Various experts within the sports medicine community have reported that the most common causes of GH joint-related impingement syndromes are "anatomic variations in the coracoacromial arch" that cause damage to the structures found within the subacromial space (Burns and Turba, 1992).

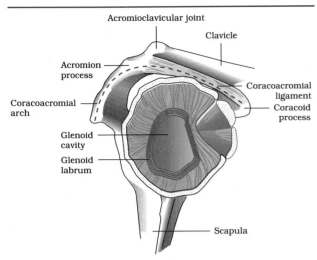

FIGURE 11.11 The coracoacromial arch and glenohumeral joint (lateral view).

Athletes who participate in sports placing an emphasis on arm movements above the shoulder level demonstrate a higher rate of impingement problems when compared with athletes who take part in sports not emphasizing such movements. A recent survey of athletes in sports requiring repetitive arm motions found the high-risk sports to include volleyball, badminton, basketball, gymnastics, squash, swimming, table tennis, tennis, and track and field events (Lo, Hsu, and Chan, 1990).

Signs and symptoms of impingement syndromes include:

1. Pain when the GH joint is abducted and externally rotated in conjunction with loss of strength.

2. Pain whenever the arm is abducted beyond 80 to 90 degrees.

3. Nocturnal pain (AAOS, 1991).

4. Pain felt deep within the shoulder (AAOS, 1991).

First aid care of impingement syndromes involving the GH joint is not required as they tend to develop over many days, weeks, or even months. Rather, any athlete complaining of the signs and symptoms listed above should be referred for a complete medical evaluation. Treatment will consist of rest, anti-inflammatory drugs, and physical therapy. If these fail, surgery to correct the problem may be prescribed. In many cases this can be done via arthroscopy; typically it involves procedures such as removal of bone spurs from beneath the acromion process, release of the coracoacromial ligament, or a resectioning of a portion of the undersurface of the acromion process (partial acromionectomy) (AAOS, 1991).

Biceps Tendon Problems The anatomy of the GH joint (Figure 11.12) includes the tendon of the long head of the biceps brachii muscle. The tendon passes into the joint capsule and is surrounded by a specialized portion of the synovium of the joint. As the tendon continues through the joint it runs across the superior surface of the humeral head; in this position the ten-

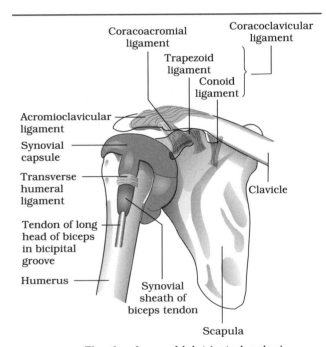

FIGURE 11.12 The glenohumeral joint (anterior view).

Information at your fingertips

The World Wide Web—To learn more about the rotator cuff and impingement syndrome, go to http://www.jbpub.com/athletictraining and click on Chapter 11.

don helps to stabilize the humeral head when the joint is abducted. The tendon of the long head of the biceps brachii originates from the supraglenoid tubercle (Gray, 1985). The short head of the biceps brachii derives from the nearby coracoid process. This tendon, however, remains anatomically separate from the GH joint.

The tendon of the long head of the biceps brachii is located directly beneath the acromion process; therefore, it can suffer a type of impingement similar to that seen in the supraspinatus tendon. As the joint is abducted the tendon may be compressed within the subacromial space. Consequently, symptoms similar to those of impingement of the supraspinatus will develop. Athletes at risk for this injury include those involved in sports that place an emphasis on repetitive overhead movements with the arms.

Another problem related to the long head tendon of the biceps brachii is **tendinitis,** which may lead to a subluxation of the tendon from the bicipital groove. In most cases tendinitis will develop slowly over a period of weeks or months. As the tendon enlarges as a result of the inflammation, it becomes less stable within the groove, where it is held by way of the transverse humeral ligament.

In chronic cases, a sudden violent force such as is commonly generated in throwing may cause the tendon to subluxate out of the groove, thereby stretching and tearing the ligament. The athlete will notice significant symptoms if the tendon should subluxate from the bicipital groove.

Signs and symptoms of biceps tendon problems include:

1. Painful abduction of the shoulder joint similar to that seen in impingement problems.

2. Pain in the shoulder joint when the athlete supinates the forearm against any resistance.

3. When actively flexing and supinating the forearm against resistance, the athlete may note a popping or snapping sensation as the tendon of the long head of the biceps brachii subluxates.

First aid care of biceps tendon problems is not a practical concern as they generally develop over time and fall into the category of a chronic injury. However, if the athlete should subluxate the biceps tendon from the bicipital groove, the initial episode of this injury can require first aid. In such cases the immediate application of ice and compression is recommended. Long-term care for this injury includes rest, anti-inflammatories, and gradually progressive exercise rehabilitation. If symptoms persist and the tendon continues to subluxate from the bicipital groove, then surgery may be required to stabilize the tendon.

Contusions of the Shoulder Region External blows around the shoulder region are a common occurrence in a variety of sports. The GH joint is well protected by muscles crossing over the joint, such as the deltoid. The nearby AC joint, however, is exposed and quite vulnerable to external blows. If the athlete should sustain a contusion to this joint, the result can be an extremely painful condition known as a **shoulder pointer.**

Signs and symptoms of shoulder contusions include:

1. History of a recent blow to the shoulder with resulting pain and decreased range of motion.

2. Spasm if muscle tissue is involved.

3. Discoloration and swelling, especially over bony regions such as the AC joint.

First aid care of shoulder contusions includes:

1. Immediate application of ice and compression directly over the area(s) involved. This is best accomplished with a bag of crushed ice and an elastic wrap.

2. In cases of severe pain apply an arm sling to relieve stress on the shoulder region.

3. If significant swelling persists for more than 72 hours in the region of the AC joint, refer the athlete to a physician. In some cases the AC ligament may have sustained a sprain.

Review Questions

1. Which two bones make up the shoulder girdle?

2. To what structure is the glenoid labrum attached?

3. Which one of the following arteries provides the blood supply to the shoulder region and upper extremity?

a. common iliac

b. ulnar

c. internal carotid

d. subclavian

e. axillary

4. Which one of the following is the correct derivation of the brachial plexus?

    a. C-5/T-2

    b. C-3/T-1

    c. C-1/T-5

    d. C-1/T-1

    e. C-5/T-1

5. List the four muscles of the rotator cuff group and identify one action common to each muscle.

6. List four signs and/or symptoms of a fractured clavicle.

7. Describe and/or demonstrate the appropriate first aid procedures for a fractured clavicle.

8. Describe the major ligaments that form the AC joint.

9. Describe briefly the two mechanisms of injury for the AC joint as discussed in the chapter.

10. Describe the common signs and symptoms of AC joint injuries.

11. Explain and/or demonstrate the appropriate first aid care for AC joint injuries.

12. List the major ligaments of the GH joint.

13. *True or false:* The most common type of GH joint dislocation is posterior.

14. Describe the common signs and symptoms of a GH joint dislocation.

15. Explain and/or demonstrate the appropriate first aid treatment of an athlete with a suspected GH joint dislocation.

16. Define the condition known as chronic GH subluxation.

17. Describe the primary ligaments of the SC joint.

18. Describe the common signs and symptoms of injury to this articulation.

19. Explain and/or demonstrate the appropriate first aid treatment of an athlete with a suspected SC joint injury.

20. Explain the five phases of an overhand throw and/or swing and give a brief description of the types of muscle contractions involved in each.

21. *True or false:* The vast majority of strains of the rotator cuff occur during the wind-up and cocking phase of the throw and/or swing.

22. List several of the signs and symptoms of rotator cuff strain as described in the chapter.

23. What anatomical structure forms a ceiling for the subacromial space?

24. *True or false:* Athletes involved in sports placing a heavy emphasis on arm movements below the shoulder level demonstrate a higher incidence of impingement syndromes.

25. List four signs and/or symptoms of impingement syndrome of the GH joint.

26. Which one of the following structures (ligaments) holds the biceps (long head) tendon in the bicipital groove?

    a. annular ligament

    b. medial collateral ligament

    c. capsular ligament

    d. transverse humeral ligament

References

American Academy of Orthopaedic Surgeons. 1991. *Athletic Training and Sports Medicine* (2d ed.). Park Ridge, Ill.: American Academy of Orthopaedic Surgeons.

Arnheim DD. 1987. *Essentials of Athletic Training* (1st ed.). St. Louis: Times Mirror/Mosby.

Bach BR, VanFleet TA, Novak PJ. 1992. Acromioclavicular injuries—controversies in treatment. *Phys Sportsmed.* 20:87-101.

Burns TP, Turba JE. 1992. Arthroscopic treatment of shoulder impingement in athletes. *Am J Sports Med.* 20:13–16.

Cain TE, Hamilton WP. 1992. Scapular fractures in professional football players. *Am J Sports Med.* 20:363–365.

Dias JJ, Gregg PJ. 1991. Acromioclavicular joint injuries in sport—recommendations for treatment. *Sports Med.* 11:125–132.

Grabiner MD. 1989. The shoulder complex. In Rasch PJ (ed.). *Kinesiology and Applied Anatomy.* Philadelphia: Lea & Febiger.

Gray H. 1985. *Anatomy of the Human Body.* Philadelphia: Lea & Febiger.

Guralnik DB, Friend JH (eds.). 1966. *Webster's New*

World Dictionary of the American Language. Cleveland: The World Publishing Company.

Lo YPC, Hsu YCS, Chan KM. 1990. Epidemiology of shoulder impingement in upper-arm sports events. *Bri J Sports Med.* 24:173–177.

National Safety Council. 1991. *First Aid and CPR.* Boston: Jones and Bartlett.

O'Donoghue DH. 1976. *Treatment of Injuries to Athletes.* Philadelphia: W. B. Saunders.

Wroble RR. 1995. Sternoclavicular injuries—managing damage to an overlooked joint. *Phys Sportsmed.* 23:19–26.

CHAPTER 12

Injuries to the Arm, Wrist, and Hand

MAJOR CONCEPTS

This chapter begins with a brief review of the gross anatomy of the region with special emphasis on arthrology. It goes on to discuss upper-arm (brachial region) injuries, focusing especially on contusions and fractures. Given the potentially serious consequences of fractures of the humerus, the chapter provides detailed instructions for proper first aid care of these injuries. Next, the chapter reviews elbow injuries, outlining current information regarding the typical mechanisms, signs and symptoms, and critical first aid procedures. Again, because there are potential catastrophic consequences of a mismanaged elbow injury, this section provides specific first aid instructions. It also discusses problems related to the muscle attachments surrounding the elbow, clinically known as epicondylitis, along with special attention paid to the possible causes, signs and symptoms, and care.

Although quite rare, forearm injuries do occasionally occur, and the chapter reviews the more frequent varieties, along with guidelines on signs and symptoms as well as first aid care. Next it discusses injuries to the wrist, emphasizing relatively common injuries such as fractures of the carpal navicular bone and dislocations of the lunate bone. Nerve injuries of the wrist region are common; carpal tunnel syndrome is perhaps the most well known. Therefore, the chapter outlines specific signs and symptoms for nerve problems involving the median and ulnar nerves.

Finally, the chapter discusses hand and finger injuries, which are both extremely common in sports.

Anatomy Review

The bones of the arm are the humerus (upper arm), the radius, and the ulna (forearm). The proximal end of the humerus (head) articulates with the glenoid fossa of the scapula to form the shoulder (glenohumeral) joint. The distal end of the humerus articulates with both of the forearm bones to form the elbow joint, which actually comprises three specific articulations—the **humeroulnar, humeroradial,** and proximal **radioulnar** joints. The distal end of the forearm articulates with the wrist (carpal) bones forming the **radio-** carpal (wrist) and distal radioulnar joints. The joints of the arm allow for a great variety of motions, including flexion/extension and pronation/supination at the elbow as well as flexion/extension and radial and ulnar deviation at the wrist. The elbow (Figure 12.1) and wrist joints are held together with several ligaments that may be subject to trauma related to sports participation. Certainly one of the more distinctive ligament structures in the human body is the annular ligament of the elbow (Figure 12.2). This ligament holds the head of the radius within the proximal radioulnar joint; in so doing it allows that articulation to pronate and supinate while simultaneously allowing the radial head to articulate with the capitulum of the humerus.

As can be seen in Figure 12.3, the musculature of the arm is extensive. The upper arm is dominated by the elbow extensor and flexors, and the forearm includes a large number of muscles that provide energy for the movements of the forearm, wrist, and hand. Many of the forearm muscles originate from the regions of the humeral epicondyles, either lateral or medial, which are located immediately proximal to the elbow joint.

The vasculature of the arm has been described in the previous chapter, as has the neural distribution.

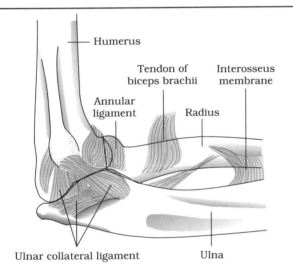

FIGURE 12.1 The elbow joint (medial view).

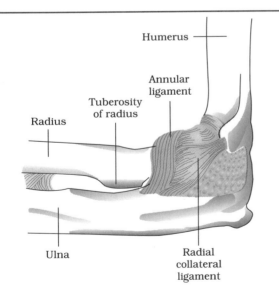

FIGURE 12.2 The elbow joint (lateral view).

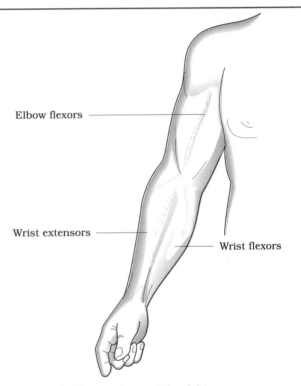

FIGURE 12.3 Surface anatomy of the right arm.

Soft-Tissue Injuries to the Upper Arm

The majority of injuries to the upper arm are either contusions or fractures. Though strains do occur to this region, they are exceedingly uncommon. Because of the nature of contact sports, blows to the arm region are a common occurrence. A typical scenerio involves a football lineman blocking with arms flexed at the elbows and receiving blows to the lateral surfaces of the upper arms. The underlying muscle tissue is compressed between the overlying skin and the bone of the humerus. Depending upon the magnitude of the blow(s), damage to the muscle tissue may be significant. If such episodes are repeated, the athlete may develop a condition known as myositis ossificans traumatica.

Myositis Ossificans Traumatica

Myositis ossificans traumatica involves chronic inflammation of muscle, leading to the development of bone-like tissue within the muscle. It is quite common in football—so much so that the condition has become known as **tackler's exostosis** (AAOS, 1991). An **exostosis** is defined as "a benign growth projecting from a bone surface characteristically capped by cartilage" (Friel, 1977). Myositis ossificans traumatica develops over a period of weeks or even months and therefore tends to be ignored in early stages of development, when it is typically dismissed as a simple bruise. It is important that the coach recognize that such an injury can develop into a more serious one and evaluate it accordingly.

Signs and symptoms of upper-arm contusions include:

1. Recent history of contusion to the region.

2. Pain, discoloration, and swelling in the region of the injury.

3. Muscle spasm and subsequent loss of strength in the affected muscle.

4. Possible neurological symptoms including loss of sensation or muscle function distal to the site of injury.

First aid care of upper-arm contusions includes:

1. Immediate application of ice and compression. This is best accomplished by using a bag of crushed ice that is secured with a wide elastic wrap tied around the arm.

2. Placing the arm in a sling to immobilize the limb for a period of 24 hours.

3. In cases of severe acute pain or symptoms that persist beyond 72 hours, refer the athlete for a complete medical evaluation.

Triceps Injuries

A less common group of injuries to the upper arm involves the triceps muscle. The mechanism of injury may be either a direct blow to the posterior elbow or a fall on an outstretched hand. Either mechanism can result in a partial or complete rupture within the muscle or its tendon. Although rare, such an injury can be extremely disabling and may be associated with either a fracture of the radial head or the olecranon process. A recent report on these injuries found that they occurred among a wide range of athletes, including a competitive weight lifter, a body builder, an alpine skier, and a volleyball player. By definition, all these injuries fall into the general category of muscle strains; depending upon their relative severity and precise location they may require immediate medical attention. In severe cases of partial or complete ruptures of the triceps or its tendon, surgical intervention may be necessary. Even in less severe cases involving only partial tears, the injury requires an extensive period of immobilization (one month) in a splint with the elbow positioned at 30 degrees of flexion (Holleb and Bach, 1990).

Signs and symptoms of injuries to the triceps muscle include:

1. The athlete may report having experienced a sudden popping in the region of the posterior humerus or elbow.

2. Significant pain in the elbow region or just proximal in the area of the triceps tendon.

3. Visible defect within the triceps muscle or within the tendon near the olecranon process.

4. Discoloration and possible swelling, although both may be delayed for a period of hours after the injury.

First aid care of an injury to the triceps muscle includes:

1. Immediate application of ice and compression. This is best accomplished with a bag of crushed ice that is secured with a wide elastic wrap tied around the arm.

2. Place the arm in a sling with the elbow positioned at approximately 90 degrees of flexion if pain can be tolerated.

3. If pain is severe, or there is a visible defect in the triceps muscle or its tendon, immediate medical referral is necessary.

Fractures of the Upper Arm

Little information is available about the frequency of humeral fractures related to sports. It would seem that activities involving collisions between participants, such as tackle football and ice hockey, or sports with a potential for high-speed falls, such as cycling or rollerblading, would carry a higher risk for such injuries. Although considered to be quite rare, humeral stress fractures have been reported related to high-intensity weight training (Bartsokas, Palin, and Collier, 1992).

Many commercial splints are available and will work well when used according to the manufacturer's specifications. The application of ice and compression is best accomplished with a bag of crushed ice that is secured with a wide elastic wrap tied around the arm. Discontinue ice application if radial nerve involvement or circulatory deficiency is observed.

2. Application of a standard sling-and-swathe bandage as described by the National Safety Council (1991).

3. As with any injury requiring the application of a splint, periodic evaluation of circulation distal to the sight of the splint is essential to guarantee that blood flow has not been impaired. This can be accomplished simply by squeezing the nail bed of

WHAT IF?

You are asked to examine the elbow of a young baseball pitcher. She has been suffering from elbow pain and reports that her elbow "locks" occasionally. When this happens she experiences sharp pain and swelling. What might be the cause of the problem and what would you recommend?

Signs and symptoms of humeral fractures include:

1. Severe pain in the region of the upper arm with a recent history of trauma to the area.

2. Deformity may be present and visible, especially when compared with the opposite extremity.

3. Loss of function or an unwillingness to use the extremity.

4. Muscle spasm in the musculature surrounding the extremity.

5. The athlete may report having felt a snap or heard a pop at the time of injury.

6. If the radial nerve is involved there may be loss of sensation into the dorsum of the forearm and wrist. This may also result in loss of strength in the wrist extensors (AAOS, 1991).

7. In cases of stress fracture, pain may not be associated with a specific traumatic incident. Instead, the athlete may report a change in a training program—for example, a sudden increase in the intensity or volume of a strength-training program.

First aid care of a humeral fracture includes:

1. Immediate application of ice and compression in conjunction with a properly constructed splint.

a finger and observing the return of blood to the fingertip.

4. Humeral fractures are serious injuries often associated with significant soft-tissue damage. In such instances, the athlete should be treated for shock and immediately transported to a health care facility.

Elbow Injuries

Elbow injuries are common in sports and range from simple abrasions or contusions to complete dislocations or fractures. In sports involving repeated throwing or swinging actions, the elbow may develop an overuse injury related to muscular attachments on the humeral epicondyles, sometimes resulting in a condition known as **epicondylitis.** The joint can also sustain sprains; the most common involve hyperextensions in which the joint is forced beyond its normal locked position in extension. Dislocations and fractures are probably the most severe types of injuries to this complex joint; if not cared for properly, either can lead to permanent complications.

Athletic Trainers Speak Out

"Wrist problems are a common occurrence in sports. Sometimes they can develop into a serious situation and may sideline an athlete for an indefinite period of time. A diver, who was a former gymnast, developed bilateral deQuervain's disease. The condition in her left wrist was more severe than in her right. It was difficult for her to go through a workout, especially the portion that included diving from the 10-meter tower. After weeks of ice, rest, and modalities with no improvement, she received a steroid injection in her left wrist and was immobilized in a thumb spica cast intermittently during a 6-week period. This also failed, and it was decided the only way of correcting this injury was to perform surgery.

The young woman successfully recovered from her surgery and rehabilitation and is now diving competitively, pain free."

—Sue Lerner, M.S., A.T.C.

Sue Lerner

Sue Lerner is Assistant Athletic Trainer at the University of Southern California.

Sprains and Dislocations

The three articulations of the elbow are bound together by several ligaments that combine to give support to the joint throughout its wide range of motion. The joint capsule of the elbow is extensive and is reinforced both medially and laterally by the ulnar and radial collateral ligaments, respectively. These two ligaments serve to protect the elbow from **valgus** and **varus** forces acting across the joint. In addition, the radial head is held in position by the annular ligament described previously.

The elbow may be sprained through a variety of mechanisms including falls, particularly when an athlete falls backwards with the elbow locked in extension. This mechanism results in a stretching and/or tearing of the anterior joint capsule as well as other soft-tissue structures in the anterior portion of the joint. Two other mechanisms for elbow sprains are valgus and varus forces that can occur suddenly in situations in which the arm is trapped in a vulnerable position, such as can happen in tackle football or wrestling.

Dislocations of the elbow are sprains in the extreme sense and involve damage to significant soft-tissue structures around the joint. The mechanism of injury is typically a fall in which the elbow is in either an extended or flexed position. The force of the impact causes the forearm bones to be driven posteriorly out of their normal position, with the olecranon process of the ulna coming to rest well behind the distal end of the humerus. The deformity is obvious, which makes the initial evaluation relatively straightforward. This injury may be associated with a fracture of either the radius or the ulna, or both.

Signs and symptoms of elbow sprains and dislocations include:

1. In cases of minor sprains, mild swelling and localized pain.

2. Difficulty in gripping objects or in making a fist.

3. In cases of dislocations, gross deformity of the elbow with abnormal positioning of the forearm bones behind the distal end of the humerus (Figure 12.4).

4. Severe pain and total dysfunction of the elbow joint.

5. Possible neurologic symptoms distal to the elbow characterized by numbness along the distribution of major nerves. The ulnar nerve appears to be the most vulnerable to this specific injury (AAOS, 1991).

First aid care for elbow sprains and dislocations includes:

1. In cases of minor sprains the immediate application of ice and compression, using a bag of crushed ice held in place with an elastic wrap, is effective.

2. Once ice and compression are properly situated, the arm should be placed in a sling-and-swathe bandage as recommended by the National Safety Council (1991).

3. In cases of obvious dislocations, the primary concern is to prevent complications, which can be extremely serious and include compression on the neurovascular structures in the elbow region.

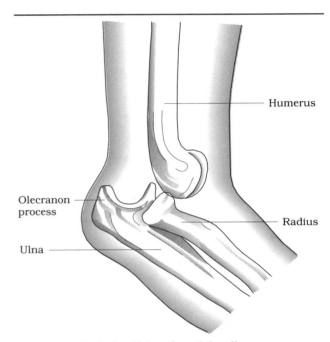

FIGURE 12.4 Posterior dislocation of the elbow.

4. Immediate application of ice and compression in combination with a properly applied splint.

5. Splinting of this injury requires special attention to avoid moving the displaced forearm bones. It is recommended by the National Safety Council (1991) that the splint be applied on either or both sides of the elbow as illustrated in Figure 12.5.

6. Elbow dislocations are serious injuries. The athlete should be treated for shock, and arrangements must be made for transportation to a medical facility.

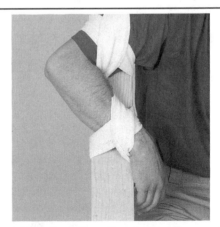

FIGURE 12.5 Splinting of an elbow injury. (Source: National Safety Council. 1994. *First Aid and CPR* (2d ed). Boston: Jones and Bartlett. 232. Reprinted with permission.)

Fractures

Elbow fractures generally involve the distal humerus, just above the epicondyles, or the proximal ulna or radius. Because of the complexity of the joint, any fracture represents potential problems for the athlete. As is the case with dislocations, neurovascular structures are in jeopardy when fractures result in displacement of bones. This is especially true if broken bones are moved inadvertently by the athlete or by someone else attempting to render first aid. A simple elbow fracture can easily be converted into an irreversible injury in such a situation. If the radial artery is compressed by broken bone ends, circulation to the forearm can be significantly reduced or stopped, resulting in a condition known as **Volkmann's contracture** (Figure 12.6). This condition involves the reaction of the forearm musculature to a lack of blood supply. If left uncorrected it becomes a permanent deformity. Therefore, it becomes imperative that elbow fractures be handled very carefully during the application of first aid procedures. Furthermore, it is important that the blood supply distal to the elbow be monitored until the athlete is transported to a medical facility.

The mechanisms of injury are similar to those of sprains and dislocations. Fractures of the olecranon process of the ulna are often associated with falls in which the elbow is in a flexed position and the impact occurs on the tip of the joint. When elbow fractures occur in adolescents, they require special attention to ensure that the injury will not adversely affect the growth centers of the bones involved.

Signs and symptoms of elbow fractures include:

1. Recent history of significant trauma to the elbow in association with significant pain and dysfunction.

2. Immediate swelling in the region of the injury.

3. In the case of displaced fractures an obvious deformity will be noted.

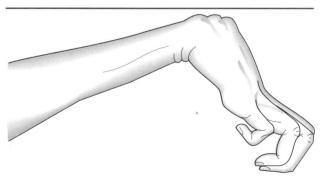

FIGURE 12.6 Volkmann's ischemic contracture.

4. In cases of problems with the blood supply, a lack of proper blood flow will be noted in the forearm and hand, both of which will feel cold and clammy. In addition, the victim will report pain or numbness in the hand.

First aid care of elbow fractures includes:

1. Immediate application of ice; however, it is critical to avoid compression around the joint owing to the increased risk for vascular compromise with this particular injury.

2. Place a bag of crushed ice over the region of injury and hold it in place with a nonelastic cloth bandage such as a commercially prepared triangular one.

3. The National Safety Council (1991) recommends applying some type of splint, taking great care to avoid moving the bones of the elbow as shown in Figure 12.5.

4. Treat the athlete for shock and arrange for transport to a medical facility.

Epicondylitis of the Elbow

The epicondyles of the humerus are located immediately proximal to the distal articular surfaces of that bone—the capitulum and the trochlea. The more prominent medial epicondyle serves as the common sight of attachment for flexor muscles of the forearm as well as for the ulnar collateral ligament. The smaller lateral epicondyle serves as the common sight of attachment for the extensor muscles of the forearm as well as for the radial collateral ligament. These bony prominences are easily located near the elbow joint (Figure 12.7).

Activities that require continuous gripping of an object along with simultaneous wrist actions, such as is common in racquet and throwing sports, place considerable stress on the tissues of the epicondylar regions. During the 1970s considerable debate existed regarding the possible negative effects on the elbow caused by excessive pitching in Little League baseball. A major concern was that the throwing motion might cause degenerative changes and subsequent inflammation within the medial epicondyle of the elbows of young players, resulting in medial epicondylitis. This condition results in significant pain around the epicondyle and can severely limit the athlete's ability to flex or pronate the wrist and hand. In the adolescent, extreme cases can lead to actual fracturing of the epicondyle away from the humerus. Concerned parents and physicians coined the phrase **Little League elbow** to

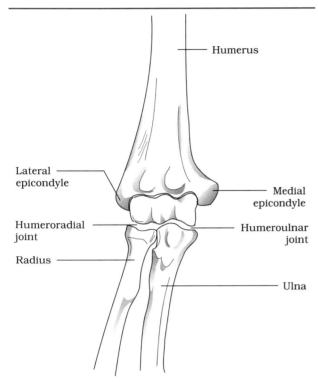

FIGURE 12.7 Epicondyles of the elbow joint.

describe the injury among these young players. Subsequent studies did produce convincing evidence of a strong relationship between the throwing mechanism and medial epicondylitis (Larson et al., 1976). As a result, rules that limited the maximum number of innings young pitchers could throw during a season were instituted.

Another sport recently identified as a cause of medial epicondylitis in some athletes is golf. The condition, known as **golfer's elbow,** has been linked to players who have problems with their swing (Hutson, 1990). Available data support the premise that epicondylitis is less common on the medial side of the elbow when compared with the lateral side. Tennis has also been identified as a cause of epicondylitis. Tennis elbow involves the lateral humeral epicondyle and the tendon of the extensor carpi radialis brevis tendon (Hannafin and Schelkun, 1996). It has been reported that from 10% to 50% of all tennis players may suffer from this condition at some point in their career (Jobe and Ciccotti, 1994).

Hutson (1990) reports that the problem is related to a variety of sports-related factors, including:

1. Overload related to the sheer frequency of shots played

2. Incorrect technique, particularly on the backhand

3. Too small a racket handle

4. Recent change of racket—for instance, from wood to graphite

5. Too tight a grip between shots

6. Muscle imbalance and/or loss of flexibility

Regardless of the type of epicondylitis, the first step in treating the problem is to identify the cause(s), including skill- and/or equipment-related problems. If the athlete treats only the symptoms without identifying the underlying problems, epicondylitis will most likely recur. After the cause(s) are identified, a program of aggressive treatment of symptoms with ice application (before and after practice) as well as strengthening exercises, including wrist curls and extensions as well as pronation and supination against mild resistance, may prove helpful. During the early phase of treatment, exercises without weight may be advised, such as squeezing a tennis ball (finger flexors) and finger extension against the resistance of the opposite hand. Any rehabilitation program should be developed and supervised by a competent sports medicine practitioner such as an athletic trainer or sports physical therapist.

Signs and symptoms of epicondylitis include:

1. Pain in the region of either the medial or lateral epicondyle. Symptoms become worse during or immediately after participation.

2. Pain radiating distally into either the flexor/pronator or extensor/supinator muscles, depending upon which epicondyle is involved.

3. Pain may be elicited in the region of the epicondyles during resisted wrist flexion or extension, depending upon which epicondyle is involved.

4. Swelling in the region of the painful epicondyle.

5. In severe and chronic cases, crepitus (feeling hardened fragments through the skin) may be noted over the region of the affected epicondyle.

First aid care of humeral epicondylitis includes:

1. Both medial and lateral epicondylitis tend to be chronic injuries resulting from overuse; therefore, first aid is not a practical solution. When symptoms worsen, however, the application of ice and compression can be helpful; this is best accomplished with a bag of crushed ice that is secured with an elastic wrap.

2. If symptoms persist, medical referral is necessary.

Information at your fingertips

The World Wide Web—For more information on tennis elbow, go to http:// www.jbpub.com/athletictraining and click on Chapter 12.

3. Long-term treatment includes rest, reduced participation in the activity, and possible use of anti-inflammatory drugs.

Osteochondritis Dissecans of the Elbow

The mechanism of throwing can lead to a type of impingement syndrome within the elbow joint occurring between the radial head and the capitellum of the humerus. The action of high-velocity extension can cause the elbow to develop a valgus overload resulting in abnormal compression of the elbow on the lateral side of the joint (Hutson, 1990). Over time and with continued throwing, the cartilage on the proximal end of the radius can become inflamed and even begin to fracture, resulting in a condition known as **osteochondritis dissecans.**

Another possible mechanism for this type of elbow injury is axial loading of the forearm. Such a mechanism is common in falls or in sports that place the forearms in a weight-bearing position, which typically occurs in gymnastics. In either case, the impact force is transmitted up the forearm and causes the head of the radius to be jammed against the humerus. Over time osteochondritis dissecans can result from such repeated insults to the joint.

Signs and symptoms of osteochondritis dissecans include:

1. During the initial phases of development the athlete will experience pain during participation.

2. Joint inflammation and stiffness may be noted, particularly 12 to 24 hours after participation.

3. In well-established cases, cartilage fragments (loose bodies) may form within the joint; these are commonly known as joint mice.

4. The athlete may experience a locking of the elbow, which occurs when a loose body is caught between the moving bone ends within the joint.

5. In advanced cases the elbow may devleop osteoarthritis.

First aid care of osteochondritis dissecans includes:

1. An athlete with a history of trauma to the elbow joint associated with the symptoms described above should be referred to the appropriate physician for a thorough diagnostic evaluation.

2. Immediate symptoms are best treated with a bag of crushed ice held in place with an elastic wrap.

3. If fragments are identified within the joint, the physician may recommend arthroscopic surgery to remove the loose bodies.

4. The conservative (nonsurgical) treatment for this condition involves rest followed by an extensive period of rehabilitative exercise designed to strengthen both the muscles surrounding the elbow and the ligaments of the joint.

Contusions of the Elbow

External blows to the elbow region are common in sports. Little protective equipment is available for the joint, and its large range of motion and irregular shape make taping and wrapping impractical. Fortunately, the vast majority of contusions result in only temporary discomfort that normally improves within a few days of the original injury. An exception, however, is the olecranon bursa, which is a large sac located between the skin and the olecranon process of the ulna. Falling on a flexed elbow or sustaining repeated blows to the olecranon area can irritate this **bursa** and cause acute **bursitis.** Although bursitis does not directly affect the integrity of the elbow joint, persistent swelling, stiffness, and pain associated with this problem can reduce the quality of athletic performance.

Signs and symptoms of olecranon bursitis include:

1. The most obvious sign of this injury is swelling located around the olecranon process of the ulna.

2. Pain and stiffness, especially when the elbow is flexed.

3. Skin temperature over the olecranon may be elevated.

4. Skin over the olecranon process may appear taut, and the joint may show signs of internal hemorrhage.

First aid care of olecranon bursitis includes:

1. Immediate care of elbow contusions includes the application of a bag of crushed ice held in place with an elastic wrap.

2. If the signs and symptoms of olecranon bursitis appear, refer the athlete to the appropriate physician.

Wrist and Forearm Injuries

The anatomy of the human wrist is highly complex. Within this compact joint exist a large number of tendons (for the wrist, fingers, and thumb) that are tightly bound together underneath bands of connective tissue known as retinaculum (transverse carpal ligaments). Also passing through this region are the major nerves and blood vessels of the hand and fingers (Figure 12.8).

Aside from simple contusions, injuries to the forearm in sports are relatively uncommon. Usually contusions can be easily treated with ice, compression, and elevation; this can be followed later with the application of protective padding. Probably the most serious forearm injuries involve fractures distal in the forearm, just proximal to the wrist joint. The most well known of these is a **Colles' fracture,** which involves a transverse fracture of the distal radius. Variations of this fracture include simultaneous fractures of both the radius and ulna as well as compound fractures of either bone: such injuries are serious and must be properly cared for to avoid complications. The mechanism of injury is highly variable; whatever the mechanism, a great deal of force will be required and many soft-tissue structures may be damaged in conjunction with the fracture.

Signs and symptoms of distal forearm fractures include:

1. The athlete will have a recent history of significant trauma to the wrist region associated with having heard a popping sound and/or felt a snapping of the bones.

2. A deformity between the arm and wrist is typical; in the case of a Colles' fracture the hand is driven backwards and outward (radial deviation). (See Figure 12.9.)

3. Swelling, often severe, develops quickly and may affect the hand and fingers.

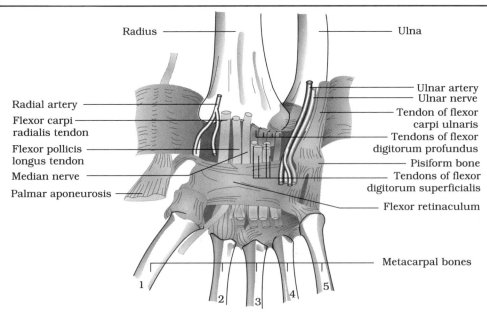

FIGURE 12.8 Right wrist (palmar view).

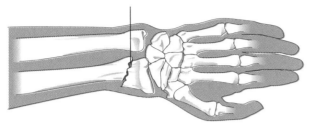

FIGURE 12.9 Colles' fracture.

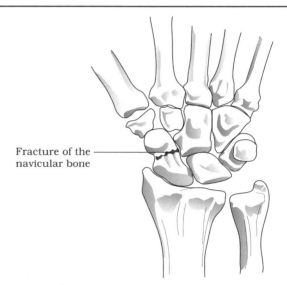

FIGURE 12.10 Fracture of the navicular bone is common in sports.

4. Pain is generally severe, and motion of the wrist, hand, or fingers will be significantly curtailed.

5. In cases in which broken bone(s) put pressure on nerves, loss of sensation may be noted in either the hand or fingers or both.

First aid care for distal forearm fractures includes:

1. Immediate application of ice, compression, and elevation. This is best accomplished with a bag of crushed ice that is held in place with an elastic wrap. Do not apply ice if you suspect either vascular or nerve supply is compromised. In addition, some type of splint must be applied in order to protect the area from further injury (see Figure 12.18).

2. Make sure that the fingertips are exposed in order to monitor the blood supply to the hand. This is easily accomplished by squeezing a nail bed and noting the return (or lack thereof) of normal reddish color to the tissue.

3. Once in place, the ice, compression, and splint should be elevated carefully using a standard sling-and-swathe bandage as recommended by the National Safety Council (1991).

4. Because of the pain and damage associated with this type of injury, it is imperative that the athlete

be treated for shock and transported to a medical facility immediately.

Wrist Fractures

Fractures of the carpal bones do occur in sports. According to O'Donoghue (1976), the most common involve the carpal navicular bone (Figure 12.10). This bone can receive considerable force when the wrist is placed into extension in sports such as tackle football (blocking) and gymnastics (vaulting and floor exercise). Simple falls can also cause fractures to this critical bone of the wrist. The fracture generally occurs within a specific site on the carpal navicular bone known as the waist, which is the narrowest section of the bone.

Other bones of the wrist may be fractured as well: fractures of the lunate, pisiform, and hamate have been reported. Regardless of which specific bone is frac-

WHAT IF?

A young gymnast grabs her left wrist immediately after completing a vault. During your examination of her wrist you note that she has pain on movement, she reports that she felt a snap as soon as her hands hit the vaulting horse, and she is point tender within the region known as the anatomical snuff-box. What would you conclude happened and what would you do for initial care?

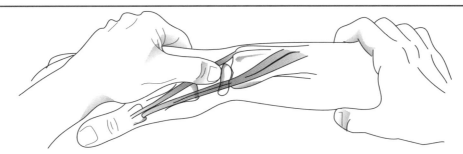

FIGURE 12.11 Palpation within the anatomical snuff-box.

tured, the signs and symptoms will be similar. Since the carpal bones are small, gross deformity is typically not present, and evaluation of these injuries is difficult. When doubt exists about the extent or nature of the injury, the best policy is to refer the athlete to a physician for a more complete diagnostic evaluation.

Signs and symptoms of wrist fractures include:

1. A recent history of trauma to the wrist, specifically forced extension associated with a snapping or popping sensation within the wrist.

2. Pain in the wrist that is aggravated by movement. A simple test for the integrity of the navicular bone involves pressing lightly into the region at the base of the thumb known as the anatomical snuff-box (Figure 12.11), which is bordered by several tendons that attach within the thumb. The radial surface of the carpal navicular bone is located within the anatomical snuff-box. Consequently, external pressure in this region may elicit a painful response from the athlete, which is a positive sign of a fracture of that bone.

3. The athlete may be unable or unwilling to move the wrist, and doing so may result in considerable pain.

4. The athlete may state that the wrist feels locked in a certain position; this can be an indication of a displaced fracture.

First aid care for wrist fractures includes:

1. Immediate application of ice, compression, and elevation in conjunction with some type of splint that immobilizes the wrist (Figure 12.18).

2. Once in place, the ice, compression, and splint should be elevated carefully by way of a standard sling-and-swathe bandage as described by the National Safety Council (1991).

3. Leave the fingertips exposed in order to facilitate monitoring blood flow to the hand beyond the level of the splint.

Wrist Sprains and Dislocations

The mechanism producing a fracture of the wrist may also produce a sprain or dislocation in that region when of lesser severity. Essentially the wrist (radiocarpal) joint is bound together by a network of large, strong ligaments known as the palmar and dorsal radiocarpal ligaments (Figures 12.12 and 12.13). In addition, several smaller ligaments bind the remaining bones of the wrist to form a well-supported series of joints known collectively as the intercarpal joints.

The most common sprain of the wrist is caused by forced hyperextension, which results in a stretching and possible tearing of the palmar radiocarpal ligament. Such an injury can, if severe enough, result in a dislocation of one or more of the carpal bones. In

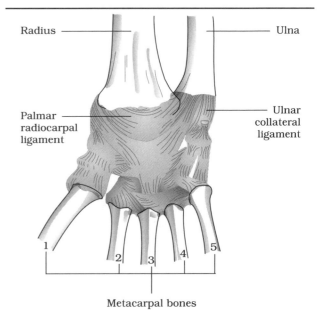

FIGURE 12.12 Palmar radiocarpal ligament.

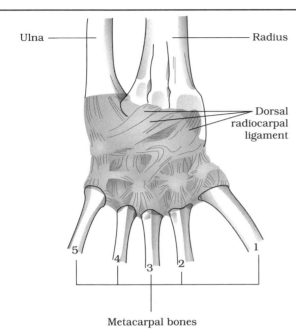

Ulna

Radius

Dorsal radiocarpal ligament

5 4 3 2 1

Metacarpal bones

FIGURE 12.13 Dorsal radiocarpal ligament.

the case of a simple sprain the carpal bones will remain in their normal position.

The most common dislocation of the wrist involves the lunate bone, which is located between the distal end of the radius and the capitate bone (O'Donoghue, 1976). The mechanism of injury is forceful hyperextension; this causes the bone to shift out of its normal position and slide toward the palmar side of the wrist. In severe cases the lunate will put pressure on the tendons and nerves of a region of the wrist known as the carpal tunnel, resulting in significant symptoms in the hand and fingers.

Signs and symptoms of wrist sprains and dislocations include:

1. The athlete will report having sustained a forced hyperextension of the wrist in conjunction with a snapping or popping sensation within the bones of the joint.

2. Movement, or attempted movements, of the wrist will be painful and meet with little success.

3. In cases of dislocations, the wrist may be locked so that the athlete will be unable to voluntarily move the wrist.

4. Numbness and/or pain may radiate from the wrist into the hand and fingers. In the case of lunate dislocations, these symptoms may involve the distribution of the median nerve, producing the symptoms known commonly as carpal tunnel syndrome.

5. Swelling of the wrist may be limited owing to the nature of the ligaments of the region.

First aid care for wrist sprains and dislocations includes:

1. Immediate application of ice, compression, elevation, and some type of splinting device designed to immobilize the wrist joint. A bag of crushed ice held in place by an elastic wrap is effective in most cases. Do not apply ice if you suspect either vascular or nerve supply is compromised. The splint may even be secured with the wrap as well.

2. Elevation is best achieved using a standard sling-and-swathe bandage.

3. In cases of significant pain or a possible dislocation, it is important to refer the athlete to a health care facility for further evaluation and treatment.

Nerve Injuries to the Wrist

Three major nerves cross the wrist from the forearm into the hand to supply both sensation and motor function to the hand and fingers. These nerves are the radial, the median, and the ulnar. Though any of these nerves may be damaged in a sports-related injury, the most commonly injured nerve is the median. This nerve passes through a region of the wrist known as the **carpal tunnel,** which also houses eight flexor tendons that pass into the hand. The tunnel is surrounded by dense, strong ligaments as well as bone.

The exact cause of **carpal tunnel syndrome** is unknown, but it probably involves swelling within the tunnel caused by tendinitis or sprains of the region. In any event, the pressure of the swelling has a negative effect on the median nerve. Although carpal tunnel syndrome can be caused by a single traumatic episode, such as a dislocated lunate bone, the majority of cases involving athletes tend to be the result of chronic, overuse injuries. Sports with a high incidence include racquet sports and those requiring the participant to grip an object tightly for extended periods of time. Unless treated properly, carpal tunnel syndrome can be extremely disabling and can often preclude an athlete from returning to the sport.

Another nerve-related injury in the wrist involves the ulnar nerve as it passes through the region on the ulnar side of the forearm. Specifically, the ulnar nerve is located in the vicinity of the pisiform bone and the hook of the hamate bone within the **tunnel of Guyon** (Hoppenfield, 1976). A blow to the wrist or tendinitis in the tendon of flexor carpi ulnaris can result in irritation to the nerve and a variety of symptoms. These include loss of sensation to a portion of the hand and fingers as well as loss of muscle strength in the fingers affected by the ulnar nerve. The region of the hand that receives sensory impulses from the ulnar nerve is the medial portion of the palm, including the region known as the hypothenar eminence as well as the medial half of the ring finger and the entire little finger.

Signs and symptoms of nerve injuries to the wrist include:

1. Loss of sensation to a portion of the hand and/or fingers that follows the distribution of a major nerve in the region. In some cases pain may radiate into the hand as well.

2. Pain and tenderness around the region of the wrist on the palm side.

3. Associated tendinitis of the wrist or recent history of trauma to the area such as a contusion or sprain.

4. Symptoms may become worse when the wrist is fully flexed or extended or an object is gripped tightly in the hand.

First aid care of nerve injuries to the wrist includes:

1. This type of injury tends to develop slowly over time. The exception is when a nerve of the wrist is aggravated by an acute injury such as a severe contusion or sprain.

2. When associated with an acute trauma, the best approach is the immediate application of ice, compression, and elevation. Do not apply ice if you suspect either vascular or nerve supply is compromised. Splinting may be necessary depending upon the specific injury.

3. Any athlete with a history of recurrent pain and stiffness in the wrist associated with the neurologic symptoms described above should be referred to a health care facility for a complete evaluation by a medical doctor.

4. If the medical diagnosis confirms a nerve-related problem, the initial care will generally involve rest, anti-inflammatory drugs, and in some cases a splint. In severe cases surgical decompression of the nerve may be required.

Unique Tendon Problems of the Wrist

By definition, **tenosynovitis** is an "inflammation between tendon and surrounding tissues with consequent loss of smooth gliding motion" (AMA, 1968). Perhaps the most common form of tenosynovitis in the wrist involves the tendons of the thumb (Figure 12.14) and is known as **deQuervain's disease.** In reality this is not a disease in the classic sense but rather a type of overuse injury specific to the wrist. deQuervain's disease most commonly involves the tendons of the extensor pollicis brevis and the abductor pollicis longus muscles as they pass across the radial styloid process. There is a third tendon in the region, the extensor pollicis longus; however, it is rarely involved in this condition.

The mechanism of injury for deQuervain's disease is vague, but it probably involves overuse of the wrist and/or thumb. Initially, the tendons and the synovial sheath around the tendons become inflamed, resulting in pain, swelling, and stiffness. As the injury progresses the tendons begin catching within the anatomic tunnel, at times with such force that the athlete will feel them as they break free. Using the thumb, particularly in flexion and extension, will be extremely

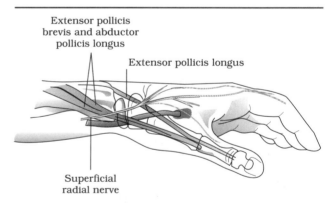

Extensor pollicis brevis and abductor pollicis longus

Extensor pollicis longus

Superficial radial nerve

FIGURE 12.14 Tendons of the thumb.

Information at your fingertips

The World Wide Web—To check out excellent graphics describing carpal tunnel syndrome, go to http://www.jbpub.com/athletictraining and click on Chapter 12.

painful, and even wrist movements will be impeded. Conservative treatment includes rest, heat and drug therapy, and splinting of the wrist to reduce movements of the thumb. In many cases this problem tends to recur and eventually may require surgical treatment to release (decompress) the tendons as they pass near the radial styloid process.

Signs and symptoms of deQuervain's disease include:

1. Pain and tenderness within the region of the radial styloid process, specifically involving the tendons of the abductor pollicis longus and the extensor pollicis brevis.

2. Swelling in the area of the radial styloid process and, in advanced cases, the development of a nodule on one or more of the tendons.

3. The athlete may report that the tendons are catching within the wrist during activity.

4. Thumb flexion in conjunction with ulnar deviation of the wrist will cause a significant increase in pain and related symptoms.

Care of deQuervain's disease includes:

1. If diagnosed early, the condition is treated with rest, immobilization with some type of splint, and drug therapy.

2. In advanced or recurring cases, surgical treatment has been found to be highly effective with this condition. The basic surgical objective is to create more room within the tunnel for the tendons.

Another unique tendon-related wrist problem is known as a ganglion. Technically, a **ganglion** is a herniation of the synovium surrounding the tendons at the wrist. When this occurs the herniated tissue will gradually begin to fill with synovial fluid, producing a protrusion often visible as a bump on the surface of the wrist (Figure 12.15). The most common sight for wrist ganglions is on the extensor tendon (dorsal) side of the wrist, although cases have been reported on the flexor tendon side of the wrist as well. Considerable debate continues concerning the specific cause of ganglions; however, it appears that they are related to the chronic strain of wrist tendons (O'Donoghue, 1976). Ganglions are highly variable in appearance. Some appear as a soft, apparently fluid-filled mass just under the skin; others materialize as a hard, painful mass over a tendon. Depending upon their specific location ganglions may interfere with an athlete's performance, but in most cases the problem is seen as primarily cosmetic.

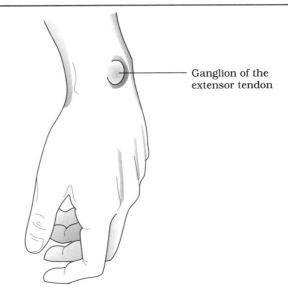

Ganglion of the extensor tendon

FIGURE 12.15 Ganglion of the wrist.

Signs and symptoms of a ganglion include:

1. The most obvious symptom is a visible swelling through the skin of the wrist in the region of the extensor or flexor tendons.

2. In more advanced cases a painful, hardened nodule may be present directly over a tendon (Figure 12.15).

Care of a ganglion includes:

1. In some cases ganglions regress on their own spontaneously.

2. In cases in which the ganglion does not interfere with performance, most physicians recommend leaving it alone.

3. In cases in which the ganglion does interfere with performance or is cosmetically unattractive, surgical removal in conjunction with repair of the synovial hernia is an option. It should be noted, however, that even after surgery ganglions may recur.

Hand Injuries

An in-depth discussion of the complexity and variety of sports-related ligamentous injuries to the hand is beyond the scope of this book. For a detailed review of hand injuries in sports, consult the article by A. Isani entitled "Prevention and Treatment of Ligamentous Sports Injuries to the Hand," which appeared in 1990 in volume 9(1) of the journal *Sports Medicine* on pages 48–61.

The hand contains 19 bones: the 5 metacarpals and the 14 separate **phalanges** of the fingers (Figure 12.16). The joints of the hand include the carpometacarpal joints at the base of the hand, the metacarpophalangeal joints (knuckles), and the interphalangeal joints of the fingers and thumb. All of these joints are freely movable and are supported by many ligaments and capsular tissues.

Movements at each of these joints are affected by the many muscles originating from the forearm that pass tendons into the hand and fingers. Also within the hand there are small, intrinsic (originating within the hand) muscles that precisely move the thumb and fingers. The nerves and vessels of the hand are continuations of the major structures that cross the wrist: the radial, median, and ulnar nerves as well as the radial and ulnar arteries.

Hand Fractures

Fractures can occur to any of the 19 bones of the hand; however, certain types of fractures are seen more commonly in sports. An injury unique to the thumb is **Bennett's fracture** (Figure 12.17). This injury often results from a blow to the hand while it is in a clenched-fist position; the force of the mechanism causes the proximal end of the first metacarpal bone to be driven into the wrist. The result is a **fracture-dislocation** of the first metacarpal bone away from the greater mul-

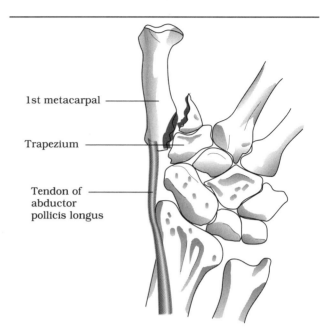

FIGURE 12.17 Bennett's fracture.

tangular (trapezium) bone of the wrist. An obvious deformity appears with this injury characterized by the thumb being shorter in appearance when compared with that of the opposite hand. Significant swelling will also be present near the base of the thumb over the carpometacarpal joint.

Fractures of the metacarpal bones of the fingers can also occur via a mechanism similar to that described for Bennett's fracture, i.e., a blow with a clenched fist. The most common injury involves the fourth and/or fifth metacarpal bone(s) near the proximal end(s) (base) and is known as **boxer's fracture.** Due to the ligamentous structure of this area displaced fractures are rare; consequently, deformity is usually not a common sign of injury. Another mechanism of injury for metacarpal fractures is a crushing force, such as having the hand stepped on by another athlete, which is common in sports such as tackle football.

Fractures of the phalanges also occur frequently in sports, particularly fractures of the proximal phalanges (O'Donoghue, 1976). Most of these fractures remain undisplaced and are easily treated with splinting; few if any long-term complications ensue. In cases in which the phalangeal fracture resists fixation and remains unstable, surgically implanted fixation is effective. This is critical since a serious complication of a finger fracture is rotational deformity, which results when the broken bone ends fail to unite in the correct position (Hutson, 1990).

Signs and symptoms of hand fractures include:

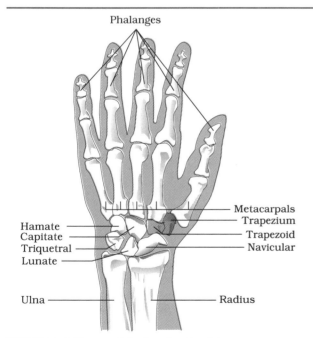

FIGURE 12.16 Bones of the hand and wrist.

1. Recent history of significant trauma to the hand followed immediately by specific pain and dysfunction of the hand and/or finger(s).

2. In cases of displaced fractures, deformity may be observable, either as a bump or protrusion within the hand or as an oddly shaped finger.

3. In cases of compound fractures the skin will be broken over the region of the fracture.

4. There will be significant inflammation associated with any fracture within the hand or finger.

First aid care for hand fractures includes:

1. Immediate application of ice, compression, elevation, and some type of splinting device. This is best accomplished using a small bag of crushed ice held in place with a narrow elastic wrap; take care to leave the fingernails exposed.

2. Elevation can be easily achieved by placing the arm in a standard sling-and-swathe bandage.

3. Depending upon the specific site of the fracture a variety of splinting techniques can be used. For example, for an isolated phalangeal fracture a procedure known as buddy taping can be used, which simply involves taping the fractured finger to an adjacent one. Fractures of the metacarpal bones are best treated by immobilzation of the entire hand (Figure 12.18).

4. The athlete should be transported to the appropriate health care facility for further medical evaluation and treatment. *It is critical that fractures of the hand be treated as serious injuries.*

Sprains and Dislocations of the Hand

Any of the many joints in the hand can be subject to sufficient trauma to cause a sprain of the supporting ligaments. If the force is severe enough a dislocation of the joint may occur as well. Although virtually any of the joints of the hand may be injured, available information regarding sports-related injuries indicates that certain types are quite common. These include gamekeeper's thumb, mallet (baseball) finger, and boutonnière deformity.

■ Gamekeeper's Thumb
The metacarpophalangeal (MP) joint of the thumb is a large, condyloid joint allowing a considerable range of motion in flexion and extension as well as a slight amount of abduction and adduction. The joint is supported by both capsular and collateral ligaments. The latter are named according to their location relative

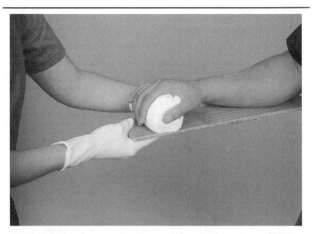
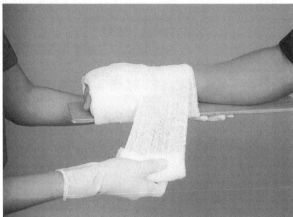
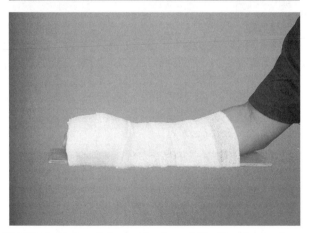

FIGURE 12.18 A splint provides immobilization for fractures of the forearm, wrist, and hand. (Source: National Safety Council. 1994. *First Aid and CPR* (2d ed.). Boston: Jones and Bartlett. Reprinted with permission.)

to the radius and ulna: the collateral ligament on the lateral side of the joint is the radial collateral ligament and the one on the medial side is the ulnar collateral ligament (Figure 12.19).

The term **gamekeeper's thumb** originated in the 1950s to describe an injury unique to gamekeepers, whose profession required them to break the necks of rabbits. Apparently this procedure resulted in considerable damage to the ulnar collateral ligament of the thumb, causing chronic instability of the MP joint (Hutson, 1990). Although there are few gamekeepers today, the injury occurs with surprising frequency in sports such as alpine skiing. The mechanism of injury involves a valgus (force applied to the medial side of the joint) stress across the MP joint of the thumb; this results in stretching, partial tearing, or even complete rupture of the ulnar collateral ligament. (In skiing, certain types of pole grips place considerable stress on the MP joint of the thumb when planting a pole.)

Injury to the ulnar collateral ligament can produce a grossly unstable thumb, particularly when an athlete attempts to grasp or hold an object. Recent evidence suggests that in 30% of the cases ligament injuries occur in conjunction with an avulsion fracture of a bone fragment from the base of the proximal phalanx (Isani, 1990). Regardless of the specific type of injury, any significant sprain of the ulnar collateral ligament within the MP joint of the thumb must be carefully evaluated by a physician in order to determine the extent of joint laxity as well as bony integrity. It is important to note that if left uncorrected this injury can lead to a chronically unstable joint that can negatively affect use of the hand.

Signs and symptoms of gamekeeper's thumb include:

1. Significant point tenderness over the region of the ulnar collateral ligament.

2. The athlete may report having felt a snap during the initial injury.

3. Significant swelling over the MP joint of the thumb.

4. Inability and/or unwillingness by the athlete to move the thumb.

First aid care for suspected gamekeeper's thumb includes:

1. Immediate application of ice, compression, and elevation. This is best accomplished by placing a small bag of crushed ice around the injured joint and securing it with an elastic wrap.

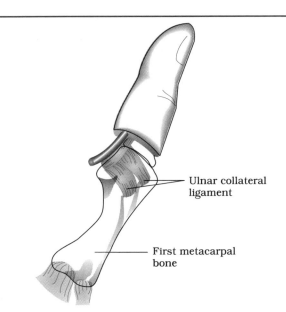

FIGURE 12.19 Damage to the ulnar collateral ligament of the metacarpophalangeal joint can result in gamekeeper's thumb.

2. The easiest method of achieving elevation is to place the arm in a simple sling.

3. Refer the athlete to a health care facility for further evaluation and treatment of the injury.

■ Mallet (Baseball) Finger

Mallet finger involves the distal phalanx of a finger, oftentimes the index or middle finger. The injury is so named because the resulting deformity gives the distal segment of the finger the appearance of a mallet. The term baseball finger arose because the injury is so common in that sport: getting hit on the fingertip by a ball is a frequent occurrence.

The anatomy of the distal finger includes the **distal interphalangeal (DIP) joint,** which functions as a hinge. The muscles acting at this joint are the flexor digitorum profundus and the extensor digitorum. These two muscles are located in the forearm; however, their tendons pass through the hand, inserting

WHAT IF?

You are coaching a junior high school basketball game. During the second half, your starting point guard injures her finger when receiving a passed ball. Upon examination you note obvious deformity with the distal phalanx pushed up so that the distal interphalangeal joint is dislocated. What is this injury and how would you care for it initially?

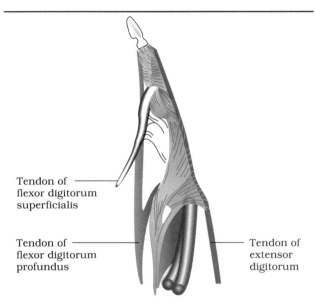

Tendon of
flexor digitorum
superficialis

Tendon of
flexor digitorum
profundus

Tendon of
extensor
digitorum

FIGURE 12.20 Tendons of the finger.

into the bases of the distal phalanges of each of the four fingers (Figure 12.20).

The mechanism of injury for mallet finger is quite precise: the tip of the finger must receive a blow at the time the finger is extending from a flexed position. The result is that the distal phalanx is suddenly and forcefully taken into flexion against the action of the extensor digitorum muscle. This can lead to an avulsion of the extensor tendon with or without a small fragment of bone from the insertion at the base of the distal phalanx. Once this injury occurs the athlete is unable to extend the affected finger; it remains in a flexed position at the DIP joint (Figure 12.21).

Signs and symptoms of mallet finger include:

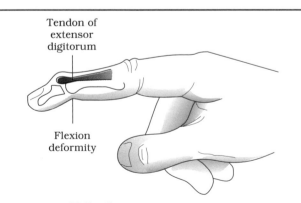

Tendon of
extensor
digitorum

Flexion
deformity

FIGURE 12.21 Mallet finger.

1. The single most important sign is the deformity itself, which is associated with a recent history of trauma to the fingertip.
2. Point tenderness on the dorsal surface of the base of the distal phalanx, directly over the site of insertion of the extensor digitorum tendon.

First aid care of suspected mallet finger includes:

1. Immediate application of ice, compression, and elevation. This is best accomplished by placing a small bag of crushed ice around the involved finger and holding it in place with a small elastic wrap.
2. Immediately splint the finger with the DIP joint extended. Do not let the distal phalanx fall back into the flexed position.
3. The easiest method of achieving elevation is to place the arm in a simple sling.
4. Refer the athlete to a health care facility for further evaluation and treatment of the injury.

▪ Boutonnière Deformity

Boutonnière deformity (French for buttonhole) involves the **proximal interphalangeal (PIP) joint** of the fingers (Hutson, 1990). The structure of the extensor digitorum tendon is unique as it crosses the dorsal surface of the PIP joint. The tendon is divided into three distinct bands: one central and two lateral bands (Figure 12.22). This arrangement allows for full flexion of the PIP joint without interference from the extensor digitorum muscle.

The mechanism for this injury is characterized by severe forced finger flexion, such as having the hand contact a playing surface during a fall with the fingers in a flexed position while an attempt is made simultaneously to extend the fingers. This results in tearing the central portion of the extensor tendon. Initial symptoms are limited; the athlete will be able to extend the injured PIP joint, but with limited strength. If left uncorrected, the PIP joint will eventually pop through the opening in the central portion of the tendon like a button popping up through a buttonhole. This results in a deformity that places the finger in a position of flexion at the PIP joint in conjunction with hyperextension at both the MP and DIP joints (Figure 12.23). Treatment for the injury consists of splinting the finger in a position of extension of the PIP joint to allow the central portion of the extensor tendon to heal. Surgical correction is not recommended (Hutson, 1990).

Signs and symptoms of boutonnière deformity include:

1. The athlete will report a violent flexion to the finger, perhaps associated with the sensation of tearing or popping over the PIP joint.

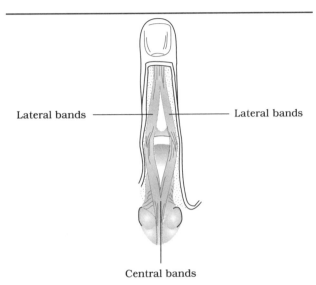

Lateral bands — — Lateral bands

Central bands

FIGURE 12.22 Bands of the extensor tendons.

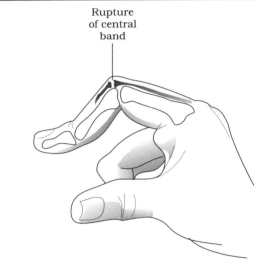

Rupture of central band

FIGURE 12.23 Boutonnière deformity.

2. The injury will be followed immediately by significant weakness in extending the injured finger at the PIP joint.

3. The PIP joint will become painful and swollen, then stiff.

4. If left unattended, the injury may progress to the classic deformity, which is characterized by hyperextension of the MP and DIP joints, with flexion of the PIP joint.

   First aid care for suspected boutonnière deformity includes:

1. Initially, this injury should be treated as any soft-tissue and/or skeletal injury of the hand or finger:

apply ice, compression, and elevation. This is best accomplished by using a small bag of crushed ice that is held in place with a small elastic wrap.

2. Elevation can be easily achieved using a simple sling.

3. If any of the above signs and/or symptoms are present, the athlete should immediately be referred to a health care facility for medical evaluation.

4. In cases in which the initial injury has not been treated and has progressed to actual deformity, medical referral is mandatory.

Information at your fingertips

The World Wide Web—For more information on the anatomy of the human hand, go to http://www.jbpub.com/athletictraining and click on Chapter 12.

Review Questions

1. List the three articulations of the elbow.

2. Explain the term myositis ossificans traumatica as it relates to a condition of the upper arm known as tackler's exostosis.

3. List the signs and symptoms of a humeral fracture.

4. Explain and/or demonstrate the first aid procedures for an athlete with a suspected fracture of the humerus.

5. Describe briefly the mechanism of injury for a posterior dislocation of the elbow.

6. List the signs and symptoms of a dislocation of the elbow.

7. *True or false:* The ulnar nerve is the most commonly damaged nerve in a dislocation of the elbow.

8. Explain and/or demonstrate the appropriate first aid care for an athlete with a suspected dislocation of the elbow.

9. Define the term Volkmann's contracture.

10. Review the signs and symptoms of either medial or lateral epicondylitis of the elbow.

11. Define osteochondritis dissecans.

12. What are the signs and symptoms of osteochondritis dissecans of the elbow?

13. What is the location of the olecranon bursa of the elbow?

14. *True or false:* A Colles' fracture involves the carpal bones of the wrist.

15. Describe the signs and symptoms of a Colles' fracture.

16. Explain and/or demonstrate the appropriate first aid procedures for an athlete with a suspected Colles' fracture.

17. Which one of the following carpal bones can be located within a region at the base of the thumb known as the anatomical snuff-box?

   a. lunate

   b. hamate

   c. capitate

   d. pisiform

   e. navicular

18. *True or false:* The most common form of wrist sprain is the result of forced hyperextension.

19. What anatomic structures within the wrist form the tunnel of Guyon?

20. Which major nerve passes through this tunnel?

21. What musculotendinous unit is most often involved in the condition known as deQuervain's disease?

22. Define the condition known as a ganglion.

23. Explain and demonstrate the appropriate first aid care for a suspected phalangeal fracture of the hand.

24. Which specific ligamentous structure is damaged in the condition known as gamekeeper's thumb?

25. Describe the signs and symptoms of gamekeeper's thumb; explain and demonstrate the appropriate first aid for an athlete suspected of having sustained such an injury.

26. Explain the mechanism of injury and the structures involved in the condition known as mallet finger.

27. Explain the mechanism of injury and the structures involved in the condition known as boutonnière deformity.

References

American Academy of Orthopaedic Surgeons. 1991. *Athletic Training and Sports Medicine* (2d ed.). Park Ridge, Ill.: American Academy of Orthopaedic Surgeons.

American Medical Association. 1968. *Standard Nomenclature of Athletic Injuries* (1st ed.). Chicago: American Medical Association.

Bartsokas TW, Palin DW, Collier DB. 1992. An unusual stress fracture site: midhumerus. *Phys Sportsmed.* 20:119–122.

Friel JP (ed.). 1977. *Dorland's Pocket Medical Dictionary.* Philadelphia: W. B. Saunders.

Hannafin JA, Schelkun PH. 1996. How I manage tennis and golfer's elbow. *Phys Sportsmed.* 24:63–68.

Holleb PD, Bach BR. 1990. Triceps brachii injuries. *Sports Med.* 10:273–276.

Hoppenfield S. 1976. *Physical Examination of the Spine and Extremities.* New York: Appleton-Century-Crofts.

Hutson MA. 1990. *Sports Injuries—Recognition and Management.* New York: Oxford University Press.

Isani A. 1990. Prevention and treatment of ligamentous sports injuries to the hand. *Sports Med.* 9:48–61.

Jobe FW, Ciccotti MG. 1994. Lateral and medial epicondylitis of the elbow. *J Am Acad Orthoped Surg.* 2:1–8.

Larson RL, et al. 1976. Little-league survey: the Eugene study. *Am J Sports Med.* 4:201–209.

National Safety Council. 1991. *First Aid and CPR.* Boston: Jones and Bartlett.

O'Donoghue DH. 1976. *Treatment of Injuries to Athletes.* Philadelphia: W. B. Saunders.

CHAPTER 13

Injuries to the Thorax and Abdomen

M A J O R C O N C E P T S

This chapter begins with an overview of the gross anatomy of the thorax and abdomen. Additionally, it discusses the internal organs associated with the thorax and abdomen that can be injured through sports participation. The internal organs and structures covered here include the heart and lungs, liver, kidneys, spleen, stomach, and diaphragm.

The chapter also discusses external injuries such as fractures to the ribs, various joint-related problems, and breast injuries and contusions. It gives signs and symptoms of internal injuries to the heart, lungs, liver, kidneys, spleen, and bladder. At times, coaches overlook serious injuries to the internal organs; many can have debilitating and even life-threatening effects if proper care is not applied.

Anatomy Review

The thorax and abdominal cavities contain the majority of the vital organs of the body. This area is enclosed by the spinal column, the rib cage, and the clavicle, which provide bony protection for the area. The vertebrae in this area include the 12 thoracic vertebrae and the 5 lumbar vertebrae located posterior to the abdomen. There are 12 pairs of ribs in both males and females; these include what are known as true ribs (the first 7). The eighth to twelfth pairs of ribs are sometimes referred to as false ribs. The first 7 (sometimes 8) pairs of ribs are connected to the spinal column posteriorly and the sternum anteriorly; therefore, they are known as true ribs. The anterior connection of the true ribs is made via a costal cartilage for each rib (Moore, 1992). The remaining ribs, specifically ribs 8 through 10, connect via a common costal cartilage. Ribs 11 and 12 do not connect to the sternum anteriorly; thus they are called floating ribs. All of the joints between the ribs and the spinal column are reinforced with strong ligamentous support. This area is further strengthened by the anterior longitudinal ligament, which runs on the anterior surface of the spinal column from the occipital bone of the skull to the pelvic surface of the sacrum.

The main joints of the thorax include the intervertebral joints, the vertebral and rib joints, the sternocostal and costochondral joints, and the sternoclavicular joints. The intervertebral joints are those between each of the vertebral bodies. These joints are stabilized by ligaments and the intervertebral disks located be-

strengthened by ligaments that allow the gliding movements of the ribs at the vertebral column. Anteriorly, the first through the seventh ribs articulate with the sternum directly from their costal cartilage. Ribs 8 through 10 articulate with the sternum through a common cartilage. These joints are known as the sternocostal joints. The point at which the rib attaches to the costal cartilage is known as the costochondral joint. Typically, there is no movement at this joint (Gray, 1974).

One of the main joints of the thorax is the **sternoclavicular joint.** This is an articulation between the clavicle and the sternum; it is discussed in Chapter 11. This is the only bony articulation between the thorax and the arm, and it is supported by strong ligaments. There is movement at this joint even though it is not viewed as a major site of movement, as are other joints within the region.

There are several muscles surrounding the thorax and abdomen. The main thoracic muscles include the intercostal muscles, both internal and external, which function primarily to lift the rib cage and assist with breathing. More superficially, the pectoralis major and minor are located in the upper chest area and mainly control arm movement. In the posterior thorax there are several muscles running the length of the spinal column that are responsible for a variety of movements as well as stabilization of the spine. Most of the deep muscles running the length of the back, including the spinalis, longissimus, and iliocostalis, and others, are responsible for keeping the spine erect. More superficially, muscles such as the latissimus dorsi, rhomboids, trapezius, and deltoid

---

Information at your fingertips

The World Wide Web—To examine an interesting review of the radiology of the thorax, visit http://www.jbpub.com/athletictraining and click on Chapter 13.

---

tween each vertebral body. The intervertebral disks are mostly fibrocartilaginous and play an important role in the weight-bearing ability of the spine.

The ribs articulate with the vertebrae in an interesting manner. Each rib articulates with two adjacent vertebrae and the intervertebral disk. These joints are

are mainly responsible for movements of the upper extremity.

In the abdominal region there are also several important muscles. The main muscles of the anterior abdominal region are the external and internal obliques and the rectus abdominis. The oblique muscles help to

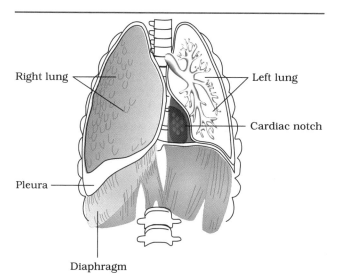

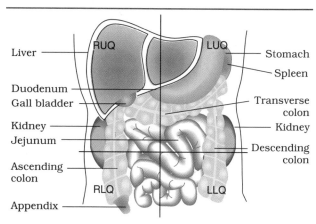

FIGURE 13.2 The four quadrants of the abdomen and the organs they house.

FIGURE 13.1 The internal organs of the thorax.

flex and rotate the trunk; they also assist with support of the abdominal viscera. The rectus abdominis is the main muscle of the anterior abdominal wall. In the abdomen the rectus abdominis acts to support the abdominal viscera and to flex the trunk. This muscle also assists in the lower extremity by helping to fixate the pelvis during movement, which allows the muscles of the lower extremity to function more effectively.

Internal Organs

The two main organs in the thorax (Figure 13.1) are the lungs and the heart. Each lung is encased in a separate and closed space called the plural sac, which assists the lungs by helping to make respiration a smooth process. The lungs oxygenate blood as it circulates; they are normally light, soft, spongy, and pinkish in a healthy person. The right lung has three lobes, and the left lung has two, which makes the right one

a little larger and heavier than the left. Located directly between the two lungs is the heart. The heart is situated in an area called the mediastinum, which also houses major blood vessels and parts of the respiratory and digestive systems (trachea and esophagus) along with nerve and lymphatic tissues. Inferior to the pleural cavities and the mediastinum is a muscle called the diaphragm. Essentially the diaphragm separates the thoracic and abdominal cavities; it is considered the main muscle of respiration. The diaphragm is basically a circular muscle with a tendon in the middle that allows the muscle to contract and assist with breathing. There are several openings for blood vessels, nerves, and digestive structures to pass through the diaphragm.

For descriptive purposes the abdominal region (Figure 13.2) is typically divided into four quadrants: the right upper and lower quadrants and the left upper and lower quadrants, with the umbilicus serving as the center point. The organs located within the right upper

Information at your fingertips

The World Wide Web—A truly interactive human anatomy web site, which incorporates images from the Visible Human Project. Go to http://www.jbpub.com/ athletictraining and click on Chapter 13.

WHAT IF?

You are coaching a tackle football game at the high school level. On the last play your quarterback was sacked and, in the process, received a severe blow to his abdomen. On further examination, he complains of extreme abdominal pain, has a rigid abdomen, and also reports pain radiating into his left shoulder and upper arm. Based on these signs and symptoms, could this athlete have a serious injury and, if so, what?

quadrant are the liver, gall bladder, and right kidney. In the right lower quadrant are the ascending colon and the appendix. In the left upper quadrant are the stomach, spleen, pancreas, and left kidney. In the left lower quadrant is the descending colon.

Common Sports Injuries

Sports injuries to the thorax and abdomen are relatively uncommon in children and adolescents. However, there are some injuries to the region that require immediate attention in order to prevent long-term disability and possibly even death. The discussion first focuses on external injuries involving the skeletal, muscular, and other external components of the region. The discussion then reviews injuries to the internal organs of the thorax and abdomen.

External Injuries

■ Fractures

Fractures to the bones of the skeleton can occur as a result of direct trauma. An athlete may fracture a rib, the sternum, the clavicle, or possibly some part of a vertebra. Fractures to any of these structures should be cared for immediately. Without proper care complications can occur: the athlete may develop a pneumothorax and/or hemothorax, both of which are life-threatening conditions. A **pneumothorax** is a presence of air in the pleural cavity; a **hemothorax** is the presence of blood in the pleural cavity (Stedman and Hensyl, 1990).

In the case of a sternal fracture, which is infrequent in sports, there are two complications that may arise. First, if the manubrium is dislocated and moves posteriorly, the possibility of an airway obstruction exists

(Booher and Thibodeau, 1989). Second, if the sternum and ribs are separated completely there is a likelihood of flail chest; the possible complications of this condition include a pneumothorax and/or hemothorax (Simoneauz, Murphy, and Tehranzadeh, 1990; Widner, 1988).

The other type of fracture to this region, which is more common in sports, is a rib fracture. Most often ribs are fractured in contact sports when two players collide and the rib cage is violently compressed. The fifth through the ninth pairs of ribs are most susceptible to fracture (Widner, 1988). However, almost any one of the ribs can be fractured under specific circumstances. As with other bones in the body, the ribs can be broken in varying degrees of severity—from greenstick to displaced fractures. If a rib fracture is suspected, the athlete must be referred to the appropriate physician as soon as possible.

Signs and symptoms of a sternum or rib fracture include:

1. Extreme localized pain at the site of injury that is typically aggravated by sneezing, coughing, forced inhalation, or sometimes movement.

2. The athlete may grasp the chest wall at the point of injury.

3. Mild swelling may occur at the site, and there may be bony deformity.

4. The athlete may complain of breathing difficulties and take rapid, shallow breaths.

First aid care for sternum or rib fractures includes:

1. Monitor the athlete's vital signs and watch for any respiratory distress.

2. Arrange for transport to a health care facility.

The athlete may also experience subluxations and dislocations at various joints in the skeleton of the thorax. Chapter 11 discusses dislocation of the sternoclavicular joint in detail. The discussion here mainly deals with costochondral separations, which involve

Athletic Trainers Speak Out

"During a routine high-school varsity football practice on a Thursday afternoon, our players were running through the pass patterns when one of the receivers caught the ball and then tripped and fell on his stomach on the ball. Initially he appeared to have had the wind knocked out of him but nothing more. I helped him from the field and sat him on a bench to let him recover. After getting his breath he still complained of pain in the upper abdominal region. It was different than the pain one might expect with a bruise. Although the possibility of an abdominal injury was considered, I felt that the mechanism did not seem to be violent enough to cause any serious injury. I decided, though, that since the athlete was not improving it might be wise to get him to the training room and contact our team physician. I escorted him to the locker room; at this time he was complaining of pain moving to the shoulder. By the time the physician saw the athlete all the signs and symptoms were present to indicate a spleen injury. Within one hour the athlete was in the operating room. Given the nonviolent nature of the drill and the lack of immediate signs, [the coaches admitted] they probably would have sent the athlete home to rest. This action would have delayed the treatment and certainly led to more serious consequences."

—Larry J. Leverenz, Ph.D., A.T.C.

Larry J. Leverenz

Dr. Leverenz is the director of athletic-training education and athletic trainer for basketball at Purdue University.

some type of disunion of the sternum and ribs. In a costochondral separation the cartilage portion of the costosternal union is either separated from the sternum medially or from the rib laterally. Obviously this requires a great deal of force, and this type of injury is usually associated with contact or collision sports. Typically, the athlete with a costochondral separation will experience a great deal of pain at the time of the injury and in many cases will complain of pain for weeks after the injury.

Signs and symptoms of a costochondral separation include:

1. The athlete will report that a pop or snap occurred.

2. A palpable defect may be felt as deformity may or may not be present; in addition, there may be swelling in the immediate area.

3. Maximum or near maximum inhalation may be very difficult.

4. Localized pain and tenderness over the area of the costochondral junction.

First aid care for a costochondral separation includes:

1. Immediately apply ice and light compression.

2. Treat for shock if necessary.

3. Arrange for transport to a medical facility.

■ Breast Injuries

The breast is subject to injury depending on the type of sport and the gender of the athlete. Women do incur breast contusions as a result of contact in some sports. Sports bras typically do not provide protection from direct contact, but they do help to support the breast during activity. Women will have various preferences regarding the type and size of sports bra that will provide the required support. Conversely, some women will elect not to wear a bra during sports participation. This decision should be left up to the athlete, based on comfort and performance. However, if the athlete elects not to wear a sports bra, she should be aware of the possible long-term effects of not supplying proper breast support during activity. Most often the major long-term effect is that the breast tissue stretches, resulting in loss of stability and natural breast contour.

Both men and women will at times experience nipple irritation. This problem is easily remedied by either changing tops or (if that is not possible) by placing a bandage over the nipple during competition so that irritation is reduced or eliminated.

Internal Injuries

There are many organs and structures that can be injured from direct trauma in collision and contact sports. It is not always easy to determine if an internal injury has occurred; therefore the coach or athletic trainer must be educated and knowledgeable about the signs and symptoms of possible injury to an internal organ. The discussion here begins with the heart and lungs and continues with the internal viscera.

■ Heart and Lung Injuries

It has been noted that sudden death among athletes is more often a result of insult to the heart than any other factor (Aubrey and Cantu, 1989). This is not a common occurrence, yet youth league baseball players and hockey players have experienced heart contusions (Karofsky, 1990). Anytime the heart is compressed via collision between the sternum and the spinal column by a violent external force—such as might be caused by being hit by a baseball or hockey puck—a cardiac contusion and or chest pain can result (Karofsky, 1990; Steine, 1992; Widner, 1988). A blunt trauma to the chest may also cause an aortic rupture (Yates and Aldrete, 1991). This injury is often fatal and must be given immediate attention if suspected. Watch any athlete with a chest injury for breathing problems, fainting, decreases in heart rate and blood pressure, and complaints of severe chest pains.

In addition to a cardiac contusion, an athlete may experience a pulmonary contusion. This injury can be a complication of a rib fracture, contusion, or some other type of pulmonary injury and typically goes undetected (Wagner, Sidhu, and Radcliffe, 1992).

There is also the possibility of spontaneous pneumothorax among high school athletes. This has been reported among both runners and weight lifters (Wagner, Sidhu, and Radcliffe, 1992). This injury is significant and must be attended to by a physician. The coach or athletic trainer must be aware of the signs and symptoms of both cardiac and pulmonary contusions as well as a pneumothorax. The progress of the athlete should be monitored over a period of days as some injuries have a tendency to exhibit complications later (Perkins and Sterling, 1991).

Signs and symptoms of a cardiac or pulmonary contusion and/or a pneumothorax include:

1. The athlete will complain of severe pain in the chest area, sometimes radiating to the thoracic spine.

2. The athlete will typically experience breathing

Information at your fingertips

The World Wide Web—Learn more about pneumothorax at http://www.jbpub.com/ athletictraining and click on Chapter 13.

problems—either shortness of breath or painful breathing exhibited by short, shallow breaths.

First aid care for an athlete with a cardiac or pulmonary contusion and/or a pneumothorax includes:

1. Treat the athlete for possible shock.

2. Monitor vital signs continuously.

3. Arrange for transport to a medical facility.

More commonly, respiratory problems can lead to chest pain in the athlete (Steine, 1992). However, whenever a coach or athletic trainer has an athlete who reports chest pain that player should be seen immediately by the team physician. Chest pain and heart conditions in athletes must be reviewed by the proper medical personnel as soon as possible.

■ Liver
The liver aids in the production of plasma proteins and the detoxification of alcohol and other substances; it also has various digestive functions (Farish, 1993). It is located in the upper right quadrant of the abdomen and can be susceptible to trauma, especially if the athlete should have hepatitis and the organ is enlarged (Kulund, 1988). The liver may be implicated if a rib fracture occurs in the upper right abdominal quadrant. Otherwise, the liver is fairly safe from injury associated with sports participation. The liver is, however, susceptible to injury by the overuse of alcohol and drugs (especially massive amounts of steroids) as well as other internal insults.

■ Kidneys
The kidneys serve to maintain the proper levels of waste, gas, salt, water, and other chemicals in the bloodstream (Farish, 1993). The kidneys are located posteriorly and somewhat inferiorly on each side of the abdomen; they can be susceptible to injury from blunt trauma or heat (via extreme exercise in the heat of the day, for example). The body can experience acute renal failure, and the kidneys will cease to function

(Appenzeller, 1988; Kulund, 1988). If an athlete has **hematuria** (blood in the urine) after being hit by an opponent in the lower back or after having exercised strenuously in the heat, he should be seen by a physician. Both of these scenarios can lead to kidney problems or damage. Many times an athlete's exercise regimen must be modified until the urine is once again clear of any blood.

■ Spleen
The chief function of the spleen is to maintain a reserve of ready-to-use blood cells for the body (Farish, 1993). It is located in the upper left quadrant of the abdomen and is somewhat protected by the ribs on the lower left side. Like most of the other internal organs, the spleen is susceptible to injury from both blunt trauma and internal disorders. An athlete who gets hit quite hard in the abdomen over the spleen can suffer a lacerated spleen. Nevertheless, the spleen has the capacity to splint or patch itself at the site of the injury because of its reservoir of red blood cells. If the spleen does patch itself and the athlete is allowed to continue participating, there remains the possibility that the patch may be disrupted by even a small amount of trauma. This can allow internal bleeding to resume, and death can occur even as long as days afterwards (Kulund, 1988). If an athlete is hit hard in the upper left quadrant and later complains of pain in the abdomen and/or left shoulder and upper third of the left arm (sometimes the right shoulder), this is indicative of **Kehr's sign.** The athlete should be referred to a physician as soon as possible.

Additionally, if an athlete is suffering from mononucleosis the spleen is probably going to be enlarged and susceptible to injury—not only from blunt trauma but from excessive movement during sports participation. The athlete with mononucleosis needs to be restricted in activity until the physician can discern if the spleen has returned to normal size during the disease progression. Please refer to Chapter 19 for more information on mononucleosis.

■ Bladder

The bladder acts as a reservoir for the urine produced by the kidneys. It is located under the midline of the abdominal quadrants; this is a well-protected area, and the bladder is rarely injured by participation in sports and athletics. If the athlete receives a direct blow to the area of the bladder and injury does occur, the signs will be pain in the localized area and possibly blood in the urine. Avoiding injury to the bladder is best accomplished by emptying it before practice or competition.

Review Questions

1. *True or false:* Men and women have the same number of ribs.

2. Explain the difference between true ribs and floating ribs.

3. List the five main joints of the thorax.

4. With what necessary function do the intercostal muscles assist in the thorax?

5. *True or false:* Both lungs are the same size and configuration.

6. What is the name of the enclosed space where each lung is located?

7. *True or false:* The diaphragm separates the heart and lungs from the abdominal viscera.

8. Explain the difference between a pneumothorax and a hemothorax.

9. List the signs and symptoms of a costochondral separation.

10. What is the best indicator of kidney damage or disorder?

11. *True or false:* The spleen is able to splint itself if injured by blunt trauma.

12. Name the infection, prevalent among college-age students, that causes the spleen to enlarge, requiring the athlete to reduce physical activity until the spleen is once again normal.

13. What is a major cause of damage to the liver among collegiate athletes?

14. List four functions of the kidneys.

15. Explain the best way to prevent bladder injury among athletes.

References

Appenzeller O. 1988. *Sports Medicine* (3d ed.). Baltimore: Urban & Schwarzenberg.

Aubrey MJ, Cantu RC. 1989. Sudden death of a hockey player. *Phys Sportsmed.* 17(2):53–64.

Booher JM, Thibodeau GA. 1989. *Athletic Injury Assessment.* St. Louis: Times Mirror/Mosby.

Farish DJ. 1993. *Human Biology.* Boston: Jones and Bartlett.

Gray H. 1974. *Anatomy, Descriptive and Surgical.* Philadelphia: Running Press.

Karofsky PS. 1990. Death of a high-school hockey player. *Phys Sportsmed.* 18:99–103.

Kulund DN. 1988. *The Injured Athlete* (2d ed.). Philadelphia: J. B. Lippincott Company.

Moore KL. 1992. *Clinically Oriented Anatomy* (3d ed.). Baltimore: Williams and Wilkins.

Perkins RM, Sterling JC. 1991. Left lower chest pain in a collision athlete. *Phys Sportsmed.* 19(3):78–84.

Simoneauz SF, Murphy BJ, Tehranzadeh J. 1990. Spontaneous pneumothorax in a weight lifter. *Am J Sports Med.* 18(6):647–648.

Stedman TL, Hensyl WR (eds.). 1990. *Stedman's Medical Dictionary* (25th ed.). Baltimore: Williams and Wilkins.

Steine HA. 1992. Chest pain and shortness of breath in a collegiate basketball player: case report and literature review. *Med Sci Sports and Exerc.* 24:504–509.

Wagner RB, Sidhu GS, Radcliffe WB. 1992. Pulmonary contusion in contact sports. *Phys Sportsmed.* 20(2):126–136.

Widner PE. 1988. Thoracic injuries: mechanisms, characteristics, management. *Athletic Training.* 23:148–151.

Yates MT, Aldrete V. 1991. Blunt trauma causing aortic rupture. *Phys Sportsmed.* 19(11):96–107.

Injuries to the Hip and Pelvis

M A J O R   C O N C E P T S

This chapter includes a basic overview of the anatomy in the region of the hip and pelvis as well as a brief description of movements by the joints and actions of the musculature in the area. It discusses some of the more common hip and pelvis injuries incurred in sports and outlines emergency procedures. The chapter also includes a section about injuries to the area that are not common in sports. Coaches need to be aware of these types of injuries because of the possible negative long-term consequences that can result from improper care. The chapter reviews injuries to the male genitalia, including both testicular contusion and torsion. It also covers hernia and nerve problems and discusses proper referral.

Anatomy Review

The hip and pelvis form a square in the way they are constructed. This area comprises the two large, irregularly shaped pelvic bones on the lateral sides, the sacrum and coccyx posteriorly, and the articulation of the pubic bones anteriorly. The pelvic bones are also known as the innominate bones and are made up of three distinct parts: the ilium, the ischium, and the pubis. In the adult the three parts are fused and come together at a lateral point called the acetabulum, which is where the head of the femur articulates with the hip to form the hip joint (Figure 14.1).

The bony pelvis has several functions in the body: the lower extremities attach here, muscle attachments are prevalent, and it provides substantial protection for the entire pelvic region. In the female the pelvis becomes important in the birth process (Moore, 1992).

The major articulations of the bony pelvis include the hip joint, the sacroiliac joints, and the symphysis pubis. The hip joint is the articulation of the head of the femur and the acetabulum in the hip bone; it is a true ball-and-socket joint that is well supported by strong ligaments. The sacroiliac joints are formed by the sacral bones and the iliac portion of the hip bones. The symphysis pubis is formed by the two pubic bones meeting in the anterior portion of the bony pelvis. All of these joints have strong ligamentous support that assists in joint stability.

There are several nerves and blood vessels that course through the bony pelvis (Figures 14.2 and 14.3).

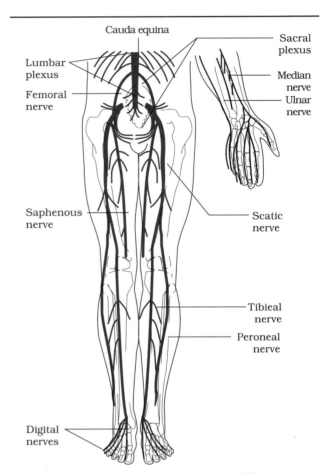

FIGURE 14.2   The nerves of the lower extremities.

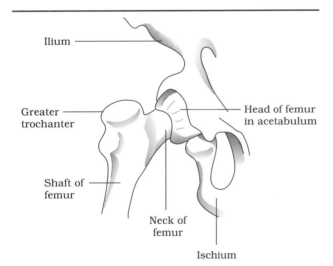

FIGURE 14.1   The ball-and-socket structure of the hip joint (anterior view).

Some of the more important nerves are made up from the cauda equina.

The spinal cord ends at the L-2 level, and the cauda equina exits the spinal cord beginning at L-2 and proceeding inferiorly (Gray, 1974). Nerves exiting the spinal cord below the L-I level typically pass through the bony pelvis. These nerves include the formation of the lumbar plexus, the sacral plexus, the coccygeal plexus, and other individual nerves. Probably the most well known of these is the sciatic nerve, which is the largest in the body and is made up of nerve roots L-4 through S-3. The sciatic nerve passes through the posterior portion of the bony pelvis and down the posterior aspect of the leg. The blood vessels of the area include both arteries and veins that supply the pelvis and lower extremities. The more well known of these vessels include the iliac artery and vein.

Many of the muscles that attach to the bony pelvis are ones that move the lower extremities. The smaller muscles consist of the medial and lateral rotators of

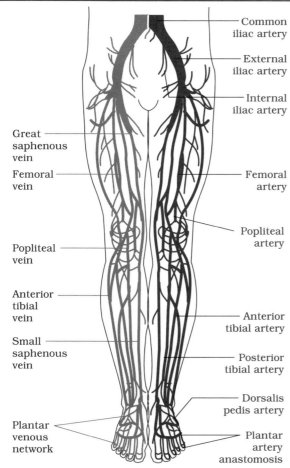

FIGURE 14.3 The blood vessels of the lower extremities.

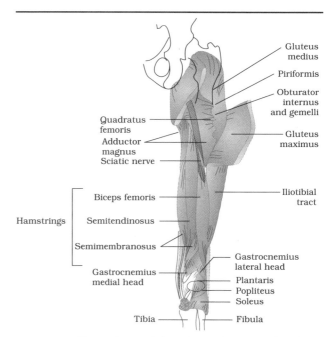

FIGURE 14.4 Hamstring and gluteal muscles (posterior view).

the femur. Some of the medial rotators include the tensor fasciae latae and gluteus minimus. These muscles are quite active in many movements of the lower extremity. The lateral rotators of the hip are small muscles located deep within the hip area that are also quite active in many movements of the lower extremity. Some of those more commonly injured include the piriformis, which attaches to the anterior surface of the sacrum and to the greater trochanter of the femur. The piriformis is a lateral rotator of the thigh; the sciatic nerve runs directly beneath the piriformis and can be irritated by the overuse of this muscle. Other external rotators of the thigh include the gemelli (superior and inferior), which attach on the ischium and run to the greater trochanter of the femur.

All of these muscles (Figure 14.4) are small in comparison with the surrounding muscles, but they do play an important part in the proper functioning of the hip and leg.

There are many muscles that attach on the pelvis

and provide musculature for the leg, back, and abdomen. The muscles responsible for many of the large movements at the hip joint include flexors, extensors, adductors, and abductors. The main hip flexors include the rectus femoris, the iliopsoas group, the tensor fasciae latae, and the sartorious (Figure 14.5). The rectus femoris attaches at the anterior inferior iliac spine and runs down the front of the leg to the common attachment of the quadriceps group at the patellar tendon. The iliopsoas group is a combination of the iliacus and the psoas muscles, which attach on the anterior lumbar spine and iliac crest and come together as they run down to the lesser trochanter of the femur. The tensor fasciae latae and sartorius attach on the anterior iliac spine. The tensor fasciae latae runs to the lateral condyle of the tibia, whereas the sartorius runs across the anterior thigh and attaches to the anterior medial aspect of the tibia. The sartorius becomes one of the muscles of the pes anserinus group.

The main muscles of hip extension are the gluteals and the hamstrings (Figure 14.4). The gluteus maximus is the main hip extensor of the gluteals. The gluteus maximus attaches on the posterior surface of the ilium and runs inferiorly to the femur. The hamstrings attach mainly on the ischial tuberosity; then two of the muscles, the semitendinosus and semimembranosus, run more medially on the posterior leg and attach near the sartorius and on the posterior/medial condyle of

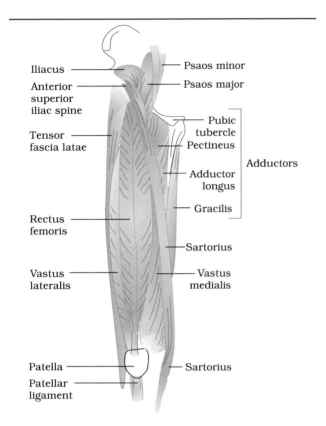

Iliacus
Anterior superior iliac spine
Tensor fascia latae
Rectus femoris
Vastus lateralis
Patella
Patellar ligament

Psaos minor
Psaos major
Pubic tubercle
Pectineus
Adductors
Adductor longus
Gracilis
Sartorius
Vastus medialis
Sartorius

FIGURE 14.5 Quadriceps muscles (anterior view).

the tibia, respectively. The biceps femoris runs more laterally on the posterior leg and attaches to the lateral aspect of the tibia and the head of the fibula.

The muscles that adduct the hip are located on the medial portion of the leg commonly called the groin area. The main muscles included in this group are the three adductors (brevis, longus, and magnus) as well as the pectineus and gracilis (Figure 14.5). The adductors attach on the pubis and run to the femur. The pectineus also attaches at the pubis and runs to the femur. The gracilis attaches on the inferior portion of the pubis and runs medially down the leg to the anterior medial portion of the tibia. The gracilis, sartorius, and

the semitendinosus comprise the pes anserinus group, to be discussed later.

Common Sports Injuries

The hip and pelvic regions are well designed anatomically: sports-related injuries to the skeletal structures of the hip and pelvis are not common. Injuries to the soft tissues in the region are more common and can be quite debilitating to the athlete. Sports-related injuries to this area commonly involve collision sports or forceful movements pursuant to an activity that requires power and speed of the lower extremities. However, one must remember that overuse injuries can also be associated with the hip and pelvis.

Skeletal Injuries

■ Fractures of the Pelvis
One of the most devastating injuries to the pelvic region is the fracture of one of the pelvic bones. Typically, a great deal of force is necessary to cause a fracture of this type. This is not a common injury related to sports participation. Still, it can occur in sports such as hockey, pole-vaulting, or football, in which there is the possibility of direct compression from another athlete, a fall from a height, or being twisted and hit by another player. Skeletal injuries to the pelvis in the adolescent population can be extremely serious, especially if the injury involves an open epiphysis. Any suspected skeletal injury to this area should be referred to a physician as quickly as possible.

Signs and symptoms of a fractured pelvis include:

1. Abnormal pain in the pelvic region after the injury.

2. There might be swelling at the site with the rare occurrence of a visual or palpable deformity at the injury.

Information at your fingertips

The World Wide Web—Check out this innovative site to learn more about the anatomy of the hip as well as hip arthritis and total hip replacement surgery. Go to http://www.jbpub.com/athletictraining and click on Chapter 14.

Athletic Trainers Speak Out

"A stress fracture is a serious injury for any athlete, both physically and mentally. Misdiagnosis and/or mismanagement of a stress fracture in the hip can become disastrous. Fortunately for athletes and trainers, this is not a common injury, but when it is suspected it must be properly diagnosed and treated. My first encounter with a hip stress fracture was several years ago and involved a female cross-country runner. This particular athlete waited to report her hip pain until it noticeably affected her workouts, fearing loss of her position on the team. After initial evaluation the athlete was referred to the team physician. She was diagnosed with a left hip fracture and was placed on non-weight-bearing activity for six weeks. During this period, her workouts on the stationary bike, in the pool, and in weight training were devised and monitored by the athletic training staff, in consultation with the team physician. Interestingly, she had better workout times after her release to full participation than she had prior to sustaining her injury. She had no further problems with the left hip. It is this kind of result that gives the athlete and coach confidence in the athletic trainer, so that injuries may be more quickly evaluated and treated."

—*Jayne E. Nelson, PA-C, A.T.C.*

Jayne E. Nelson

Jayne E. Nelson is the director of the student health care center at Boise State University.

3. Pain is elicited when the iliac crests are pressed together by the examiner.

4. Associated injuries to internal organs such as the bladder are possible and should be ruled out only by the proper medical personnel. Blood in the urine (hematuria) must be immediately reported.

First aid care for a fractured pelvis includes:

1. Treat for possible shock and internal bleeding.

2. Monitor the athlete's vital signs regularly.

3. Transport the athlete to the hospital on a long spine board with the foot of the board elevated to eliminate pooling of blood in the lower extremities.

A fracture of the pelvis is a serious injury and should be evaluated by a physician as soon as possible. Treatment will depend on the severity of the injury and should be complete before the athlete returns to practice or competition. Under no circumstances should an athlete with a suspected fracture of the pelvis return to competition before seeing a physician.

■ Hip Pointer

Probably the most common injury to the region is a contusion to the superior/anterior portion of the iliac crest, which is commonly referred to as a **hip pointer.** Typically, with this injury the athlete receives a direct blow to the area from an opponent's helmet or falls to the ground with great force. This can be an extremely painful and debilitating injury for the athlete, but it is not one that will require emergency attention or cause major complications if further activity is necessary.

Signs and symptoms of a hip pointer include:

1. Swelling at the site of injury.

2. Discoloration at the site of injury.

3. Pain and discomfort at the site of injury.

4. The athlete may walk with a slight limp on the affected side. Coughing, sneezing, and laughing may also produce pain at the site of injury.

First aid care for a hip pointer includes:

1. Immediately apply ice to the injured area.

2. Have the athlete rest and avoid activity that involves the lower extremities.

3. If the injury is severe, walking with crutches may be necessary for a few days.

Long-term care for this type of injury is rather simple. The contusion has in most cases caused minimal damage to an area where several muscles attach directly to bone tissue. The muscular attachments in the abdominal region are the cause of pain when the athlete coughs, sneezes, or laughs. The player will usu-

ally be able to participate on a limited basis within one to two weeks depending on the severity of the injury. It is important to note that if an athlete wishes to continue participating in sports while recovering from a hip pointer, the area should be padded well so that further damage will not occur if a similar incident happens before recovery is complete. This can be easily accomplished by securing a doughnut-shaped piece of foam padding over the area (Figure 14.6). Additionally, it is helpful to place hard plastic over the doughnut pad to provide even more protection to the area.

■ Osteitis Pubis

Another type of skeletal injury to this area is **osteitis pubis**—a condition resulting from continued stress and possibly some degeneration in the symphysis pubis joint. This injury is commonly a result of overuse and chronic strain on the joint. Long-distance runners, basketball players, and other athletes who experience repetitive pelvic movements in sports may complain of this condition.

Localized pain over the symphysis pubis as well as vague pain in the lower abdominal region and sometimes in the groin area unrelated to any specific injury are the most common symptoms associated with osteitis pubis (Pearson, 1988). An athlete complaining of symptoms should be referred to the appropriate doctor for complete evaluation. Because this is a chronic problem first aid is typically not necessary, but the athlete will benefit from rest, ice, and anti-inflammatory medications such as aspirin or ibuprofen. This disorder typically responds well to therapy with very few if any long-term side effects.

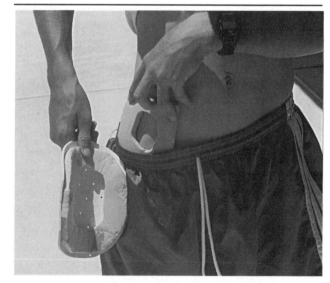

FIGURE 14.6 An athlete inserts a hip-pointer pad.

Infinitely more serious is a hip dislocation. This injury is actually quite rare in athletic events; however, it may occur to an athlete participating in contact sports. If a violent collision occurs between two players or between a player and another object—e.g., the boards surrounding a hockey rink—this type of injury can happen. Typically, when this injury occurs the hip joint is in flexion, and the force is applied through the femur. Most often the hip will dislocate posteriorly, and the athlete will experience extreme pain and loss of movement in the affected extremity.

Signs and symptoms of a dislocated hip include:

1. Abnormal pain at the site of injury.

2. Swelling at the site of injury with a palpable defect.

3. Knee of the involved extremity is angled toward the opposite leg.

4. This injury is typically quite visible to the observer.

First aid care for a dislocated hip includes:

1. Treat for possible shock.

2. Immobilize the athlete and transport to the nearest medical center.

3. Care should be given to monitor blood flow to the leg at all times.

■ Avulsion Fractures

There is always the possibility of muscle avulsions (in which a piece of bone is torn off with the tendon attached) during forceful activity. Again, these types of injuries are uncommon in sports but can occur in specific activities such as sprinting and tackle football.

Signs and symptoms of avulsion fractures in the pelvic region include:

1. Pain and swelling at the site of injury.

2. Inability to produce a specific movement that is usually accomplished easily.

3. Point tenderness over the affected area.

4. Movement of the muscle closer to its opposite attachment when contracted. This is not easily detected in many avulsion injuries.

5. The athlete may report having felt or heard a snap or pop at the time of injury.

First aid care of avulsion fractures includes:

1. Immediately apply ice and require the athlete to rest.

2. Limit motion as much as possible. Walking with crutches may be necessary.

WHAT IF?

You are coaching a high school sophomore in the high hurdles on a cool, rainy afternoon in early spring. As the young man completes a start and five consecutive high hurdles he grabs the back of his right leg, just below the buttock, and falls to the ground in obvious pain. You go to his aid immediately and upon examination you note that he is extremely tender in the region of the ischial tuberosity (origin of the hamstring muscles). He reports that he felt something tear and heard a pop while crossing the last hurdle, with immediate sharp pain. He has no history of a previous injury to this region. However, he has been complaining of tight hamstrings for the past several weeks. What type of injury may be present? What should be done for first aid? Should this athlete be referred to a physician?

Soft-Tissue Injuries

Because of the size and functions of the musculature in the hip and pelvic region, soft-tissue injuries are not very common in sports. The ligamentous support of the hip, sacrum, and other structures in the area is very strong; as a result, sprains rarely occur here. However, there are several muscles that attach in the area of the pelvis, including the musculature on both the anterior and posterior aspects of the thigh, and these are subject to avulsion.

3. Have the athlete evaluated by a physician as soon as possible to determine the extent of the injury if an avulsion fracture is suspected.

Avulsion fractures are debilitating and should be treated conservatively to reduce the amount of scar tissue that can result from these injuries. It is very wise to allow an athletic trainer or physical therapist to rehabilitate the athlete according to the recommendations of a physician. Without proper treatment and rehabilitation, this type of injury can be a problem in an athlete's future career.

■ Injuries to the Male Genitalia

An injury that is experienced by male athletes and is typically transient in nature is testicular contusion. Most male athletes competing in contact sports considered high-risk activities for testicular trauma wear a cup protector. However, this device does not always provide complete protection, nor do athletes always wear one. When the athlete receives a contusion to the testicular region there is extreme pain and usually a complete loss of mobility for a short period of time. Typically this pain and the resulting partial loss of movement are transitory; however, severe damage such as a ruptured testicle can be caused by extreme trauma to the testicles.

Signs and symptoms of testicular/scrotal contusions include:

1. Extreme pain and point tenderness.

2. Athlete may get into the fetal position and grasp his testicles.

3. The athlete will report a direct blow to the testicles.

First aid care for testicular/scrotal contusions includes:

1. Allow the athlete to rest on the sideline until he is ready to return to activity.

2. In severe cases, apply ice and allow the athlete to remain lying down in the locker room or athletic training facility when possible.

3. If there is swelling or lasting pain, refer the athlete to a physician as soon as possible.

The pain and debilitation associated with injuries to the testicles are transitory and should resolve without much intervention in a relatively short period of time (typically a few minutes). If the pain and debilitating effects last much longer than a few minutes, the athlete must see a physician to determine if severe damage has been sustained by the testicles at the time of injury.

Testicular torsion or twisting of the testicles can occur and should be recognized quickly; if this happens the athlete should be referred to a physician immediately. One of the testicles may, for any number of reasons, get twisted within the scrotum; as a result, the blood supply is compromised to or from the area, causing swelling to occur in the scrotum. The swelling may become quite uncomfortable, and the athlete needs to be transported to a medical facility as quickly as possible for treatment. Swelling in the scrotum can have serious side effects if not cared for immediately.

■ Hernias

A **hernia** is the protrusion of abdominal viscera through the abdominal wall; this typically occurs in the groin area. In males inguinal hernias are more common; femoral hernias are more prevalent among female athletes (McCarthy, 1990). Most hernias will be detected during a preparticipation physical evaluation. However, if an athlete is suffering from a hernia he will most likely have an abnormal protrusion in the groin area and experience pain in the groin and/or testicles. The athlete should seek proper medical advice promptly to discern how soon the hernia will have to be repaired.

■ Nerve Problems

A common complaint among many athletes is a burning or tingling sensation radiating from the hip and buttocks area and going down the back of the leg. These symptoms are often the result of irritation of the sciatic nerve. There may be any one of several reasons why this nerve becomes inflamed or painful. Typically, if an athlete continues to pursue the activity that has caused the irritation, then the pain will radiate farther down the leg to the foot and become more debilitating over time. The athlete must seek the advice of a physician and will need to rest and perform stretching and strengthening exercises depending on the cause of the problem.

Even though injuries to the hip and pelvis are relatively uncommon as a result of sports participation, it is important to realize that injuries to this area do occur and that they can be debilitating to the athlete. Always take into consideration the possibility of severe

Information at your fingertips

Want to learn more about hernias and their surgical correction? Go to http:// www.jbpub.com/athletictraining and click on Chapter 14.

injury when counseling an athlete about an injury to the hip and pelvis. First aid emergency care is important when treating these injuries. With most athletes rehabilitation is also important if participants are to continue the enjoyment of specific sports.

Review Questions

1. What type of joint is the hip joint?
2. Name the bones that make up the hip joint.
3. Explain the actions of the gluteal muscles.
4. Outline the location of the muscles that cause flexion, extension, adduction, and abduction of the hip.
5. List the bones in the hip area that are susceptible to fracture.
6. What structures are injured when an athlete suffers a hip pointer?
7. List the symptoms of osteitis pubis.
8. Explain the difference between testicular contusion and testicular torsion.
9. Define hernia and outline what a coach should do if one is suspected.
10. What should be done if an athlete is experiencing pain radiating down the back of the leg?

References

Gray H. 1974. *Anatomy, Descriptive and Surgical.* Philadelphia: Running Press.

McCarthy P. 1990. Hernias in athletes: what you need to know. *Phys Sportsmed.* 18(5):115–122.

Moore KL. 1992. *Clinically Oriented Anatomy* (3d ed.). Baltimore: Williams and Wilkins.

Pearson RL. 1988. Osteitis pubis in a basketball player. *Phys Sportsmed.* 16(7):69–71.

Injuries to the Thigh, Leg, and Knee

MAJOR CONCEPTS

There are numerous injuries to the thigh and knee occurring in a variety of sports to both male and female participants. Because this area is difficult to protect and is a major component of body contact with opponents, it can experience repeated trauma in contact and collision sports, thereby compounding earlier injuries. Knowledge about injuries to the thigh and knee is important for coaches dealing with young athletes.

This chapter begins with a brief anatomy overview that covers bones, ligaments, tendons, muscles, nerves, and blood vessels of the region; it goes on to describe the kinesiology of movements created by the muscles through the major joints.

The chapter continues with a description of soft-tissue injuries to the thigh that can become debilitating if not cared for properly, including contusions, strains, and various joint-related injuries. The knee joint, much like the foot and ankle, is required to provide both maximum stability and maximum mobility, thereby increasing the possibility of injury to this joint. The chapter covers problems such as osteochondritis dissecans, inflamed bursae, and patellar dislocation along with injuries caused by chronic exercise. The knee joint is a complex configuration of bones, ligaments, and muscle tendons, any of which may be injured during sports participation. The chapter describes the four major ligaments of the knee and injuries to those ligaments; it also discusses the menisci (cartilage) within the knee joint that can be injured during sports participation. The chapter concludes with a discussion of prophylactic and functional knee bracing.

Anatomy Review

The lower extremity is an area where many athletes experience some type of injury during their sports career. Injuries can occur to the thigh, knee, lower leg, ankle, or foot. The bones of this extremity include the femur, tibia, fibula, patella, and those of the foot (Gray, 1974). The femur or thigh bone is the longest, strongest, and heaviest bone in the body. It has a rounded, ball-like head that attaches to the hip bone with the help of a very strong network of ligaments. The head of the femur is attached to the shaft of the femur by a region known as the neck, which is highly susceptible to fractures. The femur becomes flatter and wider as it proceeds toward the knee, where it articulates with the tibia.

The thigh has a great deal of blood and nerve tissue going through it, both anteriorly and posteriorly. The anterior portion of the thigh contains the long saphenous vein and several branches of the femoral nerve. In the posterior section of the thigh there is the deep femoral artery and the major nerve to the leg, the sciatic nerve. Most of the blood vessels and nerves are quite well protected by the musculature of the thigh.

The muscles of the thigh can be broken down by three basic regions. First, the anterior muscles of the thigh, commonly called the **quadriceps** (Figure 15.1), have two functions. The vastus lateralis, vastus intermedius, vastus medialis, and rectus femoris work together to extend the leg at the knee joint. Three of these muscles (vastus medialis, intermedius, and lateralis) attach on the femur and run down the thigh to the quadriceps tendon. The rectus femoris is the main working muscle of this group: it helps the hip flexors to flex the thigh and assists in steadying the hip joint in this position. The rectus femoris attaches on the hip bone at the anterior inferior iliac spine and runs down the leg to the quadriceps tendon. The other muscle in the anterior portion of the thigh is the sartorius; it also attaches on the hip bone and runs somewhat diagonally down the thigh to the anterior medial portion of the tibial condyle. This muscle is responsible for flexing, abducting, and laterally rotating the thigh at the hip.

Next, the main muscles of the medial aspect of the thigh include the adductor longus, adductor brevis, adductor magnus, and the gracilis (Moore, 1992). These muscles attach on the pelvis and run to the femur; they are discussed in Chapter 14. The main function of these muscles is to adduct and help with flexion of the thigh. The third group of muscles in the thigh are in the posterior aspect of the thigh and are

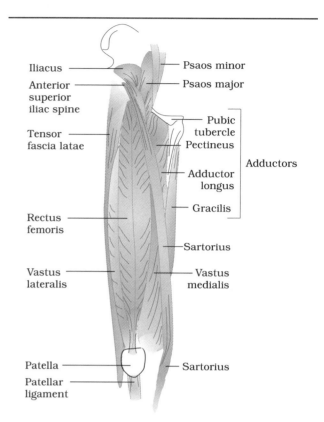

FIGURE 15.1 The quadriceps muscles of the anterior thigh serve two functions: they extend the leg at the knee joint and the rectus femoris portion of the quadriceps flexes the thigh at the hip.

commonly known as the **hamstrings.** These include the semitendinosus, semimembranosus, and biceps femoris (Moore, 1992). All these muscles attach on the pelvis and run down the leg to the tibia; they are discussed in Chapter 14. The main function of this group of muscles is to flex the leg at the knee.

The knee is a very complex joint: it can be damaged through any number of accidents occurring during sports participation. The femur and the tibia articulate with each other (tibiofemoral joint) here, and the patella and the femur also have an articulation (patellofemoral joint). The patella is a sesamoid bone, which means that it is totally enclosed within a tendon, in this case the quadriceps tendon. The patella does not articulate with the tibia. There are many ligaments supporting the knee joint; however, four major ligaments serve as the primary stabilizers of this joint. They include the tibial or medial collateral ligament, the fibular or lateral collateral ligament, the anterior cruciate ligament, and the posterior cruciate ligament (Figure 15.2).

The tibial collateral ligament (medial) extends from

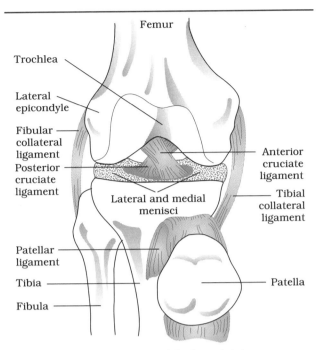

FIGURE 15.2 Major ligaments of the knee joint.

runs superiorly and anteriorly, passing the anterior cruciate ligament on the medial side and attaching to the internal aspect of the medial femoral condyle. The function of these two ligaments is primarily to reduce or prevent anterior and posterior displacement of the femur or the tibia.

Two semicircular fibrocartilaginous disks commonly called cartilage, and more specifically termed the **menisci,** are located within the space between the tibia and femur. The menisci assist with the lubrication and nourishment of the knee joint, aid in the distribution of weight and stress applied to the joint surfaces, and help with the biomechanics of the joint (Hertling and Kessler, 1990; Norkin and Levangie, 1992). Injuries to these disks, specifically the medial and lateral menisci, have caused the demise of many athletic careers.

Tendons of the muscles mentioned earlier in the description of the thigh run across the knee. Between the tendons and bone there are several bursae, which reduce the friction of muscle tendons rubbing over a prominent area of bone, thereby adding some padding for the exposed bony areas of the knee.

the medial epicondyle of the femur down to the medial condyle of the tibia. The fibular collateral ligament (lateral) begins at the lateral epicondyle of the femur and extends to the head of the fibula. The fibular collateral ligament is the stronger of the two. Both ligaments help limit motion and/or disruption of the knee joint when movement at the joint is in a side-to-side direction, which is medically termed **valgus** and **varus.**

The cruciate ligaments, unlike the collateral ligaments (which are located on the medial and lateral aspects of the knee joint proper), are situated on the inside of the joint. The anterior cruciate ligament attaches on the anterior portion of the intercondylar area of the tibia and runs superiorly and posteriorly to the internal aspect of the lateral femoral condyle. The posterior cruciate ligament attaches on the posterior aspect of the intercondylar area of the tibia and

Common Sports Injuries

Injuries to the thigh and knee can occur in almost any sport. In addition, this area can sustain injuries that are a result of overuse, trauma caused by an opponent, or trauma produced by the power and explosive movements required in some sports. The knee is an often-injured joint, and knee problems have caused a great many athletes to shorten their sports careers.

Because the knee is part of a complex mechanical system, which includes the foot, ankle, lower leg, hip, and pelvis, there are times when another part of this system causes problems that can eventually be exhibited in the knee. For this reason, it is wise to obtain competent medical advice when athletes are experiencing knee pain or chronic problems with the joint.

Information at your fingertips

The World Wide Web—To learn more about the anatomy of the knee, visit this site: http://www.jbpub.com/athletictraining and click on Chapter 15.

Skeletal Injuries

■ Femoral Fractures

The femur is the longest bone in the body and is therefore subject to being fractured; however, this requires a great deal of force and is not a common occurrence in sports. If a fracture does occur to the shaft of the femur as a result of sports participation, the injury will be quite obvious: the athlete will be in a great deal of pain, and ambulation will be difficult with the affected leg. The athlete should not attempt to ambulate on a femoral fracture. In such instances the athlete must be transported to the nearest medical facility with the leg splinted and without bearing any weight on the affected limb.

The neck of the femur can also be fractured. This occurs more often in sports than a fracture of the shaft, although neither happens frequently. Older children and teenagers are at risk for this injury as the fracture can occur through a growth plate. Among younger athletes these fractures can be the result of direct trauma or overuse. If direct trauma is the cause the athlete will typically have a foot planted and then get hit in the hip or upper thigh with a great deal of force. When this injury does occur it needs to be evaluated by a physician as soon as possible. One complication of a fracture in the neck of the femur is **avascular necrosis** of the femoral head; this is caused by a decrease in the blood supply to the femoral head, which can result in tissue death.

Signs and symptoms of a fracture of the femur include:

1. Pain at the site of injury.
2. Difficulty ambulating on the affected leg.
3. Swelling and/or deformity may occur.
4. Athlete may report a traumatic event as the cause.
5. The athlete may report having heard or felt a severe pop or snap at the time of injury.

First aid care for a fracture of the femur includes:

1. Be prepared to treat the athlete for shock if necessary.
2. Splint the injured leg, preferably with a traction splint.
3. Apply sterile dressings to any related open wounds.
4. Monitor vital signs and circulation to the lower leg.
5. Arrange for transport to the nearest medical facility.

■ Patellar Fractures

Other skeletal problems that may arise include a fracture of the patella and dislocation of the knee or tibiofemoral joint. Although the patella can be fractured, this is not a common occurrence in sports participation. In most cases a patellar fracture is caused by violent trauma, and the athlete will be incapacitated for a short period of time following the trauma. There will be a great deal of pain associated with this injury, and the athlete will need to see a physician as soon as possible.

■ Dislocation of Tibiofemoral Joint

Dislocation of the knee or **tibiofemoral joint** is possible and can compromise the blood flow to the lower leg in some instances. If there is a dislocation of the tibiofemoral joint this will be outwardly apparent, and the athlete will experience marked pain. This injury must be splinted, and the athlete must be referred to the nearest medical facility without delay. Circulation and innervation to the knee and lower leg must not be compromised for even a brief period of time.

Soft-Tissue Injuries to the Thigh

Most of the soft-tissue injuries to the thigh are either the result of contact with an opponent or explosive

WHAT IF?

You are coaching a junior high school basketball game. During the first half your starting point guard drives in for a lay up, colliding with an opponent. The point of contact was her left thigh, which was struck severely by her opponent's knee. Upon further examination you note tightness and swelling in the quadriceps muscles and an unwillingness by the athlete to put weight on her leg. Based on this history and the signs and symptoms, what would you conclude? What would be the appropriate first aid in this situation?

Athletic Trainers Speak Out

"The athletic trainer [and coach] can provide valuable assistance in the proper management of an acute sports injury by stabilizing the injury, providing support to the injured person, and preventing further trauma, either self-inflicted or by outside influences."

—*Dennis Sealey, A.T.C.*

Dennis Sealey has been the head athletic trainer at the University of Washington in Seattle for 13 years.

Dennis Sealey

movement by the athlete causing a self-inflicted muscle strain. Many sports, such as football and hockey, use some type of protective padding to prevent contact with an opponent to the thigh region. However, complete prevention is not always possible, and injuries do occur.

■ Myositis Ossificans

When an athlete receives a blow to the quadriceps muscle group from an opponent's knee, hip, or other anatomical part and there is a contusion to the musculature, bleeding and damage often occur. Depending on the force of impact and the muscles involved, the contusion may be of varying degrees of severity. In any case, the athlete must be counseled about the care of this injury and the long-term complications of improper care of a muscular contusion, which can include a condition called **myositis ossificans.** The initial muscular contusion causes bleeding; if not cared for properly, or if further insult occurs, there will be an increase in the amount of blood lost in the same area. Over a long period of time continued bleeding and insult to the area can result in calcification within the muscle, abnormal bone growth, and further disability (Finerman and Shapiro, 1990).

Signs and symptoms of a muscular contusion include:

1. The athlete will report a forceful impact to the area.

2. Muscular tightness and swelling may be present.

3. Decreased ability to forcefully contract the muscle.

4. Difficulties in ambulating with the affected leg.

First aid care for a muscular contusion includes:

1. Apply ice and compression immediately.

2. If the injury is severe place the athlete on crutches.

3. Have the athlete rest and avoid any contact with the area.

With this type of injury the athlete must be allowed plenty of rest and time to permit natural bodily processes to remove blood from the area so that healing will be complete. As further direct contact to the area may increase the risk of myositis ossificans, the area should be padded if the athlete continues to participate. Moreover, the player should be well aware of the long-term consequences of continued trauma to the area and should initiate treatment quickly if additional insult occurs.

ties requiring multiple changes in speed and/or direction. It is not uncommon for a track, soccer, football, or volleyball athlete to complain of tight, sore, or strained muscles in the groin region. The groin muscles are critical movers in speed and change of direction movements and are not easy to warm up and stretch. Special attention must be given to these muscles by the individual athletes as they are preparing for practice or competition.

These groin injuries can be debilitating if not cared for properly and quickly. Typically, when a strain to one or more of the groin muscles occurs the athlete will feel a sharp pain in the medial side of the thigh,

WHAT IF?

You're at a track meet, watching your best high school hurdler compete in the low hurdles final. As the runners approach the halfway mark your runner clears the hurdle and suddenly falls to the ground, grabbing the back of his right thigh. Upon further examination the athlete reports that he felt something pop in the back of his thigh and you note a visible defect there. Based on this history, what is the most likely injury? What would be the appropriate first aid?

■ Muscular Strains to the Thigh

Almost any of the muscles in the thigh region are susceptible to strains. Most of the strains to athletes, however, are to the hamstrings and adductor muscles. Strains to the adductor muscles are commonly known as groin pulls. Most strains occur to the muscle itself and not the tendon. Such strains are usually the result of muscles being stretched too far, which is the case with the adductor muscles. However, strains can be the result of miscommunication between **agonistic muscles** and **antagonistic muscles,** which is the case with many muscle strains involving the hamstrings.

If the muscle is stretched too far the fibers of the muscle are damaged and bleeding occurs; the result is loss of contractibility, stiffness, and impaired movement. In the case of the previously mentioned miscommunication between agonistic and antagonistic muscles, the quadriceps musculature is contracting while the hamstrings are also contracting, causing the weaker muscle to be torn and damaged. Typically, the hamstrings are the weaker of the two groups; therefore, this is the musculature that is usually strained, with subsequent bleeding and hematoma formation.

There are many athletes who experience chronic tightness and repetitive strains to the muscles of the thigh adductor (groin) region. Specifically, the adductor brevis, longus, and magnus muscles can exhibit problems, especially in athletes participating in activi-

possibly associated with a "tearing" feeling. Not long after this incident the athlete will complain of soreness, stiffness, and a lack of movement in the area. At times, even with continued use in even the most restricted situation, the muscle or muscles will take a long time to heal completely. This is because the muscles affected are being used unconsciously for many daily activities, movements of which cause small microtraumas that do not allow the damaged muscle to heal. To this end, constant attention must be paid to this injury until a complete recovery is made.

During and after recovery, athletes will need to implement a stretching program that specifically targets the adductor muscles. Stretching must be an integral part of the recovery from this and any other muscle strain injury because of the need to reduce scarring of the affected muscles.

Signs and symptoms of muscle strains to the thigh include:

1. A sharp pain in the affected muscle.

2. Swelling and inflammation in the immediate area.

3. Weakness and inability of the muscle to contract forcefully.

4. After a few days there may be discoloration of the area.

5. In severe cases, a visible defect is noted in the muscle.

First aid care for muscle strains to the thigh includes:

1. Apply ice and compression immediately.
2. Have the athlete rest and use crutches if necessary.
3. Have the athlete evaluated by a member of the medical team.

Proper care for any injury to the thigh is important. Because a strain to the hamstrings or groin muscles is not considered serious, sometimes these injuries are not cared for properly. The result can be a shortened career for the athlete.

Patellofemoral Joint Injuries

There are several injuries to the **patellofemoral joint,** both chronic and acute, that can become debilitating. Intervention is required if the athlete is to return to participation at peak level. Some of the problems causing injury are the result of faulty mechanics or growth in adolescents and are not due to anything that could be prevented initially. Many of the injuries to the patellofemoral joint, however, can be helped via intervention by the athletic trainer or physician, and the athlete can be participating at peak level in a very short time.

BOX 15.1   Case Study of a Ruptured Rectus Femoris Muscle

There is always a chance that a muscle injury can be more severe than first suspected. This soccer player thought he had severely contused and strained his quadriceps muscle group during a soccer match when an opponent stepped on his thigh. There was abnormal swelling and a great deal of pain associated with the initial injury. Standard first aid procedures included ice, compression, and rest until the athlete regained movement. A week later the athlete attempted to play again on a wet field; at one point, when he planted his leg to start running he felt something tear. At that point he decided to take some time off to let the injury heal. Months later, when the athlete was still having problems with pain and a lack of contractile ability, it was discovered that the injury to the quadriceps muscle was much more severe than the initial evaluation. In this case study, the rectus femoris muscle had torn from its attachment at the patellar tendon and not been repaired in time to salvage the muscle attachment. As can be viewed in Figure 15.3, the muscle belly of the rectus femoris muscle draws up the leg when the athlete forcefully extends the lower leg. The athlete now must deal with a weak quadriceps mechanism and a strange feeling in his thigh each time he contracts his quadriceps muscles in that leg. This injury has eliminated his participation in collegiate soccer.

■ Osteochondritis Dissecans

The condition **osteochondritis dissecans** has also been called joint mice because small pieces of bone that have been dislodged or chipped from the joint are floating within the joint capsule. Damage to the joint surfaces caused by this osteochondral fragment can be a serious problem. When the joint surfaces are damaged and no longer make smooth contact with each other, further pain and joint damage are almost always inevitable. The piece of bone does not always have to be freely floating within the joint space: it just may be dislodged yet still attached to the original bone and causing painful movement. If in fact the piece of bone is freely floating within the joint space, it can cause a blocking or locking action that limits the movement at the knee joint. The reason for this is not fully understood, although most experts believe it is a direct result of either internal or external trauma. When this occurs in juvenile athletes, the majority heal without surgical intervention (Garrett, 1991). However, if the following signs and symptoms are present the athlete should visit a physician to determine the best course of treatment.

Signs and symptoms of osteochondritis dissecans include:

1. Chronic knee pain with exertion that is generalized, not specific.
2. There may be chronic swelling present.
3. The knee may lock if there is a loose body within the joint.
4. The quadriceps group may atrophy.
5. One or both femoral condyles may be tender to palpation when the knee is flexed.

First aid care for osteochondritis dissecans includes:

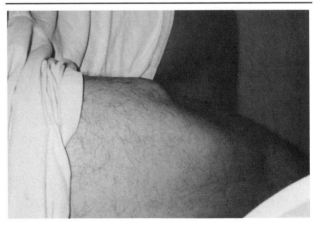

FIGURE 15.3 A soccer player with a ruptured rectus femoris muscle.

1. Apply ice and compression.

2. If the athlete has difficulty walking or the knee is locking, have the player use crutches.

3. Have the athlete see a physician for proper treatment.

■ Inflamed Bursae

A **bursa** is a small fluid-filled sac located at strategic points throughout the body that assists in the prevention of friction between bony surfaces, tendons, muscles, or skin that pass over it. There are several bursae in the knee joint; however, only a few are commonly irritated (Figure 15.4). A bursa can become inflamed due to trauma or infection. The inflammation can also be the result of chronic overuse and irritation of the bursa. In the case of trauma, a football player may hit a knee quite hard on another player's helmet or on the playing surface, thereby causing the prepatellar bursa to become swollen and enlarged (Figure 15.5). The prepatellar bursa is located just between the skin and the patella and is susceptible to direct trauma.

Most of the other bursae located within the knee are susceptible to chronic injury. The constant use of the legs and knees in some exercises creates too much friction in the area, and the bursae respond by becoming inflamed. It is also possible for these bursae to become inflamed from direct trauma, although this is not as common.

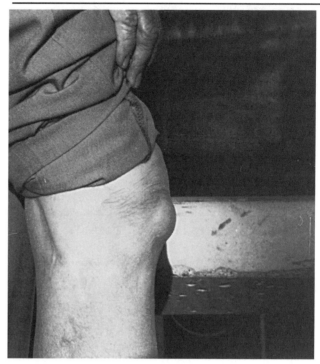

FIGURE 15.5 Prepatellar bursitis.

Signs and symptoms of an inflamed bursa include:

1. Swelling and tenderness at the site.

2. Increased pressure externally typically causes pain.

3. The athlete may report direct trauma or a chronic buildup of swelling.

First aid care for an inflamed bursa includes:

1. Application of ice and compression.

2. Reduction of activity for a short period of time.

3. In chronic cases anti-inflammatory agents may be helpful.

■ Patellar Dislocation/Subluxation

When an athlete makes a quick, cutting motion to one side or another, a great deal of abnormal force is generated within the knee. As a result of this sudden abnormal force, the patella can move laterally instead of superiorly and inferiorly as it normally does. If the patella moves too far laterally it can become dislocated. Whether the patella remains dislocated, or returns to its normal position spontaneously, tends to be related to the number of times this type of incident has occurred in the past. In many cases, if the athlete is a chronic subluxor the patella will reduce (i.e., return to a normal position) without intervention. If it is the

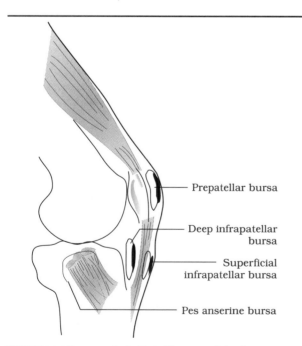

FIGURE 15.4 Commonly irritated bursae of the knee.

Prepatellar bursa

Deep infrapatellar bursa

Superficial infrapatellar bursa

Pes anserine bursa

first time the patella has dislocated it may or may not reduce itself. In most instances of patellar dislocation, the athlete will know that the patella has moved out of the normal position and will be somewhat disabled.

Signs and symptoms of a dislocation/subluxation of the patella include:

1. Athlete will report a great deal of pain and an abnormal movement of the patella when the injury occurred.

2. There will be associated swelling.

3. The knee and patella will be extremely tender, especially the lateral aspect.

First aid care for a dislocation/subluxation of the patella includes:

1. Apply ice immediately.

2. Compression and elevation will also be helpful.

3. Splint the entire leg.

4. Arrange for transport to the nearest medical facility.

When a patellar dislocation occurs, the patella will most often move laterally. In addition, when an athlete

ments of the patellar tendon to the tibial tuberosity.

Osgood-Schlatter's disease is technically defined as an epiphyseal inflammation of the tibial tubercle (Stedman and Hensyl, 1990). For this to occur there must be a growth plate at the site of the tibial tubercle; consequently, this condition is unique to children and adolescents. Constant jumping creates a pull on the patellar tendon and its attachment at the tibial tuberosity. During the growth phase there is an epiphyseal plate that is being pulled on simultaneously by the attachment of the patellar tendon at the tibia. This irritation causes inflammation and swelling to occur just below the patella.

Jumper's knee is also an irritation of the patellar tendon complex between its attachments on the tibia and the patella. This problem is common to the athlete who must jump a great deal as part of sports participation. Typically, the athlete will experience pain at one of three sites within this complex. The pain may be localized over the superior or inferior pole of the patella or at the tibial tuberosity (David, 1989). Regardless of the exact location of this condition, the athlete complains greatly of pain associated with jumping.

WHAT IF?

You are teaching a junior high school weight training class. One of the young boys in your class comes to you complaining of a chronic aching he has had for several days in the anterior knee, inferior to the patella, at the insertion of the patellar tendon. The boy reports the pain is worse in the mornings, especially when walking up and down stairs. Based on this history, what is the likely cause of this pain? What would you recommend for this child?

experiences a patellar dislocation there most likely will be accompanying soft-tissue damage to the medial aspect of the knee. If not cared for properly, this injury can become a chronic problem.

■ Osgood-Schlatter's Disease and Jumper's Knee

The attachment of the patellar tendon at the tibial tubercle can be the site of two similar problems associated with athletes who do a great deal of jumping, although this is not a prerequisite to experiencing either Osgood-Schlatter's disease or jumper's knee. The main difference in these two conditions is the exact location of the injury. Osgood-Schlatter's disease is typically a problem at the junction of the patellar tendon and the tibial tuberosity, whereas jumper's knee can exhibit itself at multiple sites within the attach-

Sign and symptoms of Osgood-Schlatter's disease or jumper's knee include:

1. Pain and tenderness about the patellar tendon complex.

2. Swelling in the associated area. In the case of Osgood-Schlatter's disease, this swelling may be more localized to the tibial tuberosity.

3. Decreased ability to use the quadriceps for running or jumping.

4. In the case of Osgood-Schlatter's disease, if the inflammation continues the area over the tibial tuberosity may become more solid when palpated.

5. Symptoms seem to be exacerbated by activity.

First aid care for Osgood-Schlatter's disease or jumper's knee includes:

1. Apply ice and compression to the area.

2. Have the athlete see a physician as soon as possible.

3. Rest is important until the inflammation subsides.

Patellofemoral Conditions

At times athletes will complain of nonspecific pain behind the patella. Sometimes this pain is due to an increased Q angle, or it can be caused by any one of a number of other problems.

As can be seen in Figure 15.6, the **Q angle** is the difference between a straight line drawn from the anterior superior iliac spine and the center of the patella compared with one drawn from the center of the patella through the center of the tibia. The larger this angle, the greater the chance of the patella being pulled too far laterally during extension of the knee; consequently, the patella rubs on the condyle of the femur causing pain and irritation. It is generally accepted that this angle is larger in females because of the width

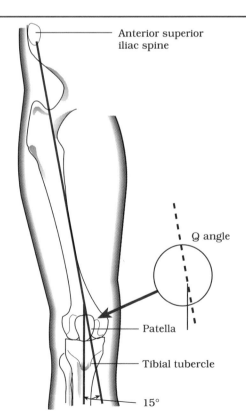

FIGURE 15.6 Measuring the Q angle at the knee.

- Anterior superior iliac spine
- Q angle
- Patella
- Tibial tubercle
- 15°

of the pelvis (Gould, 1990; Magee, 1992). Most authorities report that a Q angle of 15 to 20 degrees is acceptable. However, this is highly individual as there are often associated problems with patellar tracking, such as weak musculature or an abnormal patellofemoral skeletal configuration.

If there is abnormal patellofemoral configuration due to some skeletal, muscular, or mechanical dysfunction, this too can create retropatellar (behind the patella) pain of an **idiopathic** nature. This typically occurs in athletes such as runners or gymnasts who perform a great deal of repetitive movements in their sports activities. If this problem is allowed to continue, the possibility of chondromalacia exists. **Chondromalacia** is a softening and wearing out of the posterior cartilage surface of the patella. This is detrimental to the athlete's ability to perform in the future as there is associated pain and tenderness with this disorder that creates difficulty in movement.

In the case of retropatellar pain and discomfort the athlete will complain of chronic pain and disability. There is not any immediate first aid care to be administered; however, the athlete may gain some comfort from rest, ice, compression, elevation, and the use of nonsteroidal anti-inflammatories. If the athlete has an abnormally large Q angle, muscular imbalances, or other predisposing conditions, he or she should seek the advice of a physician to assist in the care of retropatellar pain disorder.

Menisci Injuries

As mentioned earlier, the menisci have partial attachments to other structures about the knee joint such as the cruciate ligaments, the tibial tubercles, and other structures; this creates problems when either the menisci or various other structures are damaged. If a violent force injures the medial collateral ligament there is also the possibility of damage to the medial meniscus because of a partial attachment between the two structures.

More commonly, a meniscus is damaged by being torn as a result of quick, sharp, cutting movements that occur when the foot is stabilized and does not turn while the body does. This movement and others that cause excessive stress in abnormal planes will tear the meniscus at different points. A torn meniscus can affect the athlete in a variety of ways. Some athletes will be able to function normally; others will not be able to completely extend the leg at the knee joint because of a tear in the meniscus that causes a blocking or locking effect.

Signs and symptoms of a suspected torn meniscus include:

1. The athlete reports that a pop or snap was heard when the knee twisted.
2. The athlete may not have any swelling, depending on the structures involved in the injury.
3. The athlete may not complain of any pain.
4. Depending on the severity of the injury, there may be a loss of range of motion and/or movement with a blocking or locking effect.
5. The athlete may be able to continue participation with the injury.
6. The athlete may report a feeling of the knee "giving out" at times.

First aid care for a suspected torn meniscus includes:

1. Apply ice and compression.
2. If the athlete has a blocked or locked knee, crutches should be used to aid in walking.
3. Encourage the athlete to see a physician as soon as possible.

Meniscus injuries do not necessarily have to end an athlete's playing season or career. New methods of surgery enable many athletes to return to participation relatively quickly. However, athletes should not be encouraged to finish the season with a suspected meniscus injury without first seeking the advice of a physician.

Knee Ligament Injuries

Several ligaments can be damaged through trauma; however, only four of the main ligaments will be discussed here. The four that are most commonly injured are the medial (tibial) collateral ligament, the lateral (fibular) collateral ligament, and the anterior and posterior cruciate ligaments. These ligaments are important stabilizers of the knee joint and are subject to many stresses, both internal and external. These ligaments, like any others in the body, can be traumatized and suffer first-, second-, or third-degree sprains. Refer to Chapter 1 for a review of ligament sprains.

The mechanisms by which ligaments can be injured include a broad range of maneuvers—from the athlete making a quick, sharp, cutting step and twisting the knee excessively to having an opposing lineman hit the knee from one side. Athletes also may be kicked in the tibia or attempt to stop an opponent and have the tibia driven forcefully anteriorly or posteriorly, all of which can damage one, or more, of the major sup-

porting knee ligaments. It is important to remember that the knee can be injured by all types of forces, both internal and external, even when it does not seem that the athlete is in danger during the activity.

■ Collateral Ligament Injuries

One of the more common injuries to knee ligaments in athletics is a sprain to the medial collateral ligament. This occurs when an opponent is blocked or hits the athlete's leg and knee from the outside. The opponent lands forcefully on the lateral side of the knee resulting in the joint being pushed medially (valgus stress); this creates excessive stress on the medial collateral ligament beyond what it can withstand (Figure 15.7).

If just the opposite mechanism occurs—and an opponent lands on the inside of a player's knee and pushes the joint laterally (varus stress)—then the lateral collateral ligament is stressed beyond the normal level and sprained.

Both of these ligament injuries render the knee unstable in side-to-side movements. Because the knee is a hinge joint and little sideways movement occurs there, this would seem to create very few problems for the athlete. However, the collateral ligaments are important in helping the knee with overall stability, and injury to either of these structures causes instability in the knee (Norkin and Levangie, 1992). The more severe the injury, the more unstable the knee.

FIGURE 15.7 Excessive stress on the medial collateral ligament.

■ Cruciate Ligament Injuries

The anterior cruciate ligament can be injured by having the tibia moved forcefully in an anterior direction. This can occur when an athlete is making a very quick cutting motion on a hard surface, when the athlete gets hit from behind in the lower leg, or when the femur gets pushed backwards while the tibia is held in place as happens in contact sports. If the opposite occurs—and the tibia is forced posteriorly—the posterior cruciate ligament can be disrupted and injured. The main function of these two ligaments is to stabilize the knee in anterior and/or posterior directions. In addition, quick rotational forces can injure the anterior cruciate ligament. A rotational injury can result from a noncontact mechanism. For example, a football player may make a very quick change in direction on a hard surface, and the upper body may go off balance, causing the knee to accept abnormal forces. If the circumstances are such that the soft-tissue structures within the knee cannot withstand the extra forces, these structures are damaged. The cruciate ligaments work in conjunction with the collateral ligaments to create a stable knee; anytime one or more of these ligaments is injured the knee becomes unstable.

Signs and symptoms of an injury to knee ligaments include:

1. Athlete will report that the knee was forced beyond normal range.

2. Athlete will complain of pain at the site of injury.

3. Swelling may occur in and around the knee.

4. Athlete may complain of an unstable feeling in the knee.

5. The athlete may report having felt a pop or tear or having heard a snapping sound.

First aid care for an injury to knee ligaments includes:

1. Apply ice and compression immediately.

2. If the knee is unstable have the athlete walk with crutches.

3. Have the athlete seek proper medical advice.

At times an athlete will receive a blow from the lateral side that will injure the medial collateral and anterior cruciate ligaments along with the medial meniscus. This has sometimes been called the terrible-triad injury. Obviously, injuring all of these structures creates a very unstable knee. Anytime an athlete has a suspected injury to knee ligaments caution must be exercised, and care by the proper medical personnel is critical.

▌Knee Bracing

One of the biggest controversies in sports medicine literature and in many athletic departments across the country is the use of prophylactic knee bracing with athletes. A prophylactic knee brace has two attachments: one above the knee and one below the knee with either unilateral or bilateral braces running in between (Figure 15.8). The braces can be constructed of either metal or plastic and are typically lightweight. The bracing is meant to augment the stabilizing effect on each side of the knee joint (Figure 15.9 a,b).

One has only to look in almost any sports medicine journal to find a recent study analyzing the effects of prophylactic knee bracing. Reports of both epidemiological and biomechanical studies are being published regularly. Many of the epidemiological studies have been criticized for lacking proper methods of study design. The biomechanical studies are criticized for not incorporating proper mechanisms and forces to study the effects of prophylactic braces.

Brodersen and Symanowski (1993) reviewed the

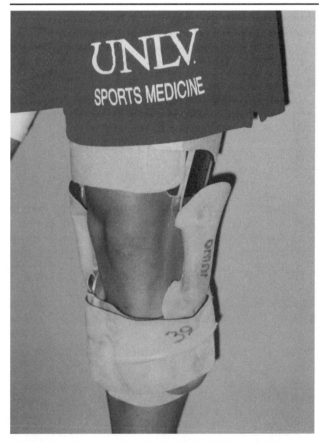

FIGURE 15.8 An example of a prophylactic knee brace.

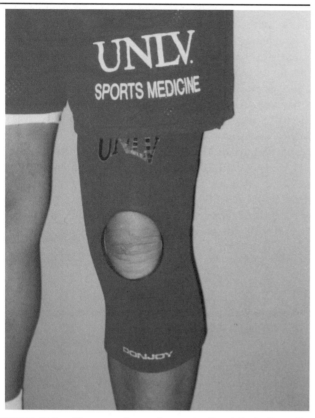

FIGURE 15.9a Neoprene knee sleeve used mainly to keep the joint warm during exercise.

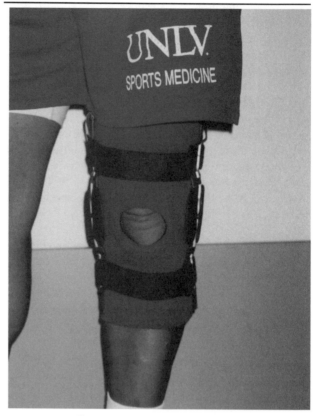

FIGURE 15.9b Some sleeves are reinforced with bracing to assist stabilization.

knee injuries experienced by football players at Iowa State University who used bilateral prophylactic knee braces between 1979 and 1987. They reported that not only did more players without braces receive more injuries but that the athletes injured without braces also stayed out for a longer period of time. In essence, knee injuries were decreased by using knee braces; if an injury did occur, this study reported it was less severe if prophylactic braces were worn.

In a comprehensive review of the epidemiological studies completed since 1978, Schootman and van Mechelen (1993) discovered many discrepancies in the research published. There were studies claiming fewer injuries among athletes who wore prophylactic knee braces, studies that could not discern any differences, and studies that reported more injuries in athletes who wore prophylactic braces.

There has also been a great deal of research on the biomechanical effects of knee braces in the recent literature. In a published study by Paulos, Cawley, and France (1991), it was reported that prophylactic lateral bracing does have some effect on the stability of knee

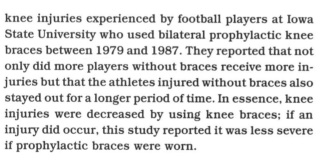

WHAT IF?

You are coaching a high school basketball game. It is late in the game; your team is on the defense, with their opponents' guard driving to the basket. Suddenly your post player, who was attempting to block the opponent's jump shot, falls to the floor, while simultaneously grabbing her left knee. Upon further examination she states that when she landed from jumping up to block the shot, her knee twisted and she felt something snap inside. You note that she also states that her knee feels very unstable. Given this information what would you conclude? What would be the appropriate first aid for this injury?

ligaments—specifically on the anterior cruciate ligament, with some benefit to the medial collateral ligament when the force is directly lateral. (The authors also recommend further clinical study to confirm their findings.) Conversely, a study by Salvaterra and colleagues (1993) points out that prophylactic braces do not stabilize the knee from a static force. Additionally, there have been reviews of the biomechanical research on prophylactic knee bracing that point out the confusion in the research published (Johnston and Paulos, 1991). There tends to be some reliability in the research indicating that at low loads applied in a directly lateral direction the prophylactic knee brace may be helpful. However, brace slippage on the leg, higher forces produced in actual field participation, the direction of forces applied in competition, and psychological effects of prophylactic braces all need to be studied further before any strong conclusions or recommendations can be made.

The benefits of functional braces (i.e., ones specially constructed to assist an athlete with an injured knee) can be as confusing as those of prophylactic braces. There is not a great deal of persuasive evidence that functional knee braces are effective in providing stability to the knee joint (Cawley, France, and Paulos, 1991). Other researchers recommend that the functional brace be part of a comprehensive rehabilitation program for an athlete who has sustained damage to the anterior cruciate ligament (Vailas and Pink, 1993). However, the athlete may be required by a physician to wear the knee brace; therefore, the coach or athletic trainer will not be responsible for deciding whether the athlete is to wear a knee brace.

Review Questions

1. List the bones that comprise the knee joint.
2. Give the common name for the muscles located on the anterior portion of the thigh.
3. Give the common name for the muscles of the posterior thigh region.
4. Give the common name for the muscles located on the medial aspect of the thigh.
5. Where do the quadriceps attach on the lower leg?
6. Define a sesamoid bone using the patella as an example.
7. Explain the articulation of the knee joint, including the involvement of the patella.
8. List and explain the attachments of the four main ligaments of the knee.
9. *True or false:* There are two menicsi located within the knee joint.
10. Explain the first aid care for a severe contusion of the thigh.
11. Explain which muscles of the thigh can experience strains through athletic participation.

12. *True or false:* If the patella dislocates it will not return to its proper position without surgical intervention.
13. Define joint mice.
14. What age group is most susceptible to Osgood-Schlatter's disease?
15. Describe how to care for an athlete with jumper's knee.
16. What population is more susceptible to Q-angle alignment problems?
17. *True or false:* An athlete with a torn meniscus will *always* have a great deal of swelling in the knee joint itself after the injury.
18. Explain the mechanism by which the medial and lateral collateral ligaments are damaged.
19. Define and list the structures damaged if an athlete experiences a terrible-triad injury.
20. Explain why an athlete should or should not choose to use a prophylactic knee brace.

References

Brodersen MP, Symanowski JT. 1993. Use of double upright knee orthosis prophylactically to decrease severity of knee injuries in football players. *Clin J Sports Med.* 3(1):31–35.

Cawley PW, France EP, Paulos LE. 1991. The current state of functional knee bracing. *Am J Sports Med.* 19(3):226–233.

David JM. 1989. Jumper's knee. *J Orthop Sports Phys Ther.* 11(4):137–141.

Finerman GAM, Shapiro MS. 1990. Sports-induced soft-tissue calcification. In Leadbetter WB, Buckwalter JA, Gordon SL (eds.). *Sports-induced Inflammation.* Park Ridge, Ill.: American Academy of Orthopaedic Surgeons. 257–275.

Garrett JC. 1991. Osteochondritis dissecans. In Whipple, TL (ed.). *Clinics in Sports Medicine: Arthroscopy Update.* Philadelphia: W.B. Saunders. 10(3):569–593.

Gould JA. 1990. *Orthopaedic and Sports Physical Therapy* (2d ed.). St. Louis: Mosby.

Gray H. 1974. *Anatomy, Descriptive and Surgical.* Philadelphia: Running Press.

Hertling D, Kessler RM. 1990. *Management of Common Musculoskeletal Disorders* (2d ed.). Philadelphia: J. B. Lippincott Company.

Johnston JM, Paulos LE. 1991. Prophylactic lateral knee braces. *Med Sci Sports and Exerc.* 23(7): 783–787.

Magee DJ. 1992. *Orthopedic Physical Assessment.* Philadelphia: W. B. Saunders.

Moore KL. 1992. *Clinically Oriented Anatomy* (3d ed.). Baltimore: Williams and Wilkins.

Norkin CC, Levangie PK. 1992. *Joint Structure and Function.* Philadelphia: F. A. Davis.

Paulos LE, Cawley PW, France EP. 1991. Impact biomechanics of lateral knee bracing. *Am J Sports Med.* 19(4):337–342.

Salvaterra GF, et al. 1993. An in vitro biomechanical study of the static stabilizing effect of lateral prophylactic knee bracing on medial stability. *Journal of Athletic Training.* 28(2):113–119.

Schootman M, van Mechelen W. 1993. Efficacy of preventative knee braces in football: epidemiological assessment. *Clin J Sports Med.* 3(3):166–173.

Stedman TL, Hensyl WR (eds.). 1990. *Stedman's Medical Dictionary* (25th ed.). Baltimore: Williams and Wilkins.

Vailas JC, Pink M. 1993. Biomechanical effects of functional knee bracing. *Sports Med.* 15(3):210–218.

Injuries to the Lower Leg, Ankle, and Foot

MAJOR CONCEPTS

For an athlete to move well there must be excellent functioning of the lower leg, foot, and ankle. The foot must provide a stable base of support and at the same time be flexible and extremely mobile. This chapter discusses the skeletal and muscular anatomy of the foot and lower leg with emphasis on the ligaments of the ankle; it also covers the compartments of the lower leg with an overview of the muscular actions of each compartment.

Sports participation can cause fractures of the bones of the lower leg and foot as a result of both acute trauma and chronic overuse. This chapter discusses such fractures as well as common sprains of ankle ligaments. Treatment of ankle sprains and control of possible future sprains are controversial issues and should be studied carefully.

Injuries to the tendons that cross the ankle joint are also quite common among athletes. This chapter reports on the recognition, care, and treatment of tendon injuries along with compartment problems and considers both the immediate and long-term effects of these disorders. It also focuses on the treatment and care of athletes with shin splints and considers ways to enhance the performance of these athletes.

Finally, the chapter discusses foot disorders such as plantar fasciitis, heel spurs, Morton's neuroma, arch problems, bunions, blisters, and calluses, providing guidelines for recognition, first aid treatment, and long-term care. It is critical to remember the importance of the lower leg, ankle, and foot when assisting the athlete to perform at peak levels: even small, seemingly insignificant injuries to this area can affect the performance.

Anatomy Review

The lower leg, ankle, and foot work together to provide a stable base of support and a dynamic system for movement (Reigger, 1988). The skeleton of the lower leg consists of the tibia and fibula bones. The tibia is the larger and stronger of the two and is commonly called the shin bone; it typically supports about 98% of body weight. The fibula is a smaller bone that supports about 2% of body weight; in addition, it acts as an attachment for various muscles and helps to provide a mechanical advantage for some of them.

The normal foot contains 26 bones (Figures 16.1 and 16.2) that are interconnected and supported by numerous ligaments. There are also many joints within the foot (Figures 16.1 and 16.2) that assist with support and movement. The ankle or **talocrural joint,**

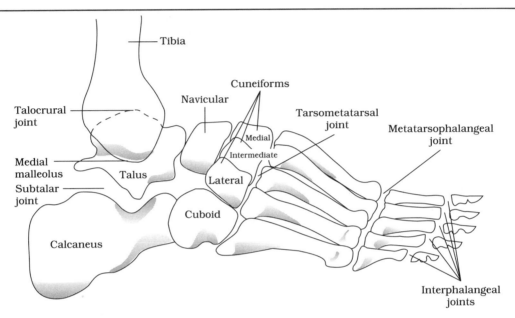

FIGURE 16.1 Major bones and joints of the foot (lateral view).

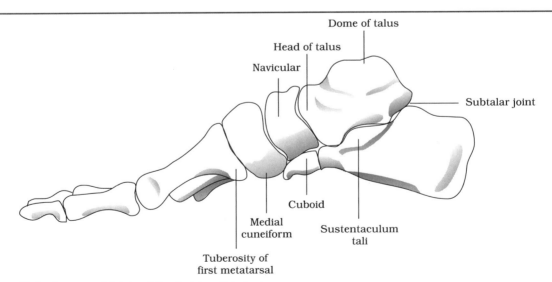

FIGURE 16.2 Major bones and joints of the foot (medial view).

where the tibia, fibula, and talus join, provides mainly plantar flexion and **dorsiflexion** of the foot. The **subtalar joint,** which is the articulation of the talus and the calcaneus, is primarily responsible for **inversion** and **eversion of the foot.** Both of these joints are synovial joints, which means they are surrounded by a capsule and supported by ligaments.

The ankle joint (talocrural) is supported on the medial side by the large and strong deltoid ligament (Figure 16.3). On the lateral side of the ankle, the joint is supported by the anterior talofibular, the posterior talofibular, and the calcaneofibular ligaments (Figure 16.4). These ligaments are not as large or as strong as the deltoid ligament. Additional lateral stability for the ankle joint is provided by the length of the fibula on

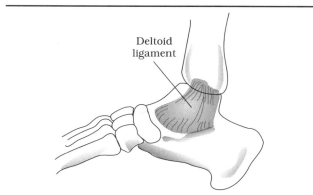

FIGURE 16.3 Major ligament of the ankle joint (medial view).

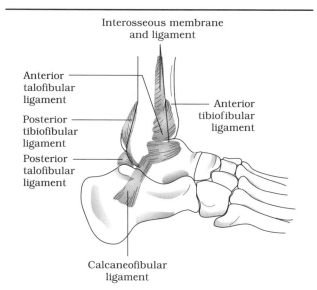

FIGURE 16.4 Major ligaments of the ankle joint (lateral view).

the lateral side of the ankle. The ankle joint is strongest when it is placed in dorsiflexion because the talus fits much tighter between the tibia and fibula in this position. Conversely, the joint is weakest when placed in plantar flexion.

The joints, ligaments, and muscles help to create and maintain the two basic arches in the foot (Gray, 1974; Moore, 1992; Reigger, 1988). The longitudinal arch has medial and lateral divisions. There is one transverse arch running from side to side. These arches assist the foot as shock absorbers; they also provide propulsion off surfaces during movement.

As can be seen in Figure 16.5, the muscles of the lower leg are divided into anterior, posterior, and lateral compartments. The muscles of the anterior compartment essentially produce dorsiflexion and extension of the toes. The muscles in this compartment include the tibialis anterior, extensor digitorum longus, extensor hallucis longus, and peroneus tertius. The anterior compartment is a very compact area with little room for any extra tissue or fluid. The nerve supply for the anterior compartment is through the deep peroneal nerve. The blood supply for the anterior compartment is supplied by the anterior tibial artery.

The posterior compartment of the lower leg mainly functions to produce plantar flexion of the foot. This compartment is commonly referred to as the calf muscles. Many anatomy books subdivide this compartment into superficial and deep sections. In the superficial section there are the gastrocnemius, soleus, and plantaris muscles. The gastrocnemius and soleus muscles have a common attachment on the calcaneus via the Achilles tendon. The plantaris muscle is small and insignificant in action and may be absent in some individuals. The deep section of this compartment houses the tibialis posterior, flexor digitorum longus, flexor hallucis longus, and popliteus muscles. With the exception of the popliteus, these muscles course behind the medial malleolus of the tibia and along the bottom of the foot: they help with plantar flexion as well as flexion of the toes. The popliteus muscle is important in knee flexion: it actually initiates knee flexion by unlocking the knee. The **innervation** for the posterior compartment is supplied by the tibial nerve, which branches off the sciatic nerve. The blood supply to the posterior compartment is via the posterior tibial artery.

The lateral compartment of the lower leg contains the peroneus longus and peroneus brevis muscles. These muscles are mainly evertors of the foot but do assist with some plantar flexion. Both of these muscles course behind the lateral malleolus of the fibula, which

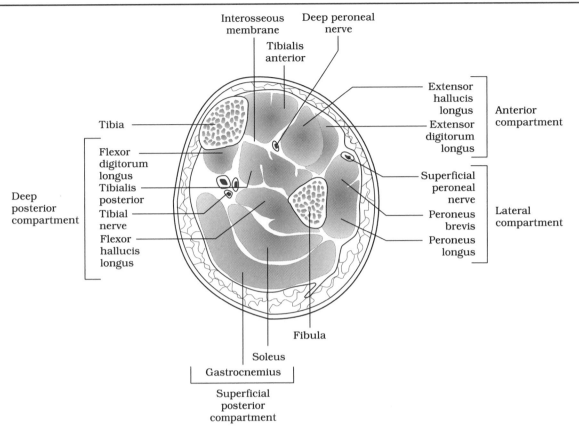

FIGURE 16.5 The muscle compartments of the lower leg.

provides a mechanical advantage for these muscles. The peroneus longus courses under the lateral side of the foot and runs across the bottom to the first metatarsal and cuneiform bones. The peroneus brevis attaches at the base of the fifth metatarsal and is subject to **avulsion.** Also in this compartment is the peroneal nerve, a superficial nerve that is susceptible to injury. The posterior tibial artery supplies blood to the peroneal muscles as there is not a major artery in the lateral compartment.

Common Sports Injuries

Many different sports-related injuries occur to the lower leg, ankle, and foot: some can be classified as traumatic, and others are chronic in nature. Traumatic injuries typically involve skeletal structures; chronic injuries usually involve damage to soft tissues in the area. However, there are definitely exceptions to this rule. There are times when overuse can be a factor in

Information at your fingertips

The World Wide Web—Visit this interesting site for more views of the anatomy of the ankle: http://www.jbpub.com/athletictraining and click on Chapter 16.

fractures, and there are occasions when trauma can be the cause of soft-tissue damage resulting in severe complications.

Skeletal Injuries

■ Fractures

Direct trauma through contact causes most fractures to the lower leg. The magnitude of contact necessary to fracture a bone such as the tibia or fibula can vary: a fracture can be caused by being kicked by an opponent in a soccer match or by having a 300-pound lineman land on a leg in a professional football game. Fractures to the foot can also occur from trauma, for example, when an opponent lands forcefully on a player's foot. However, violent trauma is not always required in fractures of the bones of the leg and foot. Stress fractures can occur from overuse or **microtrauma.** In running, for example, each time the foot strikes the ground it produces a small amount of trauma to the bone. This trauma damages a few bone cells, which the body must repair as quickly as possible. When the body cannot maintain the repair process and keep up with repeated micro-trauma to a specific bone, a **stress fracture** results (Gould, 1990).

It is also important to note here that prepubescent children can experience fractures to the growth plate of a bone as a result of either direct and violent trauma or overuse. These are termed Salter-Harris fractures—or many times just Salter fractures—in young athletes. Salter-Harris injuries have a multiple-level rating system depending on the type and severity of the fracture.

negative consequences for the athlete. These are serious fractures and should be seen by the appropriate medical provider without delay.

Signs and symptoms of a fracture in the lower leg or foot include:

1. Swelling and/or deformity at the location of the trauma.

2. Discoloration at the site of the fracture.

3. Possible broken bone end projecting through the skin.

4. Athlete reporting that a snap or a pop was heard or felt.

5. The athlete may not be able to bear weight on the affected extremity.

6. In the case of a stress fracture or a growth plate fracture that did not result from a traumatic event, the athlete will complain of extreme point tenderness and pain at the site of suspected injury.

First aid care for a suspected fracture of the lower leg or foot includes:

1. Watch and treat for shock if necessary.

2. Apply sterile dressings to any related wounds, i.e., an open fracture.

3. Carefully immobilize the foot and leg using a splint.

4. Arrange for transport to a medical facility.

In the event that bones are fractured the physician will apply a cast, and the athlete will be immobilized for a specified time. When the fracture has healed properly, the physician will release the athlete for rehabilitation, practice, and competition in that order. There

W H A T   I F ?

One of your high school soccer players has just injured his ankle, apparently while moving the ball down field. He has fallen to the ground and is in obvious pain, holding his right ankle. During your examination you note swelling and discoloration in the region of the lateral malleolus as well as point tenderness over the area of the lateral ankle ligaments. Based on this history and the signs and symptoms, what is the likely injury? What is the appropriate first aid for such injuries?

This type of fracture is common in the lower leg among adolescent athletes and can be problematic if not cared for properly. Early closure of the growth plate due to the trauma and damage received from the injury is possible. If this occurs, there is the possibility of different leg lengths resulting as well as other long-term

are extreme cases of athletes participating in sporting events with a broken bone in the lower leg or foot. This may happen in professional sports in which athletes get paid for participation in the activity. Participation while a fracture is healing is not recommended as it may slow the healing process.

Soft-Tissue Injuries

■ Ankle Injuries

One of the most common sports injuries to the lower leg and ankle is a sprained ankle. Sprains are abnormal stresses placed on ligamentous structures causing various levels of damage. (Refer to Chapter 1 for a detailed description of sprains.) Sprains can occur to the lateral or medial ligaments of the ankle depending on which direction the foot moves when abnormal stress is placed on the ligaments and the foot rolls to one side.

By analyzing the anatomical relationships of the components of the ankle, it can be seen that the non-contractile structures on the lateral aspect of the ankle are most susceptible to injury. The formation of the bones of the ankle help to stabilize the ankle: the fibula extends inferiorly approximating the lateral talus completely. Also, the ligaments on the lateral side—the anterior talofibular, the posterior talofibular, and the calcaneofibular ligaments—are not as large or strong as the deltoid ligament on the medial side of the ankle joint. With the wide anterior superior aspect of the talus being securely wedged in the mortise formed by the inferior surfaces of the tibia and fibula, the joint is most stable in a dorsiflexed position, weak in a position of plantar flexion. Therefore, when comparing the typical movements of the foot with the anatomical structure of the ankle joint, it becomes clear that the lateral ligaments are more prone to damage via excessive movement than the deltoid ligament on the medial aspect of the ankle. It has been estimated that 80% to 85% of ankle sprains experienced occur to the lateral ligaments (Ryan et al., 1986).

Ankle sprains can occur in virtually any sport and can limit the abilities of the athlete in performance until resolution of the injury is complete. As the severity of the ankle sprain increases so does the instability of the ankle. It is generally accepted that an eversion ankle sprain is more severe, with greater instability, and should be cared for more conservatively (Ryan et al., 1986). However, an inversion ankle sprain is more common, with the lateral ligaments being involved in 80% to 85% of all ankle sprains.

Signs and symptoms of a lateral ankle sprain include:

1. First-degree sprain: pain, mild disability, point tenderness, little laxity, little or no swelling.

2. Second-degree sprain: pain, mild to moderate disability, point tenderness, loss of function, some laxity (abnormal movement), swelling (mild to moderate).

3. Third-degree sprain: pain and severe disability, point tenderness, loss of function, laxity (abnormal movement), swelling (moderate to severe).

First aid care for a lateral ankle sprain includes:

1. Immediately apply ice, compression, and elevation. A horseshoe- or doughnut-shaped pad kept in place by an elastic bandage aids at this stage in the compression and reduction of fluid (Figure 16.6).

2. Have the athlete rest and use crutches to ambulate with a three- or four-point gait if a second- or third-degree sprain has occurred.

3. If there is any question concerning the severity of the sprain, splint and transport the athlete to a medical facility for further evaluation by a physician.

The control of subsequent ankle sprains seems to be a source of a great deal of research and debate in sports medicine literature (Orteza, Vogelbach, and Denegar, 1992). There are those who prefer to use the standard ankle-taping procedure as a prophylactic treatment for ankles with no history of previous injury; others choose to augment the taping procedure to prevent future ankle sprains if one has occurred before (Moss, 1992). Most researchers agree that the best known method of ankle support, the prophylactic adhesive-taping procedure, supports the ankle for only a short period of time after exercise begins (Frankeny et al., 1993; Paris, 1992). Other researchers believe that there are now very good ankle braces (Figures 16.7 through 16.9) on the market that provide the necessary protection at a much lower cost (Burks et al., 1991; Gross et al., 1992; Gross, Lapp, and Davis, 1991; Paris, 1992). Some researchers are now maintaining that bracing is better than taping for the prevention of ankle

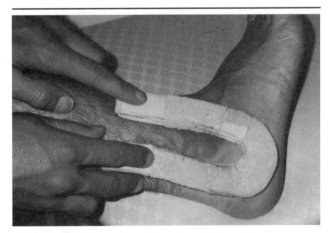

FIGURE 16.6 A horseshoe-shaped pad is used to decrease inflammation after an ankle sprain.

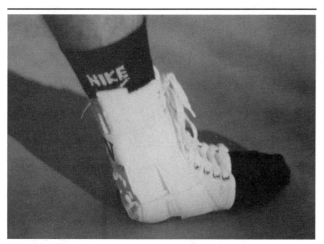

FIGURE 16.7 Lace-up type ankle braces are useful for prevention of ankle sprains.

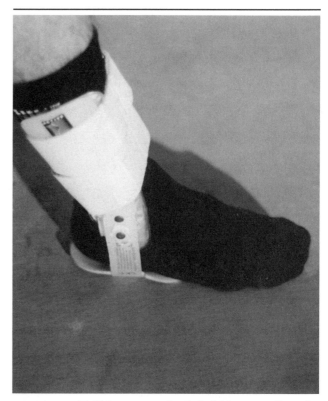

FIGURE 16.9 Rigid braces are also helpful in prevention of ankle sprains.

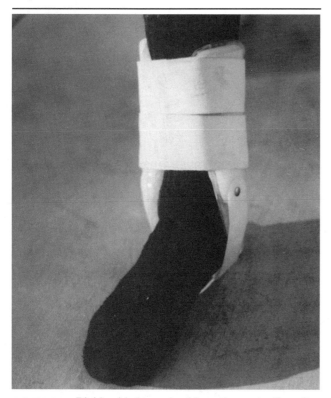

FIGURE 16.8 Rigid ankle brace used for extra protection after an ankle has been sprained.

injuries owing to the reduction in range of motion, either at excessive points or within normal ranges (Gehlsen, Pearson, and Bahamonde, 1991).

Whatever the choice of the coach or athlete, there are many factors that must be considered in preventing ankle sprains. These include the type of activity, the compliance of the athlete in wearing braces or prophylactic taping, the cost to the school or athlete, and the effectiveness of the brace as reported in research studies. Even though most coaches believe that adhesive taping is effective in reducing ankle-related injuries, there are some serious consequences of poorly applied adhesive tape, including blisters, tape cuts, and loss of circulation. If ankle taping is to be part of an athlete's protective equipment, then it should be applied properly in order to perform correctly.

■ Tendon-Related Injuries

The Achilles tendon is commonly injured by long-distance runners, basketball players, and tennis players (Leach, Schepsis, and Takai, 1991). The onset of tendinitis may be slow among runners but much more rapid among basketball or tennis players, who make a great many short-burst movements requiring jumping or rapid motion from side to side.

Some controversy exists about the actual injury that constitutes Achilles tendinitis. The Achilles tendon itself, which attaches the gastrocnemius and soleus muscles to the calcaneus, can become inflamed. However, either the tendon sheath or the subcutaneous

Information at your fingertips

The World Wide Web—Check out the excellent graphic as well as the text description at this site: http://www.jbpub.com/athletictraining and click on Chapter 16.

bursa dorsal to the tendon can become inflamed, both of which can be part of Achilles tendinitis (Leach, Schepsis, and Takai, 1991). Most agree that athletes who dramatically increase their running distance or workout times and who do so running on hard, uneven, or uphill surfaces are prone to Achilles tendinitis (Bazzoli and Pollina, 1989).

Superficially, Achilles tendinitis can produce an increased temperature in the immediate area; moreover, the tendon is painful upon touch and movement and appears thickened. The pain associated with this condition is localized to a small area of the tendon and typically intensifies when movement is initiated after rest (Bazzoli and Pollina, 1989). These signs and symptoms can be seen over an extended period of time (days to weeks) or over a shorter time period (days). Early detection of this problem usually enhances resolution of the symptoms and assists the athlete in returning earlier to practice and competition.

Treatment for chronic Achilles tendinitis is immediate rest until the swelling subsides. Usually the application of ice, nonsteroidal anti-inflammatories (e.g., aspirin or ibuprofen), and a small heel lift will assist in the reduction of swelling and the return to practice and competition. Stretching has also been shown to be beneficial to athletes with Achilles tendinitis (Taylor et al., 1990). Controlled stretching on a slant board or against a wall each day will aid in return to participation. Additionally, if an athlete must exercise or run, it is advised that this be done in a controlled environment, perhaps in a swimming pool. Many times runners or other athletes will not accept complete rest as the route to healing. In such cases decreasing the amount of work may be the only way that even a small amount of healing will occur. Without the proper amount of rest, the body has a hard time repairing injury, thereby increasing the amount of time the athlete experiences difficulty with the condition. Running in water is an option for those athletes who must maintain conditioning or want to work out even though they are injured. Other exercises may be completed by doing them at slower rates or in controlled situations, in

which the stress placed on the Achilles tendon is limited.

Explosive jumping or direct trauma from some type of impact can cause traumatic injuries to the Achilles tendon by tearing or rupturing the tendon. These types of injuries have been known to occur in many different sports.

Signs and symptoms of a ruptured Achilles tendon include:

1. Swelling and deformity at the site of injury.

2. The athlete will report a pop or snap associated with the injury.

3. Pain in the lower leg, which may range from mild to extreme.

4. Loss of function, mainly in plantar flexion.

First aid care for a suspected rupture of the Achilles tendon includes:

1. Immediate application of ice and compression to the area.

2. Immobilizing the foot by an air cast or splint.

3. Arranging for transportation to the nearest medical facility.

The long-term effects of a ruptured Achilles tendon depend on the severity or completeness of the rupture. If surgery is necessary, the athlete will most likely be out of commission for the rest of the season. In any case the athlete will need to be careful and aware of the value of stretching and warming up in any future sports activity.

Other tendon problems typically occur with the tendons on the lateral side of the ankle, including those of the peroneus longus and peroneus brevis muscles. These muscles originate on the lateral aspect of the tibia and fibula; the tendons then run an inferior course behind the lateral malleolus in the peroneal groove and attach on the lateral and posterior aspects of the foot. There is a small retinaculum band attaching on the fibula and running posteriorly to the calcaneus, which assists in holding the tendons in place. As these tendons run their course behind the lateral malleolus there is a possibility of their dislocating and/or subluxing due to trauma or extreme force and actually popping across the lateral malleolus. This can be very painful, but it is not usual for the athlete to experience.

The athlete with tendon problems should be seen by a member of the medical team, and a course of action outlined. Sometimes these problems can be controlled by taping or bracing and strengthening of the musculature in the area. Recurrent problems warrant further investigation by the physician; other modes of controlling recurrent subluxation are possible.

■ Compartment Syndrome

Another possible problem that can result from chronic or acute conditions is compartment syndrome. This syndrome is associated with the lower leg, which is divided into four very distinct compartments (Figure 16.5). The majority of compartment syndrome occur in the anterior compartment, which has very little room to expand if there is any extra swelling or effusion into it. This can be caused by chronic overuse that creates swelling of tissues in the compartment or by trauma that triggers bleeding and effusion (Black and Taylor, 1993). Some athletes chronically overuse the muscles in the anterior compartment. The resulting extra fluid creates a lack of space and places extreme

Signs and symptoms of compartment syndrome include:

1. Pain and swelling in the lower leg.
2. The athlete may complain of chronic or acute injury to the area.
3. There may be a loss of sensation or motor control to the lower leg and/or foot.
4. There can be a loss of pulse to the foot.
5. Inability to extend the great toe or dorsiflex the foot.

First aid care for compartment syndrome includes:

1. Apply ice and elevate. Do not apply compression as the area is already compromised with too much pressure.
2. If the foot becomes numb, there is loss of movement, or there is loss of pulse to the foot, seek medical help immediately.
3. Seek proper medical advice early as these problems can worsen very quickly.

■ Shin Splints

Another very common disorder of the lower leg is **shin splints,** a term used to describe exercise-induced leg pain. Kues (1990) defines shin splints as "medial or posteromedial leg pain brought about by walking, running, or related activities and that decreases with rest."

WHAT IF?

A high school gymnast has just struck the front of her lower left leg on the lower bar of the uneven parallel bars. She immediately grabs her leg and complains loudly of extreme pain. On further examination you note that she has swelling and discoloration directly over the muscles of the anterior compartment. In addition, she states that she is unable to extend her big toe. What is the likely cause of these signs and symptoms? What would be the most appropriate first aid for this injury?

pressure on the blood vessels and nerves in the compartment, thereby compromising their functions. In addition, trauma to the anterior portion of the leg (by being kicked or hit with a ball, for example) can create blood loss and swelling into the compartment. A similar scenario can cause the same results in the other compartments of the lower leg, which are so tightly packed with muscles, nerves, and blood vessels that there is little room for expansion when extra fluid is present.

This is a dubious disorder that does not have definite parameters to follow in determining the exact problem that may exist in the lower leg. Kues (1990) and DeLarcada (1982) report various reasons for this leg pain— from skeletal involvement and muscular disorders to compartment pressures. However, to date there has not been a positive link between any one specific cause and the resulting leg pain. Moreover, it is generally accepted that with rest the pain will subside and the athlete will be able once again to participate.

Signs and symptoms of shin splints include:

1. Lower leg pain either medially or posteromedially.

2. Typically a report of a chronic problem that gets progressively worse.

3. The pain and discomfort can be bilateral or unilateral.

First aid care for shin splints includes:

1. Apply ice and have the athlete rest.

2. Use of nonsteroidal anti-inflammatory medications may help.

To help the athlete work through shin splints suggest a change in workout routine. Recommend that the athlete run in water, reduce running, or eliminate the irritating stimulus altogether and use another type of exercise until there is an improvement. The athlete may also want to have his or her gait analyzed to look for biomechanical deficiencies such as overpronation. There are a myriad of related problems that can exacerbate the pain and discomfort associated with shin splints. If the problem worsens the athlete must seek professional medical advice so that long-term complications do not arise. An athletic trainer can assist the athlete with shin splints through preventative taping procedures and some therapies. However, long-term treatment with adhesive tape is not advised: the skin of the lower leg will become irritated, and many times this does not alleviate the initial problem causing the pain and discomfort. Each athlete responds differently to taping and therapy; therefore, a controlled progression of alternative taping procedures and therapy is important.

■ Plantar Fasciitis

The plantar fascia is a dense collection of tissues, including muscles and tendons, that traverses from the plantar aspect of the metatarsal heads to the calcaneal tuberosity. If this collection of tissues becomes tight or inflamed by overuse or trauma, it can produce pain and disability in the bottom of the foot known as **plantar fasciitis.** To determine whether the condition is plantar fasciitis, you must take a thorough history. Ask the athlete if he or she experiences almost unbearable pain in the plantar aspect of the foot with the first steps taken upon getting out of bed in the morning, and whether the pain eases with each of the following steps. Also inquire if there is point tenderness on the plantar aspect of the calcaneal tuberosity. If both of these symptoms exist, there is a high probability that plantar fasciitis is the problem (Bazzoli and Pollina, 1989; Middleton and Kolodin, 1992).

Treatment of plantar fasciitis is typically conservative; it includes rest, anti-inflammatories, and the use of cold and heat alternatively to enhance healing. A heel pad and stretching the Achilles tendon complex can assist in recovery and resolution. Athletes will be tempted to continue exercising with this injury. However, the more the injury is aggravated by further insult to the same area the longer it will take to heal, even when the healing process is being augmented with assorted therapeutic agents.

■ Heel Spurs

Heel spurs can also be related to plantar fasciitis: sometimes with chronic cases of inflammation there is ossification at the site of the attachment on the

Information at your fingertips

The World Wide Web—Learn more about this most common problem. Go to http:// www.jbpub.com/athletictraining and click on Chapter 16.

▌ Foot Disorders

There are many bones, joints, ligaments, muscles, and other tissues in the foot. It is important to remember that athletes participating in different sports will have different injuries associated with the foot. Some injuries are more common to specific sports.

plantar aspect of the calcaneus (Bazzoli and Pollina, 1989; Middleton and Kolodin, 1992). This results in long-term disability for many athletes since the heel spur can become problematic at any time during the exercise or activity program. Additionally, these small ossifications can occur on the posterior aspect of the calcaneus just below the attachment of the Achilles

Athletic Trainers Speak Out

"Most common injuries to the lower leg, often minimized by athletes and coaches, are traumatic contusions, or compartment syndrome. These injuries are commonly caused by kicks to the lower leg. Due to the anatomical compartments of the lower leg there is little room for expansion caused by hemorrhage.

An improperly recognized or treated contusion can result in increased pressure to nerves and blood vessels. This is especially true with injuries to the anterior compartment of the lower leg. These injuries can become life-long disabilities if not properly recognized and treated. As the effusion increases pressure, the area may need to be surgically decompressed. All trainers need to be aware of and concerned about the possibility of compartment syndrome when treating trauma to the lower leg. This is one area of the body where external pressure from elastic wraps should not be used as a method for control of swelling. The wrap may only increase the internal pressure and further hasten the symptoms of compartment syndrome."

—Dale Mildenberger, M.S., A.T.C.

Dale Mildenberger

Dale Mildenberger is Head Athletic Trainer for Utah State University.

tendon. These too can become disabling to an athlete. The athlete needs to consult a physician to determine the proper treatment plan if these spurs become too incapacitating. Doughnut-shaped pads placed beneath the heel and some therapeutic interventions may assist the athlete to participate fully, but rarely do they ameliorate the problem.

■ Morton's Foot

Morton's foot typically involves either a shortened first metatarsal bone or an elongated second metatarsal bone. The result is that the majority of weight-bearing is done on the second metatarsal instead of along the first metatarsal and spreading out to the remainder of the foot. This problem can result in pain throughout the foot and difficulty in **ambulation.** The use of padding can help the athlete, but to have the problem correctly addressed the athlete should see a physician so that the proper treatment can be prescribed.

Also associated with this area is a condition called **Morton's neuroma.** This is a problem with the nerve, usually between the third and fourth metatarsal heads. As a result, pain radiates to the third and fourth toes. A **neuroma** is an abnormal growth on the nerve itself. Tight-fitting shoes have been blamed for irritation of the nerve in many cases of Morton's neuroma. Consequently, going barefoot is one of the best methods of pain relief for this problem. This condition is most often taken care of by a doctor, who should always be consulted regarding the early detection of foot problems.

■ Arch Problems

There are several problems associated with arches of the foot that athletes can experience. However, problems with arches are not always due to flat feet. Essentially, arch problems can be classified into two categories: **pes planus** (an abnormally flat foot) and **pes cavus** (an abnormally high arch in the foot). Both problems present difficulties to some athletes. Others with similar foot conditions may never complain of problems associated with arches.

Athletes with flat feet may have too much **foot pronation,** causing difficulties in the navicular bone and some of the joints around the ankle itself. This will lead to generalized discomfort about the foot and ankle. There have been several taping procedures developed to augment the arch in athletes. How long the effects of taping will enhance the arch has been evaluated by at least one research team whose findings were consistent with those for other ankle-taping procedures. There seems to be limited effectiveness in adhesive-strapping techniques for the athlete who jogs for

a minimum of 10 minutes continuously (Ator et al., 1991). However, the athlete who participates in a different sport requiring a different set of exercise criteria may benefit from this taping technique. It is definitely a low-cost alternative and could prove a good method of determining if the athlete could benefit from an **orthosis** or some other type of augmentation for flat feet. A NATABOC-certified athletic trainer can assist in providing direction in this taping procedure. Coaches should not attempt to apply adhesive tape to an athlete until they have received the proper training. Many athletes with flat feet can be helped in the long term by **orthotics** and proper shoe selection. It should be noted that there is no evidence that the flat-footed athlete is a slower runner or has less motor ability than the athlete with a regular or high arch.

In many cases, the athlete with an excessively high arch also has foot problems. A foot with too much arch is often associated with plantar fasciitis and clawing of the toes. There have also been cases of athletes with too much arch having generalized discomfort about the foot and ankle because of the inability of the foot to absorb forces owing to the tightness of joints there. These athletes can also benefit from some orthotic help and proper shoe selection. The height of an athlete's arch need not hinder athletic performance if the proper attention and care are provided.

■ Bunions

Bunions are not very common in athletes at the high school and college level. Bunions can be simply a matter of inflamed bursae, or they can involve complicated bone and joint deformities. Many times bunions are caused by improperly fitting footwear. By getting the athlete into correctly fitting shoes the signs of a bunion should resolve. If an athlete has had a bunion for an extended period of time (weeks to months), then the athlete should seek the advice of a physician in the care of this condition.

■ Blisters and Calluses

Blisters and calluses are very common formations on athletes' feet. Excessive amounts of movement can produce a great deal of friction between the layers of skin in the foot and the shoe, resulting in the formation of either a blister or callus. If a blister forms, the layers of skin have been separated, and the friction has built up a fluid deposit. Always observe the color of the fluid within a blister. Most often the fluid will be clear, but on occasion it will be dark, which means there is blood in this small cavity. Many times the pain and discomfort from a blister will prevent the athlete from participating in sports. If the blister is large, the fluid should be drained and the area padded well to prevent further friction and blister formation. When a blister is drained, it is best to leave the top layer of skin in place until a new layer develops, thereby reducing the possibility of introducing infection into the area. In addition, place a doughnut-shaped pad made of felt, or a large pad of thin adhesive felt, directly over the blister to reduce friction. In case the blister opens inadvertently, care needs to be taken to ensure that the area is clean and the possibility of infection is reduced. Apply an antibacterial lotion and an antibiotic ointment over the area, along with sterile dressings.

When draining a blister be sure to follow the recommended precautions regarding HIV and hepatitis B:

1. Always use sterile instruments and keep the environment sterile.

2. Use latex gloves or some other barrier so that body fluids are not contacted.

According to the National Safety Council (1991), the following procedures should be followed when caring for a blister:

1. Initially wash the area with soap and warm water and sterilize the area with rubbing alcohol.

2. Using a sterile needle, puncture the base of the blister and gently drain by applying light pressure. This may need to be repeated several times in the first 24 hours. Do not remove the top of the blister; apply antibiotic ointment to the top of the blister and cover with a sterile dressing.

3. Check the area daily for redness or pus to determine if infection is occurring at the site.

4. After three to seven days, gently remove the top of the blister, apply an antibiotic ointment, and cover with a sterile dressing.

5. Watch the area closely for signs of infection such as redness or pus and pad the area well with gauze pads or moleskin. This will allow for healing to occur without further irritation.

If the blister is small, padding the area to prevent further friction will usually suffice until the blister heals. Athletes should be encouraged to report the formation of any new blisters as soon as possible so that padding and protection can be provided. It is definitely best to help prevent blisters by having properly fitted footwear and giving new shoes a short break-in period before using them in practice or competition.

In addition to the formation of blisters, there can be an excessive buildup of tissue on the bottom of the feet, which is commonly known as a callus. Calluses tend to build up over a bony area of the foot and should not be allowed to become large and extremely thick.

If this happens, the callus can begin to move with the shoe and not with the foot. This creates an area of friction between the callus and layers of skin, causing a blister to form between the callus and the next lower layer of skin. This can cause problems as the blister is difficult to drain and can be very painful to the athlete. To prevent this from happening, a callus should be shaved regularly to allow for only a small amount of buildup, which then acts as a padding for the area. If a callus gets too large the athlete will begin to complain of pain and discomfort in the area.

Preventative Ankle Taping

Applying preventative ankle taping to athletes is a popular practice among many high school, collegiate, and professional athletic trainers. Athletes commonly have their ankles taped as a routine procedure before practice or competition to prevent or reduce ankle injuries. The advantages and disadvantages of preventative ankle taping have been discussed widely and a continuum of recommendations—from not using taping as a preventative measure to always taping both ankles when participating in any sport—is advocated by various athletic trainers. Some athletic trainers promote the use of lace up and other rigid braces rather than preventative taping. Paris, Vardaxis, and Kikkaliaris (1995) indicated through their research that ankle braces are just as effective, if not more so, as preventative taping in reducing inversion range of motion over a 30- to 60-minute time period (Paris, 1992). It has also been demonstrated that ankle braces do not detract from an athlete's ability to run, jump, or perform other skills as necessary during athletic competition.

Preventative ankle taping is an important skill that must be learned properly, practiced until a level of mastery is gained, and then applied in an athletic team setting. Taping is an art and a science and each strip of tape has its own function. The following preventative taping outline is intended to provide the beginning student with the theoretical basis for the reasons the tape is applied (Figures 16.10 through 16.14). If students are interested in developing taping skills, it is recommended that they work under the direct supervision of a NATABOC-certified athletic trainer to learn and practice the art of taping.

As can be seen in Figure 16.10, the use of prewrap and anchoring strips is important in starting the taping procedure correctly. An adherent is used to help the prewrap to stay in place. If an adherent is not used, the tape will, in most situations, loosen and slide, diminishing the effectiveness of the taping procedure.

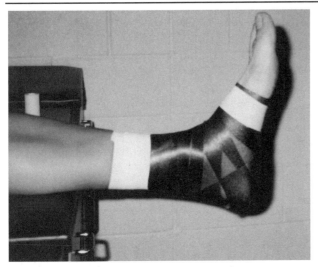

FIGURE 16.10a The application of prewrap and anchoring strips starts the ankle-taping procedure.

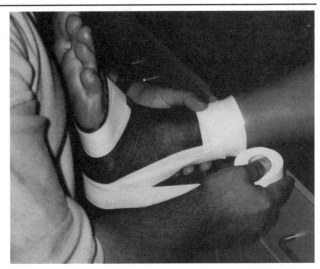

FIGURE 16.10b The use of stirrups to maintain a normal or slightly elevated foot position.

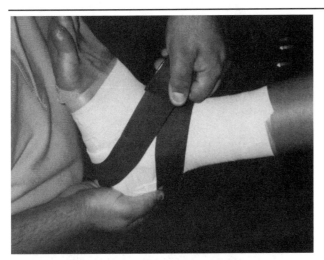

FIGURE 16.11a Applying the heel locks requires practice to perform correctly.

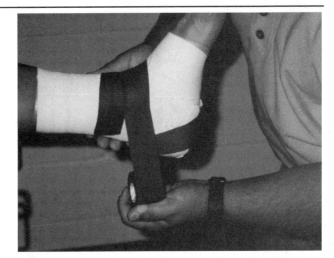

FIGURE 16.11b

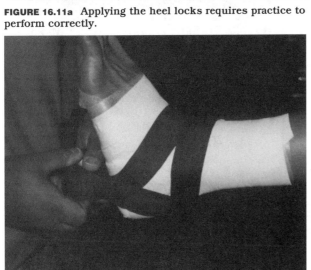

FIGURE 16.11c

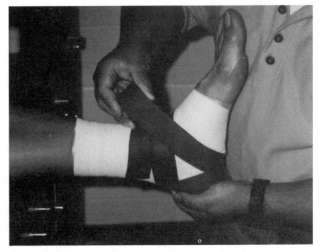

FIGURE 16.11d

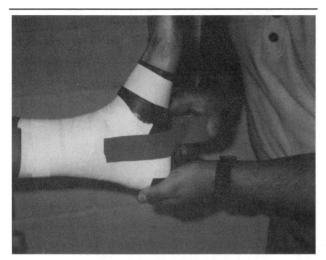

FIGURE 16.12a Applying the figure eights also takes practice and proper direction of pull on the tape to be performed correctly.

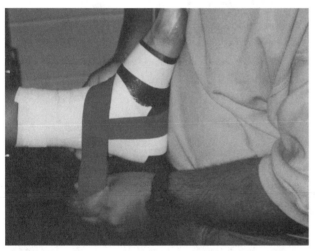

FIGURE 16.12b

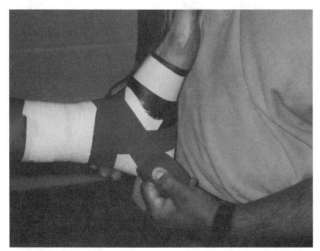

FIGURE 16.12c

In Figure 16.10b, the use of stirrups is intended to maintain the foot in a normal or slightly everted position. Stirrups are combined with horseshoe strips, which help to hold the stirrups in place and reduce the gaps in the tape on the posterior portion of the procedure. Figure 16.11 demonstrates the use of heel locks, which assist in stabilizing the subtalar joint. Heel locks are followed by the use of figure eights (Figures 16.12 and 16.13), which are intended to help stabilize the talocrural joint and the transverse tarsal joint. From this point on, the procedure involves using finishing strips to make sure there are no gaps or holes between strips of tape, securing the tape at the bottom, and using a final covering to ensure that tape ends do not get rolled or wrinkled as the athlete puts on socks and shoes (Figure 16.14).

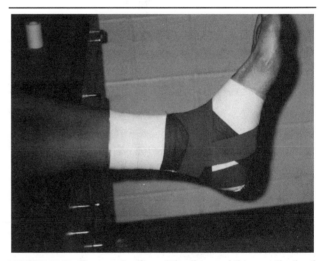

FIGURE 16.13 Demonstration of the figure eight over the heel locks.

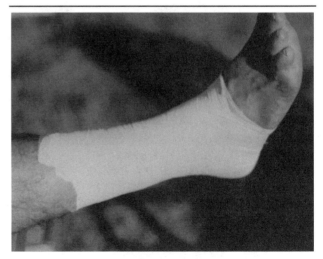

FIGURE 16.14 A completed ankle-taping procedure.

Review Questions

1. Name the two bones located in the lower leg.

2. Explain where the fibula is located and approximately how much body weight is supported by this bone.

3. What is the technical name for the ankle joint?

4. Name the strongest and largest of the ankle ligaments.

5. Draw or outline the compartments of the lower leg and describe the actions that the muscles in each compartment have on the foot.

6. Which compartment of the lower leg presents the most problems with fluid accumulation?

7. Outline the signs and symptoms of a fracture of the lower leg.

8. *True or false:* An inversion ankle sprain is more common than an eversion ankle sprain.

9. Explain which type of ankle sprain is more severe.

10. Describe where the Achilles tendon attaches and the signs, symptoms, and treatment of Achilles tendinitis.

11. Explain the possible long-term complications if problems with anterior compartment syndrome are left untreated.

12. Explain what types of changes (e.g., biomechanical, training) an athlete may need to make in order to alleviate and prevent further episodes of shin splints.

13. Outline the key signs and symptoms of plantar fasciitis and explain how heel spurs are associated with this condition.

14. What structures are involved in Morton's foot?

15. Explain the difference between pes cavus and pes planus.

16. Explain the difference between a blister and a callus.

17. Outline how a blister should be cared for when it is drained.

18. Explain how blisters can be prevented.

19. *True or false:* It is not possible for a callus to form over a blister.

20. *True or false:* Callus formation on the plantar aspect of the foot should be trimmed regularly to reduce friction.

References

Ator R, et al. 1991. The effect of adhesive strapping on medial longitudinal arch support before and after exercise. *J Orthop Sports Phys Ther.* 14(1):18–23.

Bazzoli AS, Pollina FS. 1989. Heel pain in recreational runners. *Phys Sportsmed.* 17(2):55–61.

Black KP, Taylor DE. 1993. Current concepts in the treatment of common compartment syndromes in athletes. *Sports Med.* 15(6):408–418.

Burks RT, et al. 1991. Analysis of athletic performance with prophylactic ankle devices. *Am J Sports Med.* 19(2):104–106.

DeLarcada FG. 1982. Iontophoresis for treatment of shin splints. *J Orthop Sports Phys Ther.* 3:183–185.

Frankeny JR, et al. 1993. A comparison of ankle-taping methods. *Clin J Sports Med.* 3(1):20–25.

Gehlsen GM, Pearson D, Bahamonde R. 1991. Ankle joint strength, total work, and ROM: comparison between prophylactic devices. *Journal of Athletic Training.* 26:62–65.

Gould JA. 1990. *Orthopaedic and Sports Physical Therapy* (2d ed.). St. Louis: Mosby.

Gray H. 1974. *Anatomy, Descriptive and Surgical.* Philadelphia: Running Press.

Gross MT, et al. 1992. Comparison of Donjoy ankle ligament protector and Aircast Sport Stirrup orthoses in restricting foot and ankle motion before and after exercise. *J Orthop Sports Phys Ther.* 16(2): 60–67.

Gross MT, Lapp AK, Davis JM. 1991. Comparison of Swede-O-Universal ankle support and Aircast Sport Stirrup orthoses and ankle tape in restricting eversion-inversion before and after exercise. *J Orthop Sports Phys Ther.* 13(1):11–19.

Kues J. 1990. The pathology of shin splints. *J Orthop Sports Phys Ther.* 12(3):115–121.

Leach RE, Schepsis AA, Takai H. 1991. Achilles tendinitis. *Phys Sportsmed.* 19(8):87–91.

Middleton JA, Kolodin EL. 1992. Plantar fasciitis—

heel pain in athletes. *Journal of Athletic Training.* 27(1):70–75.

Moore KL. 1992. *Clinically Oriented Anatomy* (3d ed). Baltimore: Williams and Wilkins.

Moss CL. 1992. Taping for excessive pronation: reverse-8 stirrup. *Journal of Athletic Training.* 27(1):85–87.

National Safety Council. 1991. *First Aid and CPR* (1st ed.). Boston: Jones and Bartlett.

Orteza LC, Vogelbach WD, Denegar CR. 1992. The effect of molded and unmolded orthotics on balance and pain while jogging following inversion ankle sprain. *Journal of Athletic Training.* 27(1):80–84.

Paris DL. 1992. The effects of the Swede-O, New Cross, and McDavid ankle braces and adhesive ankle taping on speed, balance, agility, and vertical jump. *Journal of Athletic Training.* 27(3):253–256.

Paris DL, Vardaxis V, Kikkaliaris J. 1995. Ankle ranges of motion during extended activity periods while taped and braced. *Journal of Athletic Training.* 30(3): 223–228.

Reigger CL. 1988. Anatomy of the ankle and foot. *Phys Ther. Journal of Athletic Training.* 68(12): 1802–1814.

Ryan AJ, et al. 1986. Ankle sprains: a roundtable. *Phys Sportsmed.* 14(2):101–118.

Taylor DC, et al. 1990. Viscoelastic properties of muscle tendon units: the biomechanical effects of stretching. *Am J Sports Med.* 18(3):300–309.

CHAPTER 17

Skin Conditions in Sports

MAJOR CONCEPTS

The skin, the largest organ of the human body, is often involved in sports injuries, which range from simple wounds to a variety of bacterial, fungal, and viral infections. This chapter discusses the basic anatomy of the skin and describes the categories of wounds and their care. Obviously, the risk of HIV and HBV infection must be considered whenever a potential exposure to blood exists. The chapter presents the latest guidelines available for the prevention of accidental exposure to human blood.

Next, the chapter covers skin conditions related to excessive exposure to ultraviolet light, with an emphasis on prevention and safety precautions. Any number of microorganisms, ranging from minute viruses and bacteria to relatively large fungi, can produce skin infections. Information in this chapter introduces the reader to the common types of skin infections in sports, with helpful descriptions of signs and symptoms as well as recommended treatment and prevention protocols. The NCAA guidelines on wrestling and skin infections are included, along with a listing of conditions to be considered. This section also covers a related group of skin conditions resulting from allergic reactions to plant toxins and other materials.

The skin, or common integument, represents the largest organ of the human body. As can be seen in Figure 17.1, two major layers of tissues, the epidermis and dermis, combine to form this complex organ, which has a total surface area of 3,000 square inches on the average adult (AAOS, 1991). Located immediately beneath the skin is a layer of subcutaneous fat that helps to insulate the body from the external envi-

The skin serves a variety of purposes, not the least of which is protecting the body from the environment. It is also essential for controlling fluid balance within the body, protecting the body from disease organisms, and regulating body temperature. Furthermore, it houses nerves of sensation that register touch, temperature, and pressure. In addition, specialized cells within the skin produce vitamin D (AAOS, 1991).

Information at your fingertips

The World Wide Web—Check out this fascinating site for electron micrographs of the skin. Go to http://www.jbpub.com/athletictraining and click on Chapter 17.

ronment. Skin thickness varies regionally on the body: thicker skin covers areas subject to pressure such as the soles of the feet and palms of the hands; thinner skin covers areas where joint mobility is essential.

The skin can be damaged in a variety of ways during participation in sports. External trauma can cause wounds, and damage can result from exposure to ultraviolet rays (sunlight) as well as burning or freezing

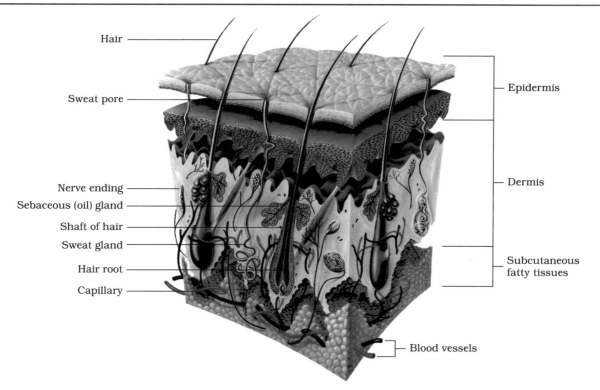

FIGURE 17.1 A cross section of human skin. (Source: National Safety Council. 1991. *First Aid and CPR.* Boston: Jones and Bartlett. 262. Reprinted with permission.)

temperatures. Skin infections can arise from a variety of organisms including viruses, **bacteria,** and fungi. In addition, allergies can also affect the skin; these may be related to contact with plants or clothing and equipment that contain chemicals to which the athlete is sensitive.

Wounds

Sports injuries can cause many types of wounds, ranging from abrasions (scrapes, burns, and strawberry) to lacerations (cuts and gashes), all of which may result in infection as well as cosmetic complications (AMA, 1968). The primary goals of initial wound care are control of bleeding followed by prevention of infection through cleaning and bandaging. A primary concern when rendering first aid care for any wound is to avoid contact with whole blood that may transmit infectious organisms such as human immunodeficiency virus (**HIV**) or hepatitis B virus (**HBV**). The majority of wounds seen in sports are abrasions caused by rubbing, scraping, and burning; lacerations produced by a blunt object tearing the skin; and incisions caused by sharp objects. A special type of abrasion, known as turf burn, has been associated with playing surfaces in stadiums made of artificial turf. Turf burns are the result of falls sustained on artificial turf that produce friction and heat.

Treatment

Treatment of wounds in sports can be considered as a two-phase process. Initial first aid care is designed to control bleeding and guard the area from further injury. This is followed later with ongoing protection of the area so that return to participation is possible while healing takes place. An important aspect of wound care is protection of fellow athletes, coaches, and other personnel from exposure to whole blood, which can result in the transmission of HIV and HBV organisms. Risk of exposure involves not only the wound itself, but also blood-soaked clothing as well as any blood that may be on playing surfaces.

Initial treatment of wounds follows first aid protocol described by the National Safety Council (1993). These are its guidelines:

1. Before rendering first aid, precautions should be taken against the possible transmission of HIV and HBV. Wear latex gloves and dispose of all waste in a storage container for biohazardous materials.

2. Remove clothing and/or equipment covering the wound.

3. Control bleeding with direct pressure over the wound site by applying some type of sterile dressing.

4. If dressing becomes soaked with blood, add more dressing on top. Do not remove blood-soaked dressings.

5. Although rare in sports, severe bleeding may not respond to direct pressure. In such cases, combine direct pressure with elevation.

6. Increased hemorrhage control can be achieved via the application of a pressure bandage to a point over either the brachial or femoral arteries depending upon location of the wound. Once pressure is applied to either of these points, it should not be released until the athlete is under the care of physician.

7. Tourniquets should be applied only as a last resort; they are rarely needed in first aid for sports-related wounds.

8. All materials used to treat the wound—gauze pads, towels, paper towels—should be stored for later disposal or cleaning in a container properly identified as containing biohazardous materials.

At the time of initial first aid, a decision must be made whether the athlete will be allowed to return to participation. Obviously, the health and safety of the athlete must be the first priority; however, the majority of sports-related wounds are not life-threatening occurrences. Another consideration is protection of other participants, coaches, and personnel from exposure to whole blood from any wound. In sports such as wrestling, tackle football, and basketball, wounds must be dealt with in such a way to protect other athletes and the coaching staff from incidental exposure. Although research indicates the risk of transmission of HIV and HBV in such situations is remote, the possibility does exist (Calabrese, Haupt, and Hartman, 1993).

Once the initial bleeding is arrested, a commercially made dressing should be applied to the wound and held in place with an adhesive bandage. Small wounds are usually treatable by simply applying a bandage; larger wounds such as a strawberry on the thigh or arm may require a large sterile gauze pad that is held in place with adhesive tape. Such bandages should be rechecked periodically during participation to ensure that they remain in proper position and bleeding has not resumed.

Lacerations and incisions, particularly those to the scalp or face, merit special attention because of their potential cosmetic impact. Such wounds should be referred to a physician for evaluation and possible stitches. As a general rule, any wound going below the dermal layer that is more than a centimeter in length—especially if it is on the face—should be seen by a physician for evaluation.

The National Safety Council (1993) provides the following guidelines for cleaning wounds:

1. Personnel rendering first aid should protect themselves from direct exposure to whole blood by wearing latex gloves.

2. Wash the wound with a sterile gauze pad saturated with soap and water. Hydrogen peroxide (3% solution) may be used to bubble away blood clots and related debris. This is especially helpful when treating abrasions containing significant amounts of dirt and other foreign material.

3. Flush the wound with large amounts of water; then dry the area with a sterile gauze pad.

4. Use isopropyl rubbing alcohol to clean the skin adjacent to the wound site; however, do not apply the alcohol directly to the wound.

5. Do not apply chemicals such as Mercurochrome, Merthiolate, or iodine to wounds; their effectiveness is minimal, and they may cause an allergic reaction.

6. Apply a sterile, dry dressing and hold it in place with some type of bandage. For smaller wounds, Band-Aid bandages are effective; for larger wounds, sterile gauze pads held in place with elastic adhesive tape are recommended. By definition, a **dressing** is a sterile material, usually gauze, used to cover a wound to control bleeding and prevent contamination. A **bandage** is used to hold the dressing in place. Bandages need not be anything more than a folded cravat, strips of cloth, or commercially made elastic adhesive tape that can be directly applied to the skin and holds well even near a moving joint.

7. Severe wounds should be treated for control of bleeding and referred immediately for medical evaluation.

■ HIV/HBV and the Athlete

Although the majority of national focus regarding these two viral infections has focused primarily on HIV,

HBV has been on the increase as well. It is estimated that 300,000 new HBV infections occur each year. In 1981, the first diagnosed case of acquired immune deficiency syndrome (AIDS) was reported. In 1976 there were approximately 2,000 people infected with HIV in the United States; however, in 1994 it is estimated that the number is 1.5 million (Cramer Products, 1994).

Virtually anyone who is sexually active, including athletes, is at risk of contracting the AIDS virus. Athletes who inject anabolic steroids may also be at risk of infection, especially when sharing needles (Calabrese, 1989). The disease is spread primarily through intimate sexual contact or blood-to-blood exposure, which can easily occur when sharing needles during IV drug use. HBV is a bloodborne pathogen and is most easily spread via blood-to-blood contact with an infected person. Both HIV and HBV are carried within the blood of infected persons; therefore, anytime such individuals sustain a bleeding wound, the possibility of transmission exists. This is especially true if another athlete who also has an open wound comes into contact with the blood of an infected person. Although the chance of such an occurrence may be remote, some precautions are necessary, especially in sports in which external bleeding is likely. Recently, the Occupational Safety and Health Administration (**OSHA**) developed a comprehensive set of guidelines for health care workers regarding prevention of exposure to HIV and HBV (U.S. Department of Labor/U.S. Department of Health and Human Services, 1991). Although coaching personnel are not commonly thought of as health care providers, virtually all coaches find themselves dealing on a regular basis with open wounds on some of their athletes. Coaches and athletes are routinely exposed to blood-contaminated towels, water bottles, playing surfaces, and blood-soaked bandaging materials. As a result, the prudent coach should make every effort to follow the basic preventative guidelines for HIV and HBV transmission that have been outlined by OSHA and are presented in Box 17.1.

Athletes participating in wrestling, tackle football, and boxing frequently sustain bleeding wounds. It is advised that coaches and officials remove players from participation when excessive bleeding is evident. Furthermore, those persons providing first aid care for such injuries should protect themselves by wearing latex gloves and perhaps even eye protection when treating a bleeding wound. In addition, athletes should be cautioned about sharing water bottles or blood-stained towels with fellow athletes (Calabrese, 1989). Athletes, coaches, and health care providers should

BOX 17.1   OSHA Guidelines for Preventing the Transmission of HIV and HBV

1. Written guidelines regarding the prevention of HIV and HVB transmission must include a detailed description of infection-control procedures to be followed by coaches as well as any other personnel working with athletes. This policy must be read by all staff members involved, and the athletic director or other supervisory personnel should monitor compliance.
2. Written plans must be rehearsed in order to ensure that all personnel are versed in correct procedures.
3. Records must be kept regarding all exposures of staff and athletes to whole blood.
4. All personnel should be notified of the availability of HVB vaccinations.
5. Labels warning of biohazardous materials should be posted prominently in areas where exposure to whole blood may occur, e.g., locker rooms and training facilities.
6. All personnel should be required to practice basic exposure-prevention protocols, including wearing latex gloves—and possibly eye shields and face masks—when treating an athlete with an open wound.
7. Blood-contaminated materials such as bandages and towels as well as sharp objects such as needles need to be placed in containers clearly marked as containing biohazardous substances.
8. Contaminated areas such as treatment tables and playing surfaces should be disinfected with a commercially prepared solution or with a solution of water and household bleach (one part bleach to 10 parts water).

Source: Cramer Products. 1992. Preparation is best policy against blood-borne diseases. *The First Aider.* 62(2): 1, 6. Reprinted with permission.

wash hands and skin as soon as possible after being exposed to the blood of an injured athlete. Conversely, coaches and health care providers with open wounds should protect athletes from possible infection by wearing latex gloves, bandages, and practicing good personal hygiene.

Education of athletes, coaches, and parents about the transmission and prevention of HIV and HBV is essential. Obviously, participation in organized sports presents a very low risk for the contraction of the viruses. Prudence dictates, however, that precautions be implemented since sports participation does carry some risk to all parties involved—athletes, coaches, and sports-medicine personnel. (See Appendix 2.)

Other Skin Conditions

Ultraviolet Light-Related Skin Problems

Outdoor sports played during the summer can result in exposure of large areas of the body to harmful rays of the sun. Typically, summer sportswear does not cover the arms and legs; in some sports such as swimming and diving major portions of the skin are unprotected. Medical evidence is substantial that even minor sunburn can be harmful to the skin; it may lead to serious, even lethal, complications such as skin-related carcinomas and melanomas (Reichel and Laub, 1992). Two different wavelengths of ultraviolet light are involved in the sunburn process: ultraviolet A (UVA) and ultraviolet B (UVB). UVB is a shorter wavelength than UVA and seems more related to the development of skin problems (Rustad, 1992).

It is well known that some individuals are at a higher risk for damage from sunlight exposure, including those with lighter skin, red hair, and freckles (Reichel and Laub, 1992). Exposure to sunlight at any time of day can result in sunburn; however, the most dangerous times are between 10:00 A.M. and 2:00 P.M.

Sunburn has two clinical phases. The first, known as the immediate erythema phase, involves reddening

Information at your fingertips

The World Wide Web—Review this site for excellent graphics and descriptions of a variety of dermatological conditions. Go to http://www.jbpub.com/athletictraining and click on Chapter 17.

of the skin, which occurs during exposure to sunlight. The second phase, called the delayed erythema phase, normally develops within a few hours of exposure and peaks at 24 hours (Reichel and Laub, 1992). Although most cases of sunburn result in mild discomfort, with symptoms diminishing within a day or two, more severe cases can include the formation of blisters associated with chills and gastrointestinal distress.

The primary concern should be focused on protection of exposed skin when an athlete is participating in outdoor sports. Certain body areas may require special protection with a commercially prepared sunscreen—particularly the outer ear, nose, lips, back of the neck, forehead, and (if not covered by clothing) the forearms and hands. Though many sunscreen products are available, athletes should use only those rated with at least a sun protection factor (SPF) of 15. The SPF rating is derived by determining the sunscreen's ability to absorb harmful ultraviolet light over time. Thus, athletes using a product with an SPF rating of 15 will receive the same amount of ultraviolet light to the skin in 15 hours outdoors as they would have in one hour of unprotected exposure. Sunblocks are also available: they contain chemicals that block all light from reaching the skin. These products contain zinc oxide or titanium dioxide. Sunscreen products may contain a variety of chemicals that either absorb or reflect UVA and UVB light; these include *para*-aminobenzoic acid **(PABA),** cinnamates, salicylates, benzophenone-3, 3% avobenzone, and dibenzoylmethane (Rustad, 1992). For best results, sunscreens should be applied in advance of exposure to sunlight. Although many products are advertised as waterproof or water-resistant, athletes who perspire heavily or who are involved in water sports should periodically (every 60 minutes) reapply the product to maintain adequate protection.

Treatment of sunburn involves application of a commercially made topical anesthetic as well as a skin lotion to help relieve burning and dryness. In severe cases, medical attention may be warranted, and treatment may include the administration of anti-inflammatory medications.

Skin Infections

A variety of organisms can cause infections of the skin—including fungi, bacteria, and viruses. Although a detailed discussion of sports dermatology is beyond the scope of this book, some of the more common afflictions—along with their signs, symptoms, and treatment—are presented. It should also be remembered that many apparent skin infections can be symptoms of more serious infectious and/or allergic conditions, including Lyme disease, herpes, or contact dermatitis, and should be referred to a doctor for evaluation.

■ Tinea (Ringworm)

Tinea, commonly known as ringworm, is an infection of the skin caused by a group of fungi. In athletes, the common locations for tinea include the groin region (tinea cruris, commonly known as jock itch) and the feet and toes (tinea pedis). Tinea infections are common in these body areas because moisture and warmth make them ideal for fungal growth. Tinea can affect other parts of the body as well, including the scalp (tinea capitis) and the extremities. Although tinea infections are not serious, if left untreated they may persist and lead to secondary bacterial infections that can be cosmetically displeasing.

Signs and symptoms of tinea infections include:

1. Small, superficial, brownish-red, elevated lesions that tend to be circular in shape.

2. When infections involve the toes, lesions may include cracking between toes associated with oozing and crusting.

3. Itching and pain are associated with both tinea pedis and tinea cruris.

4. Scaling of the skin over the lesions may also be noted.

W H A T   I F ?

You are the wrestling coach at Johnson High School. Several of your athletes have reported similar skin lesions on their faces and arms. They appear as superficial, brownish-red, circular-shaped lesions. What might be causing these lesions and what, if any, action would you take?

Athletic Trainers Speak Out

"Skin problems in wrestlers, such as fungal infections, seem to run a cyclic course through a season. No one is resistant and outbreaks tend to happen at the worst possible time, just before competition. Skin problems often go undiagnosed and unattended until the lesions start to spread or look bad enough to seek advice. This is a perplexing problem for coaches and athletes. Prevention is best spearheaded by early recognition. Who should be charged with this duty? Everyone associated with the team should be sensitized to skin lesions as a fact of life in wrestling. Together, they should promote personal hygiene and develop a ready resource to assist with early recognition."

—Danny T. Foster, Ph.D., L.A.T.

Danny T. Foster

Dr. Foster is Head Athletic Trainer at the University of Iowa.

Treatment of tinea infections—according to Rustad (1992)—involves:

1. Vigilant cleaning of the involved areas, followed by drying.

2. Applying an over-the-counter topical treatment such as Tinactin®.

3. Applying a moisture-absorbing powder to the area.

4. Wearing clothing made of natural fibers such as cotton.

■ Tinea Versicolor (TV)

This particular fungal infection is considered to be the most common warm-weather-related skin problem among teenagers and young adults (Rustad, 1992). **Tinea versicolor** gets its name from the symptoms it produces on the skin of the affected person. These include circular lesions that appear either lighter or darker than adjacent unaffected skin. The infection is usually confined to the upper trunk, neck, and upper abdomen (AMA, 1968). Treatment for TV involves the use of prescription drugs, administered either topi-

Information at your fingertips

The World Wide Web—Learn more about fungal infections of the skin. Go to http:// www.jbpub.com/athletictraining and click on Chapter 17.

cally or orally, designed to destroy the fungus. Weeks to months may be required for normalization of skin color in the affected areas, sometimes causing the athlete to doubt the effectiveness of the treatment.

■ Bacterial Infections

Bacterial infections of the skin are relatively common in sports that involve close physical contact between participants. Known collectively as **pyoderma** (pus-producing infection of the skin), these infections are normally caused by two common bacteria, *Staphylococcus aureus* and *Streptococcus.* The former is related to conditions such as furuncles, carbuncles, and folliculitis; the latter causes impetigo, ecthyma, and cellulitis.

All of these conditions are characterized by infected, **purulent** (pus-producing) lesions on the skin. For example, in folliculitis the lesions are located at the base of a hair follicle. Furuncles are similar in appearance; however, they form large nodules around the hair follicles and may burst as the infection develops. Impetigo is similar in appearance, but may develop in areas with little or no hair.

BOX 17.2 Precautions Regarding Pyoderma

---

1. Once identified, the athlete will probably be treated with an oral antibiotic.
2. All clothing and towels used by the athlete should be isolated.
3. Equipment used by the athlete—such as mats in wrestling—should be cleaned with a strong disinfectant.
4. The athlete should not be allowed to return to participation until the infection is controlled.

Source: Olerud JE. 1989. Common skin problems encountered in young athletes. In Smith NJ (ed.). *Common Problems in Pediatric Sports Medicine.* Chicago: Year Book Medical Publishers. 228–229. Reprinted with permission.

Regardless of the specific condition, all pyodermal infections share a common characteristic: the presence of lesions that are obviously infected and associated with drainage and pus formation. Any athlete demonstrating such symptoms should be removed from participation and referred for medical evaluation. If pyoderma is the diagnosis, the precautions outlined in Box 17.2 immediately should be instituted.

■ Viral Infections

Two of the more common viral-related skin problems in sports are plantar warts and herpes gladiatorum. As a skin problem, warts are quite common in the general population and occur as the result of infection by a specific group of viruses known collectively as the human papillomavirus **(HPV),** of which over 55 specific types have been identified. The majority of plantar warts are caused by two types: HPV-1 and HPV-4. The infection is contagious; however, some individuals seem more susceptible, with an **incubation period** ranging from 1 to 20 months (Ramsey, 1992). The most well-known characteristic of a wart is the abnormal buildup of epidermis around the region of actual infection; warts can vary in size from 1 millimeter in diameter to as large as 1 centimeter or more. Plantar warts are simply warts that occur on the plantar surfaces of the feet. Although warts elsewhere generally rise up from the skin, the pressure of bearing weight drives the plantar wart inward on the bottom of the feet, often resulting in annoying if not painful symptoms. Signs and symptoms of plantar warts are somewhat vague; however, the warts are usually first noticed because they become painful when an athlete is walking or running. Upon inspection, small thickened areas of skin may be noticeable, with tiny black or dark red dots appearing within the area (Ramsey, 1992). Contrary to popular myth, these small dark spots are not seeds but rather small capillaries that have been destroyed within the wart. Sometimes a group of warts will develop, causing a relatively large area to become involved. This is referred to as a mosaic wart.

Treatment of plantar warts ranges from the application of chemicals designed to dissolve the wart to actual surgical removal, although the latter is not recommended by the medical community. A variety of prescription products is available, most of which contain salicylic, pyruvic, and lactic acids. These compounds soften and errode the wart (the process is known technically as keratolysis); the ultimate goal is complete removal of the growth. Other treatment options exist, including the use of chemicals designed to stop the growth of the wart. Sometimes liquid nitrogen is applied to freeze the affected tissue; this is followed by surgical removal. Even a form of **laser** surgery has been developed for use on plantar warts (Ramsey, 1992).

Interestingly, in many athletes plantar warts terminate on their own with no long-term symptoms. Athletes who find plantar warts to be detrimental to participation in sports should consult a doctor to determine the best course of treatment. Coaches and athletes should not attempt treatment since this may result in a worsening of the condition, infection, and even permanent scarring.

Herpes gladiatorum is the name given to herpes infections among athletes such as wrestlers. This virus, herpes simplex virus type 1 (**HSV-1**), is well known as the causative agent of the common cold sore or fever blister, which typically occurs on the outer lip area. Lesions are often associated with physical trauma, sunburn, emotional disturbances, fatigue, or infection (AMA, 1968). A unique aspect of herpes infection is its ability to remain dormant for long periods, sometimes months or even years, between active periods when lesions reappear. The infection is most contagious when open lesions are present. Once exposed to the virus, the incubation period may be as long as two weeks. Initial symptoms of the infection include the development of a lesion, often on the face, which is characterized by blistering associated with a red, infected area of skin. Open, draining lesions may persist for a few days; afterwards they become crusted and begin to heal. In addition, more systemic symptoms are often noted in highly susceptible individuals. These include general fatigue, body aches, and inflammation of lymph glands associated with tenderness (White, 1992). Obviously these symptoms could significantly impair performance, which makes prevention and treatment critical.

Outbreaks of herpes must be controlled, or the infection can be devastating in a sport such as wrestling, in which acute outbreaks can involve many athletes. Coaches and athletes must be educated about the early signs and symptoms of HSV-1 infections. Moreover, any type of open lesion must be evaluated to rule out the possibility of infection. Athletes with active infections must be removed from participation until lesions have healed, a process that may take up to five days. It has been noted that once the crust of the lesion has come off it is safe to resume activity (Olerud, 1989). Drugs are available for control of the infection; however, they must not be used without the supervision of a physician. In addition to drug therapy, athletes should be advised to take the precautions outlined in Box 17.3.

Wrestling and Skin Infections

Due to the nature of the sport of wrestling, participation with an active skin infection presents special hazards to the athletes involved. Common sense should prevail in such situations and any open sore or skin lesion that cannot be covered adequately should be grounds for removal from participation until the infection subsides. The National Collegiate Athletic Association (NCAA) has published specific criteria for disqualification because of skin infections among wrestlers (NCAA, 1995). The NCAA recommends that any infected area that cannot be protected adequately should be considered as cause for disqualification from practice and/or competition. The NCAA

BOX 17.3 Precautions Regarding HSV-1 Infections

1. Athletes whose infections appear to be related to exposure to sunlight should use a sunscreen whenever outdoors.
2. Consume foods containing high levels of lycine and low levels of arginine. This can be accomplished by eliminating nuts, seeds, and chocolate from one's diet. In addition, lycine supplements can be purchased from health-food stores.
3. The application of ice directly to areas where early signs of lesions are noted may arrest further development of sores.

Source: Olerud. 1989. Common skin problems encountered in young athletes. In Smith NJ (ed.). *Common Problems in Pediatric Sports Medicine.* Chicago: Year Book Medical Publishers. 226. Reprinted with permission.

WHAT IF?

A member of the cross-country team asks you to examine a strange rash he has developed on his legs. He reports that it developed about 12 to 24 hours after he used a topical analgesic with a wintergreen odor. What is a likely cause of this condition and what would you recommend to this athlete?

has included all of the following as infections worth considering under their recommendations (NCAA, 1995):

1. Bacterial skin infections
   a. impetigo
   b. erysipelas
   c. carbuncle
   d. staphylococcal disease
   e. folliculitis (generalized)
   f. hidradentitis suppurative
2. Parasitic skin infections
   a. pediculosis
   b. scabies
3. Viral skin infections
   a. herpes simplex
   b. herpes zoster (chicken pox)
   c. molluscum contagiosum
4. Fungal skin infections
   a. tinea corporis (ringworm)

Allergic Reactions

Allergic skin reactions can be caused by exposure to any number of chemical agents from a variety of sources. For those susceptible, contact with the of-fending chemical results in a condition known as **contact dermatitis.** Plants such as poison ivy, poison oak, and poison sumac contain potent chemicals that cause reactions in susceptible people. Certain types of sports equipment and related clothing may also contain compounds causing allergic reactions.

According to the National Safety Council (1993), allergies to poison ivy, poison oak, and poison sumac result in skin reactions in 90% of adults. The sap of the plant contains the offending chemical; therefore, any direct contact with the plant can cause sap to be

deposited onto the skin. Contact with contaminated clothing or other materials can also result in reactions. The average time period between exposure and development of symptoms is 24 to 48 hours; the earliest symptoms include itching and redness in the affected area. These symptoms are followed by the development of blisters, which often break open and subsequently become crusted. Healing takes place within one to two weeks from the time of the initial reaction.

Athletes who know they are allergic to plants should learn to recognize poison ivy, poison oak, and poison sumac to avoid contact with them when participating in outdoor activities. Organizers of events that may place athletes in areas where these plants grow should alert participants to the potential problem. A good example is cross-country running, a traditional autumn sport in high schools across the nation. It is common for training runs, as well as races, to take the runners through areas where plants such as poison ivy flourish. Obviously, these athletes need to be able to recognize such vegetation. Coaches and organizers should also make every effort to keep courses well away from areas where such plants may grow. The precautions in Box 17.4 outline the recommended prevention and care of plant-related allergies.

Allergies related to chemicals contained in sports

BOX 17.4 Precautions Regarding the Prevention and Care of Plant-Related Allergies

1. Recognize and avoid the offending plants.
2. Protect the skin with clothing.
3. Apply lotion containing linoleic acid (Stokogard) to exposed skin prior to exposure.
4. Wash clothing and the skin, including under the fingernails, immediately after possible exposure.

Source: Rustad OJ. 1992. Outdoors and active: relieving summer's siege on skin. *Phys Sportsmed.* 20(5):176. Reprinted with the permission of McGraw-Hill, Inc.

TABLE 17.1 Sensitizers That Active Patients Frequently Encounter and Sample Alternatives

Sensitizer	Alternative	Model or Source of Alternative
RUBBER ADDITIVES IN		
Tennis shoes	Polyurethane shoes	All Puma shoes (Etonic, Tretorn, Puma, Inc, Brockton, MA) "Wimbledon Player" model 7028 (Nike, Inc, Beaverton, OR)*
Support hose	Lycra and nylon hose	Jobst, Inc (Toledo, OH)
Masks and mouthpieces	Silicone masks and mouthpieces	Dow Chemical Co (Midland, MI)†
Swim caps	Silicone swim caps	Speedo (Authentic Fitness Corp, Van Nuys, CA)
Swim goggles	Air-blown neoprene swim goggles	Speedo Hilco "Swim N' Sun" (Hilsinger Corp, Plainville, MA)
	Polyvinyl chloride swim goggles	Speedo "Freestyle Antifog" model 750127
Diving suits	Ethylbutyl thiourea-free diving-suit material	Material number G231-N‡ (Rubatex Co, Bedford, VA)
	Ethylene vinyl acetate diving-suit material	Material number R-5012-A (Rubatex Co)
Nose clips, earplugs, and fins	Plastic nose clips, earplugs, and fins	Various
TOPICAL ANALGESICS		
Methyl salicylate (oil of wintergreen)	Menthol-only products	Various
	Hot packs, cold packs	Various
Menthol	Oral magnesium salicylate pain relievers	Regular Strength Doan's analgesic Extra Strength Doan's analgesic (CIBA Consumer Pharmaceuticals, Edison, NJ)
	Hot packs, cold packs	Various
FORMALDEHYDE RESINS		
Athletic tape	Acrylate tape	Micropore (3M Co, St. Paul)
EPOXY RESINS		
Face masks	Silicone adhesives	Various
Helmets	Silicone adhesives	Various

*Taylor J: Rubber, in Fisher AA: Contact Dermatitis, ed 3. Philadelphia, Lea & Febiger, 1986, pp 634–636
†Fisher AA: Aquatic dermatology. Clin Dermatol 1987;5(3):36–40
‡This diving suit contains the rubber additive mercaptobenzothiazole, a known sensitizer.
Source: Fisher AA. 1993. Allergic contact dermatitis: practical solutions for sports-related rashes. *Phys Sportsmed.* 21(3):67. Reprinted with permission.

equipment or clothing have been receiving increased attention in sports-medicine literature. It has been reported that products containing rubber, topical analgesics (pain relievers), resins found in athletic tape, and epoxy used in face gear are associated with allergic reactions in sensitive athletes. The chemicals initiating the allergic reaction are called sensitizers. They can produce classic symptoms of contact dermatitis:

swelling and redness of the skin (**erythema**) followed by the development of pimple- or blister-like lesions. Symptoms normally occur approximately seven days after the initial exposure. In athletes with a history of previous allergic reactions, repeat exposures may yield symptoms within 24 hours (Fisher, 1993).

Major sensitizers include synthetic rubber additives commonly found in certain brands of tennis shoes, swim caps, swim goggles, nose clips, and ear-plugs as well as topical analgesics containing either salicylates or menthol. Adhesive athletic tapes made with formaldehyde resins and face gear and helmets made with epoxy resins can also initiate allergic reactions (Fisher, 1993). For athletes with known allergies to any of these products, it is essential that alternative gear be identified if possible. Listed in Table 17.1 are the common sensitizers as well as sources and brand names of alternative products.

An athlete suspected of having allergic contact dermatitis should be referred to a dermatologist for specific diagnosis and treatment, which includes identification of the sensitizer and treatment of symptoms with anti-inflammatory drugs.

Review Questions

1. Review the primary goals of initial wound care.

2. List the precautions that should be taken when treating an athlete with an open wound to avoid possible transmission of HIV and HBV.

3. Describe and differentiate between a wound dressing and bandage.

4. *True or false:* With respect to the types of sunlight causing sunburn, evidence suggests that UVB is more connected with the development of skin-related problems.

5. Discuss the two clinical phases of sunburn as described in the chapter.

6. Explain the acronym PABA.

7. *True or false:* The term pyoderma implies a pus-producing infection of the skin.

8. Describe the recommended treatment(s) for plantar warts.

9. *True or false:* There is no evidence that synthetic materials such as tennis shoes, swim caps, and swim goggles can cause allergic skin reactions.

10. *True or false:* The first case of AIDS was reported in the United States in 1981.

References

American Academy of Orthopaedic Surgeons. 1991. *Athletic Training and Sports Medicine.* Park Ridge, Ill.: American Academy of Orthopaedic Surgeons.

American Medical Association. 1968. *Standard Nomenclature of Athletic Injuries.* Chicago: American Medical Association.

Benson M (ed.). 1995. *1995–96 Sports Medicine Handbook* (8th ed.). Overland Park: The National Collegiate Athletic Association.

Calabrese LH. 1989. AIDS and athletes. *Phys Sportsmed.* 17(1):127–132.

Calabrese LH, Haupt HA, Hartman L. 1993. HIV in sports: what is the risk? *Phys Sportsmed.* 21: 172–180.

Cramer Products. 1992. Preparation is best policy against blood-borne diseases. *The First Aider.* 62(2): 1, 6.

Cramer Products. 1994. OSHA regulations continue to raise questions. *The First Aider.* 64(2):1, 10.

Fisher AA. 1993. Allergic contact dermatitis: practical solutions for sports-related rashes. *Phys Sportsmed.* 21(3):65–72.

National Safety Council. 1993. *First Aid and CPR* (2d ed.). Boston: Jones and Bartlett.

Olerud JE. 1989. Common skin problems encountered in young athletes. In Smith NJ (ed.). *Common Problems in Pediatric Sports Medicine.* Chicago: Year Book Medical Publishers. 222–229.

Ramsey ML. 1992. Plantar warts: choosing treatment for active patients. *Phys Sportsmed.* 20(11):69–88.

Reichel M, Laub DA. 1992. From acne to black heel: common skin injuries in sports. *Phys Sportsmed.* 20(2):111–118.

Rustad OJ. 1992. Outdoors and active: relieving summer's siege on skin. *Phys Sportsmed.* 20(5): 163–176.

U.S. Department of Labor/U.S. Department of Health and Human Services. 1991. *Joint Advisory Notice Protection Against Occupational Exposure to Hep-atitis B (HBV) and Human Immunodeficiency Virus (HIV).* Washington, D.C.: Federal Register 56:235.

White J. 1992. Vigilance vanquishes herpes gladia-torum. *Phys Sportsmed.* 20(1):56.

CHAPTER 18

Thermal Injuries

Sports and athletic events are staged under a wide range of environmental conditions, indoors as well as a nearly infinite variety of outdoor settings. This chapter explores the body's response to extremes of both heat and cold, with particular attention given to life-threatening conditions. It is critical to note that a significant percentage of the deaths directly attributable to sports today result from heat-related problems.

In addition, the chapter discusses cold-related problems, including hypothermia, frostbite and frostnip, and a relatively unknown condition called cold urticaria.

During two days in late August one of your football players, an offensive lineman, suddenly staggers away from the blocking sled, falls to the ground, and is unable to get to his feet. During your primary survey you note that he is semiconscious, his skin is dry, reddish in color, and hot to the touch. He is able to tell you that he is thirsty and that he has not had any water for over an hour. It is 95° F, approximately 78% humidity, and there is little wind. Given this scenario, most likely what is the problem? If you are correct, what is the appropriate first aid for this athlete?

Because of the great range of environmental conditions within which sports take place, a variety of temperature-related health emergencies occur each year; some result in death. The majority, if not all, of these deaths could be prevented if coaches, athletes, and administrators would take the time to consider the environmental conditions prior to allowing an event to begin. Normal metabolism can be maintained within only a very narrow range of body **core temperatures,** ranging from between 98.0°F to 98.6°F when measured orally (Guyton, 1986). Heat is a natural product of metabolism; during exercise the metabolic rate can increase significantly, resulting in elevations of body temperature to as high as 104°F. Excess heat must be eliminated from the body during exercise, or the body temperature can rise to dangerous levels in a short period of time. The body can rid itself of excess heat by taking advantage of basic physics through a complex process known as thermoregulation. Thermoregulation is controlled primarily by the temperature-regulating centers within the hypothalamus of the brain (Wilmore and Costill, 1988). A variety of neurologic sensors throughout the body, both in the deep tissues and the skin, provide information regarding body temperature to the hypothalamus (Guyton, 1986). Excess heat can be lost through **radiation** (via infrared light), **conduction** (absorbed into surrounding objects), **convection** (moving air currents), and **evaporation** (sweating). Each of these methods is effective, although during most exercise on dry land evaporation is the most efficient. Its effectiveness as a form of thermoregulation can be severely compromised by extremes in relative humidity. Relative humidity represents the amount of water vapor suspended in the air, and it determines how much water can effectively evaporate from the skin during exercise. The higher the relative humidity, the less ability the surrounding air has to absorb fluid (sweat) from the skin surface. As a result, the higher the relative humidity the

greater the potential for heat-related problems. In cases of outdoor activity during times of both extremely high temperatures and high humidity, coaches need to make modifications in the demands of the exercise session or consider delaying activity until conditions improve.

Athletes need to be given adequate time to adjust their systems to a major change in temperature. This process, known as **acclimatization**, can take from one to six weeks and occurs naturally when a person is exposed to continuous and significant climatic changes. As a general rule, those with a higher level of fitness tend to acclimatize more quickly; adolescents, obese individuals, and those with certain metabolic disorders take longer to readjust their systems. As a result of proper acclimatization, the sweating mechanism can yield 1.5 to 2 liters (L) of sweat per hour, with a heat loss of at least 10 times the normal rate (Guyton, 1986). During times of high ambient temperature, athletes need to consume from 4 to 10 L of fluids per day in order to avoid dehydration (Montain, Maughan, and Sawka, 1996). To put this amount into perspective, 4 L of fluid is roughly equivalent to consuming 17 eight-ounce glasses of water. While this amount may seem large, it is important to remember that this figure represents a consumption over a 24-hour period and much of the food consumed during this time also contains some fluid.

Athletes, regardless of geographic region, can be susceptible to temperature-related disorders. For example, temperature extremes at both ends of the scale are common in the northern climates depending upon time of year. Conversely, participants living in the so-called sun belt (southern climates) are routinely exposed to the combination of high temperature and high humidity. There, a typical scenario might involve a high school football player who has lost fitness over the summer and begins practices twice daily in August, when the temperature is 96°F and the relative humidity is 90%. Such athletes need to practice in the early morning or evening hours whenever possible in order to avoid the heat of the day. In addition, they need to be encouraged to drink water frequently (a minimum of 10 ounces every 30 minutes) during practices (Figure 18.1). Evidence suggests that body fluid losses, representing as much as 2% of body weight, can occur before the athlete perceives the need to drink. Athletes may lose from 2% to 6% of body weight during exercise, which is significant in light of evidence that demonstrates that such losses can impair performance by as much as 50%. It is critical to note that the process of heat acclimatization does **not** decrease the body's fluid needs; in fact, fluid needs are increased as the rate of sweating increases with improved fitness (Montain, Maughan, and Sawka, 1996).

Heat-Related Health Problems

Heat-related health problems take three basic forms: heat cramps, heat exhaustion, and heat stroke (Hubbard and Armstrong, 1989). They are presented here in the order of least severity, beginning with heat cramps.

Heat Cramps

Heat cramps, the least severe of the three, generally develop within the muscles being exercised, e.g., the leg muscles in runners or the shoulder muscles in

Information at your fingertips

The World Wide Web—Try taking the "fluid balance test." Go to http://www.jbpub.com/athletictraining and click on Chapter 18.

FIGURE 18.1 During hot-weather activity, adequate hydration is essential.

swimmers. The physiology of heat cramps is not clear; however, they are thought to occur as a result of water and mineral loss caused by sweating. As previously stated, air temperature and relative humidity work together to increase the likelihood of heat-related problems in athletes. The body rids itself of excess heat primarily through the evaporation of sweat from the skin surface. Under conditions of high relative humidity, however, the evaporation process becomes less effective, thereby contributing to elevations in body temperature. As can be seen in Table 18.1, apparent air temperature can vary significantly depending upon the relative humidity.

Signs and symptoms of heat cramps include:

1. Severe muscle cramps in the arms or legs.

2. Muscle cramping may occur in the abdominal muscles.

3. Profuse sweating.

Management of heat cramps involves:

1. Immediate cessation of exercise.

2. Consumption of fluids, either water, fruit drinks, or electrolyte beverages.

3. Static stretching of the involved muscles.

Heat Exhaustion

Heat exhaustion, as the term implies, involves generalized fatigue that occurs during exercise when excessive body fluids have been lost through sweating and not adequately replaced. Though not in itself a life-threatening condition, heat exhaustion can be a precursor to heat stroke, which is a true medical emergency. The prudent coach should constantly monitor athletes for the signs and symptoms of heat exhaustion when they must practice and compete in extreme climatic conditions of high heat and/or high humidity.

Signs and symptoms of heat exhaustion— according to Hubbard and Armstrong (1989) and the National Safety Council (1991)—include:

1. Moist, clammy skin.

2. Muscle fatigue (general).

3. Nausea or related gastrointestinal distress.

4. Dizziness and occasionally loss of consciousness.

5. Increased respiratory rate and rapid pulse.

6. Body temperature ranging from 96.6°F to 102°F.

Management of heat exhaustion involves:

1. Immediate cessation of exercise.

TABLE 18.1 Heat Index

| Relative Humidity | Air Temperature | | | | | | | | | | |
	70	75	80	85	90	95	100	105	110	115	120
	Apparent Temperature*										
0%	64	69	73	78	83	87	91	95	99	103	107
10%	65	70	75	80	85	90	95	100	105	111	116
20%	66	72	77	82	87	93	99	105	112	120	130
30%	67	73	78	84	90	96	104	113	123	135	148
40%	68	74	79	86	93	101	110	123	137	151	
50%	69	75	81	88	96	107	120	135	150		
60%	70	76	82	90	100	114	132	149			
70%	70	77	85	93	106	124	144				
80%	71	78	86	97	113	136					
90%	71	79	88	102	122						
100%	72	80	91	108							

*Degrees Fahrenheit.
Above 130°F = heat stroke imminent
105°–130°F = heat exhaustion and heat cramps likely and heat stroke with long exposure and activity
90°–105°F = heat exhaustion and heat cramps with long exposure and activity
80°–90°F = fatigue during exposure and activity
Source: National Safety Council. 1991. *First Aid and CPR*. Boston: Jones and Bartlett. 160. Reprinted with permission.

Athletic Trainers Speak Out

"A far too common type of injury is heat illness. This must be recognized in its early stages so that it can be easily managed. Refusing to recognize the signs and symptoms can quickly lead to heat stroke, which is a medical emergency and causes the most deaths among high-school athletes. As a student athletic trainer, I experienced several situations in which aggressive treatment was prohibited by a well-meaning but ignorant coaching staff. We were often not allowed to administer assistance to the athletes until they dropped or lost consciousness. We were scolded for touching them to help break their falls as they fainted. These athletes fortunately did recover, but had to be hospitalized for three to seven days. The coaching staff was also replaced before the end of the academic year. [This problem] can be entirely avoided with proper preventive measures and aggressive management of those suspected of manifesting early signs and symptoms of heat stress."

—*Christine Stopka, Ph.D., A.T.C., C.S.C.S.*

Christine Stopka

Dr. Stopka is an associate professor with the Department of Exercise and Sports Science at the University of Florida.

2. Moving the athlete to a cool place.

3. Placing the athlete in a supine position, with legs elevated 8 to 12 inches.

4. Loosening clothing and cooling the athlete with wet towels or ice packs.

5. If the athlete is not fully recovered within 30 minutes, seek immediate medical attention.

Heat Stroke

Heat stroke involves the body's inability to cool itself, with subsequent radical elevations in body temperature, sometimes exceeding 106°F. Two types of heat stroke have been identified, classic and exertional. Classic heat stroke occurs among nonathletes and is generally seen in obese people, the chronically ill or elderly, or diabetics. Such people often have circulatory problems and difficulty controlling body temperature. Exertional heat stroke is the form seen in athletes when they are exercising in a warm environment. It is usually related to excessive fluid loss due to heavy sweating and extreme environmental conditions. Experts have reported that heat stroke occurs most often at temperatures in excess of 95°F (AAOS, 1991). It is critical to remember that heat

5. Severe motor disturbances and loss of coordination.

6. Rapid and strong pulse.

It must be emphasized that heat stroke can result in permanent damage to the central nervous system (**CNS**) as well as other systems within the body. Death can result if the body temperature is not controlled quickly; therefore, correct initial management of heat stroke is critical.

Management of heat stroke involves:

1. Summoning emergency medical services.

2. Moving the athlete to a cool, humidity-controlled environment.

3. Wrapping the athlete in wet sheets or towels or placing cold packs in areas with abundant blood supply, e.g., neck, armpits, head, or groin.

4. Treating for shock and monitoring temperature, not allowing it to drop below 102°F.

5. Keeping the athlete in a semiseated position.

Prevention of Heat Disorders

Ironically, heat-related illness causing death among athletes is a totally preventable problem. Application

Information at your fingertips

The World Wide Web—Learn more about prevention of heat-related illness. Go to http://www.jbpub.com/athletictraining and click on Chapter 18.

stroke is a true medical emergency and must be treated accordingly.

Signs and symptoms of heat stroke include:

1. Sweating may or may not be present (Hubbard and Armstrong, 1989).

2. Hot, dry skin, or clammy (if sweat is present on skin).

3. Mental confusion and possible loss of consciousness.

4. Gastrointestinal distress, including nausea and vomiting.

of a few simple guidelines and a dose of common sense are all that is needed to avoid possible tragedy.

In order to prevent heat disorders, athletes should comply with the following guidelines:

1. Consume fluids and avoid **dehydration** when participating in activities in warm and humid environments. Experts recommend the consumption of 10 ounces of water every 30 minutes of activity (AAOS, 1991).

2. Avoid heavy exertion during times of extreme environmental conditions, especially when the temperature is above 95°F and there is high humidity.

TABLE 18.2 Factors That Increase the Risk of Heat Stroke

DRUGS
Drugs such as cocaine or speed tend to increase physical activity and reduce the awareness of fatigue.

ALCOHOL
Decreases cardiac output and can cause hyperthermia.
Causes electrolyte disturbances in skeletal muscle.
Causes dehydration.

ILLNESS
Particularly dangerous when fever is present.
Athletes are often reluctant to report illness for fear of losing their position on the team or being seen as a shirker.

PRESCRIPTION MEDICATIONS
Some cold medications act like amphetamines and increase heat production.
Antihistamines interfere with body cooling by reducing sweat production.
Many drugs for suppressing nausea or diarrhea also reduce sweating. So do many tranquilizers.
Diuretics are associated with loss of salt, potassium, and water.

LACK OF PHYSICAL CONDITIONING
Poor physical condition predisposes an athlete to heat stroke.
Poor condition leads to inefficient performance that results in more heat production per unit of work performed.

INAPPROPRIATE CLOTHING
Being overdressed prevents the evaporation of sweat from the skin.

ENVIRONMENTAL FACTORS
High temperature, high humidity, no breeze.
Physical exertion in the sun during the hottest part of the day.

GENETICS
Obesity, or large, heavy physique.
Male gender.
Sickle cell trait.

Source: Knochel JP. 1996. Management of heat conditions. *Athletic Therapy Today*. 1(4):31. Reprinted with permission.

3. Remember that restrictive garments can impair circulation of air, thus reducing the evaporation of sweat. Be aware that dark colors on uniforms and helmets may facilitate heat buildup.

4. Be reminded that fitness has a positive effect on the ability to function in extreme conditions. The process of developing a tolerance to extremes of climate, or acclimatization, normally requires a period of weeks.

Obviously, prevention of heat stroke must be a top priority for all those involved in organized sports. The legal community has shown little tolerance for coaching personnel who are found to be negligent in the implementation of prudent heat stroke prevention procedures. All personnel should be well versed in the major risk factors for heat stroke; these are listed in Table 18.2.

Cold-Related Health Problems

Just as extremes in both heat and humidity can create problems for athletes, so can temperatures that are significantly lower than the body's core temperature. Exposure to cold can result in several conditions, including hypothermia, which can be a life-threatening situation.

Hypothermia

Hypothermia, another aspect of thermal-related injury, has to do with losing body heat too rapidly, resulting in total body cooling. Clinically, hypothermia involves a lowering of the body core temperature significantly below the norm of 98.6°F. Mild hypothermia begins to occur when core temperature drops to 95°F. Historically, the study of hypothermia has been limited to military personnel in the North Sea and those taking part in expeditions in extremely cold environments (Thornton, 1990). Recently, however, cases of clinical hypothermia have been documented in athletes involved in outdoor aerobic events like long-distance runs. Participants with the greatest risk are extremely lean athletes who have very little insulating body fat to help conserve heat. Surprisingly, hypothermia can occur at temperatures well above freezing. The combination of wind and moisture can cause rapid heat loss and the onset of hypothermia, during which the hypothalamus induces shivering in the skeletal muscles to generate heat. If this is unsuccessful, shivering will cease at around 87°F to 90°F; then uncontrolled body cooling occurs.

Signs and symptoms of hypothermia—according to the National Safety Council (1991) and Thornton (1990)—include:

1. In *mild cases,* the athlete will display shivering, loss of motor control, slurring of speech, and mental problems such as confusion and loss of memory.

2. In *severe cases,* shivering will cease, and muscles will become stiff, giving the appearance of rigor mortis. Skin will become blue, and respiration and pulse rates will decrease. The athlete will be semiconscious or unconscious.

Management of hypothermia involves:

1. Moving the athlete to a source of heat and out of the cold environment.

2. Removing any clothing that may be wet.

3. Wrapping the athlete in warm, dry clothing or blankets.

4. Using an electric blanket or hot packs placed around the head and neck, armpits, groin, and chest.

Management of severe hypothermia (body temperature below 90°F) involves:

1. Transporting the athlete immediately to a health care facility.

2. Making no attempt to rewarm the athlete but preventing further heat loss by moving the athlete to a warm environment and gently removing cold, wet clothing.

3. Treating the athlete gently since cardiac-related problems are likely at low body temperatures.

4. Monitoring vital signs and being prepared to administer artificial respiration or CPR.

As is the case with heat-related disorders, the best approach to the treatment of hypothermia is prevention. This can be accomplished in the majority of cases by following a few simple rules.

To prevent hypothermia, athletes should comply with the following guidelines:

1. Assess the risk by learning to use the wind-chill chart shown in Table 18.3. As can be seen, even on days when the temperature is moderate, the wind-chill factor can significantly increase the risk of hypothermia.

2. Do not embark on an outdoor activity of long duration, such as running or cycling, alone. Train with a friend or at least tell someone where you are going and when you plan to return.

3. Learn to recognize the early warning signs of hypothermia. If you have uncontrolled shivering in conjunction with loss of motor control, get to a warmer environment immediately.

4. Dress with appropriate cold-weather clothing. The new synthetic materials now available allow body moisture to be brushed away from the skin surface while retaining body heat. It is also advised that you carry extra dry clothing whenever possible. When practical, keep your hands, feet, and head protected with extra insulation.

5. Make sure you remain properly hydrated and keep sufficient calories in your system to generate body heat. It is best to consume food and drink at regular intervals during long outdoor exposures. Also, avoid drugs such as alcohol, which creates the illusion of warmth but in fact contributes to heat loss.

Personnel rendering first aid to a victim of hypothermia should be versed in assessing body core temperature rectally. Oral thermometers are of little practical value when dealing with this form of medical emergency.

▌Frostbite and Frostnip

Exposure to extremely cold temperatures can result in skin-related problems, known commonly as frostbite and frostnip. The American Academy of Orthopaedic Surgeons (1991) defines **frostbite** as "freezing of tissues from excessive exposure to cold." Symptoms of frostbite include an initial feeling of burning and pain,

TABLE 18.3 Wind-Chill Factor

Estimated Wind Speed (in MPH)	Actual Thermometer Reading (°F)											
	50	40	30	20	10	0	−10	−20	−30	−40	−50	−60
	Equivalent Temperature (°F)											
calm	50	40	30	20	10	0	−10	−20	−30	−40	−50	−60
5	48	37	27	16	6	−5	−15	−26	−36	−47	−57	−68
10	40	28	16	4	−9	−24	−33	−46	−58	−70	−83	−95
15	36	22	9	−5	−18	−32	−45	−58	−72	−85	−99	−112
20	32	18	4	−10	−25	−39	−53	−67	−82	−96	−110	−124
25	30	16	0	−15	−29	−44	−59	−74	−88	−104	−118	−133
30	25	13	−2	−18	−33	−48	−63	−79	−94	−109	−125	−140
35	27	11	−4	−20	−35	−51	−67	−82	−98	−113	−129	−145
40	26	10	−6	−21	−37	−53	−69	−85	−100	−116	−132	−148

(Wind speeds greater than 40 mph have little additional effect.)

Little danger (for properly clothed person). Maximum danger of false sense of security.

Increasing danger. (Flesh may freeze within 1 minute.)

Great danger. (Flesh may freeze within 30 seconds.)

Source: National Safety Council. 1991. *First Aid and CPR*. Boston: Jones and Bartlett. 156. Reprinted with permission.

followed by progressive loss of sensation. Damage in frostbite is caused by actual freezing of tissues as well as lack of blood (oxygen) supply to the tissues as a result of clotting. **Frostnip** is generally considered less severe than frostbite and involves freezing of only outer layers of skin, without damage to underlying tissue. Both these conditions can occur when the nose, ears, fingers, and feet are exposed to temperatures below 32°F for a long enough time period for freezing to occur. Skin temperatures must range between 28° and 21°F in order for tissue freezing to occur. A temperature of −20°F is required for total freezing of exposed areas (Deivert, 1996). Medical evidence indicates that the most severe damage related to frostbite occurs when the frozen tissue thaws and then refreezes prior to medical treatment.

Fortunately, the risk of frostbite is minimal in most organized outdoor activities such as team sports. Typically such activities are held near school or community facilities so that participants can return to a warm environment before any significant freezing takes place. The probability of frostnip occurring is quite high, however, even under such circumstances because participants may not realize the severity of tissue cooling taking place. During activities in extreme conditions in which temperatures are below freezing and wind chill is a factor, athletes should be instructed by coaching personnel to watch closely for the early warning signs of both frostbite and frostnip. Remem-

ber, the early signs of these problems are often noted by someone other than the victim.

The National Safety Council (1991) has published criteria to aid in the early identification of both frostbite and frostnip; its guidelines are listed in Box 18.1. Tissue freezing can be categorized as either superficial

---

BOX 18.1 First Aid for Frostbite and Frostnip

1. Get medical attention immediately.
2. If medical help is nearby, do not attempt any sort of rapid rewarming.
3. If medical help will be delayed, then slow rewarming is necessary. This involves the following steps:
   - Remove clothing or constricting items, such as rings, which can impair circulation.
   - Place frostbitten parts in warm (102° F–106° F) water.
   - Keep water temperature constant by adding additional warm water when necessary.
   - Warming usually requires 20–40 minutes and should be continued until the tissues are soft and pliable.
   - For frostbite of facial areas, apply warm, moist cloths directly to the tissues involved.

Source: National Safety Council. 1991. *First Aid and CPR*. Boston: Jones and Bartlett. 153, 155. Reprinted with permission.

or deep, depending on the duration and extent of exposure.

Signs and symptoms of superficial freezing include:

1. Skin color is white or grayish yellow.

2. Pain may occur early and later subside.

3. Affected part may feel very cold and numb. There may be a tingling, stinging, or aching sensation.

4. Skin surface will feel hard or crusty, and underlying tissue will be soft when depressed gently and firmly.

Signs and symptoms of deep freezing include:

1. Affected part feels hard, solid, and cannot be depressed.

2. Blisters appear in 12 to 36 hours.

3. Affected part is cold with pale, waxy skin.

4. A painfully cold part suddenly stops hurting.

Cold Urticaria

Another related problem of the skin associated with exposure to cold temperatures is **cold urticaria,** which involves a skin reaction of localized **edema** (fluid accumulation) associated with severe itching. The areas involved are usually those directly exposed to the cold or those not well protected by clothing. The exact mechanism of cold urticaria is unknown but appears to be an allergic reaction to cold temperatures. Some individuals are more susceptible, including people with mononucleosis, syphilis, varicella (chicken pox), and hepatitis. In addition, those using certain drugs, such as penicillin and oral contraceptives, also demonstrate a higher incidence of cold urticaria (Escher and Tucker, 1993).

Fortunately, symptoms of cold urticaria tend to be self-limiting, with the acute symptoms resolving within a few hours after rewarming of the affected areas. For athletes who repeatedly suffer such symptoms, medical referral may be warranted. Treatment may include taking drugs such as antihistamines to control edema and itching. Athletes may also find certain types of outdoor clothing to be more effective in protecting the skin.

Review Questions

1. Describe the normal range for body core temperature.

2. Explain how the body rids itself of excess heat.

3. What is the relationship between relative humidity and the process of evaporation?

4. *True or false:* Heat exhaustion is potentially more serious than simple heat stroke.

5. *True or false:* Heat cramps may be managed with rest, consumption of fluids, and static stretching of the involved muscles.

6. What is the recommended water intake during physical activity?

7. What is the fluid ounce equivalent of 4 L?

8. A fluid loss of from 2% to 6% can impair physical performance by how much?

9. At what core temperature does hypothermia begin?

10. At what body temperature does the shivering response cease?

11. What is the relationship between hypothermia and cardiac function?

12. Describe the signs and symptoms of cold urticaria.

References

American Academy of Orthopaedic Surgeons. 1991. *Athletic Training and Sports Medicine.* Park Ridge, Ill.: American Academy of Orthopaedic Surgeons.

Deivert RG. 1996. Adverse environmental conditions and athletes. *Athletic Therapy Today.* 1(4):5–10.

Escher S, Tucker A. 1993. Preventing, diagnosing, and

treating cold urticaria. *Phys Sportsmed.* 21: 125–133.

Guyton AC. 1986. *Textbook of Medical Physiology.* Philadelphia: W. B. Saunders.

Hubbard RW, Armstrong LE. 1989. Hyperthermia: new thoughts on an old problem. *Phys Sportsmed.* 16(6): 97–113.

Montain SJ, Maughan RJ, Sawka MN. 1996. Fluid replacement strategies for exercise in hot weather. *Athletic Therapy Today.* 1(4):24–27.

National Safety Council. 1991. *First Aid and CPR.* Boston: Jones and Bartlett.

Thornton JS. 1990. Hypothermia shouldn't freeze out cold-weather athletes. *Phys Sportsmed.* 18(1): 109–113.

Wilmore JH, Costill DL. 1988. *Training for Sport and Acitivity: The Physiological Basis of the Conditioning Process.* Dubuque: William C. Brown.

CHAPTER 19

Other Medical Concerns

MAJOR CONCEPTS

Athletes, like everyone else, occasionally become ill with infections that involve the respiratory and/or gastrointestinal systems. This chapter provides participation guidelines along with examples of typical signs and symptoms of the more common types of infections. The identification of several cases of Lyme disease within the athletic community has spurred growing concern over the last few years. This bacterial infection is transmitted primarily by ticks and can have serious, long-term implications for athletes. The chapter outlines early and late signs and symptoms, along with tips on how to avoid exposure to the disease-carrying ticks.

Next, the chapter examines several illnesses caused by viruses, including infectious mononucleosis and infectious strains of hepatitis A and B. All of these conditions pose a serious health risk to athletes; their signs and symptoms can assist the coach in identification.

The chapter concludes with a discussion of the current thinking regarding sports participation by athletes suffering from exercise-induced asthma (EIA), diabetes, or epilepsy. The emphasis is on identification of the major signs and symptoms of each of these conditions as well as management and special precautions related to sports participation.

Exercise and Infectious Disease

Infectious disease is illness caused by some type of microorganism: virus, bacteria, fungi, or protozoa. Although it is generally thought that physical activity helps to improve one's resistance to common infections, athletes remain vulnerable to the same illnesses as the general population. Research is ongoing in an effort to better identify the effects of long-term exercise on the immune system (Heath et al., 1991; Nieman and Nehlsen-Cannarella, 1991). The vast majority of infectious conditions affecting athletes involve either the respiratory or gastrointestinal systems.

Respiratory Infections

According to Afrasiabi and Spector (1991), respiratory infections can be categorized as upper respiratory infections (**URI**) involving the nose, throat, ears and sinuses, tonsils, and associated lymph glands, or lower respiratory infections (**LRI**) involving the lungs, bronchi, and larynx. The majority of upper and lower respiratory infections in athletes are caused by viruses.

participation in a sport demanding a high degree of balance, e.g., figure skating, gymnastics, or diving (Nelson, 1989). In addition, there is recent evidence that viral infections decrease both **endurance** and **muscular strength** (Eichner, 1993). Since most sports require some degree of both, it seems unlikely that optimal performance will be possible during periods of acute infection. Athletes involved in national or international events also must be warned not to treat themselves with over-the-counter medications such as decongestants or analgesics since many of these drugs have been banned by sports regulatory organizations. Box 19.1 lists over-the-counter cold medications banned by the National Collegiate Athletic Association (NCAA).

Infections of the upper respiratory system that persist for more than a few days may be related to bacterial infections such as streptococci. Symptoms of such infections are generally more pronounced, with visible lesions in the back of the throat (strep throat), severe sore throat, fever and chills, general discomfort, and swollen lymph glands in the neck and lower jaw. Athletes demonstrating such symptoms should not be allowed to participate, especially in team sports in which they are in close contact with other athletes because such infections are routinely contagious. Medical evaluation is essential; it usually includes a physical as-

WHAT IF?

You are coaching track at a small college in the Midwest. Your best miler has been suffering from an upper respiratory infection for several days and, worse, the regional qualifying meet is in three days. What would you recommend to this young athlete and, further, what would you caution him regarding over-the-counter medications?

■ Upper Respiratory Infections

Upper respiratory infections (URI) produce classic symptoms of the common cold or **rhinitis**—sore throat, stuffy nose, mild cough, mild fatigue, and fever. As a general rule, these infections are self-limited and last only a few days. Since the infection is related to a virus, antibiotic therapy will have no effect on the organism causing the illness. Athletes with colds should be cautioned not to borrow drugs such as antibiotics from a friend or parent since this could result in drug-related poisoning or allergic reactions.

Athletes with URI can normally participate in competitive sports unless specific symptoms place them at obvious risk. For example, if an athlete has an ear infection affecting the vestibular system that results in **vertigo** (loss of balance), it may be unwise to allow

sessment, throat culture (to identify the infectious agent), and in most cases a prescription for an antibiotic medication. The athlete should be advised to rest and drink plenty of nonalcoholic fluids until the major symptoms begin to subside. Return to activity can usually occur within a few days of treatment.

■ Lower Respiratory Infections

Infections of the lower respiratory system can impair performance for periods ranging up to several weeks. Normally related to a viral infection of the bronchi, the symptoms include cough, fever, and **malaise** (general discomfort). Obviously, athletes involved in aerobic sports—running, swimming, cycling, or cross-country skiing—will be directly and negatively affected by such an infection. As was the case with upper respiratory

---

BOX 19.1   OTC Cold Medications Banned by the NCAA

Actifed	Dristan	Primatene Mist
Alka-Seltzer Plus	Duration	Robitussin
Chlortrimeton	Four-Way Cold	Sucrets Decongestant
Co-Tylenol	Halls Mentho-Lyptus	Sudafed
Comtrex	Head & Chest	Triaminic
Congesprin	Neo-Synephrine	Vicks Formula 44
Contac	Novahistine	Vicks Daycare
Coricidin	Nyquil	Vicks Nightime
Day Care Cold		

Source: Nelson MA. 1989. A young gymnast with an acute upper respiratory infection. In Smith NJ (ed.). *Common Problems in Pediatric Sports Medicine.* Chicago: Year Book Medical Publishers. 208. Reprinted with permission.

---

infections, athletes with lower respiratory infections (LRI) should be isolated from their peers and referred to a physician for complete evaluation and treatment. Such cases are normally treated with rest and medication designed to control coughing and to relieve the associated aches and pains. A more serious, sometimes life-threatening, form of infection to this area of the body is **pneumonia** (inflammation of the lungs), which can be related to either bacterial or viral infection. Generally, symptoms of pneumonia are more profound and also include coughing up of discolored sputum (AAOS, 1991). Diagnosis of pneumonia must be made by a physician, and treatment includes rest, medication, and, in severe cases, hospitalization. Decisions regarding when to return to activity should be made on the advice of the attending physician as well as the athlete (or parents in the case of a minor).

Gastrointestinal Infections

Illnesses of the gastrointestinal **(GI)** system are typically related to viral, bacterial, or protozoan infections. Known collectively as **gastroenteritis** (inflammation of the stomach and intestines) these infections produce similar symptoms: one of the most common forms is simple stomach flu, which is caused by a virus. Symptoms include abdominal cramping, nausea (often associated with vomiting), fever and chills, and diarrhea. When such symptoms occur, the best approach is to remove the athlete from participation until symptoms abate. The athlete should be encouraged to drink plenty of nonalcoholic fluids as dehydration can occur when vomiting and/or diarrhea persist. If symptoms continue for more than a few days, the athlete should consult a physician. Related conditions that may be more serious are caused by bacteria (in the case of typhoid fever) and protozoa (in the case of giardiasis).

As a general rule, an athlete with GI symptoms—including severe (explosive or bloody) diarrhea, fever, extreme dehydration, and chills—should be referred to a physician for a complete physical evaluation and diagnosis.

A large and diverse number of problems of the gastrointestinal system can produce symptoms that mimic those of simple stomach flu. Evidence suggests that in some athletes the stress of physical activity may be the causative mechanism (Anderson, 1992). Other research has documented the reduction of GI symptoms in groups of athletes involved in aerobic activity (Halvorsen et al., 1990). Common GI-related problems include **gastritis** (inflammation of the stomach lining), **colitis** (inflammation of the colon), and **colic** (intra-abdominal pain). As with any recurrent and persistent clinical symptoms, referral to a physician is the prudent choice of action.

Related Infectious Diseases

Several other types of infections can affect athletes, and all present special problems with respect to identification, management, and prevention. The newest of this group is Lyme disease; although rarely a life-threatening illness, it can severely limit one's ability to participate in sports. Others include infectious mononucleosis, known in the 1960s as the kissing disease because of this common mode of transmission, and hepatitis A and B, both of which are extremely dangerous conditions.

■ Lyme Disease
Lyme disease is a bacterial *(Borrela burgdorferi)* infection transmitted by the common deer tick (sometimes called bear tick in the western United States), which is widespread throughout the United States. Lyme dis-

ease gets its name from the town where the first cases were identified in 1975: Lyme, Old Lyme, and East Haddam, Connecticut (Pinger, Hahn, and Sharp, 1991). Since that time Lyme disease has surpassed Rocky Mountain spotted fever as the most prevalent tick-borne infectious disease in the United States.

The disease is transmitted via a tick bite. Once infected, initial symptoms may appear as early as three days later; however, they may be absent for as long as one month after the bite. Regardless of the time period, the early symptom is the development of a circular area of reddened skin at the site of the bite. This is technically known as erythema chronicum migrans (ECM) and signifies the first stage of the infection. ECM will continue to develop for days; it can vary in size from a few inches to a foot or more. Additional symptoms include chills, fever, general aches and pains (malaise), and general fatigue. If left untreated the disease will become systemic and can affect the heart and central nervous system. In the majority of untreated cases arthritis will develop, with the knee being the most commonly affected joint (Pinger, Hahn, and Sharp, 1991). These symptoms may appear together or separately and can be accompanied by a repeated appearance of ECM. It is important to note that untreated Lyme disease can persist for years within the body and produce symptoms of a variety of disorders, thereby making recognition and diagnosis difficult.

Athletes who are involved in outdoor sports held in wooded areas are at risk of exposure to the deer tick; they should be taught how to perform a thorough inspection of their bodies for the presence of a tick. This may require assistance when inspecting hard-to-see areas, such as the hairline at the back of the neck, behind the ears, and the posterior torso. The deer tick is very small—about the size of a pinhead in the nymph stage, which is the time it is best able to transmit the disease. If a tick is found, it should be removed immediately as it has been found that length of attachment plays a role in likelihood of infection. Box 19.2 outlines recommended procedures for removal of a tick.

Treatment of Lyme disease involves the administration of antibiotic drugs. Cases have been reported in which even drug therapy was ineffective. Obviously, the best approach is prevention of the disease by avoiding an infectious tick bite. Sports organizations that promote outdoor activities during the summer months in wooded areas should check with local medical authorities regarding reports of deer tick activity. Every effort should be made to hold events in areas where the likelihood of tick exposure is minimal. Athletes should be encouraged to conduct tick checks

---

BOX 19.2 Guidelines for Tick Removal

- Do *not* use the following popular methods of tick removal, which have proven useless:
  1. Petroleum jelly
  2. Fingernail polish
  3. Rubbing alcohol
  4. A hot match
- Pull the tick off, employing the following methods:
  1. Use tweezers or, if you have to use your fingers, protect your skin by using a paper towel or disposable tissue. Although few people ever encounter ticks infected with a disease, the person removing the tick may become infected by germs entering through breaks in the skin.
  2. Grasp the tick as close to the skin surface as possible and pull away from the skin with a steady pressure or lift the tick slightly upward and pull parallel to the skin until the tick detaches. Do *not* twist or jerk the tick since this may result in incomplete removal.
  3. Wash the bite site and your hands well with soap and water. Apply alcohol to further disinfect the area. Then apply a cold pack to reduce pain. Calamine lotion might aid in relieving any itching. Keep the area clean.

Source: National Safety Council. 1993. *First Aid and CPR* (2d ed.). Boston: Jones and Bartlett. 123, 125. Reprinted with permission.

---

regularly when they are participating in high-risk areas.

Several other viral-related illnesses can increase the chance of serious injury, even death, among athletes. Infectious mononucleosis is caused by the Epstein-Barr virus. Hepatitis A (HAV) and hepatitis B (serum hepatitis) (HBV) are both caused by viruses as well. The illnesses produce symptoms that can seriously impair performance; in the case of HBV infection, the disease can result in death.

■ Infectious Mononucleosis

Infectious mononucleosis is extremely common in the United States among young people, with a reported incidence in the general population of 90% by age 30, and 3% per year among college students (Eichner, 1996; McKeag and Kinderknecht, 1989). The initial symptoms of the infection are similar to the common cold—sore throat, fever, chills, and enlarged lymph nodes in the neck and jaw region. Infected persons often complain of extreme fatigue as well and may first notice the problem when they find it difficult to participate in sports. As the disease progresses other organs may become involved, including the liver and spleen.

Athletic Trainers Speak Out

"In 1992 one of our offensive linemen was diagnosed with adult diabetes. I realized I would not only learn about the disease but also counsel this young man, who would be challenged to change his lifestyle dramatically during the course of his senior season and from that point forward. Knowing very little about diabetes, I sought as much information as possible from as many resources as I found available. My best resource was a professor of pharmacology who also had diabetes and was an active individual. [Learning about the disease] was the easy part. This young man jumped through many hurdles in the first few months. Still, there were several times when he wanted to quit football. I would not let him. I challenged him to never give up. Fortunately, he was surrounded by supportive players and coaches. His special moment of glory came against the University of Washington in the 1992 Apple Cup. He was chosen to serve as co-captain for his final game, which was known as the Snow Bowl, and helped lead his team to victory."

—Mark J. Smaha, M.S., A.T.C.

Mark J. Smaha

Mark Smaha is the director of athletic medicine at Washington State University and a former president of NATA.

Transmission of the disease usually occurs via contact with discharge from an infected person's mouth (airway). Once exposed, the incubation is variable; however, it usually ranges between two and six weeks (AAOS, 1991). Once the illness develops, its duration ranges from 5 to 15 days, with recovery beginning thereafter. Treatment is essentially symptomatic once the diagnosis is made by a physician; the emphasis is on rest and pain control with some type of analgesic drug. Fortunately, infectious mononucleosis is a self-limited disease with no long-term effects.

A major concern with this illness, however, is its effect on the spleen. It has been well documented that acute cases result in enlargement of the spleen (splenomegaly) in 40% to 60% of all cases (McKeag and Kinderknecht, 1989). When the spleen experiences an episode of blunt trauma, as is common in many contact sports, splenomegaly predisposes this organ to rupture. Data regarding rupture is sparse; however, the available information indicates an incidence of rupture in the infected population to be approximately 1/1000 cases (Eichner, 1996). (See Chapter 13.) Therefore, the attending physician is faced with the dilemma of determining when it is safe for an athlete to return to participation after recovering from infectious mononucleosis. It has been documented that most spleen ruptures occur between the 4th and 21st day of the illness; consequently athletes never should be allowed to participate during this period (McKeag and Kinderknecht, 1989). Obviously the coach, athlete, and parents must rely on the attending physician regarding the best time to resume participation.

Prevention of the spread of infectious mononucleosis is difficult when dealing with athletes involved in team sports in which they are in close contact with one another on a daily basis. Athletes should know that the major mode of transmission of this disease involves coming into contact with an infected person's saliva, as in kissing. Preventive steps include advising athletes not to share water bottles or any other beverage containers. As a general precaution, towels and jerseys should not be shared by the athletes since such items may be contaminated with respiratory discharge containing the virus. In addition, athletes should be taught the importance of reporting any symptoms of illness to the coach so he or she can decide a given athlete's participation status.

■ Hepatitis Infection

Hepatitis infection, either HAV or HBV, is serious, although HBV or serum hepatitis is considered to be the more serious and potentially life-threatening variety. HAV is transmitted via feces and is a serious problem among food handlers who fail to wash their hands after going to the bathroom. Serum hepatitis is transmitted through the blood and sexual fluids of an infected person; it is routinely transmitted among IV drug users or accidentally by health care workers working with contaminated needles. It is also possible that transmission of HBV may occur during blood transfusions from an infected person. Guidelines for preventing the transmission of HBV were presented in Chapter 17.

Once infected, the incubation period for HAV is 15 to 50 days; for HBV it is 45 to 160 days (Benenson, 1975). Symptoms of both HAV and HBV infection are varied, but symptoms of both strains include nausea, abdominal pain, vomiting, fever, and malaise. If untreated, both strains will begin to affect the liver, resulting in jaundice (yellowing of the skin). This indicates liver involvement; in severe cases this vital organ may be severely damaged, leading in some cases to death. Treatment for either form of hepatitis infection is limited; for HAV it appears that immediate innoculation with immune serum globulin (ISG) may confer passive immunity. There is some evidence that this also may be effective in treating cases of HBV exposure. Obviously, an athlete with HAV or HBV infection should be removed from participation and given prompt medical treatment. Because of the vulnerability of the liver during hepatitis infection, all decisions regarding return to participation for recovering athletes should be made by the attending physician.

Information at your fingertips

The World Wide Web—Check out this impressive site to learn more about hepatitis. Go to http://www.jbpub.com/athletictraining and click on Chapter 19.

Exercise-Induced Asthma

Exercise-induced asthma (**EIA**) is defined by Afrasiabi and Spector (1991) as "a temporary increase in airway resistance after several minutes of strenuous exercise and is usually felt after stopping exercise." The highest incidence of EIA is found, not surprisingly, among chronic asthmatics: about 80% will develop an attack during exercise. However, EIA afflicts 12% to 15% of the general population as well (Afrasiabi and Spector, 1991).

The typical scenario for the onset and symptoms of EIA begins with exercise of sufficient magnitude to be considered intense. During exercise the airway will typically dilate; however, upon cessation of exercise airway restriction or bronchospasm will occur within minutes. EIA has been found to be more common among athletes engaging in continuous exercise lasting at least six to eight minutes and less common among athletes involved in intermittent forms of exercise typical of team sports (Lemanske and Henke, 1989). Although the exact cause of EIA is unknown, it is hypothesized that a variety of stimuli may initiate an attack, including cold air temperature, low humidity, and pollution as well as certain foods such as

shrimp, egg whites, almonds, and bananas (Afrasiabi and Spector, 1991; Van Camp, 1989). Type of activity can also be a factor, as EIA is common among susceptible runners and less so among cyclists and walkers (Afrasiabi and Spector, 1991). Because indoor swimming pools usually provide a warm, humid environment, swimming in this setting is less likely to initiate an EIA attack.

Signs and symptoms of EIA include:

1. Coughing and tightness in the chest.
2. Shortness of breath.
3. Fatigue and stomachache (in children).
4. Some athletes may become alarmed.

Management of EIA generally involves the use of any one of a variety of drugs that prevent airway restriction or bronchospasm. Effective drugs are available and can be administered either orally or with an inhaler. It is important to note that certain drugs have been banned by some international sports-regulating agencies, such as the International Olympic Committee. Refer to Table 19.1 for a list of currently approved drugs.

Highly susceptible individuals may be required to avoid certain activities such as running or cycling, or at least be cognizant of environmental conditions and

TABLE 19.1 Prophylactic Pharmacologic Management of Exercise-Induced Asthma

	Delivery System*	When to Administer (min before exercise)	Duration of Effect (hr)
BETA₂-ADRENERGICS			
Albuterol†	MDI	15	4–6
Albuterol	PO	30	4–6
Epinephrine	MDI	10	1–3
Metaproterenol sulfate	MDI	10	2–4
Metaproterenol sulfate	PO	30	2–4
Terbutaline sulfate†	MDI	15	3–6
Terbutaline sulfate	PO	30	4–6
Cromolyn sodium†	S, MDI, A	10–20	4–6
THEOPHYLLINE†			
Short-acting	PO	30	4–12
Long-acting	PO	60–120	(24‡)
ANTICHOLINERGICS			
Ipratropium bromide	MDI	60	§??

*MDI = metered-dose inhaler; PO = oral; S = spinhaler; A = aerosol.
†Approved by the International Olympic Committee for managing asthma (albuterol and terbutaline sulfate are approved in MDI form only).
‡Hypothesized.
§Unknown.
Source: Afrasiabi R, Spector SL. 1991. Exercise-induced asthma. *Phys Sportsmed.* 19(5):56. Reprinted with permission.

EIA Treatment

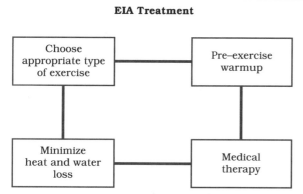

FIGURE 19.1 Overall treatment approaches for individuals with exercise-induced asthma. (Source: Lemanske RF, Henke KG. 1989. Exercise-induced asthma. In Gisolfi CV, Lamb DR (eds.). *Perspectives in Exercise Science and Sports Medicine, Volume 2: Youth Exercise and Sport.* Indianapolis: Benchmark Press. 483. Reprinted with permission.)

avoid such activity on cold, dry days. Sports involving short bursts of activity, followed by periods of rest, are excellent alternatives for high-risk athletes. For outdoor activities on cold, dry days, wearing a mask or scarf has been recommended (Afrasiabi and Spector, 1991). Warm-up exercises have also been found to help reduce the likelihood of an attack (Lemanske and Henke, 1989). A schematic diagram of the major treatment approaches regarding EIA is shown in Figure 19.1.

The appropriate steps in the management of an athlete suffering an acute attack of EIA are shown in Figure 19.2.

The Athlete with Diabetes

Diabetes is defined by the National Safety Council (1993) as "the inability of the body to appropriately metabolize carbohydrates." Blood glucose levels in a typical diabetic patient may fluctuate widely, ranging from excessive levels of blood glucose (**hyperglycemia**) to exceedingly low levels (hypoglycemia). Though a detailed explanation of the specific mechanisms for con-

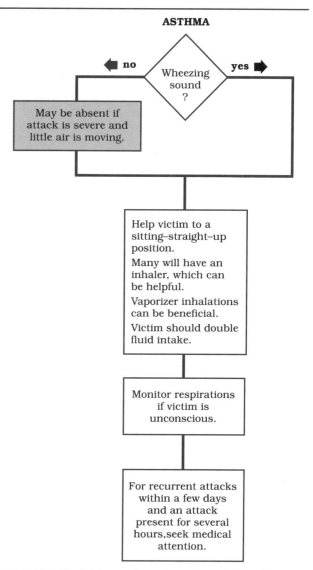

FIGURE 19.2 First aid procedures for asthma victims. (Source: National Safety Council. 1993. *First Aid and CPR* (2d ed.). Boston: Jones and Bartlett. 200. Reprinted with permission.)

trolling levels of blood glucose is beyond the scope of this book, suffice it to say that the ability to manufacture and/or utilize the hormone insulin is not possible for the diabetic athlete.

WHAT IF?

You are coaching high school softball. During practice one afternoon your right fielder comes to you complaining of extreme hunger and acting strangely. You notice during your conversation that she is perspiring heavily although it is a cool, cloudy afternoon. You know from her preseason physical evaluation that she has diabetes. What condition would these signs and symptoms indicate? What would be the appropriate first aid for this young athlete?

Exercise is now generally considered to be beneficial for children with insulin-dependent diabetes; however, certain problems can arise if exercise intensity, diet, and insulin dosage are not carefully monitored. This is best accomplished by working with a physician prior to the beginning of the playing season. Recent research by Robbins and Carleton (1989) has determined that any of three general reactions are possible in the diabetic athlete who initiates an exercise session:

1. The athlete anticipates correctly the amount of insulin needed to keep levels of blood glucose between 100 and 200 milligrams per deciliter. In this situation, glucose utilization in muscles is equal to that produced by the liver.

2. If the athlete does not take into account the effects of exercise and starts working out with a low level of insulin and an elevated blood glucose, liver glucose production may actually increase. This may lead to a dangerously elevated level of blood glucose, a condition known as hyperglycemia.

3. In some cases, an athlete who begins exercising with a low level of insulin may react just the opposite to the above scenerio. Liver glucose production may decrease while muscle glucose demand increases, causing dangerously low levels of blood glucose and leading to a condition known as hypoglycemia.

Research has shown that the type of exercise may determine what type of insulin response will occur (Horton, 1989). It has been found that sustained exercise of moderate intensity results in maintenance of, or even a decrease in, levels of blood glucose. It is recommended that diabetic athletes involved in triathlons or marathons decrease their insulin levels and increase caloric intake before a race or training session.

Interestingly, brief bouts of high-intensity exercise (80% or greater VO$_2$max) result in an increase in blood glucose levels. Sports such as tackle football, soccer, and basketball may contribute to this reaction; thus, athletes participating in these sports must be monitored to ensure they do not develop hyperglycemia and its complications.

Box 19.3 lists a variety of strategies that will help reduce the chances of developing hypoglycemia or hyperglycemia either during or after an exercise session.

The diabetic athlete will benefit from learning how to monitor blood glucose levels; this is most easily accomplished through a test involving a finger-sticking technique. Periodic monitoring of blood glucose levels allows the athlete to adjust caloric and insulin

---

BOX 19.3   Suggested Strategies to Avoid Hypoglycemia or Hyperglycemia During and After Physical Exercise

1. Adjustments to the Insulin Regimen
   a. Take insulin at least 1 h before exercise. If less than 1 h before exercise, inject insulin in muscle that will not be extensively used during exercise.
   b. Decrease the dose of both short-acting and intermediate-acting insulin before exercise.
   c. Alter daily insulin schedule.
2. Meals and Supplemental Feedings
   a. Eat a meal 1–3 h before exercise and check to see that blood glucose is in a safe range (100 to 250 mg/dL) before starting exercise.
   b. Take supplemental carbohydrate feedings during exercise, at least every 30 min if exercise is vigorous and of long duration. Monitor blood glucose during exercise if necessary to determine size and frequency of feedings needed to maintain safe glucose levels.
   c. Increase food intake for up to 24 h after exercise, depending on intensity and duration of exercise, to avoid late-onset post-exercise hypoglycemia.
3. Self-monitoring of blood glucose in urine ketones.
   a. Monitor blood glucose before, during, and after exercise to determine the need for and effect of changes in insulin dosage and feeding schedule.
   b. Delay exercise if blood glucose is <100 mg/dL or >250 mg/dL and if ketones are present in blood. Use supplemental feedings or insulin to correct glucose and metabolic control before starting exercise.
   c. Learn individual glucose responses to different types, intensities, and conditions of exercise. Determine effects of exercise at different times of the day (e.g., morning, afternoon, or evening) and effects of training versus competition on blood glucose responses.

Source: Horton ES. 1989. Exercise and diabetes in youth. In Gisolfi CV, Lamb DR (eds.). *Perspectives in Exercise Science and Sports Medicine, Volume 2: Youth Exercise and Sport.* Indianapolis: Benchmark Press. 563. Reprinted with permission.

---

intake prior to, during, and even after exercise. Athletes should learn to estimate the caloric content of foods and the caloric demands of a given exercise session. With this information, the athlete can adjust diet prior to an event to compensate for the typical abnormal metabolic response seen in diabetics.

Coaches, parents, and fellow athletes need to be versed in the early recognition and first aid treatment of both hypoglycemia and hyperglycemia. Although both conditions present unique signs and symptoms, either condition can become life threatening. Hyperglycemia (high blood sugar) can lead to a condition known as diabetic coma or ketoacidosis. This occurs when fatty acids are metabolized to provide energy and yield ketones, which make the blood more acidic. Hypoglycemia occurs when too little sugar is available or too much insulin has been introduced into the body. In either case the body has too little glucose, and insulin shock can occur.

Signs and symptoms of hyperglycemia include:

1. Symptoms develop slowly.

2. Fruity breath odor (indicates ketoacidosis).

3. The athlete will complain of extreme thirst and will have the urge to urinate frequently.

4. Nausea and/or vomiting.

5. Loss of consciousness.

Management of hyperglycemia involves:

1. Summoning emergency medical services.

2. Treating for shock and monitoring vital signs.

Signs and symptoms of hypoglycemia include:

1. Symptoms develop quickly.

2. The athlete may demonstrate unusual behavior—e.g., aggression or confusion followed by loss of consciousness.

3. Profuse perspiration.

4. Loss of motor coordination.

5. Extreme hunger.

Management of hypoglycemia involves:

1. If the athlete is conscious, immediately administer a food or beverage containing sugar—e.g., soda or fruit juice.

2. If the athlete does not improve within minutes, summon emergency medical services, treat for shock, and monitor vital signs.

A management flow chart covering the major treatment approaches for diabetic-related emergencies is shown in Figure 19.3.

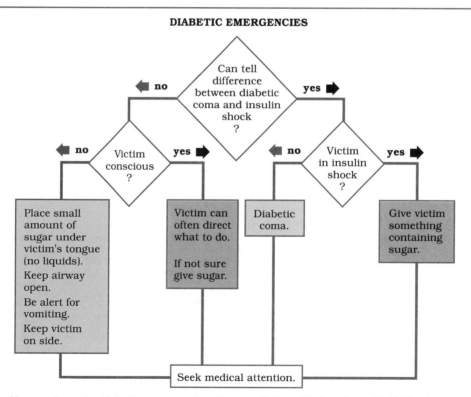

DIABETIC EMERGENCIES

FIGURE 19.3 First aid procedures for diabetic emergencies. (Source: National Safety Council. 1993. *First Aid and CPR* (2d ed.). Boston: Jones and Bartlett. 198. Reprinted with permission.)

Epilepsy and Sports Participation

Epilepsy is a disorder of the brain associated with a wide variety of symptoms. The most well known symptom is a **seizure**—a sudden episodic change in behavior or internal psychic state associated with an abrupt paroxysmal discharge of electrical activity in the brain (Gates, 1991). Seizures take many forms and may involve motor systems, perceptions, even the mood of the athlete. Epilepsy is not as common as popularly believed; it affects only 5 out of every 1,000 among the general population (Linschoten et al., 1990).

There are three forms of epileptic seizure the coach is likely to encounter among athletes (Gates, 1991). The first, a generalized tonic-clonic seizure known historically as the grand mal, involves perhaps the most dramatic type of epileptic disorder. This seizure is characterized by generalized convulsions involving a fall to the ground and uncontrolled shaking of the arms and legs as well as body twitching. During the seizure the person is unconscious, although the eyes may be open, thereby creating the illusion that the person is awake. The typical grand mal seizure lasts from two to five minutes (National Safety Council, 1993).

The second type, called an absence attack, was previously known as a petit mal seizure. The classic symptoms are sudden loss of awareness of immediate surroundings associated with a blank stare that lasts for a few seconds. Immediately following the seizure the person will recover and may not know one has occurred.

The third form is known as a complex partial seizure. An athlete suffering this type of seizure will suddenly lose contact with surroundings and demonstrate any number of unusual behaviors, including mumbling, picking at or removing clothing, or walking around in an apparently random fashion. This type of seizure may last for up to five minutes, after which time the athlete will recover but will remain confused and disoriented, possibly for a considerable time. The athlete will have no memory of activity during the seizure.

From the coach's standpoint, two major concerns must be addressed regarding an athlete with epilepsy: safety in the chosen activity and proper first aid care should a seizure occur. Many questions have been raised within both the lay and medical communities regarding what activities may pose a risk for the epileptic athlete. With the advent of anticonvulsant drugs, the vast majority of these athletes can control seizures. It has been reported that over half of epileptics taking antiseizure medication can remain free from seizures; another 30% will have infrequent attacks (Gates, 1991). The prevailing medical evidence suggests that high-risk activities for athletes afflicted with epilepsy include aquatic sports, sports in which falling is possible, and contact and collision sports (Gates, 1991; Linschoten et al., 1990).

Obviously, a seizure occurring while an athlete is in the water carries the risk of drowning; therefore, athletes who may suffer seizures should always swim with a buddy and alert pool personnel of their condition. However, it is generally advised that the benefits to a young athlete with epilepsy who is interested in water sports, such as competitive swimming, far outweigh any risks.

Athletes interested in sports capable of producing a dangerous fall, such as cycling, ice-skating or speed skating, skydiving, and horseback riding, should be discouraged from participating. In such activities the risks of injury related to a seizure exceed whatever benefits may be derived from participation.

A persistent myth has been that epileptics should not be involved in contact and collision sports since the potential jarring of the brain may increase the likelihood of seizure. Research, however, does not support this premise; in fact, it appears that athletes wth epilepsy have no more risk of participation in such sports than does anyone else (Gates, 1991). Of course, the epileptic athlete involved in such activities should take the same safety precautions as other athletes by wearing helmets, face masks, and mouth guards.

Information at your fingertips

The World Wide Web—Check out the home page of the **Epilepsy Foundation of America**. Go to **http://www.jbpub.com/athletictraining** and click on **Chapter 19.**

BOX 19.4   First Aid for Epilepsy: What To Do When Someone Has a Seizure

---

GENERALIZED TONIC-CLONIC SEIZURE

During the seizure the person may fall, stiffen, and make jerking movements. A pale or bluish complexion may result from difficulty in breathing.

Help the person into a lying position and put something soft under the head.
Remove glasses and loosen any tight clothing.
Clear the area of hard or sharp objects.
Don't force anything into the person's mouth.
Don't try to restrain the person. You cannot stop the seizure.

After the seizure the person will awaken confused and disoriented.

Turn the person to one side to allow saliva to drain from the mouth.
Arrange for someone to stay nearby until the person is fully awake.
Don't offer any food or drink until the person is fully awake.

An ambulance usually is not necessary. Call 911 or local police or ambulance only if:

the person does not start breathing within 1 minute after the seizure. If this happens, call for help and start mouth-to-mouth resuscitation.
the person has one seizure right after another.
the person requests an ambulance.

COMPLEX PARTIAL SEIZURE

During the seizure the person may

have a glassy stare or give no response or an inappropriate response when questioned.
sit, stand, or walk about aimlessly.
make lip-smacking or chewing motions.
fidget with clothes.
appear to be drunk, drugged, or even psychotic.

Remove harmful objects from the person's pathway or coax the person away from them.
Don't try to stop or restrain the person.
Don't approach the person if you are alone and the person appears angry or aggressive.

After the seizure the person may be confused or disoriented.

Stay with the person until he or she is fully alert. Call 911 or local police or ambulance only if the person is aggressive and you need help.

Source: Gates JR. 1991. Epilepsy and sports participation. *Phys Sportsmed*. 19:101. Reprinted with the permission of McGraw-Hill, Inc.

There is no reason why any youngster with epilepsy should be excluded from most school or community sports programs. In fact, such children can benefit a great deal from participation, particularly with regard to their self-esteem. It is important for coaching personnel to educate all participants about epilepsy in the event that an athlete suffers from a seizure. In this way, fear and anxiety on the part of teammates can be avoided.

First aid care for epileptic seizures is determined by the type of seizure and the immediate circumstances. Obviously, a generalized tonic-clonic seizure that takes place in the water will require quite different first aid than a complex partial seizure that occurs in the wrestling arena. For the most part, first aid for any type of seizure involves protection of the athlete from self-injury followed by psychological support. Specific first aid protocols for the athlete with epilepsy are shown in Box 19.4.

Review Questions

1. Define the acronyms URI and LRI.
2. What types of organisms are related to the above infections?
3. Define the term gastroenteritis.
4. Describe briefly the history of Lyme disease within the United States.

5. What is the mode of transmission for Lyme disease?

6. Describe the major signs and symptoms of Lyme disease.

7. *True or false:* Lyme disease is caused by a virus.

8. What is the causative agent of infectious mononucleosis?

9. What is the risk related to collision sports and mononucleosis?

10. Describe the common signs and symptoms of EIA.

11. What are the recommended levels of blood glucose for the athlete with diabetes?

12. List the signs and symptoms of hyperglycemia.

13. List the signs and symptoms of hypoglycemia.

14. What is the difference between in-field management for the above two conditions?

15. Define epilepsy.

16. What are the management guidelines for an athlete suffering an epileptic seizure?

References

Afrasiabi R, Spector SL. 1991. Exercise-induced asthma. *Phys Sportsmed.* 19(5):49–60.

American Academy of Orthopaedic Surgeons. 1991. *Athletic Training and Sports Medicine.* Park Ridge, Ill.: American Academy of Orthopaedic Surgeons.

Anderson CR. 1992. A runner's recurrent abdominal pain. *Phys Sportsmed.* 20:81–83.

Benenson AS (ed.). 1975. *Control of communicable diseases in man.* Washington, D.C.: American Public Health Association.

Eichner ER. 1996. Infectious mononucleosis—recognizing the condition, reactivating the patient. *Phys Sportsmed.* 24:49–54.

Eichner ER. 1993. Infection, immunity, and exercise: what to tell patients? *Phys Sportsmed.* 21:125–133.

Gates JR. 1991. Epilepsy and sports participation. *Phys Sportsmed.* 19:98–104.

Halvorsen FA, et al. 1990. Gastrointestinal disturbances in marathon runners. *Bri J Sports Med.* 24:266–268.

Heath GW, et al. 1991. Exercise and the incidence of upper respiratory tract infections. *Med Sci Sports and Exerc.* 23:152–157.

Horton ES. 1989. Exercise and diabetes in youth. In Gisolfi CV, Lamb DR (eds.). *Perspectives in Exercise Science and Sports Medicine, Volume 2: Youth Exercise and Sport.* Indianapolis: Benchmark Press. 97–113.

Lemanske RF, Henke KG. 1989. Exercise-induced asthma. In Gisolfi CV, Lamb DR (eds.). *Perspectives in Exercise Science and Sports Medicine, Volume 2: Youth Exercise and Sport.* Indianapolis: Benchmark Press. 465–596.

Linschoten R, et al. 1990. Epilepsy in sports. *Sports Med.* 10:10–19.

McKeag DB, Kinderknecht J. 1989. A basketball player with infectious mononucleosis. In Smith NJ (ed.). *Common Problems in Pediatric Sports Medicine.* Chicago: Year Book Medical Publishers. 191–203.

National Safety Council. 1993. *First Aid and CPR* (2d ed.). Boston: Jones and Bartlett.

Nelson MA. 1989. A young gymnast with an acute upper respiratory infection. In Smith NJ (ed.). *Common Problems in Pediatric Sports Medicine.* Chicago: Year Book Medical Publishers. 204–209.

Nieman DC, Nehlsen-Cannarella SL. 1991. The effects of acute and chronic exercise on immunoglobulins. *Sports Med.* 11(3):183–201.

Pinger RR, Hahn DB, Sharp RL. 1991. The role of the athletic trainer in the detection and prevention of Lyme disease in athletes. *Athletic Training.* 26:324–331.

Robbins DC, Carleton S. 1989. Managing the diabetic athlete. *Phys Sportsmed.* 17(12):45–54.

Van Camp SP. 1989. Prescribing physical activity. In Ryan AJ, Allman FL (eds.). *Sports Medicine.* San Diego: Academic Press. 529–550.

National Safety Council *CPR*

Background Information

What Is CPR?

Cardiopulmonary resuscitation (CPR) combines rescue breathing (also known as mouth-to-mouth) and external chest compressions. *Cardio* refers to the heart and *pulmonary* refers to the lungs. *Resuscitation* means to revive. Proper and prompt CPR serves as a holding action by providing oxygen to the brain and heart until advanced cardiac life support can be provided.

When to Start CPR

Trained people need to be able to:
- recognize the signs of cardiac arrest,
- provide CPR, and
- call for emergency medical services (EMS).

About two-thirds of deaths that are the result of a heart attack in a nonhospital setting occur within two hours of the first signs and symptoms.

Victims have a good chance of surviving if:
- CPR is started within the first 4 minutes of heart stoppage, and
- they receive advanced cardiac life support within the next 4 minutes.

Brain damage begins within 4–6 minutes after the heart stops and is certain after 10 minutes when no CPR is given.

Start CPR as soon as possible!

EMS System

The emergency medical services (EMS) system consists of several components:

Source: National Safety Council. 1994. *CPR Review Manual.* Boston: Jones and Bartlett. Reprinted with permission.

- first responders (law enforcement agency or fire service member or others designated in industry, government, and the private sector),
- EMS dispatcher located at the local emergency communications center,
- emergency medical technicians (EMTs) with various levels of training working with well-equipped emergency vehicles, and
- hospital emergency department staff (e.g., physicians, nurses).

EMS Telephone Numbers

Activate the EMS system by using:
- 9-1-1 (covers majority of people in the United States), or
- seven-digit local number found on the inside front cover of the telephone directory, since not all communities have 9-1-1, or
- 0 (zero or operator) as a last resort if unable to use the other numbers.

What Information to Give

Give to the EMS dispatcher:
- **The victim's location.** Give address, names of intersecting streets or roads, and other landmarks if possible.
- **Telephone number you are calling from.** This prevents false calls, and also allows the center to call back for additional information if needed.
- **What happened.** Tell the nature of the emergency (e.g., heart attack, drowning, etc.).
- **Number of persons needing help and any special conditions.**

■ **The victim's condition** (e.g., conscious, breathing, etc.) **and what is being done for the victim** (tell about CPR, rescue breathing).

Hang up the phone only after the dispatcher tells you to do so.

Disease Precautions

Disease Precautions During CPR Training

■ There is concern about contracting diseases, such as HIV, which results in AIDS, hepatitis B virus (HBV), and respiratory tract infections (e.g., influenza, mononucleosis, and tuberculosis) from a CPR manikin during CPR training.

■ The American Heart Association reports that CPR manikins have never been found to transmit any bacterial, fungal, or viral disease.

■ CPR classes should follow the manikin manufacturers' recommendations for using and maintaining their manikins.

■ The viral agent causing AIDS, known as HIV, is delicate and is inactivated in less than 10 minutes at room temperature by several kinds of disinfectants used for cleaning manikins.

Disease Precautions During Actual CPR

■ Laypersons are most likely to perform CPR in the home and will usually know the health status of the victim.

■ It should be assumed that certain body fluids may have the potential to spread disease either to the victim or the rescuer.

■ HBV-positive saliva has not been shown to be infectious. A theoretical risk of HIV and HBV spread exists during rescue breathing if either the victim or rescuer has breaks in the skin, on or around the lips, or inside the mouth.

■ Transmission of HBV and HIV infection during rescue breathing has not been documented.

■ The Centers for Disease Control (CDC) and the Occupational Safety and Health Administration (OSHA) constructed guidelines that include the use of latex gloves and resuscitation masks with valves capable of diverting exhaled air from contacting the rescuer.

■ Rescuers should not fear the transmission of a disease, but many may be unwilling to help a person in need because of that fear. Rescuers should learn how to use a mouth-to-barrier device (face mask or face shield).

■ Two types of mouth-to-barrier devices exist:

1. **Mask devices.** These have a one-way valve so that exhaled air does not enter the rescuer's mouth. Those without one-way valves offer little protection.

2. **Face shields.** These have no exhalation valve and air can leak around the shield.

■ If a rescuer refuses to start rescue breathing, he or she should:

1. activate the EMS system,

2. open the airway, and

3. give chest compressions until another rescuer arrives who will give rescue breathing.

When to Stop CPR

■ Victim revives (regains pulse and breathing). Though revival is hoped for, most victims also require advanced cardiac procedures before ever regaining their heart and lung functions.

■ Replaced either by another trained rescuer or by EMS system.

■ Too exhausted to continue.

■ Scene becomes unsafe for the rescuer.

■ A physician tells you to stop.

■ Cardiac arrest lasting longer than 30 minutes (with or without CPR except in cases of severe or profound hypothermia). This is a National Association of EMS Physicians' recommendation.

How Can an Untrained Rescuer Help?

Untrained rescuer can help by:

■ going for help,

■ checking breathing and pulse following directions from trained rescuer, and

■ performing CPR following directions from trained rescuer.

If exhausted, an untrained rescuer can give chest compressions while the trained rescuer gives rescue breaths. Tell the untrained rescuer to watch how to:

■ find hand position;

■ keep fingers off victim's chest;

■ keep arms straight and shoulders over victim's chest; and

■ perform 5 chest compressions at proper rate and depth, stop while trained rescuer gives 1 breath, then starts another cycle of 5 chest compressions.

If untrained rescuer adequately performs chest compressions, allow him/her to continue helping you.

Precautions During Training

- Do not practice mouth-to-mouth resuscitation on people—practice on a manikin.
- Do not practice chest compressions on people—practice on a manikin.
- Do not practice abdominal or chest thrusts on people.
- Wash your hands before class.
- Clean the manikin before using it according to your instructor's directions (use either a solution of liquid bleach and water or rubbing alcohol).
- Do not put anything (chewing gum, food, drink, tobacco) in your mouth when manikins are being used.

Disease Precautions During CPR Training

Do *not* use a training manikin *if* you have:

- sores on the hands, lips, or face (such as a cold sore),
- an upper respiratory infection (such as a cold or sore throat),
- known positive hepatitis B virus,
- been infected by HIV or have AIDS,
- an infection or recent exposure to an infectious source.

Clean manikin between each student use:

1. Scrub the manikin's entire face and inside of mouth vigorously with a 4″ × 4″ gauze pad wet with 70% alcohol (isopropanol or ethanol).
2. Place the wet gauze pad over the manikin's mouth and nose for at least 30 seconds.
3. Allow manikin's face to dry.

During training, students should practice and become familiar with mouth-to-barrier devices.

CPR Performance Mistakes

Rescue breathing mistakes:

- inadequate head tilt, airway not open;
- failing to pinch nose shut;
- not giving full breaths;

- too fast or too forceful;
- failing to watch chest and listen for exhalation;
- failing to maintain tight seal around victim's mouth (and/or nose).

Chest compression mistakes:

- pivoting at knees instead of hips (rocking motion);
- wrong compression site;
- bending elbows;
- shoulders not above sternum (arms not vertical);
- fingers touching chest;
- heel of bottom hand not in line with sternum;
- quick, stabbing compressions;
- hand not staying in contact with chest between each compression.

Dangerous Complications

- Vomiting may occur during CPR. If it happens it is usually before CPR has begun or within the first minute after beginning CPR. Inhaling vomit (aspiration) into the lungs can produce a type of pneumonia that can kill even after successful rescue efforts. Vomiting happens at death or near death.

  In case of vomiting:

  1. Turn victim onto his/her side and keep him/her there until vomiting ends.
  2. Wipe vomit out of victim's mouth with your fingers wrapped in a cloth to quickly clear the airway.
  3. Reposition victim onto his/her back and resume rescue breathing/CPR if needed.

- Stomach (gastric) distention describes stomach bulging from air, especially common in children.

  1. Caused by:
     a. rescue breaths given too fast;
     b. rescue breaths given too forcefully;
     c. partially or completely blocked airway.
  2. Dangerous because:
     a. air in stomach pushes against lungs, making it difficult or impossible to give full breaths;
     b. possibility of inhaling vomit into the lungs.
  3. Prevent or minimize by:
     a. trying to blow just hard enough to make chest rise;
     b. retilt head to open airway;
     c. using mouth-to-nose method;

d. slow rescue breathing (1½ to 2 seconds per breath for adults). Pause between breaths so you can take another breath.

e. Do **not** try to push air out of stomach. Retilt the head and continue slow rescue breathing. If victim vomits, turn victim on his/her side, clean out mouth with your fingers covered by a cloth, roll victim onto back, and continue rescue efforts.

■ Inhalation of foreign substances (known as aspiration).

1. particulate matter aspiration—can stop up airway;

2. nongastric liquid aspiration—mainly due to fresh- and saltwater drowning;

3. gastric acid aspiration—effects of gastric acid on lung tissue can be equated with a chemical burn.

Help prevent vomiting by placing nonbreathing victim on his/her left side. This position keeps stomach from spilling contents into esophagus by keeping the bottom end of esophagus above stomach.

■ Chest compression-related injuries can happen even with proper compressions

Injuries may include:

1. rib fractures;

2. rib separation;

3. bruised lung;

4. lung, liver, and spleen lacerations.

Prevent or minimize:

1. Use proper hand location on chest—if too low the sternum's tip can cut into liver.

2. Keep fingers off victim's ribs by interlocking fingers.

3. Press straight down instead of sideways.

4. Give smooth, regular, and uninterrupted (except when breathing) compressions. Avoid sudden, jerking, jabbing, or stabbing compressions.

5. Avoid pressing chest too deeply.

■ Dentures, loose or broken teeth, or dental appliances. Leave tight-fitting dentures in place to support victim's mouth during rescue breathing. Remove loose or broken teeth, dentures, and/or dental appliances.

Basic Life Support Procedures and Techniques

1

Adult Rescue Breathing and CPR

If you see a motionless person . . .

■ **Check Responsiveness**

■ If head or neck injury is suspected, move only if absolutely necessary.

■ Tap or gently shake victim's shoulder.

■ Shout near victim's ear, "Are you OK?"

2

■ **Activate EMS System for Help**

■ Ask a bystander to call the local emergency telephone number, usually 9-1-1.

■ If alone, shout for help. If no one comes quickly, call the local emergency telephone number. If someone comes quickly, ask him/her to call.

3

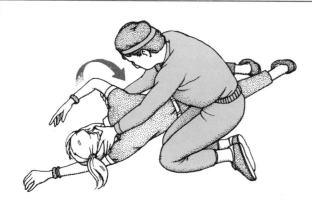

■ Roll Person onto Back

- Gently roll victim's head, body, and legs over at the same time. Do this without further injuring the victim.

4

■ Open Airway (use head-tilt/chin-lift method)

- Place hand nearest victim's head on victim's forehead and apply backward pressure to tilt head back.
- Place fingers of other hand under bony part of jaw near chin and lift. Avoid pressing on soft tissues under jaw.
- Tilt head backward without closing victim's mouth.
- Do *not* use your thumb to lift the chin.

■ If You Suspect a Neck Injury

Do *not* move victim's head or neck. First try lifting chin without tilting head back. If breaths do not go in, slowly and gently bend the head back until breaths can go in.

5

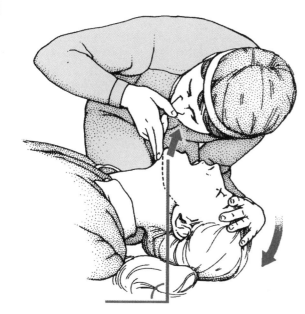

■ Check for Breathing (take 3–5 seconds)

- Place your ear over victim's mouth and nose while keeping airway open.
- *Look* at victim's chest to check for rise and fall; *listen* and *feel* for breathing.

6

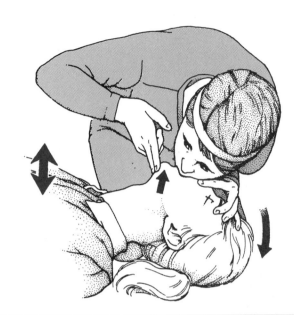

■ Give Two Slow Breaths

- Keep head tilted back with head-tilt/chin-lift method to keep airway open.
- Pinch nose shut.
- Take a deep breath and seal your lips tightly around victim's mouth.
- Give 2 slow breaths, each lasting 1½ to 2 seconds (you should take a breath after each breath given to victim).
- Watch chest rise to see if your breaths go in.
- Allow for chest deflation after each breath.

■ First Breath Did Not Go In

Retilt the head and try 1 more breath. If still unsuccessful, suspect choking, also known as foreign body airway obstruction (use *Unconscious Adult Foreign Body Airway Obstruction* procedures).

7

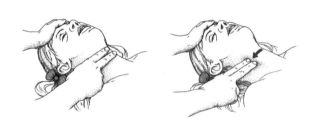

■ Check for Pulse

- Maintain head tilt with hand nearest head on forehead.
- Locate Adam's apple with 2 or 3 fingers of hand nearest victim's feet.
- Slide your fingers down into groove of neck on side closest to you (do not use your thumb because you may feel your own pulse).
- Feel for carotid pulse (take 5–10 seconds). Carotid artery is used because it lies close to the heart and is accessible.

8

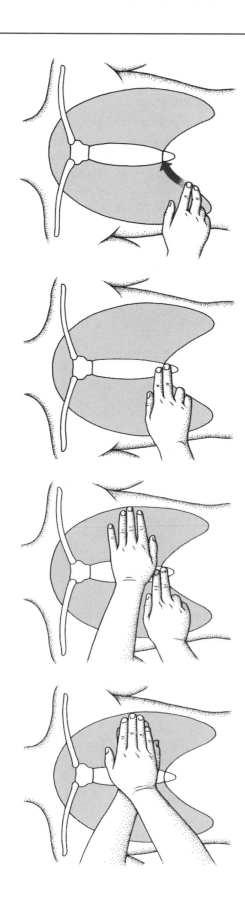

Perform rescue procedures based upon what you found:

▪ If There Is a Pulse But No Breathing

Give one rescue breath (mouth-to-mouth resuscitation) every 5 to 6 seconds. Use the same techniques for rescue breathing found in Step 6 above but only give one. Every minute (10 to 12 breaths) stop and check the pulse to make sure there is a pulse. Continue until:

▪ Adult starts breathing on his or her own.

OR

▪ Trained help, such as emergency medical technicians (EMTs), arrive and relieve you.

OR

▪ You are completely exhausted.

▪ If There Is No Pulse, Give CPR

▪ Find hand position

1. Use your fingers to slide up rib cage edge nearest you to notch at the end of sternum.

2. Place your middle finger on or in the notch and index finger next to it.

3. Put heel of other hand (one closest to victim's head) on sternum next to index finger.

4. Remove hand from notch and put it on top of hand on chest.

5. Interlace, hold, or extend fingers up.

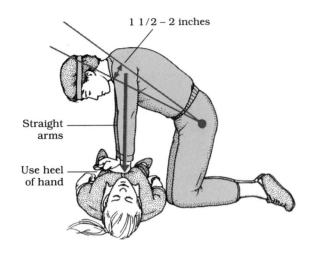

1 1/2 – 2 inches

Straight arms

Use heel of hand

■ Do 15 compressions.

1. Place your shoulders directly over your hands on the chest.

2. Keep arms straight and elbows locked.

3. Push sternum straight down 1½ to 2 inches.

4. Do 15 compressions at 80 per minute. Count as you push down: "one and, two and, three and, four and, five and, six and, seven and, ... fifteen and."

5. Push smoothly; do not jerk or jab; do not stop at the top or at the bottom.

6. When pushing, bend from your hips, not knees.

7. Keep fingers pointing across victim's chest, away from you.

■ Give 2 slow breaths.

■ Complete 4 cycles of 15 compressions and 2 breaths (takes about 1 minute) and check the pulse. *If there is no pulse,* restart CPR with chest compressions. Recheck the pulse every few minutes. *If there is a pulse,* give rescue breathing.

■ Give CPR or rescue breathing until:

Victim revives.

OR

Trained help, such as EMTs, arrives and relieves you.

OR

You are completely exhausted.

Conscious Adult Foreign Body Airway Obstruction (Choking)

If person is conscious and cannot speak, breathe, or cough . . .

1

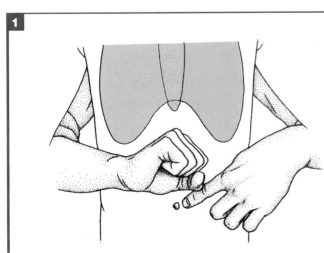

■ **Give Up to 5 Abdominal Thrusts** (Heimlich maneuver):

■ Stand behind the victim.

■ Wrap your arms around victim's waist. (Do not allow your forearms to touch the ribs.)

■ Make a fist with 1 hand and place the thumb side just above victim's navel and well below the tip of the sternum.

■ Grasp fist with your other hand.

■ Press fist into victim's abdomen with 5 quick upward thrusts.

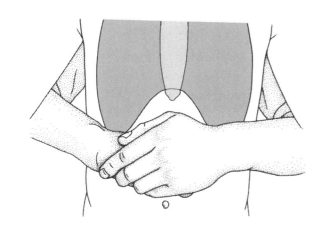

- Each thrust should be a separate and distinct effort to dislodge the object.

After every 5 abdominal thrusts, check the victim and your technique.

Note: For women in an advanced state of pregnancy and obese victims consider using chest thrusts.

 2

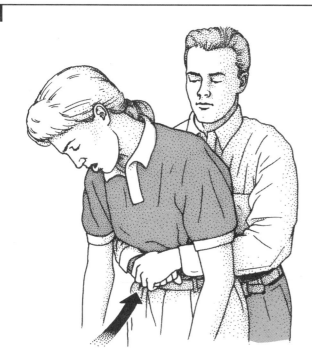

■ **Repeat Cycles of Up to 5 Abdominal Thrusts Until:**

- Victim coughs up object.

OR

- Victim starts to breathe or coughs forcefully.

OR

- Victim becomes unconscious (activate EMS and start methods for an unconscious victim with a finger sweep first).

OR

- You are relieved by EMS or other trained person. Reassess victim and your technique after every 5 thrusts.

Unconscious Adult Foreign Body Airway Obstruction (Choking)

If person is unconscious and breaths have not gone in . . .

1

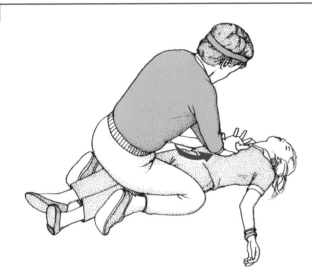

■ **Give Up to 5 Abdominal Thrusts** (Heimlich maneuver):

- Straddle victim's thighs.
- Put heel of one hand against middle of victim's abdomen slightly above navel and well below sternum's notch (fingers of hand should point toward victim's head).
- Put other hand directly on top of first hand.
- Press inward and upward using both hands with up to 5 quick abdominal thrusts.
- Each thrust should be distinct and a real attempt made to relieve the airway obstruction. Keep heel of hand in contact with abdomen between abdominal thrusts.

Note: For women in advanced stages of pregnancy and obese victims consider using chest thrusts.

2

■ **Perform Finger Sweep**

- Use only on an unconscious victim. On a conscious victim, it may cause gagging or vomiting.
- Use your thumb and fingers to grasp victim's jaw and tongue and lift upward to pull tongue away from back of throat and away from foreign object.
- If unable to open mouth to perform the tongue-jaw lift, use the crossed-finger method by crossing the index finger and thumb and pushing the teeth apart.
- With index finger of your other hand, slide finger down along the inside of one cheek deeply into mouth and use a hooking action across to other cheek to dislodge foreign object.
- If foreign body comes within reach, grab and remove it. Do not force object deeper.

3

■ **If the Above Steps Are Unsuccessful**

Cycle through the following steps in rapid sequence until the object is expelled or EMS system arrive:

- Give 1 rescue breath.
- Do up to 5 abdominal thrusts.
- Finger sweep.

Adult Basic Life Support Proficiency Checklist

S = **self-check**

P = **partner check**

I = **instructor check**

Adult Rescue Breathing	S	P	I
1. Check responsiveness	☐	☐	☐
2. Activate EMS	☐	☐	☐
3. Roll victim onto back	☐	☐	☐
4. Airway open	☐	☐	☐
5. Breathing check	☐	☐	☐
6. 2 slow breaths	☐	☐	☐
7. Check pulse at carotid artery	☐	☐	☐
8. Rescue breathing (1 every 5 to 6 seconds)	☐	☐	☐
9. Recheck pulse and breathing after first minute, then every few minutes	☐	☐	☐

Adult One-Rescuer CPR	S	P	I
1. Check responsiveness	☐	☐	☐
2. Activate EMS	☐	☐	☐
3. Roll victim onto back	☐	☐	☐
4. Airway open	☐	☐	☐
5. Breathing check	☐	☐	☐
6. 2 slow breaths	☐	☐	☐
7. Check pulse at carotid artery	☐	☐	☐
8. Hand position	☐	☐	☐
9. 15 compressions	☐	☐	☐
10. 2 slow breaths	☐	☐	☐
11. Continue CPR (3 more cycles for total of 4)	☐	☐	☐
12. Recheck pulse	☐	☐	☐
13. Continue CPR (start with compressions)	☐	☐	☐
14. Recheck pulse after first minute, then every few minutes	☐	☐	☐

Conscious Adult Choking Management	S	P	I
1. Recognize choking	☐	☐	☐
2. Up to 5 abdominal thrusts	☐	☐	☐
3. Reassess	☐	☐	☐
4. Repeat cycles of up to 5 thrusts; reassess after each cycle	☐	☐	☐

Unconscious Adult Choking Management	S	P	I
1. Check responsiveness	☐	☐	☐
2. Activate EMS	☐	☐	☐
3. Roll victim onto back	☐	☐	☐
4. Airway open	☐	☐	☐
5. Breathing check	☐	☐	☐
6. Try 1 slow breath. If unsuccessful, retilt head and try 1 more	☐	☐	☐
7. Up to 5 abdominal thrusts	☐	☐	☐
8. Finger sweep	☐	☐	☐
9. Try 1 slow breath.	☐	☐	☐
10. Repeat "5 thrusts, sweep, 1 breath" sequence	☐	☐	☐

Differences Between Adult and Child (1–8 Years) Basic Life Support

IF child . . .	THEN . . .
is **not** responsive	**activate EMS system after 1 minute of resuscitation** (in adults, activate EMS system immediately after determining unresponsiveness)
is **not** breathing, but has a pulse	■ give **1 to 1½ seconds breaths** (in adults give 1½ to 2 seconds breaths) ■ give **1 breath every 3 seconds** (in adults give 1 breath every 5 to 6 seconds)
does **not** have a pulse	■ after locating the tip of the breastbone, lift your fingers off and put heel of the **same hand** on breastbone immediately above where index finger was (adult requires one hand to locate and the other hand placed next to it) ■ give **chest compressions with 1 hand** (nearest feet) while keeping other hand on child's forehead (adult requires 2 hands on victim's chest for compressions) ■ **compress breastbone 1 to 1½ inches** (adults require 1½ to 2 inches) ■ give **1 breath after every 5 chest compressions** (one-rescuer adult CPR requires 2 breaths after every 15 compressions)
has a foreign body airway obstruction (choking), and after giving up to 5 abdominal thrusts (Heimlich maneuver), the airway still remains obstructed	look into mouth; **remove foreign body only if seen with finger sweep—do not perform blind finger sweeps** (in an adult, you can perform blind finger sweeps)

Child Basic Life Support Proficiency Checklist

S = self-check

P = partner check

I = instructor check

Child Rescue Breathing	S	P	I
1. Check responsiveness	☐	☐	☐
2. Send a bystander, if available, to call EMS	☐	☐	☐
3. Roll victim onto back	☐	☐	☐
4. Airway open	☐	☐	☐
5. Breathing check	☐	☐	☐
6. 2 slow breaths	☐	☐	☐
7. Check pulse at carotid artery	☐	☐	☐
8. Rescue breathing (1 every 3 seconds)	☐	☐	☐
9. Call EMS after 1 minute	☐	☐	☐
10. Recheck pulse and breathing after first minute, then every few minutes	☐	☐	☐

Child One-Rescuer CPR	S	P	I
1. Check responsiveness	☐	☐	☐
2. Send a bystander, if available, to call EMS	☐	☐	☐
3. Roll victim onto back	☐	☐	☐
4. Airway open	☐	☐	☐
5. Breathing check	☐	☐	☐
6. 2 slow breaths	☐	☐	☐
7. Check pulse at carotid artery	☐	☐	☐
8. Hand position using same hand used to locate tip of sternum	☐	☐	☐
9. 5 compressions with only 1 hand	☐	☐	☐
10. 1 slow breath	☐	☐	☐
11. Continue CPR for 1 minute (for total of 12)	☐	☐	☐
12. Call EMS	☐	☐	☐
13. Recheck pulse	☐	☐	☐
14. Continue CPR (start with compressions)	☐	☐	☐
15. Recheck pulse after first minute, then every few minutes	☐	☐	☐

Conscious Child Choking Management	S	P	I
1. Recognize choking	☐	☐	☐
2. Up to 5 abdominal thrusts	☐	☐	☐
3. Reassess	☐	☐	☐
4. Repeat cycles of up to 5 thrusts; reassess after each cycle	☐	☐	☐

Unconscious Child Choking Management	S	P	I
1. Check responsiveness	☐	☐	☐
2. Send a bystander, if available, to call EMS	☐	☐	☐
3. Roll victim onto back	☐	☐	☐
4. Airway open	☐	☐	☐
5. Breathing check	☐	☐	☐
6. Try 1 slow breath. If unsuccessful, retilt head and try 1 more	☐	☐	☐
7. Up to 5 abdominal thrusts	☐	☐	☐
8. Check mouth for foreign object (finger sweep only if object is seen)	☐	☐	☐
9. Try 1 slow breath	☐	☐	☐
10. Repeat "5 thrusts, mouth check, 1 breath" sequence	☐	☐	☐

How to Remember the Basic Life Support Steps

■ Basic Life Support for an Adult Victim

R   **R**esponsive

A   **A**ctivate EMS system (usually call 9-1-1)

P   **P**osition victim on back

A   **A**irway open (Use head-tilt/chin-lift or jaw-thrust method)

B   **B**reathing check (look, listen, and feel for 3–5 seconds)

- If breathing and spine injury not suspected, place in recovery position.
- If not breathing, give 2 slow breaths; watch chest rise:
  - If 2 breaths go in, proceed to step **C**.
  - If first breath did not go in, retilt head and try 1 more breath.
  - If second breath did not go in, give 5 abdominal thrusts; perform tongue-jaw lift followed by a finger sweep; give 1 breath. Repeat 5 thrusts, sweep, 1 breath sequence.

C   **C**irculation check (at carotid artery for 5–10 seconds)

- If there is a pulse, but no breathing, give rescue breathing (1 breath every 5–6 seconds).
- If there is no pulse, give CPR (cycles of 15 chest compressions followed by 2 breaths).

After 1 minute (4 cycles of CPR or 10–12 breaths of rescue breathing), check pulse.

- If no pulse, give CPR (15 : 2 cycles) starting with chest compressions.
- If there is a pulse, but no breathing, give rescue breathing.

■ Basic Life Support for a Child or Infant Victim

E   **E**stablish unresponsive

S   **S**end bystander, if available, to activate the EMS system (usually call 9-1-1)

P   **P**osition victim on back

A   **A**irway open (use head-tilt/chin-lift or jaw-thrust method)

B   **B**reathing check (look, listen, and feel for 3–5 seconds)

- If breathing and spine injury not suspected, place in recovery position.
- If not breathing, give 2 slow breaths; watch chest rise:
  - If 2 breaths go in, proceed to step **C**.
  - If first breath did not go in, retilt head and try 1 more breath.
  - If second breath did not go in, then . . .

For a child: give 5 abdominal thrusts; perform tongue-jaw lift and if object is seen perform a finger sweep; give 1 breath. Repeat 5 thrusts, mouth check, 1 breath sequence.

For an infant: give 5 back blows and 5 chest thrusts; perform tongue-jaw lift and if object is seen perform a finger sweep; give 1 breath. Repeat 5 blows, 5 thrusts, mouth check, 1 breath sequence.

C   **C**irculation check (for 5–10 seconds)

- *For a child:* at carotid pulse
  For an infant: at brachial pulse
- If there is a pulse, but no breathing, give rescue breathing (1 breath every 3 seconds).
- If no pulse give CPR (cycles of 5 chest compressions followed by 1 breath).

After 1 minute (20 cycles of CPR or 20 breaths of rescue breathing), check pulse.

- If alone, activate the EMS system.
- If no pulse, give CPR (5 : 1 cycles) starting with chest compressions.
- If there is a pulse, but no breathing, give rescue breathing.

Two-Rescuer CPR Procedures

(Laypersons should learn only one-rescuer CPR. Professional rescuers such as EMTs and other health care professionals should learn both one-rescuer and two-rescuer CPR.)

Entry of Second Trained Rescuer to Perform Two-Rescuer CPR

#1 Performing one-rescuer CPR

#2 Says:

- "I know CPR"
- "EMS system has been activated"
- "Can I help?"

#1

- Completes CPR cycle (15 compressions and ends on 2 breaths)
- Says, "Take over compressions"
- Checks pulse and breathing (5 seconds)
- If pulse absent, #1 rescuer says, "no pulse, continue CPR"

#2

- Gives 5 compressions (at 80–100 per minute rate)
- After every 5th compression, pauses for #1 rescuer to give 1 full breath

#1

- Monitors victim while #2 performs compressions:

  (a) watches chest rise during breaths

  (b) feels carotid pulse during compressions

- Gives 1 full breath after every 5th compression given by #2 rescuer

Two Rescuers Starting CPR at the Same Time

#1 (ventilator)

- Assesses victim; if no breaths, gives 2 full breaths; if no pulse, tells #2 to start compressions

- Gives 1 full breath after every 5th compression given by #2

#2 (compressor)

- Finds hand position and gets ready to give compressions
- Gives 5 compressions after #1 says to start them
- Pauses after every 5th compression for #1 to give 1 full breath

Switching During Two-Rescuer CPR

#2 (compressor)

- Signals when to change by saying, "Change and, two and, three and, four and, five," or "Change on the next breath"

- After #1 gives breath, #2 moves to victim's head and completes pulse and breathing check (5 seconds), and if absent says, "No pulse, begin CPR"

- Gives a full breath after every cycle of 5 compressions

#1 (ventilator)

- Gives 1 full breath at the end of 5th compression and moves to victim's chest

- Finds hand position and gets ready to give compressions

- Begins cycles of 5 compressions after every breath

How an Untrained Rescuer Can Help

- Go for help
- Monitor pulse and breathing, with some direction
- Give CPR with directions (untrained rescuer can learn compressions easier with trained rescuer giving breaths)

CPR Review

Item	Infant (0–1 year)	Child (1–8 years)	Adult (>8 years)
How to open airway?	Head-tilt/chin-lift method	Head-tilt/chin-lift method	Head-tilt/chin-lift method
How to check breathing?	Look at chest and listen and feel for air (3–5 seconds)	Look at chest and listen and feel for air (3–5 seconds)	Look at chest and listen and feel for air (3–5 seconds)
What kinds of breaths?	Slow, make chest rise and fall	Slow, make chest rise and fall	Slow, make chest rise and fall
Where to check pulse?	Brachial artery (5–10 seconds)	Carotid artery (5–10 seconds)	Carotid artery (5–10 seconds)
Hand position for chest compressions?	1 finger's width below imaginary line between nipples	1 finger's width above tip of sternum	1 finger's width above tip of sternum
Compress with?	2 fingers	Heel of 1 hand	Heels of 2 hands, one hand on top of the other
Compression depth?	½–1 inch	1–1½ inches	1½–2 inches
Compression rate?	100 per minute	100 per minute	80–100 per minute
Compression : breath ratio?	5 : 1	5 : 1	15 : 2
How to count for compression rate?	1,2,3,4,5, breathe	1 and, 2 and, 3 and, 4 and, 5 and, breathe	1 and, 2 and, 3 and, 4 and, 5 and, 6 and, . . . 15 and, breathe, breathe
How often to reassess?	After the first minute, then every few minutes	After the first minute, then every few minutes	After the first minute, then every few minutes
After reassessment, resume CPR with?	Compressions	Compressions	Compressions
How often to give only breaths during rescue breathing?	Every 3 seconds	Every 3 seconds	Every 5 seconds

National Safety Council *Bloodborne Pathogens*

Introduction

What Is the OSHA Bloodborne Pathogens Standard?

Who Needs This Manual?

Why Do I Need This Manual?

Meeting OSHA Standards

What Is the OSHA Bloodborne Pathogens Standard?

The 1991 OSHA (Occupational Safety and Health Administration) regulations include a section specific to bloodborne pathogens, section 1910.1030. This standard provides requirements for employers to follow to ensure employee safety with regard to occupational exposure to bloodborne pathogens.

Who Needs This Manual?

Any employee who has potential for occupational exposure to blood or other potentially infectious materials (OPIM) is required to receive training according to the bloodborne pathogens standard. The following job classifications may be associated with tasks that have occupational exposure to blood or OPIM, but the standard is not limited to employees in these positions.

- Physicians, physicians' assistants, nurses, nurse practitioners, and other health care employees in clinics and physicians' offices
- Employees of clinical and diagnostic laboratories
- Housekeepers in health care facilities
- Personnel in hospital laundries or commercial laundries that service health care or public safety institutions
- Tissue bank personnel
- Employees in blood banks and plasma centers who collect, transport, and test blood. Free-standing clinic employees (for instance, hemodialysis clinics, urgent care clinics, health maintenance organization (HMO) clinics, and family planning clinics)

- Employees in clinics in industrial, educational, and correctional facilities (for example, those who collect blood, and clean and dress wounds)
- Employees assigned to provide emergency first aid
- Dentists, dental hygienists, dental assistants, and dental laboratory technicians
- Staff of institutions for the developmentally disabled
- Hospice employees
- Home health care workers
- Staff of nursing homes and long-term care facilities
- Employees of funeral homes and mortuaries
- HIV and HBV research laboratory and production facility workers
- Employees handling regulated waste
- Medical equipment service and repair personnel
- Emergency medical technicians, paramedics, and other emergency medical service providers
- Firefighters, law enforcement personnel, and correctional officers

Note: Good Samaritan Acts are not covered under the standard.

Why Do I Need This Manual?

This manual provides a written reference for your personal use during both this session of bloodborne pathogens training and later, at the worksite.

Meeting OSHA Standards

The 1991 OSHA Bloodborne Pathogens Standard mandates annual training for all employees with occupational exposure to blood or OPIM.

Source: National Safety Council. 1997. *Bloodborne Pathogens*. Boston: Jones and Bartlett. Reprinted with permission.

Annual training is necessary to ensure employee safety.

A good rule of thumb to determine whether your job requires exposure to blood or OPIM is to ask yourself if you would be reprimanded for not helping someone who is bleeding, or for failing to open packages that might contain blood or OPIM.

The training must be offered at no cost to the employee during regular work hours.

We encourage all employees to receive the training in any site where exposure to blood or OPIM is possible. Employees whose duties do not require exposure to blood or OPIM also should be made aware of worksite hazards as well as the meaning of the terms biohazard, red bags, labeling and disposal of regulated waste to protect themselves from inadvertent exposures. The standards include the potential for exposure, not just actual exposure. For example, a front desk receptionist may not have an actual exposure to a bleeding patient, but the potential for exposure may exist.

This training must be presented in language appropriate in content and vocabulary to the educational and literacy level of the employee. If employees are proficient only in a foreign language, training must be presented in that foreign language.

The employer must provide additional training when there is a change in the tasks and procedures that affects the employees' occupational exposure.

The training program must provide employees with the following:

1. An accessible copy of the regulatory text and an explanation of its contents

2. A general explanation of the epidemiology and symptoms of bloodborne disease

3. An explanation of the modes of transmission of bloodborne pathogens

4. An explanation of the employer's Exposure Control Plan and the means by which the employee can obtain a copy of the written plan (supplied by your company directly or through the instructor)

5. An explanation of the appropriate methods for recognizing tasks and other activities that may involve exposure to blood and other potentially infectious materials

6. An explanation of the use and limitations of methods that will prevent or reduce exposure including appropriate engineering controls, work practices, and personal protective equipment

7. Information on the types, proper use, location, removal, handling, decontamination, and disposal of personal protective equipment

8. An explanation of the basis for selection of personal protective equipment

9. Information on the hepatitis B vaccine, including information on its efficacy, safety, method of administration, the benefits of being vaccinated, and that the vaccine and vaccination will be offered free of charge to employees covered by the standard

10. Information on the appropriate actions to take and persons to contact in an emergency involving blood or other potentially infectious materials

11. An explanation of the procedure to follow if an exposure incident occurs including the method of reporting the incident and the medical follow-up that will be made available

12. Information on the post-exposure evaluation and follow-up that the employer is required to provide for the employee following an exposure incident

13. An explanation of the signs, labels, and/or color-coding required

14. An opportunity for interactive questions and answers with the person conducting the training session (during and after training session)

Note: Failure to meet the standards may result in fines to the employer.

The Ryan White Act

The Centers for Disease Control (CDC) is in the process of preparing the final list of diseases required by the passage of the Public Law 101-381, the Ryan White Comprehensive AIDS Resources Emergency Act. The Act creates a notification system for emergency response employees listed as police, fire, and the EMS system, who are exposed to diseases such as *M. tuberculosis,* hepatitis B or C, and HIV.

Bloodborne Pathogens

What Are Bloodborne Pathogens?

Hepatitis B Infection

Human Immunodeficiency Virus (HIV)

Learning Objective

You will be able to explain the transmission, course, and effects of bloodborne pathogens.

What Are Bloodborne Pathogens?

- Bloodborne pathogens are disease-causing microorganisms that may be present in human blood. They may be transmitted with any exposure to blood or OPIM.

- Two pathogens of significance are hepatitis B virus (HBV) and human immunodeficiency virus (HIV).

- Several bloodborne diseases other than HIV and HBV exist, such as hepatitis C, hepatitis D, and syphilis.

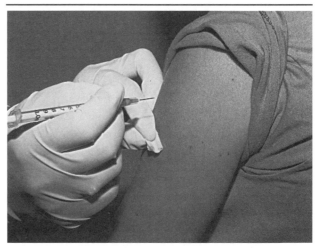

Immunization against HBV is possible.

Hepatitis B Infection

- Hepatitis B virus (HBV) is one of five viruses that cause illness directly affecting the liver.

- Hepatitis B virus is a major cause of viral hepatitis for which prevention is possible through immunization. Hepatitis results in swelling, soreness, and loss of normal functions of the liver.

- The symptoms of hepatitis B include weakness, fatigue, anorexia, nausea, abdominal pain, fever, and headache.

- Jaundice, a yellow discoloration of the skin, is a symptom that may develop.

- Hepatitis B may have no symptoms and therefore may not be diagnosed.

- A person's blood will test positive for the HBV surface antigen within 2 to 6 weeks after symptoms of the illness develop.

- Approximately 85% of patients recover in 6 to 8 weeks.

- A major source of HBV is chronic carriers. Chronic carriers will have the antigen present at all times and can unwittingly transmit the disease to suscep-

tible persons through needle, or other penetrating injury, and intimate contact.

- Chronic active hepatitis may be the consequence of a problem with the immune system that prevents the complete destruction of virus-infected liver cells.

Key Facts

- Approximately 8,700 health care workers contract hepatitis B each year, and about 200 will die.

- Cases of acute hepatitis B infection have increased 37% from 1979 to 1989.

- It is estimated that 200,000 to 300,000 new infections occurred annually from 1980 to 1991.

- It is estimated that 1 to 1.25 million persons in the United States have chronic hepatitis B and are potentially infectious to others.

Key Facts

- It is estimated that 1 in 250 persons in the United States is infected with HIV.
- There are at least 65 case reports of health care workers whose HIV infection is associated with occupational exposure.
- According to the World Health Organization, 10 to 12 million people around the world are infected with HIV.
- Approximately 200,000 AIDS patients have been reported to the CDC thus far, 84 of whom are health care workers with no other identified reason for infection.
- The CDC reports that prisons have a higher incidence of HIV infection than any other public institutions. In a 1990 survey, 5.8% of prison inmates were found to be infected.

Human Immunodeficiency Virus (HIV)

- Human immunodeficiency virus (HIV) is a virus that infects immune system T_4 blood cells in humans and renders them less effective in preventing disease.
- It is the virus identified as responsible for acquired immunodeficiency syndrome (AIDS).
- Symptoms of HIV might include night sweats, weight loss, fever, fatigue, gland pain or swelling, and muscle or joint pain.
- People with HIV may feel fine and not be aware that they have been exposed to HIV for as many as 8 to 10 years.
- It may take as long as a year for a blood test to become positive for HIV antibodies. Therefore, more than one test may be required to determine if a person has been infected.

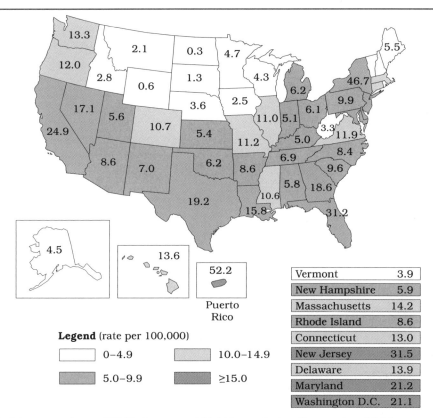

Vermont	3.9
New Hampshire	5.9
Massachusetts	14.2
Rhode Island	8.6
Connecticut	13.0
New Jersey	31.5
Delaware	13.9
Maryland	21.2
Washington D.C.	21.1

Legend (rate per 100,000)
- 0–4.9
- 5.0–9.9
- 10.0–14.9
- ≥15.0

Acquired immunodeficiency syndrome (AIDS). Cases per 100,000 population. Reported to CDC by state, United States, 1990.

Prevention

Engineering Controls

Work Practice Controls

Personal Protective Equipment

Universal Precautions

Learning Objective

You will be able to identify four ways to prevent an exposure incident to bloodborne pathogens.

To minimize exposure to bloodborne pathogens there are four strategies of prevention. These strategies are used in combination to offer you maximum protection.

- Engineering controls attempt to design safety into the tools and workspace organization. An example is a sharps container.

- Work practice controls are the use of equipment with engineered protections. An example would be immediately putting contaminated sharps into a sharps container.

- When occupational exposure remains after using engineering and work practice controls, employers must provide personal protective equipment. Personal protective equipment is used to protect you from contamination of skin, mucous membranes, or puncture wounds.

- Universal Precautions is a strategy to structure your approach to working with all human blood and certain body fluids. Another method of infection control is called Body Substance Isolation (BSI). This method defines all body fluids and substances as infectious. BSI includes all fluids and materials covered by the standard.

All these strategies combined promote worker safety and provide a safer working environment.

Engineering Controls

Engineering controls are structural or mechanical devices the company provides. Examples include handwashing facilities, eye stations, sharps containers, and biohazard labels.

Handwashing is a primary means of prevention.

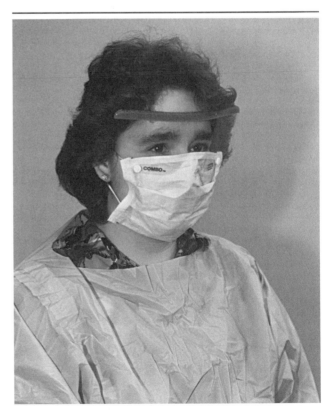

Protective equipment is provided for your protection.

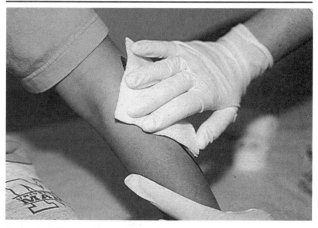

Universal Precautions protect everyone.

Work Practice Controls

Work practice controls are the behaviors necessary to use engineering controls effectively. These include, but are not limited to, using sharps containers, using an eye wash station, and washing your hands after removing personal protective equipment.

Personal Protective Equipment

Personal protective equipment is equipment provided by your employer at no cost to you. It is to your advantage to use this equipment. Report to your supervisor when any equipment is not in working order.

Personal protective equipment includes materials such as latex gloves, masks, aprons, gowns, and face shields.

Universal Precautions

Universal Precautions is the concept that all blood and certain body fluids are to be treated as if contaminated with HIV, HBV, or other bloodborne pathogens.

Body Substance Isolation can be used as an alternative to Universal Precautions. This method treats all fluids and substances as infectious and is acceptable under the standard.

Universal Precautions

Universal Precautions

Materials That Require Universal Precautions

Materials That Do Not Require Universal Precautions

Personal Protective Equipment

Learning Objective

You will be able to describe the concept of Universal Precautions and explain the materials that require precautions.

Universal Precautions

Universal Precautions is an aggressive, standardized approach to infection control. According to the concept of Universal Precautions, you should treat all human blood and certain body fluids as if they are known to contain HIV, HBV, or other bloodborne pathogens.

■ Body Substance Isolation

Another method of infection control is called Body Substance Isolation (BSI). This method defines all body fluids and substances as infectious. BSI includes not only the fluids and materials covered by this standard but expands coverage to all body fluids and substances.

BSI is an acceptable alternative to Universal Precautions provided facilities using BSI adhere to all other provisions of this standard.

Materials That Require Universal Precautions

Universal Precautions apply to the following potentially infectious materials:

- Blood
- Semen
- Vaginal secretions
- Cerebrospinal fluid
- Synovial fluid
- Pleural fluid
- Any body fluid with visible blood
- Any unidentifiable body fluid
- Saliva from dental procedures

- Feces
- Nasal secretions
- Sputum
- Sweat
- Tears
- Urine
- Vomitus

Materials That Do Not Require Universal Precautions

Universal Precautions do *not* apply to the following body fluids unless they contain visible blood:

Personal Protective Equipment

You must use personal protective equipment such as gloves or a mask whenever you might be exposed to blood or OPIM. (See table: Determining the Need for Universal Precautions.)

Determining the Need for Universal Precautions

Incident	Universal Precautions Needed?	Suggested Action
Nurse is going to change dressing on a recent wound.	YES	Nurse should wear latex gloves and/or other personal protective equipment whenever at risk of exposure to blood or potentially infectious materials.
Teacher is approached by young, hysterical student with a bloody nose.	YES	If required to attend to the student, the teacher should reassure child, put on latex gloves, and follow the routine procedures at your facility.
An ambulance attendant is called to a home where an elderly man appears to have had a heart attack. The man is conscious and able to speak.	NO	There is no immediate blood or infectious materials; the attendant may need to perform CPR in the event of cardiac or respiratory arrest. **Note:** In the event of cardiac or respiratory arrest, work practice controls and personal protective equipment may be required.
A police officer pulls over a car that has a burned out headlight.	NO	It is unlikely that the police officer will come in contact with blood or potentially infectious materials.
A laboratory worker is testing urine for evidence of infection. The specimen appears to have a trace of blood.	YES	The laboratory worker should be using personal protective equipment whenever dealing with any specimens with visible blood.

Immunization

■ **Hepatitis B Vaccines**

■ **Who Should Receive the Vaccine?**

■ **Contraindications**

■ **Side Effects of the Vaccine**

Learning Objective

You will be able to describe the types of hepatitis B vaccine, their usage, and contraindications.

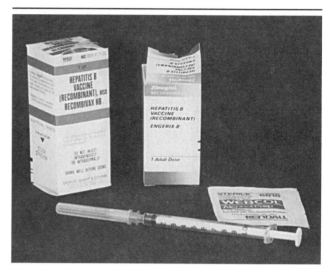

Hepatitis B vaccine is available from a variety of manufacturers.

All people who have routine occupational exposure to blood or other potentially infectious materials have the right to receive the immunization series against hepatitis B at no personal expense. The standard includes temporary and part-time workers.

Prescreening is not required, and your employer may not make prescreening a requirement for receiving the vaccine. If you choose to have prescreening, the testing must be done at an accredited laboratory.

The standard requires that your employer offer the vaccine to you at a convenient time, during normal work hours. If travel is required away from the worksite, your employer is responsible for that cost. The standard includes temporary and part-time workers.

Your employer cannot require you to use your health insurance to pay for the cost of the vaccine. Your employer cannot require you to pay and then be reimbursed if you remain employed for a specific time. Nor are you required to reimburse your employer for the cost of the vaccine if you leave your job.

You may refuse the series by signing the hepatitis B vaccine declination form. If you change your mind while still covered under the standard at a later date, you may still receive the vaccine at no cost.

Hepatitis B Vaccines

Recombivax HB vaccine provided by Merck Sharp & Dohme and Engerix-B by Smith-Kline, Inc. are the vaccines used to prevent infection with the hepatitis B virus. Either vaccine is given in three doses over a 6-month period; the first is given at an agreed-on date, the second is given 1 month later, and the third dose is given 5 months after the second dose. The vaccine

is administered by needle into a large muscle such as the deltoid in the upper arm.

In persons receiving the vaccine, 87% will develop immunity after the second dose of the vaccine, and 96% will develop immunity after the third dose.

Who Should Receive the Vaccine?

The hepatitis B vaccine series is recommended for the following groups. This list is suggestive and by no means inclusive.

■ Health care personnel

■ Custodial staff that have possible exposure to bloodborne pathogens such as those working in health care settings or laboratories

■ Dental, medical, and nursing students

■ Any personnel exposed to blood or blood products such as laboratory and blood bank personnel

■ Lifeguards, firefighters, teachers, police officers, sports team coaches, and trainers

Hepatitis B vaccine is recommended for anyone with occupational exposure to bloodborne pathogens.

Contraindications

You should not receive the vaccine if you are sensitive to yeast or any other component of the vaccine. Consultation with a physician is required for persons with heart disease, fever, or other illness.

If you are pregnant or breastfeeding an infant, you should consult your physician before receiving the vaccine.

Side Effects of the Vaccine

The side effects of the vaccine are minimal and may include localized swelling, pain, bruising, or redness at the injection site. The most common systemic reactions include flu-like symptoms such as fatigue, weakness, headache, fever, or malaise.

Bloodborne Pathogens: Immunization

DECISION FOR HEPATITIS B IMMUNIZATION

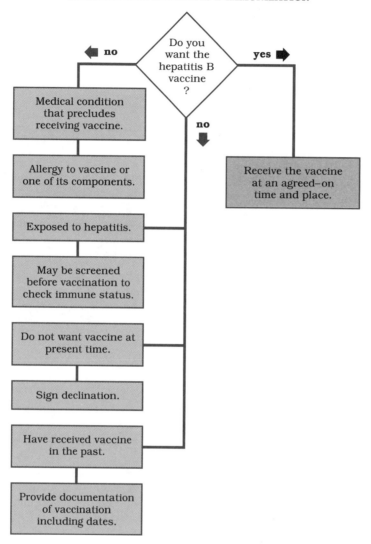

Exposure Control

Engineering and Work Practice Controls

Personal Protective Equipment

Limited Exceptions to Using Personal Protective Equipment

Learning Objective

You will be able to describe the controls that reduce exposure to bloodborne pathogens.

Engineering and Work Practice Controls

OSHA requires safety to be engineered into the tools and workspaces. Work practice controls are the required behaviors necessary to take full advantage of the engineered controls. Both are used to eliminate or minimize exposure to bloodborne pathogens. If risk of occupational exposure exists even when engineering and work practice controls are instituted, workers must use personal protective equipment for their protection and safety.

Your employer is responsible for the full cost of instituting engineering and work practice controls. Engineering controls must be examined and maintained or replaced on a regular schedule to ensure effectiveness and safety. This task may be assigned to you by your employer. It is a violation of the standard if effective monitoring does not take place.

▪ Handwashing and Handwashing Facilities

Employers are required to provide handwashing facilities that are readily accessible to all employees. The standard specifies that the handwashing facility must be situated so that employees do not have to use stairs, doorways, and corridors, which might result in environmental surface contamination.

If the provision of handwashing facilities is not feasible (such as in an ambulance or police car), the employer must provide either an appropriate antiseptic hand cleanser with clean cloth or paper towels, or antiseptic towelettes. If you use antiseptic hand cleansers or towelettes, you must wash your hands with soap and warm water as soon as possible after contact with blood or OPIM.

Groups that may use alternative washing methods such as antiseptic hand cleaners and towelettes are ambulance-based paramedics, EMTs, firefighters, po-

Handwashing is a primary means of preventing transmission of bloodborne pathogens.

lice, and mobile blood collection personnel. All groups must wash with soap and warm water as soon as possible after contact with blood or OPIM.

Employers shall ensure that employees wash hands and any other contaminated skin with soap and warm water (or flush mucous membranes with water) as soon as possible following contact with blood or OPIM. Employees must wash hands and skin surfaces after the removal of gloves or other personal protective equipment.

▪ Work Practice Controls

All procedures involving blood or OPIM shall be performed in such a way as to minimize or eliminate splashing, spraying, splattering, and generation of droplets of these substances.

Mouth pipetting or suctioning of blood or OPIM is prohibited. This procedure should *never* occur unless it is part of a specialized procedure such as DeLee suctioning. However, even then there must be a one-way valve between the patient and the practitioner.

Eating, drinking, smoking, applying cosmetics or lip balm, and handling contact lenses are *prohibited* in work areas where there is a reasonable likelihood

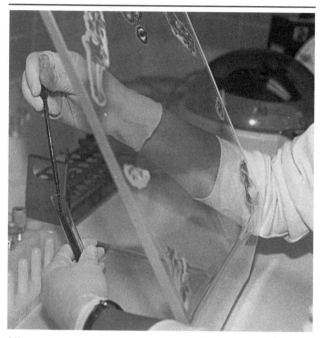

All procedures should be performed to minimize splashing.

of occupational exposure to blood or OPIM. Hand cream is not considered a cosmetic and is permitted under the standard. It should be noted, however, that some petroleum-based hand creams can adversely affect glove integrity.

Food or drink must not be kept in refrigerators, freezers, shelves, cabinets, countertops, or benches where blood or OPIM is present.

You must remove all personal protective equipment and wash your hands prior to leaving the work area. To prevent contamination of employee eating areas do not enter eating or break areas while wearing personal protective equipment.

■ Contaminated Needles or Sharps

OSHA defines contaminated sharps as any contaminated object that can penetrate the skin, including, but not limited to, needles, scalpels, broken capillary tubes, and exposed ends of dental wires.

Contaminated needles or other contaminated sharps must not be bent, recapped, or removed unless it can be demonstrated that no alternative is feasible or that such action is required by a specific medical procedure. If a procedure requires shearing or breaking of needles, this procedure must be specified in the company's Exposure Control Plan.

Needle removal or recapping needles must be accomplished through a one-handed technique or the

use of a mechanical device. (See Skill Scan on One-Handed Technique.)

Reusable sharps must be placed in clearly labeled, puncture-resistant, leakproof containers immediately or as soon as possible after use until they can be reprocessed. *Never* blindly reach into a container containing contaminated sharps.

▌ Personal Protective Equipment

Personal protective equipment is specialized clothing or equipment worn or used by you for protection against hazard. This includes equipment such as latex gloves, gowns, aprons, face shields, masks, eye protection, laboratory coats, CPR microshield, and resuscitation bags.

Whenever you need to wear a face mask, you must also wear eye protection. If you are wearing your personal glasses, you must use side shields and plan to decontaminate your glasses and side shields according to the schedule determined by your employer.

Personal protective equipment is acceptable if it prevents blood or OPIM from contaminating work clothes, street clothes, undergarments, skin, eyes, mouth, or other mucous membranes.

Your employer is responsible for providing personal protective equipment at no expense to you. Equipment must be provided in appropriate sizes and placed within easy reach for all employees.

Hypoallergenic gloves, glove liners, powderless gloves, or other similar alternatives shall be provided to you if you are allergic to gloves normally provided.

Your employer is responsible for cleaning, laun-

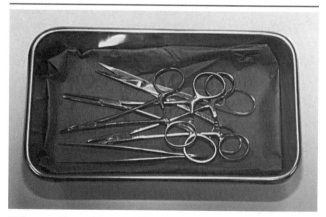

Using caution with reusable sharps can prevent injury and disease.

Key Facts

- Studies have shown that gloves provide a barrier, but that neither vinyl nor latex procedure gloves are completely impermeable.

- Disinfecting agents may cause deterioration of the glove material; washing with surfactants could result in wicking or enhanced penetration of liquids into the glove via undetected pores, thereby transporting blood and OPIM into contact with the hand. For this reason, disposable (single-use) gloves may not be washed and reused.

- Certain solutions such as iodine may cause discoloration of gloves without affecting their integrity and function.

dering, disposing, and replacing of personal protective equipment at no charge to you.

If blood or OPIM contaminates your clothing, you must remove it as soon as feasible and place it in an appropriately designated area or container.

If a pullover scrub or shirt becomes contaminated, you must remove it in such a way as to avoid contact with the outer surface—for example, rolling up the garment as it is pulled toward the head for removal. However, if the blood penetrates the scrub or shirt and contaminates the inner surface, the penetration itself would constitute an exposure. If the scrub or shirt cannot be removed without contamination of the face, it is recommended that the shirt be cut and removed.

If your personal protective equipment has been penetrated by blood or OPIM, it is recommended that you check your body for cuts or scrapes or other nonintact skin when removing your equipment.

You must remove all personal protective equipment before leaving the work area to prevent transmission of bloodborne pathogens to coworkers in other departments and family, and to prevent contamination of environmental surfaces.

Limited Exceptions to Using Personal Protective Equipment

There are a few exceptions to the use of personal protective equipment when the use of such equipment would prevent the proper delivery of health care or public safety services, or would pose an increased hazard to the personal safety of the worker. Examples of such situations could include:

- A sudden change in patient status such as when an apparently stable patient unexpectedly begins to hemorrhage profusely, putting the patient's life in immediate jeopardy

- A firefighter, rescuing an individual who is not breathing from a burning building, discovers that the resuscitation equipment is lost or damaged and must administer CPR

- A bleeding suspect unexpectedly attacks a police officer with a knife, threatening the safety of the officer and/or coworkers.

Skill Scan: One-Handed Technique

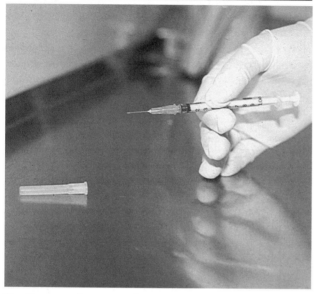

Needle removal or recapping must be accomplished through the use of a mechanical device or one-handed technique to prevent puncture wounds.

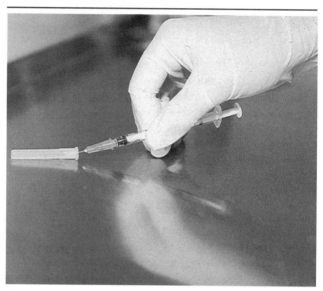

The one-handed technique uses a nearby wall or heavy object to stabilize the needle cover.

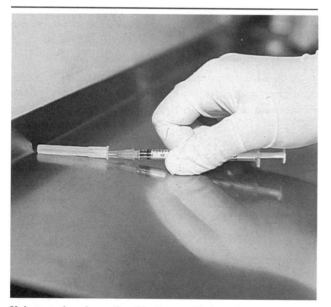

Using one hand, gently slide the needle into the needle cover.

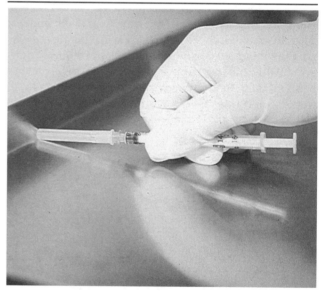

Using the wall as support, apply gentle pressure to secure the needle cover. Dispose of the needle and syringe in nearest sharps container.

Skill Scan: Cleaning a Contaminated Spill

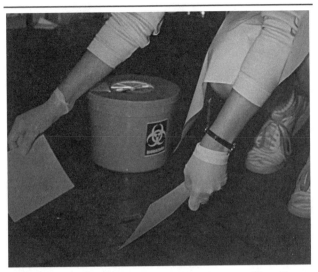

When cleaning up broken glass, wear gloves and/or other personal protective equipment.

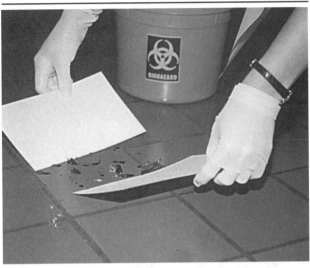

Do not clean up broken glass with your hands. Instead use a dust pan and brush, cardboard (as shown), or tongs.

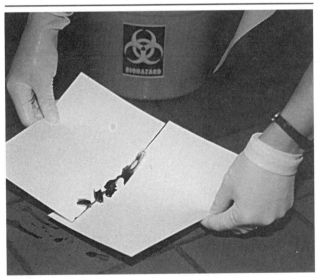

Vacuum cleaners are prohibited for the cleaning up of broken glass.

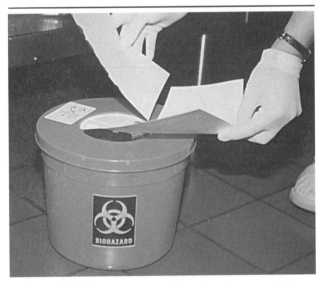

Broken glass must be placed in an appropriate sharps container. Placing broken glass in a plastic bag may put others at risk for exposure.

Skill Scan: Removing Contaminated Personal Protective Equipment

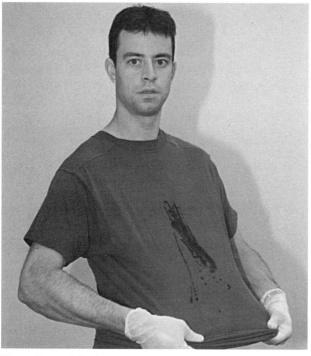

If a pullover shirt becomes contaminated, you must remove it in such a way as to avoid contact with the outer surface.

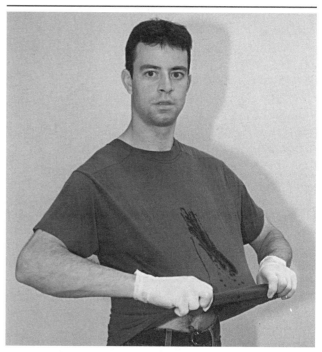

Rolling the garment as it is pulled toward the head will decrease the chance of contact with the contaminated area.

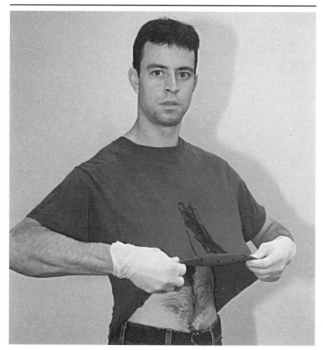

After rolling up the shirt, carefully pull it over the head to avoid contact with the face or mucous membranes.

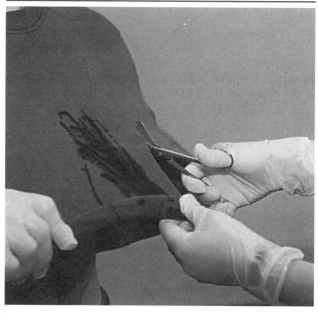

If the shirt cannot be removed without contamination, it is recommended that the shirt be cut off.

Housekeeping

Work Surfaces

Sharps

Laundry

Learning Objective

You will be able to explain how cleaning work surfaces and equipment will protect you from disease.

Work Surfaces

Your employer will identify which work surfaces could become contaminated with blood or OPIM. This could include, but is not limited to, wastebaskets, exam tables, counters, floors, ambulance interiors, and police cars.

A regular cleaning schedule will need to be established and followed. The schedule must consider location, type of surface, type of soil present, and procedure and tasks performed. The cleaning schedule must occur at least weekly or after completion of tasks, after contamination of surfaces, or at the end of a shift if there is a possibility of contamination.

While cleaning up potentially infectious materials, you will wear reusable latex gloves and use an EPA-approved solution. An example of an inexpensive approved solution is 10% bleach and water. You should use disposable towels to clean up the spill and then dispose of the towels in a biohazard-labeled bag.

Do not clean up broken glass with your hands. Instead use a dust pan and brush, cardboard, or tongs. Vacuum cleaners are prohibited for the cleaning of broken glass under the standard.

Broken glass must be placed in a sharps container. Placing broken glass in a plastic bag may put others at risk for an occupational exposure incident.

Sharps

Reusable sharps including pointed scissors that have been contaminated must be decontaminated before reuse. Before cleaning, store the sharps in a container

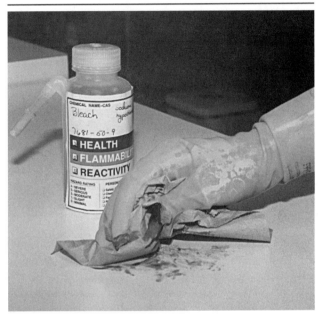

Care must be used when cleaning up contaminated spills.

with a wide opening and encourage people to use care in removing items.

Before decontamination, all visible blood or OPIM must be rinsed off, as large amounts of organic debris interfere with the efficacy of the disinfecting/sterilization process. *Never* blindly reach into any container.

Disposable sharps must be placed in puncture-resistant containers labeled as biohazardous to protect others.

Laundry

Laundry and waste materials may be separated into contaminated and noncontaminated labeled containers. Remember that the goal of these regulations is to protect you and others from contamination, so use plastic bags or double plastic bags (if the outside of the first bag becomes contaminated) to prevent leakage of wet/damp laundry.

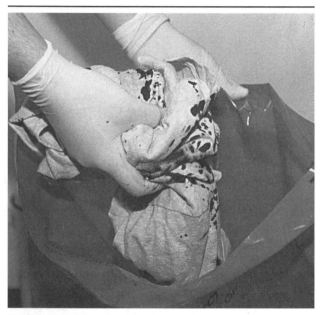

Contaminated laundry should be clearly labeled and placed in leakproof containers.

You must wear gloves when handling laundry or waste materials. Do not handle laundry any more than necessary. Home laundering of personal protective equipment is prohibited.

Contaminated laundry should be sent to a facility following the OSHA Standard.

DISPOSAL OF SHARPS CONTAINERS

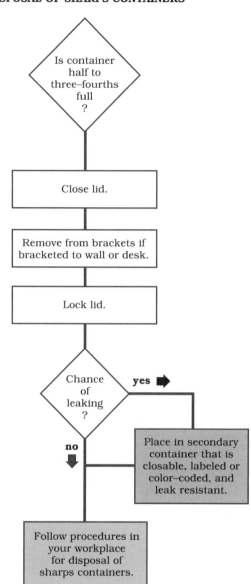

HANDLING USED SHARPS

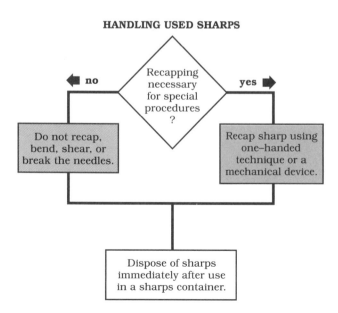

HANDLING CONTAMINATED LAUNDRY

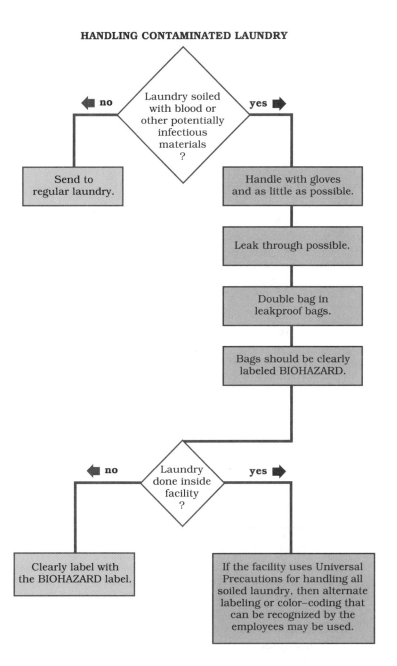

Labeling

What Is an Acceptable Container?

When Is Labeling Necessary?

Using Sharps Containers

Labeling Regulated Waste

Learning Objective

You will be able to recognize and explain the appropriate labels and containers for contaminated items.

What Is an Acceptable Container?

A sharps container must meet four criteria to be considered acceptable.

It must be closable, puncture resistant, leakproof on sides and bottom, and labeled or color-coded.

A sharps container may be made of a variety of products including cardboard or plastic, as long as the four criteria are met. Duct tape may be used to secure a sharps container lid, but it is not acceptable if it serves as the lid itself.

When Is Labeling Necessary?

Labels must be provided on containers of regulated waste, on refrigerators and freezers that are used to store blood or OPIM, and on containers used to store, dispose of, transport, or ship blood or OPIM.

Equipment that is being sent to another facility for servicing or decontamination must have a label attached stating which portions of the equipment remain contaminated in order to warn other employees of the hazard and the precautions they need to take.

Using Sharps Containers

Contaminated sharps must be discarded immediately in an acceptable sharps container. Sharps containers must be easily accessible to personnel and located as close as feasible to the immediate area where sharps are used or can be reasonably anticipated to be found.

Sharps containers must be maintained upright throughout use and replaced routinely. The replacement schedule must be clearly outlined in the Exposure Control Plan.

If leakage is possible, or if the outside of the container has become contaminated, the sharps container must be placed in a secondary container.

Areas such as correctional facilities, psychiatric units, or pediatric units may have difficulty placing sharps containers in the immediate use area. If a mobile cart is used by health care workers in these units, an alternative would be to lock a sharps container in the cart.

Laundries that handle contaminated laundry must have sharps containers easily accessible due to the incidence of needles mixed with laundry.

Facilities that handle shipments of waste that may contain contaminated sharps must also have sharps containers easily accessible in the event a package accidentally opens and releases sharps.

Labeling Regulated Waste

Regulated waste containers are required to be labeled with the biohazard label or color-coded to warn employees who may have contact with the containers of the potential hazard posed by their contents.

Even if your facility considers all of its waste to be regulated waste, the waste containers must still bear the required label or color-coding in order to protect new employees and employees from outside facilities.

Regulated waste that has been decontaminated need not be labeled or color-coded. However, your employer must have controls in place to determine if the decontamination process is successful.

■ Exceptions to Labeling Requirements

Blood and blood products that bear an identifying label as specified by the Food and Drug Administration and that have been screened for HBV and HIV antibodies and released for transfusion or other clinical uses are exempted from the labeling requirements.

When blood is being drawn or laboratory procedures are being performed on blood samples, then the individual containers housing the blood or OPIM do not have to be labeled provided the larger container into which they are placed for storage, transport, shipment, or disposal (for example, a test tube rack) is labeled.

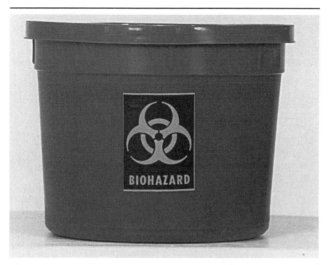

Biohazard symbols must be fluorescent orange or orange-red with letters or symbols in a contrasting color. These are attached to any container that is used to store or transport potentially infectious materials.

Biohazard labels may be attached to bags containing potentially infectious materials. The label must be fluorescent orange or orange-red in color and clearly visible.

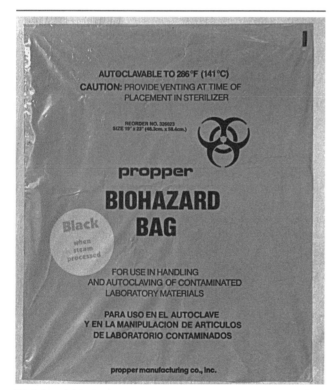

Biohazard labels must be fluorescent orange or orange-red in color and attached as close as feasible to the container by string, wire, adhesive, or other method that prevents their loss or unintentional removal.

Biohazard labels may be attached to waste containers containing potentially infectious materials. The label must be fluorescent orange or orange-red and clearly visible.

Transmission

Mode of Transmission of Bloodborne Pathogens

Protecting Yourself

Handwashing

HBV Versus HIV

Learning Objective

You will be able to explain how bloodborne pathogens are transmitted.

Mode of Transmission of Bloodborne Pathogens

Bloodborne pathogens are transmitted when blood or OPIM come in contact with mucous membranes, nonintact skin, or by handling or touching contaminated items or surfaces. Nonintact skin includes, but is not limited to, cuts, abrasions, burns, rashes, paper cuts, and hangnails. Bloodborne pathogens are also transmitted by injection under the skin by puncture wounds or cuts from contaminated sharps.

The majority of occupational HIV transmission has occurred through puncture injury. However, there have been documented HIV transmissions from nonsexual, nonpercutaneous exposures to fresh blood or body fluid contamination with HIV. Transmission has been documented to occur after contact with HIV-contaminated blood through nonintact skin and mucous membranes. One worker became HIV positive after a splash of HIV contaminated blood to the eyes. It should be clear that contact with blood or OPIM should be avoided.

You can protect yourself from transmission of bloodborne pathogens.

Protecting Yourself

To protect yourself from transmission of bloodborne pathogens, you should observe Universal Precautions and wear personal protective equipment.

Handwashing

Handwashing is one of the most effective methods of preventing transmission of bloodborne pathogens. It is required that you wash your hands after removal of gloves and other personal protective equipment.

HBV Versus HIV

Hepatitis B virus (HBV) is more persistent than HIV and is able to survive for at least a week in dried blood on environmental surfaces or contaminated instruments. It is unlikely that HIV will be transmitted by handling or touching contaminated surfaces whereas HBV is.

A source of HBV is chronic carriers. Chronic carriers have the antigen present at all times and can unwittingly transmit the disease to susceptible persons through transfusion, needle or other penetrating injury, and intimate contact.

A number of other bloodborne diseases other than HIV and HBV exist, such as hepatitis C, hepatitis D, and syphilis.

Exposure Determination

What Is an Occupational Exposure Incident?

Assessing Exposure Determination

Learning Objective

You will be able to determine whether an exposure incident could occur within your job.

What Is an Occupational Exposure Incident?

An occupational exposure incident occurs if you are in a work situation and come in contact with blood or other potentially infectious materials.

For OSHA 200 record-keeping purposes, an occupational bloodborne pathogens exposure incident (e.g., needlestick, laceration, or splash) shall be classified as an injury since it is usually the result of an instantaneous event or exposure.

Once an occupational exposure to blood or other potentially infectious materials has occurred, the employee's name and job classification are listed on the OSHA 200 log. All staff in the same job classification as the exposed employee are now covered under the standard and must receive the training and be offered the hepatitis B immunization series at no cost.

Assessing Exposure Determination

Occupational exposure can occur in many different job situations. Examples of professions in which a person might be exposed to blood or OPIM could include, but

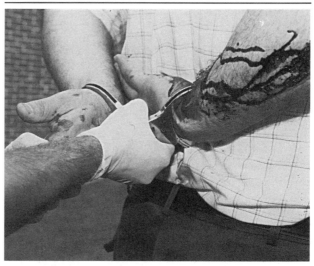

Are you at risk?

are not limited to, physicians, nurses, police officers, ambulance attendants, EMTs, fire and rescue personnel, laboratory personnel, morticians and embalmers, and teachers. All persons in these professions need to be aware of their possible risk of exposure.

Any exposure is enough to place your job under the requirements of the standard. If you have ever been exposed to blood or OPIM, ask yourself why you have been exposed. Is the task that you were doing a normal part of your occupation? Was a package not properly labeled? Are you trained to prevent injury to yourself?

Post-Exposure Reporting

Minimizing Exposure

Reporting an Incident

Medical Care after an Incident

Confidentiality

Learning Objective

You will be able to describe the steps to take after an exposure incident and the importance of reporting it.

Minimizing Exposure

If you have an exposure incident to another person's blood or OPIM, immediately wash the exposed area with warm water and soap.

To minimize exposure, flush affected area immediately with water.

If the exposed area was in your mouth, rinse your mouth with water or mouthwash (whichever is most readily available).

If the exposure was in your eyes, flush with warm water (or normal saline if available). A quick rinse is probably not adequate; you want to irrigate the area completely with water.

Reporting an Incident

Next report the incident to your supervisor. OSHA requires the following information:

1. How, when, and where the incident occurred.

2. With whose blood or body secretions did you come in contact? If you do not know, do not worry. Just explain why you do not know.

3. Your blood may be tested for HBV and/or HIV only with your consent. You may refuse. But you may also have the blood drawn and stored for 90 days. If you change your mind within the 90 days, HIV testing will be done. If you elect not to have the blood tested, the sample will be disposed of without testing after 90 days.

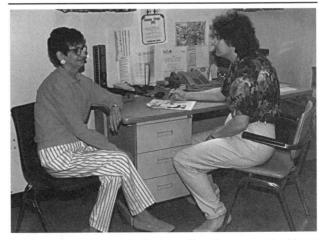

It is important to report all occupational exposure incidents immediately.

4. The source individual's blood will also be tested if available (unless already known to be HIV or HBV positive) and the results of the test will be made known to you. State laws may vary; please check with your instructor regarding confidentiality laws in your state.

Medical Care after an Incident

You are entitled to medical care after an exposure incident. When you go for treatment the following information will be made available to the caregiver:

1. A copy of the OSHA guidelines section 1910.1030

2. A description of how the incident occurred as it relates to your employment

3. The results of the source individual's testing (if available)

4. All medical records that pertain to this one incident

The following is a list of the records that your employer is required to have on file about each employee:

1. The name and social security number of each employee

2. A copy of the employee's hepatitis B vaccination status including the dates of all the hepatitis B vaccinations and any medical records relative to the employee's ability to receive the vaccination

3. A copy of all results of examinations, medical testing, and follow-up procedures after an exposure incident

4. The employer's copy of the health care provider's written opinion regarding the incident

Confidentiality

It is the employer's responsibility to ensure that employee medical records are kept confidential. Your records cannot be disclosed without your express written consent to any person within or outside the workplace except as required by law.

Requirements
The Exposure Control Plan

Learning Objective

You will be able to state the requirements of the Exposure Control Plan.

The Exposure Control Plan

Each employer having an employee with occupational exposure to blood or OPIM shall establish a written Exposure Control Plan designed to eliminate or minimize employee exposure.

The Exposure Control Plan shall contain at least:

1. An exposure determination including:
  a. A list of job classifications in which occupational exposure may occur, and will occur
  b. A list of all tasks and procedures in which occupational exposure occurs and that are performed by employees in the job classifications listed above.

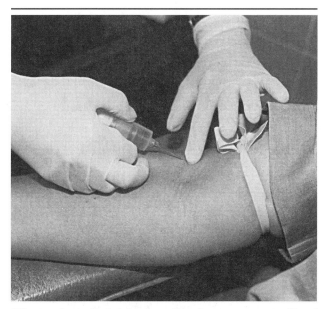

All procedures that risk occupational exposure are outlined in the Exposure Control Plan.

2. This Exposure Control Plan shall be written as if personal protective equipment is not used. Personal protective equipment should be used as a back-up method only, not primary protection.

3. The schedule and method of implementation of methods of compliance including:
   a. Universal Precautions
   b. Engineering Controls
   c. Work practice controls
   d. Hepatitis B vaccination and post-exposure evaluation and follow-up
   e. Communication and record keeping procedures

4. Each employer shall ensure that a copy of the Exposure Control Plan is accessible to employees in accordance with 29 CFR 1910.30 (the OSHA Bloodborne Pathogen Standard).

5. The Exposure Control Plan shall be renewed and updated annually and whenever necessary to reflect new or modified tasks and procedures that affect occupational exposure, and to reflect new or revised employee positions with occupational exposure.

6. The Exposure Control Plan shall be made available to the Assistant Secretary of Labor and the Director on request.

Tuberculosis (TB)

What Are the 1994 CDC TB Guidelines?

What Is the Occupational Safety and Health Act of 1970?

Who Needs This Section?

Meeting the General Duty Clause

What Is Tuberculosis?

Prevention

Screening

Post-Exposure Reporting

Requirements

This section contains information about tuberculosis (TB), an airborne disease. Since 1985, the incidence of TB in the general U.S. population has increased approximately 14%, reversing a 30-year downward trend. Recently, drug-resistant strains of mycobacterium tuberculosis *(M. tuberculosis)* have become a serious concern and cases of multi-drug-resistant (MDR) TB have occurred in 40 states. This overview of the risks of tuberculosis exposure (although it is not a bloodborne pathogen) has been included because many employees with occupational exposure to bloodborne pathogens may potentially have occupational exposure to persons with TB disease.

Nationwide, at least several hundred health care workers (HCW) have become infected with TB and have required medical treatment after workplace exposure to TB. Twelve (12) of these HCWs have died from TB disease. In general, persons who become infected with TB have approximately a 10% risk for developing TB disease in their lifetimes.

What Are the 1994 CDC TB Guidelines?

The Occupational Safety and Health Administration (OSHA) has not released a standard specific to tuberculosis (as of this printing); however, the Centers for Disease Control and Prevention (CDC) has released the 1994 TB Guidelines for the protection of HCWs. OSHA believes the CDC's 1994 TB Guidelines reflect an industry recognition of the hazard as well as appropriate, widely recognized, and accepted standards of practice to be followed by employers in carrying out their responsibilities under the Act.

The CDC is not a regulatory agency. The focus of the 1994 CDC TB Guidelines is to minimize the number of HCWs exposed to *M. tuberculosis,* while maintaining optimal care of patients with active infection with *M. tuberculosis.* The Guidelines can be found in the "Morbidity and Mortality Weekly Report," vol. 43, October

28, 1994. No. RR-13 Recommendations and Reports: *Guidelines for Preventing the Transmission of Mycobacterium Tuberculosis in Health-Care Facilities.*

What Is the Occupational Safety and Health Act of 1970?

OSHA is a regulatory agency. OSHA regulations are written to protect the employee from recognized hazards in the workplace. OSHA can and does enforce the worker protection by invoking the Occupational Safety and Health Act of 1970, or the General Duty Clause. The General Duty Clause (Public Law 91-596) states that "each employer shall furnish to each of his employees employment and a place of employment which are free from recognized hazards that are causing or are likely to cause death or serious physical harm to his employees: shall comply with occupational safety and health standards promulgated under this Act. Each employee shall comply with occupational safety and health standards and all rules, regulations, and orders issued pursuant to this Act which are applicable to his own actions and conduct."

Methods are available to minimize the hazards posed by employee exposure to TB. It is the employer's responsibility to see that these protections are in place and are readily available. It is your (the employee's) responsibility to utilize these protections.

Who Needs This Section?

Any employee who has potential for occupational exposure to *M. tuberculosis* needs this section. The 1994 CBC TB Guidelines specify five potentially hazardous work areas:

- Health care facilities
- Long-term care facilities for the elderly
- Homeless shelters
- Drug and treatment centers
- Correctional facilities

The following is a list of HCWs whose tasks may lead them to occupational exposure to *M. tuberculosis.* The potential for occupational exposure is not limited to employees in these positions:

- Physicians
- Nurses
- Aides
- Home health care workers

- Dental workers
- Technicians
- Workers in laboratories and morgues
- Emergency medical service personnel (EMTs)
- Students
- Part-time personnel
- Temporary staff not employed by the health care facility
- Persons not directly involved with patient care, but who are potentially at risk for occupational exposure to *M. tuberculosis* (e.g., air ventilation system workers)

Meeting the General Duty Clause

The 1994 CDC TB Guidelines specify steps to be taken in order to minimize exposure to *M. tuberculosis.* In order to ensure a safe working environment and meet the OSHA General Duty Clause requirements, employers should provide the following:

1. An assessment of the risk for transmission of *M. tuberculosis* in the particular work setting
2. A protocol for the early identification of individuals with active TB
3. Training and information to ensure employee knowledge of the method of TB transmission, its signs and symptoms, medical surveillance and therapy, and site-specific protocols, including the purpose and proper use of controls. (*Note:* Failure to provide respirator training is citable under OSHA's general industry standard on respirators.)
4. Medical screening, including preplacement evaluation; administration and interpretation of Mantoux skin tests
5. Evaluation and management of workers with positive skin tests or a history of positive skin tests who are exhibiting symptoms of TB, including work restrictions for infectious employees
6. AFB (acid-fast bacilli) isolation rooms for suspected or confirmed infectious TB patients. These AFB isolation rooms, and areas in which high-hazard procedures are performed, should be single-patient rooms with special ventilation characteristics that are properly installed, maintained, and evaluated to reduce the potential for airborne exposure to *M. tuberculosis.*
7. Institution of Exposure Controls specific to the workplace, which include the following:

- **Administrative Controls** are policies and procedures to reduce the risk of employee exposure to infectious sources of *M. tuberculosis.* An example is a protocol to ensure rapid detection of people who are likely to have an active case of TB.

- **Engineering Controls** attempt to design safety into the tools and workspace organization. An example is High Efficiency Particulate Air (HEPA) filtration systems.

- **Personal Respiratory Protective Equipment** is used by the employee to prevent exposure to potentially infectious air droplet nuclei, for example, a personal respirator.

What Is Tuberculosis?

- *M. tuberculosis* is the bacteria responsible for causing TB in humans.

- TB is a disease that primarily spreads from person to person through droplet nuclei suspended in the air.

- TB may cause disease in any organ of the body. The most commonly affected organ is the lung, and accounts for about 85% of all infection sites. Other sites may include lymph nodes, the central nervous system, kidneys, and the skeletal system.

- TB is a serious and often fatal disease if left untreated.

- Symptoms of TB include weight loss, weakness, fever, night sweats, coughing, chest pain, and coughing up blood.

- The prevalence of infection is much higher in the close contacts of TB patients than in the general population.

- There is a difference between TB infection (positive TB skin test) and TB disease.

■ Transmission

TB is spread from person to person in the form of droplet nuclei in the air. When a person with TB coughs, sings, or laughs, the droplet nuclei are released into the air. When another uninfected person *repeatedly* breathes in the droplet nuclei, there is a chance of their becoming infected with TB.

For an employee to develop TB infection, he or she must have close contact to a sufficient number of air droplet nuclei over a long period of time. The employee's health is also considered as contributing to the susceptibility for TB infection and the possible devel-

opment of TB disease. Among the medical risk factors for developing TB are diabetes, gastrectomy (removal of the stomach), long-term corticosteroid use, immunosuppressive therapy, cancers and other malignancies, and HIV infection.

■ Symptoms

Symptoms of TB also occur in people with more common diseases such as a cold or flu. The difference is that the symptoms of TB disease last longer than those of a cold or flu and must be treated with prescription antibiotics. The usual symptoms of TB disease include cough, production of sputum, weight loss, loss of appetite, weakness, fever, night sweats, malaise, fatigue, and, occasionally, chest pain. Hemoptysis, the coughing up of blood, may also occur, but usually not until after a person has had TB disease for some time.

■ Diagnosis

TB disease is diagnosed when there is a positive AFB sputum smear, or when three successive early morning sputum specimens are cultured and there is a growth of *M. tuberculosis* from at least one culture. When extrapulmonary (not in the lungs) TB is being considered, it may also be diagnosed by culture techniques. The difference is that the specimen is cultured from the site where TB is considered the cause of the infection.

Prevention

The 1994 CDC TB Guidelines recommend a hierarchy of controls to minimize TB transmission. These strate-

---

Key Facts

Relationship to HIV

1. People infected with HIV and *M. tuberculosis* are at a very high risk of developing active TB. Seven to 10 percent of persons infected with both TB and HIV will develop active disease each year.

2. Extrapulmonary TB (i.e., outside the lungs) is more common in people with HIV infections.

3. Miliary TB and lymphatic TB are more common in HIV-infected people.

4. The HIV epidemic is a major contributing factor to the recent increase in cases of active TB.

gies are used in combination to promote workplace safety and to provide the employee with maximum protection against occupational exposure to *M. tuberculosis*. Under these guidelines, the control of TB is to be accomplished through the early identification, isolation, and treatment of persons with TB; use of engineering and administrative procedures to reduce the risk of exposure; and through the use of respiratory protection. The CDC 1994 TB Guidelines also stress the importance of the following measures: (1) use of risk assessments for developing a written TB control plan; (2) TB screening programs for HCWs; (3) HCW training and education; and (4) evaluation of TB infection-control programs.

Screening

■ Who Should Receive TB Screening?
According to the 1994 CDC TB Guidelines, HCWs are at increased risk for TB infection and should be provided with TB skin testing. This testing must be provided at no cost to employees at risk of exposure. The general population of the United States is thought to be at low risk for TB and should not be routinely tested.

■ Frequency of Testing
The frequency of testing is determined by the number of active cases of TB within a worksite of the facility. HCWs should receive TB skin testing prior to work in an area at increased risk for active cases of TB. A two-step TB skin testing process should be used (see What Is the Booster Effect?). Testing should be repeated each year, or more frequently for an employee assigned to a high-risk worksite or after a known exposure to a person with active TB.

■ What Is the TB Skin Test?
The tuberculin skin test of choice is the Mantoux test, which uses an intradermal injection of purified protein derivative (PPD). There are three strengths of PPD available; intermediate-strength (5 tuberculin units) PPD is the standard test material.

    A skin test is done by injecting a very small amount of PPD just under the skin (usually the forearm is used). A small bleb (bubble) will be raised. The bleb will disappear. The injection site is then checked for reaction by your clinician about 48 to 72 hours later. If you fail to have the injection site evaluated in 72 hours, and no induration (swelling) is present, the tuberculin skin test will need to be repeated.

■ What Types of Reactions Occur?
Induration, the hard and bumpy swelling at the injection site, is used for determining a reaction to the PPD. Interpretation of results is best understood when the general health and risk of exposure to active TB cases are considered in the assessment. The injection site may also be red, but that does not determine a reaction to the PPD, nor indicate a positive result. We recommend that the interpretation guidelines of the American Thoracic Society–CDC Advisory panel be used to assess the measured induration at the injection site.

■ What Does a Positive Result Mean?
A positive skin test means an infection with *M. tuberculosis* has occurred, but does not prove TB disease. Referral for further medical evaluation is required to determine a diagnosis of TB disease. People found to have TB disease must be provided effective treatments. These treatments would be provided to the employee by the employer if the illness was found to be work related.

■ Possible False Positive Results
Close contacts of a person with TB disease, who have had a negative reaction to the first skin test, should be re-tested about 10 weeks after the last exposure to the person with TB disease. The delay between tests should allow enough time for the body's immune system to respond to an infection with *M. tuberculosis*. A second test will result in a positive reaction at the injection site if an infection with *M. tuberculosis* has occurred.

■ Contraindications to TB Screening
If you have tested positive to the TB skin test in the past it is *not recommended* that you receive the test again. Also, pregnancy does not exclude a HCW from being tested. Many pregnant workers have been tested for TB without documented harm to the fetus. You should consult with your doctor if you are pregnant and have any questions about receiving a TB skin test.

Post-Exposure Reporting

■ What Determines an Occupational Exposure?
Occupational exposure to *M. tuberculosis* is defined as employees working in one of the five types of facilities whose workers have been identified by the CDC as having a higher incidence of TB than the general population, and whose employees have exposure defined as follows:

1. Potential exposure to the exhaled air of an individual with suspected or confirmed TB disease

2. Exposure to a high-hazard procedure performed on an individual with suspected or confirmed TB disease, which could generate potentially infectious airborne droplet nuclei

■ What Is the Booster Effect?

Sensitivity to the TB skin test may decrease over time, causing an initial skin test to be negative but at the same time stimulating or boosting the immune system's sensitivity to tuberculin, thereby producing a positive reaction the next time the test is given. When repeated skin testing is necessary, concern about the booster effect and the misinterpretation of skin test results can be avoided by using a two-step testing process. This is why your employer should require the two-step test as soon as you start employment. The two-step test helps to eliminate any confusion over whether an employee was infected at the worksite or was previously infected.

■ Post-Exposure Evaluation and Testing

Records of employee exposure to TB, skin tests, and medical evaluations and treatment must be maintained by your employer.

Active tuberculosis disease is an illness that must be reported to public health officials. Every state has reporting requirements.

For OSHA Form 200 recordkeeping purposes, both tuberculosis infections (positive TB skin test) and tuberculosis disease are recordable. A positive skin test for tuberculosis, even on initial testing (except preassignment screening), is recordable on the OSHA 200 log because of the presumption of work-relatedness in these settings, unless there is clear documentation that an outside exposure occurred.

Requirements

■ TB Exposure Control Plan

Employers having employees with exposure to TB shall establish a written Exposure Control Plan designed to eliminate or minimize employee exposure. This plan involves:

- Schedule and method of implementation of the control plan
- PPD testing
- Respiratory protection
- Communication of hazards to employees
- Post-exposure evaluation and follow-up
- Record keeping

Health Evaluation History

Name _____ Date _____ Birth date _____

School _____ Grade _____ Sex _____

Family history of diabetes, heart attack, sudden death, sickle cell disease, trait of other diseases _____

_____

Medical History

Chronic illness _____

Injuries _____

Surgery _____

Do you take any medicine _____ Vitamins _____ Supplements _____

Circle if you have had any of the following symptoms:

Allergies	Heat exhaustion	Vomiting blood	Pain with urination
Seizures	Heatstroke	Constipation	Menstrual problems
Headaches	Cough or wheeze	Diarrhea	Last menses _____
Concussion	Chest pain	Blood in stool	Back pain
Dizziness	Spitting blood	Blood in urine	Joint pain
Fainting	Stomachache		

Sports to be played: _____

Diet History
Servings Per Day

Servings Per Week

Vegetables	Fruit	Milk, Dairy	Bread, Cereal	Junk Food	Red Meat	White Meat
None	None	None	None	None	None	None
1–2	1–2	1–2	1–2	1–2	1–2	1–2
3–4	3–4	3–4	3–4	3–4	3–4	3–4
4+	4+	4+	4+	4+	4+	4+

Name _____

Height _____ Weight _____ BP _____ % Body fat _____

Vision 20/ _____ Left 20/ _____ Right _____ Contacts _____ Glasses _____

Posture and Gait

Scoliosis _____	Shoulder higher _____	Genu valgum _____
Kyphosis _____	Iliac crest higher _____	Genu varum _____
Lordosis _____	Pronation _____	Toe in _____

Comments _____

Source: Donahue P. 1990. Preparticipation exams: how to detect a teen-age crisis. *Phys Sportsmed.* 18(4):54–55. Reprinted with permission.

Flexibility

	Normal	Tight	Very Tight
Neck	_____	_____	_____
Low back	_____	_____	_____
Hamstrings	_____	_____	_____
Quadriceps	_____	_____	_____
Adductors	_____	_____	_____
Iliotibial band	_____	_____	_____
Heel cord	_____	_____	_____

Comments _____

Medical Examination

	Normal	Abnormal		Normal	Abnormal
Heart, eyes, ears, nose, throat	_____	_____	Spine	_____	_____
			Genitalia	_____	_____
			Skin	_____	_____
Cardiovascular	_____	_____	Neuro	_____	_____
Respiratory	_____	_____	Tanner stage _____		
Abdomen	_____	_____			

Comments _____

Joint Examination

	Left			Right	
	Normal	Abnormal		Normal	Abnormal
Shoulder	_____	_____		_____	_____
Elbow	_____	_____		_____	_____
Wrist	_____	_____		_____	_____
Hip	_____	_____		_____	_____
Knee	_____	_____		_____	_____
Ankle	_____	_____		_____	_____

Comments _____

Appraisal _____

Recommendations _____

_____ Full sports activity   _____ May participate in all activity except _____

_____ No sport activity until _____ Referred to _____

Return _____   to check _____

_____ MD

How to Identify Pathogenic Weight-Control Behavior

Female athletes have gone to extraordinary lengths to lower their body fat stores in an effort to improve performance. A pattern of eating disorders has emerged from this desperate, health-threatening situation. The following protocol was developed to advise the athletic training staff how to identify symptoms in athletes who suffer from one or more features of pathogenic weight-control behavior. Many of the items do not by themselves prove the presence of an eating disorder, but identification of one or more may justify further attention to the possible presence of a problem.

Reports or observation of the following signs or behaviors should arouse concern:

1. Repeatedly expressed concerns by an athlete about being or feeling fat even when weight is below average.

2. Expressions of fear of being or becoming obese that do not diminish as weight loss continues.

3. Refusal to maintain even a minimal normal weight consistent with the athlete's sport, age, and height.

4. Consumption of huge amounts of food not consistent with the athlete's weight.

5. Clandestine eating or stealing of food (e.g., many candy wrappers, food containers, etc., found in the athlete's locker, around his or her room); repeated disappearance of food from the training table.

6. A pattern of eating substantial amounts of food, followed promptly by trips to the bathroom and resumption of eating shortly thereafter.

7. Bloodshot eyes, especially after trips to the bathroom.

8. Vomitus or odor of vomit in the toilet, sink, shower, or wastebasket.

9. Wide fluctuations in weight over short time spans.

10. Complaints of light-headedness or disequilibrium not accounted for by other medical causes.

11. Evidence of use of diet pills (e.g., irritability fluctuating with lethargy over short periods of time).

12. Complaints or evidence of bloating or water retention that cannot be attributed to other medical causes (e.g., premenstrual edema).

13. Excess laxative use or laxative packages seen in the athlete's area, locker, wastebasket, etc.

14. Periods of severe calorie restriction or repeated days of fasting.

15. Evidence of purposeless, excessive physical activity (especially in a thin athlete) that is not part of the training regimen.

16. Depressed mood and self-deprecating expression of thoughts following eating.

17. Avoiding situations in which the athlete may be observed while eating (e.g., refusing to eat with teammates on road trips, making excuses such as having to eat before or after the team meal).

18. Appearing preoccupied with the eating behavior of other people such as friends, relatives, or teammates.

19. Certain changes in the athlete's physical appearance (e.g., rounding or pouch-like dilation at or just under the angle of the jaw, ulceration or sores at the corners of the mouth or on the tongue, thinning or loss of hair).

20. Known or reported family history of eating disorders or family dysfunction.

If an athlete who seems to have an eating disorder is practicing one or more pathogenic weight-control techniques, the following recommendations are in order:

1. The coaching or training staff person who has the best rapport with the athlete should arrange a private meeting with him or her.

2. The tone of the meeting should be entirely supportive. Express concern for the best interests of the individual and make it clear that this concern transcends the issue of the individual as an athlete.

3. In as nonpunitive a manner as possible, indicate to the athlete what specific observations were made that aroused your concern. Let the individual respond.

Source: Rosen et al. 1986. Pathogenic weight-control behavior in female athletes. *Phys Sportsmed.* 14(1):82–83. Reprinted with permission.

4. Affirm and reaffirm that the athlete's role on the team will not be jeopardized by an admission that an eating problem exists. Participation on a team should be curtailed only if evidence shows that the eating disorder has compromised the athlete's health in a way that could lead to injury should participation be continued.

5. Try to determine if the athlete feels that he or she is beyond the point of being able to voluntarily abstain from the problem behavior.

6. If the athlete refuses to admit that a problem exists in the face of compelling evidence, or if it seems that the problem either has been long-standing or cannot readily be corrected, consult a clinician with expertise in treating eating disorders. Remember, most individuals with this problem have tried repeatedly to correct it on their own and failed. Failure is especially demoralizing to athletes, who are constantly oriented toward success. Let the individual know that outside help is often required and that this need should not be regarded as a failure or lack of effort.

7. Arrange for regularly scheduled follow-up meetings apart from practice times, or, if the athlete is seeing a specialist, obtain advice as to how you may continue to help.

8. Be aware that most athletes resorting to pathogenic weight-control techniques have been told at various times that they had a weight problem. It is important to know what role, if any, past or present coaches or trainers may have played in the development of this problem. Let the athlete know that you realize that the demands of the sport may well have played a role in the development of this behavior.

What not to do:

1. Question teammates instead of talking directly to the athlete.

2. Immediately discipline the athlete if you find evidence that a problem exists.

3. Indicate to the athlete that you know what's going on, but tell nothing as to how or why you've become suspicious.

4. Tell the athlete to straighten up and that you'll be checking back from time to time.

5. Conclude that if the athlete really wants to be okay, he or she will make it happen, and failure to improve shows a lack of effort.

6. Dissociate yourself and the demands of the sport from any aspect of the development of the problem.

7. Refuse to obtain outside assistance but rather "keep it in the family."

Summary

Despite a growing body of evidence admonishing the behavior, weight cutting (rapid weight reduction) remains prevalent among wrestlers. Weight cutting has significant adverse consequences that may affect competitive performance, physical health, and normal growth and development. To enhance the education experience and reduce the health risks for the participants, the ACSM recommends measures to educate coaches and wrestlers toward sound nutrition and weight control behaviors, to curtail weight cutting, and to enact rules that limit weight loss.

Introduction

For more than half a century, rapid weight loss, weight cutting as practiced by wrestlers, has remained a concern among educators, health professionals, exercise scientists, and parents (14,28,55,63). Since the American College of Sports Medicine first published the position statement Weight Loss in Wrestlers (3) in 1976, a plethora of research articles has been published on this topic. On a weekly basis, rapid weight loss in high school and collegiate wrestlers has been shown to average 2 kg and may exceed 2.7 kg among 20% of the wrestlers (41,55,61). One-third of high school wrestlers have reported repeating this process more than 10 times in a season (41,61). These practices have been documented over the past 25 years (61,62), and during that time their prevalence appears to have changed little (41,55,61).

Weight Loss in Wrestlers

While wrestlers may believe they have excess fat, studies show that in the off-season high school wrestlers have 8% to 11% body fat, well below their high school

peers, who average 15% (6,21,24,60). Estimates made during the season have found body fat to be as low as 3% and average 6% to 7% (17,23,27,38,42,43,58). Consequently, loss of fat contributes minimally to weight reduction while the primary methods for weight loss (e.g., exercise, food restriction, fasting, and various dehydration methods) affect body water, glycogen content, and lean body mass (23,51,56,67,69). These weight loss techniques are used by 25% to 67% of wrestlers (32,41,61,69). Use of pharmacological agents, including diuretics, stimulants, and laxatives to reduce weight has been reported among a few of these athletes (32,41,55). The weight loss techniques have been passed down from wrestler to wrestler, or coach to wrestler, and have changed little over the past 25 years. Seldom do parents and health professionals provide input on how to lose weight appropriately (32,41,61). Recently, a small but growing number of females have begun to participate in wrestling. No data exist on the weight control behaviors of this select group of wrestlers. If these females also practice weight cutting, the same health and performance concerns apply to them as to their male counterparts.

Wrestlers practice these weight loss techniques believing their chances of competitive success will increase. Ironically, weight cutting may impair performance and endanger the wrestler's health. Weight loss in wrestlers can be attributed to reductions in body water, glycogen, lean tissue, and only a small amount of fat. The combination of food restriction and fluid deprivation creates a synergistic, adverse physiologic effect on the body, leaving the wrestler ill-prepared to compete. In addition, most forms of dehydration, e.g., sweating and catharsis, contribute to the loss of electrolytes as well as water (5,9). Wrestlers hope to replenish body fluids, electrolytes, and glycogen in the brief period (30 min–20 h) between the weigh-in and competition. However, reestablishing fluid homeostasis may take 24 to 48 h (10); replenishing muscle glycogen may take as long as 72 h (11,25), and replacing lean tissue might take even longer. In short, weight cutting appears to adversely influence the wrestler's energy reserves and fluid and electrolyte balances.

The singular or combined effects of weight cutting on physiological function and performance are presented in Table 1. These functions are indicators of

Source: American College of Sports Medicine. 1996. Position Stand on Weight Loss in Wrestlers. *Med. Sci. Sports. Exerc.* 28(2)ix–xii. This pronouncement was written for the American College of Sports Medicine by: Robert A. Oppliger, Ph.D., FACSM, (Chair), H. Samuel Case, Ph.D., FACSM, Craig A. Horswill, Ph.D., Gregory L. Landry, M.D., and Ann C. Shelter, M.A., R.D. Reprinted with permission.

TABLE 1 Effects of "Weight Cutting" on Physiological Performance

[a,c]	Little or no increase (1,17,50,53,63,68) and possible reduction in muscle strength (23,46,66)
[a,c]	Little or no increase (26,44,46) and possible decrease in anaerobic power capacity (35,66)
[b,c]	Lower plasma and blood volume (2,31,49,65), increased resting and submaximal heart rate (2,49), decreased cardiac stroke volume (2), resulting in decreased ability to sustain work at a constant rate, i.e., reduced endurance capacity (45,47)
[a]	Lower oxygen consumption (36,57)
[c,d]	Impaired thermoregulatory processes, which could decrease endurance capacity and increase the risk of heat illness during practice (7,48,49)
[c]	Decreased renal blood flow and kidney filtration of blood (70–72)
[a,b]	Depletion of muscle (23) and possibly liver glycogen (25), which will reduce muscle endurance capacity (19,29), the body's ability to maintain blood glucose levels, and accelerate the breakdown of the body's protein (4,15)
[a,c,d]	Depletion of electrolytes resulting in impaired muscle function (5), coordination (29), and possibly cardiac arrhythmias

Superscript identifies methods that contribute to this physiological effect: [a] = food restriction or fasting; [b] = exercise; [c] = dehydration; [d] = catharsis (diuretic or laxatives).

performance on the mat; however, no research to date has investigated the relationship between wrestling performance and weight loss. Although the scientific data are not conclusive, these weight cutting practices may also alter hormonal status (59), diminish protein nutritional status (20), impede normal growth and development (18), affect psychological state (19,32,37, 41,55), impair academic performance (8,13,64), and have severe consequences such as pulmonary emboli (12), pancreatitis (34), and reduce immune function (30). Use of diuretics may result in more profound effects on the cardiovascular systems and electrolyte balance than other forms of weight loss (5,7).

For these reasons, the National Federation of State High School Associations supports the opinion that each state implement rules that include an effective weight control program (39). Several states have successfully instituted programs that require body composition assessment and nutrition education (personal communications, 40), and more states appear poised to follow. Scientists, physicians, dieticians, coaches, athletic administrators, trainers, and other health professionals should work toward implementation of these recommended changes nationwide.

Conclusions and Recommendations

Because of the equivocal benefits and the potential health risks created by the procedures used for "weight cutting" by wrestlers (particularly adolescents), the ACSM makes the following recommendations:

1. Educate coaches and wrestlers about the adverse consequences of prolonged fasting and dehydration on physical performance and physical health.

2. Discourage the use of rubber suits, steam rooms, hot boxes, saunas, laxatives, and diuretics for "making weight."

3. Adopt new state or national governing body legislation that schedules weigh-ins immediately prior to competition.

4. Schedule daily weigh-ins before and after practice to monitor weight loss and dehydration. Weight lost during practice should be regained through adequate food and fluid intake.

5. Assess the body composition of each wrestler prior to the season using valid methods for this population (42,60). Males 16 years old and younger with a body fat below 7% or those over 16 with a body fat below 5% need medical clearance before being allowed to compete. Female wrestlers need a minimal body fat of 12% to 14% (33).

6. Emphasize the need for daily caloric intake obtained from a balanced diet high in carbohydrates (> 55% of calories), low in fat (< 30% of calories) with adequate protein (15% to 20% of calories, 1.0 to 1.5 $g \cdot kg^{-1}$ body weight) determined on the basis of RDA guidelines and physical activity levels (16,22,54). The minimal caloric intake for wrestlers of high school and college age should range from 1,700 to 2,500 $kcal \cdot d^{-1}$, and rigorous training may increase the requirement up to an additional 1,000 calories per day (16). Wrestlers should be discouraged by coaches, parents, school officials, and physicians from consuming less than their minimal daily needs. Combined with exercise, this minimal caloric intake will allow for gradual weight loss. After the minimal weight has been attained, caloric intake should be increased sufficiently to support the normal developmental needs of the young wrestler (16).

The ACSM encourages:

Permitting more participants per team to compete by adding weight classes between 119 lb. and 151 lb. or by allowing more than one representative at a given weight class just as swimming and track teams do in competition.

Standardization of regulations concerning the eligibility rules at championship tournaments so that severe and rapid weight loss is discouraged at the end of the season (e.g., a wrestler dropping one or more weight classes).

Cooperative efforts between coaches, exercise scientists, physicians, dietitians, and wrestlers to systematically collect data on the body composition, hydration state, energy and nutritional demands, growth, maturation, and psychological development of wrestlers.

Through this position statement, the ACSM hopes to further the sport of wrestling by providing a positive educational environment for the primary, secondary, or collegiate wrestler. The ACSM believes these recommendations will enable the athlete to better focus on skill acquisition, fitness enhancement, psychological preparation, and the social interactions offered by the sport.

Acknowledgment

This position stand replaces the 1976 ACSM position paper, "Weight Loss in Wrestlers."

This pronouncement was reviewed for the American College of Sports Medicine by members-at-large, the Pronouncements Committee, and by: Jack Harvey, M.D., FACSM, Michael Sharratt, Ph.D., FACSM, Suzanne Steen, Ph.D., and Charles Tipton, Ph.D., FACSM.

References

1. Ahlman, K. and M.J. Karvonen. Weight reduction by sweating in wrestlers and its effect on physical fitness. *J. Sports Med.* 1:58–62, 1961.

2. Allen, T.E., D.P. Smith, and D.K. Miller. Hemodynamic response to submaximal exercise after dehydration and rehydration in high school wrestlers. *Med. Sci. Sports Exerc.* 9:159–163, 1977.

3. American College of Sports Medicine. Position statement: weight loss in wrestlers. *Med. Sci. Sports* 8:xi–xiii, 1976.

4. Cahill, G. F. Starvation in man. *N. Engl. J. Med.* 282:668–675, 1970.

5. Caldwell, J. E., E. Ahonen, and U. Nousiainen. Differential effects of sauna-, diuretic-, and exercise-induced hypohydration. *J. Appl. Physiol.* 57:1018–1023, 1984.

6. Cisar, C. J., G. O. Johnson, A. C. Fry, et al. Preseason body composition, build, and strength as predictors of high school wrestling success. *J. Appl. Sports Sci. Res.* 1:66–70, 1987.

7. Claremont, A. D., D. L. Costill, W. J. Fink, and P. Vanhandel. Heat tolerance following diuretic induced dehydration. *Med. Sci. Sports Exerc.* 8:239–243, 1976.

8. Conners, C. K. and A. G. Bouin. Nutritional effects on behavior of children. *Psychiatry Res.* 17:193–201, 1982.

9. Costill, D. L., P. Cote, and W. J. Fink. Muscle water and electrolytes following varied levels of dehydration in man. *J. Appl. Physiol.* 40:6–11, 1976.

10. Costill, D. L. and K. E. Sparks. Rapid fluid replacement following thermal dehydration. *J. Appl. Physiol.* 34:299–303, 1973.

11. Coyle, E. F. and E. Coyle. Carbohydrates that speed recovery from training. *Physician Sportsmed.* 21:111–123, 1993.

12. Croyle, P. H., R. A. Place, and A. D. Hilgenberg. Massive pulmonary embolism in a high school wrestler. *J.A.M.A.* 241:827–828, 1979.

13. DeFeo, P., V. Gallia, and G. Mazzotta. Modest decrements in plasma glucose concentration cause early impairment in cognitive function and later activation in glucose counterregulation in absence of hypoglycemic symptoms in normal man. *J. Clin. Invest.* 82:436–444, 1988.

14. Doshner, N. The effect of rapid weight loss upon the performance of wrestlers and boxers and upon the physical proficiency of college students. *Res. Q.* 15:317–324, 1944.

15. Felig, P., O. E. Owen, J. Wahren, and G. F. Cahill. Amino acid metabolism during prolonged starvation. *J. Clin. Invest.* 48:584–594, 1969.

16. Food and Nutrition Board. *Recommended Dietary Allowances*, 10th Ed. Washington, DC: National Academy of Sciences, 1989, pp. 24–37, 65, 66.

17. Freischlag, J. Weight loss, body composition, and health of high school wrestlers. *Physician Sportsmed.* 12:121–126, 1984.

18. Hansen, N. C. Wrestling with "making weight." *Physician Sportsmed.* 6:106–111, 1978.

19. Horswill, C. A., R. C. Hickner, J. R. Scott, D. L. Costill, and D. Gould. Weight loss, dietary carbohydrate modifications and high intensity physical performance. *Med. Sci. Sports Exerc.* 22:470–476, 1990.

20. Horswill, C. A., S. H. Park, and J. N. Roemmich. Changes in the protein nutrition status of adolescent wrestlers. *Med. Sci. Sports Exerc.* 22: 599–604, 1990.

21. Horswill, C. A., J. Scott, P. Galea, and S. H. Park. Physiological profile of elite junior wrestlers. *Res. Q. Exerc. Sports* 59:257–261, 1988.

22. Houck, J. and J. Slavin. Protein nutrition in the athlete. In: *Sports Nutrition for the 90s: The Health Profession's Handbook.* J. R. Berning and S. N. Steen (Eds.). Gaitherburg, MD: Aspen Publishers, 1991, pp. 1–12.

23. Houston, M. E., D. A. Marrin, H. J. Green, and J. A. Thomson. The effect of rapid weight reduction on physiological functions in wrestlers. *Physician Sportsmed.* 9:73–78, 1981.

24. Hughes, R. A., T. J. Housh, and G. O. Johnson. Anthropometric estimations of body composition across a season. *J. Appl. Sports Sci. Res.* 5:71–76, 1992.

25. Hultman, E. and L. Nilsson. Liver glycogen as glucose-supplying source during exercise. *Limiting Factors of Physical Performance.* 1973, pp. 179–189.

26. Jacobs, I. The effects of thermal dehydration on performance of the Wingate anaerobic test. *Int. J. Sports Med.* 1:21–24, 1980.

27. Kelly, J. M., B. A. Gorney, and K. K. Kalm. The effect of a collegiate wrestling season on body composition, cardiovascular fitness, muscular strength, and endurance. *Med. Sci. Sports Exerc.* 10:119–124, 1978.

28. Kenny, H. E. The problem of making weight for wrestling meets. *J. Health Phys. Ed.* 1:24, 1930.

29. Klinzing, J. E. and W. Karpowicz. The effect of rapid weight loss and rehydration on a wrestling performance test. *J. Sports Med.* 26:139–145, 1986.

30. Kono, I., H. Kitao, M. Matsuda, S. Haga, and H. Fukushmia. Weight reduction in athletes may adversely affect phagocytic function of monocytes. *Physician Sportsmed.* 16:56–65, 1988.

31. Kozlowski, S. and B. Saltin. Effects of sweat loss on body fluids. *J. Appl. Physiol.* 19:1119–1124, 1964.

32. Lakin, J.A., S. N. Steen, and R. A. Oppliger. Eating behaviors, weight loss methods, and nutritional practices of high school wrestlers. *J. Community Health Nurs.* 7:223–234, 1990.

33. McArdle, W. D., F. I. Katch, and V. L. Katch. *Exercise Physiology: Energy, Nutrition, and Human Performance,* 3rd Ed. Malvern, PA: Lea & Febiger, 1991, p. 488.

34. McDermott, W. V., M. K. Bartlett, and P. J. Culver. Acute pancreatitis after prolonged fast and subsequent surfeit. *N. Engl. J. Med.* 254:379–80, 1956.

35. McMurray, R. G., C. R. Proctor, and W. L. Wilson. Effects of caloric deficit and dietary manipulation on aerobic and anaerobic exercise. *Int. J. Sports Med.* 12:167–172, 1991.

36. Melby, C. L., W. D. Schmidt, and D. Corrigan. Resting metabolic rate in weight-cycling collegiate wrestlers compared with physically active, noncycling control subjects. *Am. J. Clin. Nutr.* 52:409–414, 1990.

37. Morgan, W. P. Psychological effects of weight reduction in the college wrestler. *Med. Sci. Sports Exerc.* 2:24–27, 1970.

38. Nagle, F. J., W. P. Morgan, R. O. Hellickson, R. C. Serfass, and J. F. Alexander. Spotting success traits in Olympic contenders. *Physician Sportsmed.* 3:31–34, 1975.

39. National Federation of High School Associations. *Wrestling Rules 1992–93.* Kansas City, MO: National Federation of High School Associations, 1992.

40. Oppliger, R. A., R. D. Harms, D. L. Herrmann, C. M. Streich, and R. R. Clark. The Wisconsin wrestling minimal weight project: a model for wrestling weight control. *Med. Sci. Sports Exerc.* 27:1220–1224, 1995.

41. Oppliger, R. A., G. L. Landry, S. A. Foster, and A. C. Lambrecht. Bulimic behaviors among high school wrestler: a statewide survey. *Pediatr. Res.* 94:826–831, 1993.

42. Oppliger, R. A., D. H. Neilsen, and C. G. Thompson. Minimal weight predicted by bioelectrical impedance and anthropometric equations. *Med. Sci. Sports Exerc.* 23:247–253, 1991.

43. Oppliger, R. A. and C. M. Tipton. Weight prediction equation tested and available. *Iowa Med.* 75:449–452, 1985.

44. S. H., Park, J. N. Roemmich, and C. A. Horswill. A season of wrestling and weight loss by adolescent wrestlers: effect on anaerobic arm power. *J. Appl. Sports Sci. Res.* 4:1–4, 1990.

45. Ribisl, P. M. and W. G. Herbert. Effect of rapid weight reduction and subsequent rehydration

upon the physical working capacity of wrestlers. *Res. Q.* 41:536–541, 1970.

46. Roemmich, J. N., W. E. Sinning. Sport seasonal changes in body composition, growth, power, and strength of adolescent wrestlers. *Int. J. Sports Med.* 17:92–99, 1996.

47. Saltin, B. Aerobic and anaerobic work capacity after dehydration. *J. Appl. Physiol.* 19:1114–1118, 1964.

48. Saltin, B. Circulatory response to submaximal and maximal exercise after thermal dehydration. *J. Appl. Physiol.* 19:1125–1132, 1964.

49. Sawka, M. N., R. P. Francesconi, K. B. Pandolf, and A. J. Young. Influence of hydration level and body fluids on exercise performance in the heat. *J.A.M.A.* 252:1165–1169, 1984.

50. Serfass, R. C., G. A. Stull, J. F. Alexander, and J. L. Ewing. The effects of rapid weight loss and attempted rehydration on strength and endurance of the hand muscle in college wrestlers. *Res. Q. Exerc. Sports* 55:46–52, 1984.

51. Sherman, W. M., D. L. Costill, W. J. Fink, F. C. Hagerman, L. E. Armstrong, and T. S. Murray. Effect of 42.2 m footrace and subsequent rest or exercise on muscle glycogen and enzymes. *J. Appl. Physiol.* 55:1219–1224, 1983.

52. Short, S. H. and W. R. Short. Four year study of university athletes' dietary intake. *J. Am. Diet. Assoc.* 82:632–645, 1983.

53. Singer, R. N. and S. A. Weiss. Effects of weight reduction on selected anthropometric, physical, and performance measures of wrestlers. *Res. Q.* 39:361–369, 1968.

54. Steen, S. N. Nutritional considerations for the low body-weight athlete. In: *Sports Nutrition for the 90s: The Health Profession's Handbook,* J. R. Berning and S. N. Steen (Eds.). Gaitherburg, MD: Aspen Publishers: 1991, pp. 160–164.

55. Steen, S. N. and K. D. Brownell. Patterns of weight loss and regain in wrestlers: has the tradition changed? *Med. Sci. Sports Exerc.* 22:762–768, 1990.

56. Steen, S. N. and S. McKinney. Nutritional assessment of college wrestlers. *Physician Sportsmed.* 14:100–116, 1986.

57. Steen, S. N., R. A. Oppliger, and K. D. Brownell. Metabolic effects of repeated weight loss and regain in adolescent wrestlers. *J.A.M.A.* 260:47–50, 1988.

58. Stine, G., R. Ratliff, G. Shierman, and W. A. Grana. Physical profile of the wrestlers at the 1977 NCAA Championships. *Physician Sportsmed.* 7:98–105, 1979.

59. Strauss, R. H., R. R. Lanese, and W. B. Malarkey. Weight loss in amateur wrestlers and its effect on serum testosterone. *J.A.M.A.* 254:3337–3338, 1985.

60. Thorland, W. G., C. M. Tipton, R. W. Bowers, et al. Midwest wrestling study: prediction of minimal weight for high school wrestlers. *Med. Sci. Sports Exerc.* 23:1102–1110, 1991.

61. Tipton, C. M. and T. K. Tcheng. Iowa wrestling study: weight loss in high school students. *J.A.M.A.* 214:1269–1274, 1970.

62. Tipton, C. M., T. K. Tcheng, and W. D. Paul. Evaluation of the Hall method for determining minimum wrestling weights. *J. Iowa Med. Soc.* 59:571–574, 1969.

63. Tuttle, W. W. The effects of weight loss by dehydration and witholding of food on the physiologic response of wrestlers. *Res. Q.* 14:158–166, 1943.

64. Tuttle, W. W., K. Daum, L. Myers, and C. Martin. Effect of omitting breakfast on the physiologic response of men. *J. Am. Diet. Assoc.* 26:332–335, 1950.

65. Vaccaro, P., C. W. Zauner, and J. R. Cade. Changes in body weight, hematocrit, and plasma protein concentration due to dehydration and rehydration in wrestlers. *J. Sports Med. Phys. Fitness* 16:45–53, 1976.

66. Webster, S., R. Rutt, and A. Weltman. Physiological effects of a weight loss regimen practiced by college wrestlers. *Med. Sci. Sports Exerc.* 22:229–234, 1990.

67. Weissinger, E., T. J. Housh, G. O. Johnson, and S. A. Evans. Weight loss behavior in high school wrestling: wrestler and parent perception. *Pediatr. Exerc. Sci.* 3:64–73, 1991.

68. Widerman, P. M. and R. D. Hagen. Body weight loss in a wrestler preparing for competition: a case report. *Med. Sci. Sports Exerc.* 14:413–418, 1982.

69. Woods, E. R., C. D. Wilson, and R. P. Masland. Weight control methods in high school wrestlers. *J. Adolesc. Health Care* 9:394–397, 1988.

70. Zambraski, E. J., D. T. Foster, P. M. Gross, and C. M. Tipton. Iowa wrestling study: weight loss and urinary profiles of collegiate wrestlers. *Med. Sci. Sports* 8:105–108, 1976.

71. Zambraski, E. J., C. M. Tipton, H. R. Jordan, W. K. Palmer, and T. K. Tcheng. Iowa wrestling study: urinary profiles of state finalists prior to competition. *Med. Sci. Sports* 6:129–132, 1974.

72. Zambraski, E. J., C. M. Tipton, T. K. Tcheng, H. R. Jordan, A. C. Vailas, and A. K. Callahan. Iowa wrestling study: changes in urinary profiles of wrestlers prior to and after competition. *Med. Sci. Sports* 7:217–220, 1975.

Generic First-Aid Kit for Sports Injuries *(Checklist)*

The following is a comprehensive listing of supplies that should enable coaching personnel to handle the majority of common sports injuries, regardless of sport. However, it is critical to note that some sports may present unique problems, such as in the case of tackle football, with respect to airway management and face mask removal. In such cases, coaching personnel should include specialty items such as a set of Trainers Angels® for face mask removal, in addition to the items listed below.

Check Item

_____ alcohol preps

_____ antibiotic ointment

_____ antifungal cream

_____ approved biohazard container (for storage of all materials exposed to blood or other body fluids)

_____ athletic tape (1.5″ width, nonelastic)

_____ Band-Aids®—variety of shapes and sizes including those for fingers, knuckles, and large joints

_____ Betadine® skin disinfectant

_____ Chapstick (with sunscreen)

_____ cloth ties for splints (can be made from old sheets)

_____ Conform® (elastic athletic tape)

_____ contact-lens cleaning kit

_____ cotton tip applicators (Q-tips®)

_____ elastic wraps (Ace® bandages in sizes ranging from 4″ to 6″)

_____ emergency information cards for all athletes—should include all pertinent information regarding each athlete, such as drug allergies, preexisting medical conditions, home phone number, insurance policy information, name and phone number of family physician

_____ face mask, one-way valve (artificial respiration)

_____ fingernail clippers

_____ foam padding material (open- and closed-cell foams)

_____ hydrogen peroxide solution

_____ inhalers (for exercise-induced asthma attack)

_____ medical soap (used for wound cleaning)

_____ medically approved eye protection (goggles)

_____ nonsterile latex examination gloves (sizes small, medium, large)

_____ nonstick sterile gauze pads (variety of sizes)

_____ note pad and pencil or pen

_____ padding material for splints (wool or cotton blankets)

_____ paper bag (for treatment of hyperventilation)

_____ pen light (with extra batteries)

_____ petroleum jelly or other lubricant for skin

_____ plastic (sandwich) bags (for use with crushed ice)

_____ prewrap (used in conjunction with athletic tape)

_____ quarters and dimes (for public phone)

_____ rolled sterile gauze (self-adhering)

_____ skin tape

_____ Spenco Second Skin™

_____ splints (Sam® Splint)

_____ sterile gauze pads (variety of sizes from 2″ × 2″ to 4″ × 4″)

_____ Steri-Strips® (for management of wounds on the face)

_____ sunscreen product (waterproof)

_____ tape scissors

_____ thermometers (oral and rectal)

_____ tongue depressors

_____ triangular bandages (cravat bandages)

_____ tweezers

_____ wooden splints (variety of sizes suitable for arm and leg fractures)

Introduction

This appendix presents guidelines for the installation, use, and storage of full-size or nearly full-size movable soccer goals. The U.S. Consumer Product Safety Commission (CPSC) believes these guidelines can help prevent deaths and serious injuries resulting from soccer goal tip over. They are intended to promote greater safety awareness among those who purchase, install, use, and maintain movable soccer goals.

These guidelines are intended for use by parks and recreation personnel, school officials, sports equipment purchasers, parents, coaches, and any other members of the general public concerned with soccer goal safety.

These guidelines are intended to address the risk of movable soccer goal tip over. They are not a CPSC standard, nor are they mandatory requirements. Therefore, the Commission does not endorse them as the sole method to minimize injuries associated with soccer goals.

Soccer Goal Injuries and Deaths

According to the 1994 National Soccer Participation Survey (Soccer Industry Council of America), over 16 million persons in the United States play soccer at least once a year. Seventy-four % (over 12 million) of these persons are under the age of 18. Soccer ranks fourth in participation for those under 18, following basketball, volleyball, and softball and well ahead of baseball, which has an annual participation of 9.7 million.

There are approximately 225,000 to 500,000 soccer goals in the United States. Many of these soccer goals are unsafe because they are unstable and are either unanchored or not properly anchored or counterbalanced. These movable soccer goals pose an unnecessary risk of tip over to children who climb on goals (or nets) or hang from the crossbar.

Source: U.S. Consumer Product Safety Commission. January 1995. Washington, D.C. 20207

The CPSC knows of four deaths in 1990 alone and at least 21 deaths during 1979 to 1994 associated with movable soccer goals. In addition, an estimated 120 injuries involving falling goals were treated each year in U.S. hospital emergency rooms during the period 1989 through 1993. Many of the serious incidents occurred when the soccer goals tipped over onto the victim. Almost all of the goals involved in these tip overs appeared to be home-made by high school shop classes, custodial members, or local welders—not professionally manufactured. These home-made goals are often very heavy and unstable.

The majority of movable soccer goals are constructed of metal, typically weighing 150 to 500 pounds. The serious injuries and deaths are a result of blunt force trauma to the head, neck, chest, and limbs of the victims. In most cases this occurred when the goal tipped or was accidentally tipped onto the victim. In one case an 8-year-old child was fatally injured when the movable soccer goal he was climbing tipped over and struck him on the head. In another case, a 20-year-old male died from a massive head trauma when he pulled a goal down on himself while attempting to do chin-ups. In a third case, while attempting to tighten a net to its goal post, the victim's father lifted the back base of the goal, causing it to tip over fatally striking his 3-year-old child on the head.

High winds can also cause movable soccer goals to fall over. For example, a 9-year-old was fatally injured when a goal was tipped over by a gust of wind. In another incident, a 19-year-old goalie suffered stress fractures to both legs when the soccer goal was blown on top of her.

Rules of Soccer

From the Federation of Internationale De Football Associations' (FIFA) *Laws of the Game, Guide for Referees, July 1993:*

Goal-posts and cross-bars must be made of wood, metal, or other approved material as decided from time to time by the International Football Association Board. They may be square, rectangular, round, half round, or elliptical in shape.

Goal-posts and cross-bars made of other materials and in other shapes are not permitted. The goal-posts must be white in color.

The width and depth of the cross-bar shall not exceed 5 inches (12 cm).

From the National Federation of State High School Associations' (NFSHSA) *1994–95 National Federation Edition—Soccer Rules Book:*

They shall consist of 2 upright (posts) 4 inches but not more than 5 inches (0.10m by 0.12m) . . . the tops of the posts shall be joined by a 4 inches but not more than 5 inches (0.10m by 0.12m) horizontal crossbar . . .

From the National Collegiate Athletic Associations' (NCAA) *Rules for Soccer:*

. . . and shall consist of two wooden or metal posts, . . . the width or diameter of the goal-posts and cross-bar shall not be less than 4 inches (10.16 cm) nor more than 5 inches (12.7 cm).

Design and Construction Guidelines

While a movable soccer goal appears to be a simple structure, a correctly designed goal is carefully con-structed with counterbalancing measures incorporated into the product. The common dimensions of a full-size goal are approximately 7.3 m (24 ft.) in width by 2.4 m (8 ft.) in height and 1.8 m (6 ft.) in depth. The stability of a soccer goal depends on several factors. One effective design alternative uses a counterbalancing strategy by lengthening the overall depth of the goal to effectively place more weight further from the goal's front posts (more weight at the back of the goal). A second design selects lightweight materials for the goal's front posts and crossbar and provides much heavier materials for the rear ground bar and frame members. This tends to counterbalance the forces working to tip the goal forward. Another design uses a heavy rear framework and folds flat when not in use, making the goal much less likely to tip over. Finally, after these various designs are considered, it is imperative that *all* movable soccer goals be anchored firmly in place at all times.

Anchoring, Securing, and Counterweighting Guidelines

A properly anchored and counterweighted movable soccer goal is much less likely to tip over. Remember to secure the goal to the ground (preferably at the rear

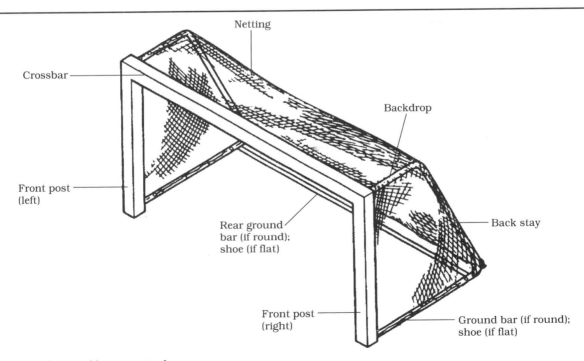

Components of a movable soccer goal.

of the goal), making sure the anchors are flush with the ground and clearly visible. It is *imperative* that *all* movable soccer goals are always anchored properly. There are several different ways to secure your soccer goal. The number and type of anchors to be used will depend on several factors, such as soil type, soil moisture content, and total goal weight.

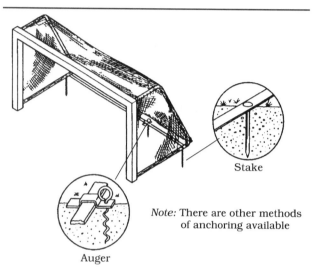

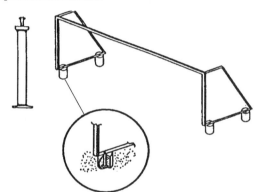

Note: There are other methods of anchoring available

Goal anchoring.

■ Anchor Types

■ **Auger style** This style anchor is helical shaped and is screwed into the ground. A flange is positioned over the ground shoes (bar) and rear ground shoe (bar) to secure them to the ground. A minimum of two auger-style anchors (one on each side of the goal) is recommended. More may be required, depending on the manufacturer's specifications, the weight of the goal, and soil conditions.

■ **Semipermanent** This anchor type is usually composed of two or more functional components. The

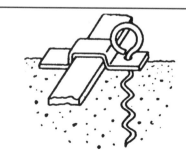

Auger style anchor.

main support requires a permanently secured base that is buried underground. One type of semipermanent anchor connects the underground base to the soccer goal by means of two tethers. Another design utilizes a buried anchor tube with a threaded opening at ground level. The goal is positioned over the buried tube and the bolt is passed through the goal ground shoes (bar) and rear ground shoe (bar) and screwed into the threaded hole of the buried tube.

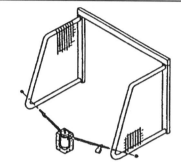

Semipermanent anchor.

Semipermanent anchor.

■ **Peg or stake style (varying lengths)** Typically two to four pegs or stakes are used per goal (more for heavier goals). The normal length of a peg or stake is approximately 10 inches (250 mm). Care should be taken when installing pegs or stakes. Pegs or stakes should be driven into the ground with a sledgehammer as far as possible and at an angle if possible, through available holes in the ground shoes (bar) and rear ground shoe (bar) to secure them to the ground. If the peg or stake is not flush with the ground, it should be clearly visible to persons playing near the soccer goal. Stakes with larger diameters or textured surfaces have greater holding capacity.

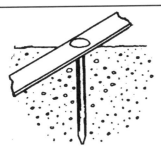

Peg or stake style anchor.

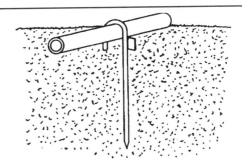

J-hook anchor.

■ **J-hook stake style** This style is used when holes are not predrilled into the ground shoes (bars) or rear ground shoe (bar) of the goal. Similar to the peg or stake style, this anchor is hammered, at an angle if possible, directly into the earth. The curved (top) portion of this anchor fits over the goal member to secure it to the ground. Typically, two to four stakes of this type are recommended (per goal), depending on stake structure, manufacturer's specifications, weight of goal, and soil conditions. Stakes with larger diameters or textured surfaces have greater holding capacity.

■ **Sandbags and counterweights** Sandbags or other counterweights could be an effective alternative on hard surfaces, such as artificial turf, where the surface can not be penetrated by a conventional anchor (i.e., an indoor practice facility). The number of bags or weights needed will vary and must be adequate for the size and total weight of the goal being supported.

■ **Net pegs** These tapered, metal stakes should be used to secure only the *net* to the ground. Net pegs should *not* be used to anchor the movable soccer goal.

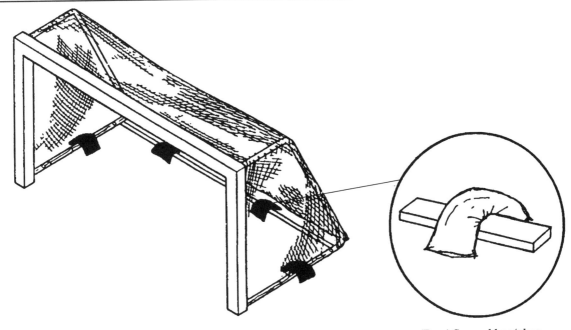

(Rear) Ground bar/shoe

Sandbag method of anchoring.

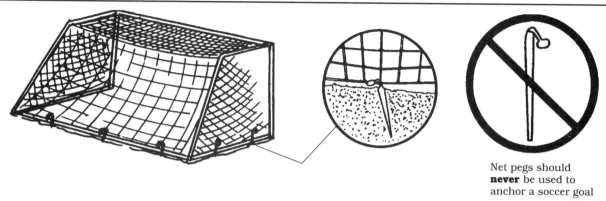

Net pegs.

Net pegs should **never** be used to anchor a soccer goal

Goal Storage Guidelines

The majority of the incidents investigated by the CPSC did not occur during a soccer match. Most of the incidents occurred when the goals were unattended. Therefore, it is imperative that all goals are stored properly when not being used. When goals are not being used always:

1. Remove the net,

2. Take appropriate steps to secure goals such as:

   a. Place the goal frames face to face and secure them at each goalpost with a lock and chain,

   b. Lock and chain to a suitable fixed structure such as a permanent fence,

   c. Lock unused goals in a secure storage room after each use,

   d. If applicable, fully disassemble the goals for seasonal storage, or

   e. If applicable, fold the face of the goal down and lock it to its base.

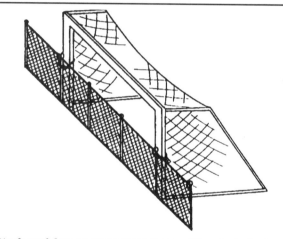

Attach goal face to permanent fence with a chain lock.

Safety Tips

- Securely anchor or counterweight movable soccer goals at *all* times.

- Anchor or chain one goal to another, to itself in a folded-down position, or to nearby fence posts, dugouts, or any other similar sturdy fixture when not in use. If this is not practical, store movable soccer goals in a place where children cannot have access to them.

- Remove nets when goals are not in use.

- Check for structural integrity and proper connecting hardware before every use. Replace damaged or missing parts or fasteners immediately.

- *Never* allow anyone to climb on the net or goal framework.

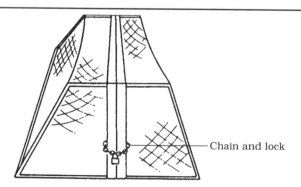

Chain and lock

Join goal faces and lock together using chain and lock.

- Ensure safety and warning labels are clearly visible (placed under the crossbar and on the sides of the down posts at eye level).

- Fully disassemble goals for seasonal change.

- Always exercise extreme caution when moving goals and allow adequate manpower to move goals of varied sizes and weights. Movable soccer goals should be moved only by authorized and trained personnel.

- Always instruct players on the safe handling of and potential dangers associated with movable soccer goals.

- Movable soccer goals should be used only on *level* (flat) fields.

List of Soccer Organizations

Federation of Internationale De Football Association
Hitzigweg 11, 8030
Zurich, Switzerland
Telephone 41-1-384-9595

National Federation of State High School Associations
11724 NW Plaza Circle
Box 20626
Kansas City, Missouri 64195-0626
Telephone (816) 464-5400

National Collegiate Athletic Association
6201 College Blvd
Overland Park, Kansas 66211-2422
Telephone (913) 339-1906

For Further Information

For further information on soccer goal anchors or to obtain **free** soccer goal warning labels, safety alerts and bulletins, and additional copies of this document, please contact:

 The Coalition to Promote Soccer Goal Safety
 c/o Soccer Industry Council of America
 200 Castlewood Dr.
 North Palm Beach, FL 33408
or call any of these Coalition members:
 (800) 527-7510
 (800) 334-4625
 (800) 243-0533
 (800) 531-4252
or write:
 U.S. Consumer Product Safety Commission
 Washington, D.C. 20207

To report a dangerous product or a product-related injury, call the CPSC's toll-free hotline at (800) 638-2772 or the CPSC's teletypewriter at (800) 638-8270. Consumers can get recall information via Internet gopher services at cpsc.gov or report product hazards to info@cpsc.gov.

Warning Labels

ALWAYS ANCHOR GOAL
Unsecured Goal Can Fall Over Causing Serious Injury or Death

NEVER CLIMB OR HANG ON GOAL
Goal Can Fall Over Causing Serious Injury or Death

Throughout their competitive careers, many athletes incur injuries, the majority of which are minor enough not to need rehabilitation. However, there are several sports-related injuries that are severe enough to require a formal rehabilitation program. Unfortunately, sometimes this program is not completed because of an athlete's, coach's, or parent's impatience for a return to play. Such a situation may arise when there is no one available who is experienced in and understands the rehabilitation process. It may be that the coach, athlete, or parent does not understand the importance of restoration before returning to activity and how a rehabilitation process can enhance an athlete's level of functioning after return. However, a knowledgeable professional, willing to spend a little extra time working with an athlete recovering from an injury, can only enhance the restoration process.

The rehabilitation or reconditioning of sports-related injuries is both an art and a science when properly completed. Rehabilitation can be defined as the restoration of an injured part to normal or near normal function. To return an athlete to activity functioning as close to 100% as possible is a valuable asset both for the athlete and the team. An untrained person may propose a strength training regimen but, without the basic understanding of the healing process and the basis for a gradual progression through a rehabilitation program, the outcome may not be positive. For example, weight training too early after injury can actually create more of a problem for an athlete by increasing damage to already injured tissues.

Rehabilitation programs can be created by working with a certified athletic trainer or a physical therapist. Sometimes, though, these are just "written recipes" for the athlete to follow that include a series of exercises. This type of program, "by the numbers," does not account for the recognition of daily gains or setbacks, swelling or pain, or other variables that might accompany the rehabilitation process. A well-structured and supervised rehabilitation program will include a set of detailed guidelines to follow, and will include a qualified therapist, who can discern variables that could be counterproductive to healing the injury. The next sections present the science of the rehabilita-

tion process as well as the art of the entire process. Finally, there are some generic sample programs for rehabilitating the ankle, shoulder, and knee.

The Science of Rehabilitation

For a detailed outline of the inflammatory process, see the section "Physiology of Sports Injury" in Chapter 8. The final phase of the inflammatory process is regeneration and repair. Here, the circulatory system brings fibroblasts to the damaged area; these fibroblasts mature and provide the necessary collagen for the repair of damaged tissues. The collagen fibers are randomly placed in the damaged area and take time to initiate collagen cross-linking to native tissue. It is during this time that it is important both to protect the damaged area and to promote movement there. The injury must be protected from further damage by undue stresses. However, the collagen is being deposited randomly, and before the collagen cross-linking is completed, controlled movement in a proper direction will assist the newly deposited collagen to assimilate a corresponding direction to the native fibers. With controlled movement as the healing process continues, the collagen fibers will align themselves in the direction of pull and, as time progresses, they will lay down a cross-linking system with native tissues. This process will provide the injured tissue both a structural base and an elastic component, allowing it to function as close to normal as possible. However, if the new collagen is allowed to migrate to the injured area and set up cross-links in a random fashion, a less pliable and structurally sound tissue will result. This uncontrolled scarring will not allow the injured soft tissue to function in as close to normal capacity as possible and, therefore, the athlete will be unable to perform at their highest level.

All of the phases in the inflammatory process, including the regeneration and repair phase, have generalized time lines depending on the severity of the injury. In this case, the regeneration and repair phase can last anywhere from one week to one year, again, depending on the severity of the injury and the intervention provided by the athletic trainer or physician.

Once the time line for the regeneration and repair phase is understood, the rehabilitation program becomes a series of steps that build on one another. The first step is designed to decrease swelling and pain to make it easier to move and exercise the injured part. When the swelling and pain are essentially absent from the injured area, the rehabilitation can proceed to the second step, reestablishing the range of motion (ROM). It is critical to restore normal, preinjury levels of ROM as any loss of joint mobility may contribute to reinjury. Range-of-motion exercises incorporate either passive movements (the coach or therapist moves the joint) or active movements (the athlete moves the joint). There are times when other, more intensive ROM measures need to be incorporated but this decision should be made by the attending physician. When an athlete has regained approximately 90% of ROM, he or she can move into the third step of the rehabilitation program. The goal of this portion of the program is to return muscle strength to the level of what it was prior to the injury. That can be accomplished best by incorporating a progressive resistive exercise (PRE) program that takes advantage of the overload principle. A variation of the PRE program is the daily adjusted progressive resistive exercise (DAPRE) program, developed by Dr. Ken Knight. The DAPRE protocol provides the athletic trainer with an objective method for adjusting the amount of weight being lifted in a given rehabilitation workout. An outline of the DAPRE protocol designed specifically for the quadriceps is shown in Table 1. Guidelines for adjusting the weight used during rehabilitation are shown in Table 2.

When strength is restored to 85% to 90% of the uninjured limb, the athlete is ready to proceed to the fourth step of the rehabilitation program: to train the nervous system to regain normal proprioception and to reestablish muscle power, speed, and skill. This is accomplished using many different types of equipment and exercises. Proprioception in the lower extremities is commonly reestablished by performing simple balance exercises such as standing on one foot or on the toes of both feet. As proprioception improves, more challenging exercises can be introduced, such as the slide board or the biomechanical ankle platform system (BAPS) board. Power can be improved by way of high velocity, high intensity resistive exercises such as Olympic lifts (power clean, high pulls, hang cleans) or with plyometric (bounding) exercises. Skill is best reestablished by practicing sport-specific drills. What type of exercise is appropriate at this stage of the rehabilitation is based on the athletic trainer's experience and an understanding of the athlete's needs upon returning to activity.

When an athlete can efficiently accomplish the tasks outlined for her in the fourth category, she is ready for a functional test to determine readiness to return to competition. These functional tests put the athlete through complete movements and drills similar to those needed in participation at a competitive level.

The five steps of the rehabilitation process are summarized as

1. Control pain and swelling
2. Increase ROM
3. Increase strength
4. Restore proprioception and reestablish muscle power, speed, and skill
5. Functional testing

TABLE 2 Guidelines for Adjustment of Working Weight

Number of Repetitions	Fourth Set Adjustment	Next Session
0–2	Decrease 2–5 kg	Redo set
3–4	Decrease 0–2 kg	Same weight
6–7	Same weight	Increase 2–5 kg
8–12	Increase 2–5 kg	Increase 2–7 kg
13+	Increase 5–7 kg	Increase 5–10 kg

Source: Knight KL. (1985). Quadriceps strengthening with the DAPRE technique: case studies with neurological implications. *Medicine and Science in Sports and Exercise.* 17(6): 646–650.

TABLE 1 Knight's DAPRE Program

Set	Weight	Repetitions
1	50% of maximum	10
2	75% of maximum	6
3	100% of maximum	Max*
4	Adjust weight	Max**

*Repetitions in the third set determine the adjusted working weight for the fourth set, according to the guidelines in Table 2.
** Repetitions in the fourth set determines the adjusted working weight for the next day according to the guidelines in Table 2.

The Art of Rehabilitation

The actual implementation of the rehabilitation program takes great skill. One must understand the injury, the time lines the injury requires for complete healing, the psychological makeup of the athlete and how that athlete will respond to the injury. In addition, it is essential to be familiar with both the equipment needed and the equipment available to assist in the rehabilitation process. It is important that the athlete have some short-term and long-term goals for rehabilitation. The coach or athletic trainer can assist the athlete in setting reasonable and attainable goals. Too many times after an injury, athletes are determined to be back in play for the next game. In many cases, such an attitude results in a delay of healing and, frequently, a reinjury or secondary injury of another structure.

If there is specific equipment needed to complete the rehabilitation process and it is not available on site, the coach or athletic trainer needs to develop a viable alternative. The alternative piece of equipment may not look as fancy, but will do the job that is necessary in the process. If an alternative piece of equipment cannot be devised, the coach or athletic trainer may need to locate and acquire the equipment to complete the rehabilitation.

The coach or athletic trainer must have the time and patience to participate fully in the rehabilitation process. There will be times when an athlete needs to slow down after a rehabilitation session because of an increase in swelling or pain. Time and patience are necessary for the healing process to continue. Goals must be set and maintained, and the athlete needs positive feedback about his or her role in the rehabilitation process.

The final portion of this appendix includes some sample generic rehabilitation protocols. These protocols are not meant to be used generally, but rather in specific rehabilitation situations. Please do not feel that by following one of these protocols step-by-step the athlete will be totally rehabilitated from an injury. These sample protocols are intended to give the reader an idea of how programs are structured and the exercises are progressed through. These programs should not be used, as presented, by an athlete until he or she is fully evaluated by an athletic trainer or physical therapist. Any rehabilitation program should be individualized and supervised by a qualified practitioner such as an athletic trainer or physical therapist.

Shoulder Rehabilitation Exercises Weight/Tubing Strengthening Program

Perform the following exercises _____ times per week. This program has been designed for *your* specific needs. *Do not* change it without your doctor's or therapist's consent and instruction. Weight strengthening exercises should be done *after* activity.

Rotator Cuff Exercises

1. *Internal Rotation*
   Stand with involved side toward the door. Grasp tubing with hand and position elbow so it is bent to 90°. Place a towel roll under your arm for correct starting position. Pull from the starting position toward your stomach, rotating the shoulder inward. Start exercises pulling from *high* to *low*. Keep exercise pain free.

   Repeat _____ sets of _____ repetitions.

2. *External Rotation*
   Stand with uninvolved side toward the door. Grasp tubing with hand and position elbow so it is bent to 90°. Place a towel roll under your arm for correct starting position. Pull from your stomach out away from your body. Rotate outward until pain or shoul-

der starts to move. Start exercise by pulling from *low* to *high*.

Repeat _____ set of _____ repetitions.

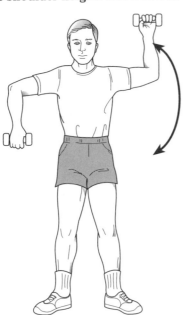

3. *Marshall Exercise*

This exercise is performed by lying on your back as in the position shown. With dumbbell weights in your hands, rotate your arms from palm of hand to back of hand lightly touching the floor. If full range of motion is painful, try to accomplish as much of the range as possible. Perform continuously for 2 to 3 minutes, checking to maintain elbows at shoulder height. Use 3 to 5 lb weights.

Shoulder Rehabilitation Exercises

Perform the following exercises _____ times per week. This program has been designed for *your* specific needs. *Do not* change it without your doctor's or therapist's consent and instruction. Shoulder strengthening exercises should *not* be done *before* sports activities. Keep all exercises pain free.

1. *Upright Rowing*

Shoulder rhythm is very important when doing this exercise. Watch the shoulders carefully to be sure you do not let one shoulder "hike up" higher than the other. *Do not* increase weight at the expense of sacrificing proper rhythm.

Lift the bar up to your chin keeping the elbows *higher* than your wrists. The weights should be held close to your body.

Repeat _____ sets of _____ repetitions.

2. *Bent Over Lateral Raises*

This exercise is also a rhythm exercise and should be done smoothly. Raise weights out to your side until your arms are level with the top of shoulder. Pause and slowly lower arms to starting position.

Repeat _____ sets of _____ repetitions.

3. *Marshall Exercise*

This exercise is performed by lying on your back, as in the position shown below.

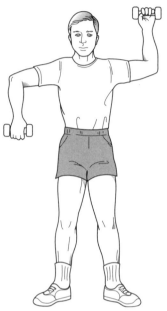

With dumbbells in your hand, rotate your arms doing 3 sets of 10 repetitions.

Repeat _____ sets of _____ repetitions.

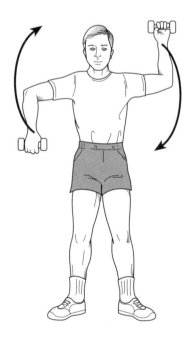

4. *Ice*

a. Fill a plastic bag with ice. Place the bag around the shoulder and wrap it with a towel.

b. Ice for 10 to 15 minutes.

c. Icing should be done immediately following the exercise, if possible.

Ankle Rehabilitation Exercises

Perform the following exercises _____ times per week. This program has been designed for *your* specific needs. *Do not* change it without your doctor's or therapist's consent and instruction. Ankle strengthening exercises should *not* be done *before* sports activities. Keep all exercises pain free.

1. *Ankle Inversion*

Sit on a chair next to the rubber bands with knee bent to 45°. Pull your foot out and away from the rubber bands. Keeping the thigh still, pivot just on the heel to the *inside* and then back to the starting position.

As above, perform with straight knee.

Repeat _____ sets of _____ repetitions.

2. *Ankle Eversion*

Bend the knee to 45° and attach rubber band to mid-foot area. Keeping the thigh still, pivot just on the heel to the *outside* and then back to starting position.

As above, perform with straight knee.

Repeat _____ sets of _____ repetitions.

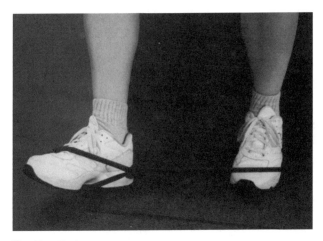

3. *Toe Raises*

Stand at the edge of a 2″-high board. Point your toes in slightly so that your feet are in a bit of a "pigeon-toed" position. Raise up and down on your tiptoes, making sure the go both directions as far as possible. Keep your weight equally distributed on both legs.

Repeat _____ sets of _____ repetitions, double leg

Repeat _____ sets of _____ repetitions, single leg

4. *Dorsiflexion*

Attach the rubber bands to the mid-foot area. Pull your toes toward your shins and back to the original position.

Repeat _____ sets of _____ repetitions.

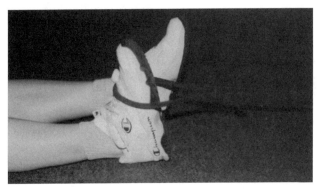

5. *Ice*

Fill a plastic bag with ice. Place the bag around the ankle and wrap it with a towel.

Ice 10 to 15 minutes.

Icing should be done no later than 15 minutes after exercises or immediately following exercises, if possible.

Knee Rehabilitation Exercises

Perform the following exercises _____ times per week. This program has been designed for *your* specific needs. *Do not* change it without your doctor's or therapist's consent and instruction. Weight strengthening exercises should *not* be done *before* sports activities. Keep all exercises pain free.

1. *Toe Raises*

Stand at the edge of a 2″-high board. Point your toes in slightly so that your feet are a bit "pigeon-

toed." Raise up and down on your tiptoes, making sure to go both directions as far as possible. Keep your weight equally distributed on both legs.

Repeat _____ sets of _____ repetitions.

2. *Short Arc Leg Extensions*

Use a knee bench through an angle of _____ degrees. Sit with your foot under the resistance pad and straighten (extend) leg. Pause, and lower weight under control.

Repeat _____ sets of _____ repetitions, single leg

Repeat _____ sets of _____ repetitions, double leg

3. *Hamstring Curls*

Use a knee bench. Lie on your stomach with your kneecaps slightly off the edge of the bench. Place your heels under the resistive pad.

Bend your knee so your heel approaches your buttocks. Pause, and lower the weight in control.

Repeat _____ sets of _____ repetitions, single leg

Repeat _____ sets of _____ repetitions, double leg

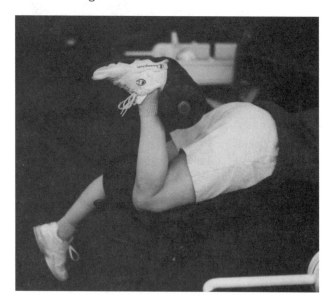

4. *Ice*

Fill a plastic bag with ice.

Place the bag around the knee and wrap it with a towel.

Ice 10 to 15 minutes.

Icing should be done no later than 15 minutes after exercises or immediately following exercise, if possible.

Source: Idaho Sports Medicine Institute, Boise, Idaho. Reprinted with permission.

A

abduction Movement of a body part away from the midline of the body.

abrasion Rubbing or scraping off of skin.

accident Occurring by chance or without intention.

acclimatization The adaptation of the body to a different environment.

acromioclavicular joint Articulation (arthrodial) formed by the distal end of the clavicle and the acromion process.

acute injury Characterized by rapid onset, resulting from a traumatic event.

adduction Movement of a body part toward the midline of the body.

ad libitum Amount desired.

adult-onset diabetes (type II) Mild form of diabetes mellitus typically occurring in adults; controlled mainly through diet and exercise.

AFB Acid fast bacilli.

afferent nerves Nerves that transport messages toward the brain.

agonistic muscles Muscles in a state of contraction as related to opposing muscles.

airborne Capable of being transmitted by air particles.

ambient Environing or surrounding (e.g., temperature that surrounds the immediate environment).

ambulation Move or walk about.

amenorrhea Absence or suppression of menstruation.

analgesia Pain inhibition.

analgesic Agent that relieves pain without causing a complete loss of sensation.

anaphylactic shock Shock caused by an allergic reaction.

anaphylaxis Increased susceptibility or sensitivity to a foreign protein or toxin as the result of previous exposure to it.

androgen A generic term for a substance that aids in the development of and controls the appearance of male characteristics.

anesthesia Partial or complete loss of sensation.

angiogenesis Formation of capillaries, which interconnect, resulting in the formation of new vessels.

anomaly Deviation from the normal.

anorexia Diminished or loss of appetite; aversion to food.

anorexia nervosa Characterized by a pattern of self-starvation with a concomitant obsession with being thin and an overwhelming fear of being fat.

anoxia Lack of oxygen.

antagonistic muscles Muscles that counteract the action of agonistic muscles.

anterior Before or in front of.

anti-inflammatories Drugs designed to prevent swelling. Two basic categories are currently in use: steroidal and nonsteroidal.

antipyretic Agent that relieves or reduces fever.

anxiety A feeling of uncertainty or apprehension.

apophysis Bony outgrowth to which muscles attach.

apophysitis Inflammation of an apophysis.

arachidonic acid Chemical released when cells are damaged that serves as a precursor to the formation of other inflammatory chemicals including leukotrienes and prostaglandins.

arrhythmic movement Irregular movement.

arthrography Radiopaque material injected into a joint to facilitate the taking of X-rays.

arthrokinematics Physiological and accessory movements of the joint.

arthroscopic examination Viewing the inside of a joint through an arthroscope using a small videocamera lens.

aspiration Taking a foreign matter into the respiratory tract during inhalation.

asymmetry (body) Lack of symmetry of sides of the body.

atrophy Decrease in size of a tissue or an organ.

aura Preepileptic seizure phenomenon involving a sensory stimulatory effect.

automatism Automatic behavior before consciousness or full awareness has been achieved after a brain concussion.

avascular Devoid of blood circulation.

avascular necrosis Death of tissue caused by the lack of blood supply.

avulsion Forcible tearing away or separation.

axilla Armpit.

B

bacteria Plural of bacterium. A Schizomycetes, unicellular microorganism that can either be parasitic or free-living and have a wide range of biochemical, often pathogenic, properties.

bacteriostatic Inhibiting or retarding the growth of bacteria.

ballistic stretching Stretching technique that uses repetitive bouncing motions.

bandage Material used to cover a wound.

Bennett's fracture Fracture and/or dislocation of the first metacarpal bone away from the greater multangular bone of the wrist.

biomechanics Branch of study that applies the laws of mechanics, internal or external, to the living body.

BLS Basic life support; its primary objective is to maintain life until medical assistance arrives at the scene of the injury.

BMR Basal metabolic rate.

boutonnière deformity Buttonhole deformity whereby the proximal interphalangeal joint of the finger is forced through the central band of the tendon of the extensor digitorum muscle.

boxer's fracture Fracture of the proximal fourth and/or fifth metacarpal bones.

bradycardia Slow heartbeat; adults below 60 BPM, children below 70 BPM.

bradykinin Inflammatory chemical released when tissues are damaged; it results in increased pain in the area and may play a role in the production of other inflammatory chemicals such as prostaglandins.

bulimia Binge-purge eating disorder.

bulimia nervosa Characterized by repeated bouts of binge eating followed by some form of purging, e.g., vomiting, use of laxatives, fasting, or vigorous and excessive exercise.

bursa Small synovial sac typically located over bony prominences that assists in cushioning and reducing friction.

bursitis Inflammation of a bursa.

C

calcific tendinitis Deposition of calcium in a chronically inflamed tendon.

calisthenic Exercise involving free movement without the aid of equipment.

carpal tunnel Anatomic region of the wrist where the median nerve and the majority of the tendons of the forearm pass into the hand.

carpal tunnel syndrome A complex of symptoms resulting from pressure on the median nerve as it passes through the carpal tunnel of the wrist, causing soreness and numbness.

catastrophic injury One involving damage to the brain and/or spinal cord that presents a potentially life-threatening situation or the possibility of permanent disability.

catecholamine Active amines, such as epinephrine and norepinephrine, that affect the nervous and cardiovascular systems.

cerebral concussion A clinical syndrome characterized by immediate and transient impairment of neurologic function secondary to mechanical forces.

cerebral contusion Bruising of brain tissue.

cerebrovascular accident Stroke.

chafing Irritation of the skin caused by friction.

charitable immunity Legal doctrine holding that a person sponsoring a charitable function should not be held accountable for negligent acts.

chiropractor One who practices a method for restoring normal health by adjusting segments of the spinal column.

Chlamydia trachomatis A genus of microorganism that can cause a wide variety of diseases in humans, one of which is venereal and causes nonspecific urethritis.

chondromalacia Abnormal softening of cartilage, typically noted between the patella and femur.

chronic injury One characterized by a slow, insidious onset, implying a gradual development of structural damage.

circadian rhythm Biological time clock of body functions.

circuit training Exercise stations that incorporate combinations of weight training, stretching exercises, calisthenics, and aerobic exercises.

circumduct Act of moving a limb such as the arm or hip in a circular manner.

CNS Central nervous system.

cold urticaria A condition in which the skin reacts to exposure to cold with localized edema associated with severe itching.

colic Intra-abdominal pain.

colitis Inflammation of the colon.

collagen The major protein of connective tissue.

Colles' fracture Transverse fracture of the distal radius.

collision sport One in which collisions between athletes are expected.

commission A legal liability arising when a person commits an act that is not legally his to perform.

communicable disease One that may be transmitted directly or indirectly from one individual to another.

computerized axial tomography (CAT) Computer-assisted X-ray scan that provides detailed images of tissues based on their relative density. Also called CAT scan.

concentric contraction Occurs when a muscle shortens and there is movement at the joint accompanied by contraction against resistance.

conduction Heating through direct contact with a hot medium.

conjunctiva Mucous membrane that lines the eyes.

connective tissue The most common tissue in the body; includes ligaments, bones, retinaculum, joint capsules, cartilage, fascia, and tendons.

contact allergen External agent that causes inflammation of the skin.

contact dermatitis Inflammation of the skin that is nonallergenic.

contact sport Sport in which athletes are expected to make physical contact but not with the intent to produce bodily injury.

contrecoup brain injury Trauma occurring when the brain continues to move within the skull following a blow to the head, resulting in injury to the brain on the side opposite the initial force.

contributory negligence Negligence arising when an injured party is at least partly responsible for an act that causes his own injury.

contusion Bruise or injury to soft tissue that does not break the skin.

convection Heating indirectly through another medium such as air or liquid.

conversion Heating by other forms of energy, e.g., electricity.

convulsions Involuntary muscular spasms or jerking.

core temperature Internal body temperature as opposed to shell or peripheral temperature.

corticosteroid Steroid produced by the adrenal cortex.

coryza Profuse nasal discharge.

counterirritant Agent that produces mild inflammation and acts in turn as an analgesic when applied locally to the skin, e.g., liniment.

crepitation Crackling sound heard during the movement of a broken bone.

critical force Magnitude of a single force by which an anatomical structure is damaged.

cryokinetics Cold application combined with exercise.

cryotherapy Therapeutic use of cold.

CSF Cerebrospinal fluid.

cubital fossa Triangular area on the anterior aspect of the forearm directly over the elbow joint.

cyanosis Bluish, grayish, or dark purple discoloration of the skin caused by a reduced amount of hemoglobin in the blood.

D

DAPRE Daily adjustable progressive resistive exercise.

débride Removal of dirt and dead tissue from a wound.

deconditioning The loss of a competitive fitness level.

degeneration Deterioration of tissue.

dehydration Decrease of fluid contained within the body.

de Quervain's disease Inflammation of sheaths surrounding the extensor tendons of the thumb.

dermatome Segmental skin area innervated by various segments of the spinal cord.

diabetes mellitus Disorder characterized by the inability of the body to appropriately metabolize carbohydrates.

diastolic blood pressure The residual pressure when the heart is between beats.

DIP Distal interphalangeal joint.

diplopia Double vision.

dislocation The displacement of contiguous surfaces of bones comprising a joint.

distal Farthest from the center, midline, or trunk.

doping The use of a drug designed to improve a competitor's performance.

dorsiflexion Bending toward the dorsum or rear; the opposite of plantar flexion.

dorsum The back of a body part.

dressing Covering, either protective or supportive, that is applied to an injury or wound.

drug Any substance that when taken into a living organism may modify one or more of its functions.

dysesthesia Impairment of the sense of touch.

dysmenorrhea Painful menstruation.

dyspnea Difficult or painful breathing.

dysrhythmia Irregular heartbeats.

E

eccentric contraction The simultaneous processes of muscle contraction and stretching of the muscle-tendon unit by an extrinsic force.

ecchymosis Black-and-blue discoloration of the skin caused by hemorrhage.

ectopic calcification Calcification occurring in an abnormal place.

edema Swelling caused by the collection of fluid in connective tissue.

effleurage Stroking massage technique.

electrolyte Solution that is a conductor of electricity.

embolus A mass of undissolved matter occluding a blood vessel.

emetic Agent that induces vomiting.

endurance The ability of the body to engage in prolonged physical activity.

enzyme An organic catalyst that can cause chemical changes in other substances without being changed itself.

epicondylitis Inflammatory response at the medial or lateral epicondyle of the humerus.

epidemiology The study of the distribution of disease or injury within a population and its environment.

epidural hematoma Bleeding between the dura and the cranial bones.

epilepsy A chronic disorder characterized by sudden attacks of brain dysfunction, including altered consciousness, abnormal motor activity, sensory phenomena, and/or inappropriate behavior.

epiphysis Cartilaginous growth region of a bone.

epistaxis Nosebleed.

erythema Swelling and red discoloration of the skin.

ethics Principles of morality and professional conduct.

etiology Science dealing with causes of disease.

eversion of the foot To turn the foot outward.

exercise-induced asthma (EIA) Acute, reversible, self-limiting bronchospasm occurring during or after exercise.

exostosis Bony outgrowths that protrude from the surface of a bone where there is not a typical bony formation.

extraoral mouth guard Protective device that fits outside the mouth.

extrapulmonary Outside of the lungs.

extravasation Escape of a fluid from its vessels into the surrounding tissues.

exudate Exuded matter such as fluid that accumulates in an area.

F

facilitation To assist the progress of or help with the healing process.

fascia Fibrous membrane that covers, supports, and separates muscles.

fasciitis Inflammation of fascia.

fibrinogen Blood plasma protein that is converted into a fibrin clot.

fibroblast Immature, fiber-producing cells of connective tissue that can mature into one of several different cell types.

fibrocartilage Type of cartilage that contains visible collagenous fibers.

fibrosis Development of excessive fibrous connective tissue; fibroid degeneration.

flexibility The range of motion (ROM) in a given joint or combination of joints.

foot pronation Combined foot movements of eversion and abduction.

foot supination Combined foot movements of inversion and abduction.

fracture A break or crack in a bone.

fracture-dislocation An injury resulting in both the fracture of a bone and dislocation at the joint.

friction Heat producing.

frostbite Freezing of tissues from excessive exposure to cold.

frostnip Less severe form of frostbite.

G

gamekeeper's thumb Sprain of the ulnar collateral ligament of the metacarpophalangeal joint of the thumb.

ganglion Herniation of the synovium surrounding a tendon and subsequent filling of the area with synovial fluid, resulting in a visible bump seen through the skin.

gastritis Inflammation of the stomach lining.

gastroenteritis Inflammation of the stomach and intestines.

genitourinary Pertaining to the reproductive and urinary organs.

genu recurvatum Hyperextension at the knee joint.

genu valgum Knock knee

genu varum Bowleg.

GI Gastrointestinal.

glenohumeral joint Articulation (spheroid) formed by the head of the humerus and the glenoid fossa of the scapula.

glycogen Storage form of glucose found in both the liver and skeletal muscles.

glycosuria Abnormally high proportion of sugar in the urine.

golfer's elbow Medial humeral epicondylitis related to incorrect golf technique.

H

hamstrings The three muscles that make up the posterior thigh: biceps femoris, semimembranosus, and semitendinosus.

HBV Hepatitis B virus.

heat cramps Muscle spasms related to excessive heat buildup within the body.

heat exhaustion Generalized fatigue related to excessive heat buildup within the body; may be a precursor to heat stroke.

heat stroke Excessive heat buildup within the body resulting in the body's inability to cool itself, with core temperatures exceeding 106° F.

heel spur Ossification into the proximal attachment of the plantar fascia.

hemarthrosis Blood in a joint.

hematolytic Pertaining to the degeneration and disintegration of the blood.

hematoma A localized collection of extravasated blood, usually clotted, that is confined within an organ, tissue, or space.

hematuria Blood in the urine.

hemoglobin The red respiratory protein of erythrocytes that transports oxygen from the lungs to the tissues.

hemoglobinuria Hemoglobin in the urine.

hemolysis Destruction of red blood cells.

hemophilia Hereditary blood disease in which coagulation is prolonged or nonexistent.

hemopoietic Forming blood cells.

hemorrhage Discharge of blood.

hemothorax Bloody fluid in the pleural cavity.

HEPA High-efficiency particulate air filter.

hernia Protrusion of a part of an organ or tissue through an abnormal opening.

herniated disk Rupture or protrusion of the nucleus pulposus through the annulus fibrosus of an intervertebral disk.

hip pointer Contusion and associated hematoma to the superior/anterior portion of the iliac crest.

hirsutism Excessive hair growth and/or presence of hair in unusual places, especially in women.

histamine Powerful inflammatory chemical that causes an increase in vascular permeability as well as vasodilation.

HIV Human immunodeficiency virus.

homeostasis Maintenance of a steady state in the body's internal environment.

HPV Human papillomavirus; approximately 55 specific types of these viruses have been identified, at least two of which are related to plantar warts.

HSV-1 Herpes simplex virus type 1; related to infections in athletes commonly known as herpes gladiatorum.

humeroradial joint Articulation (arthrodial) formed by the proximal end of the radius and the distal end of the humerus, specifically the capitulum.

humeroulnar joint Articulation (ginglymus) formed by the proximal end of the ulna, specifically the trochlear notch, with the distal end of the humerus, specifically the trochlea.

hyperallergenic Material(s) that result in allergic reactions.

hyperemia Unusual amount of blood in a body part.

hyperextension Extreme stretching of a body part.

hyperflexibility Flexibility beyond a joint's normal range.

hyperglycemia Excessively high level of blood sugar.

hyperhidrosis Excessive sweating; excessive foot perspiration.

hyperkeratosis Increased callus development.

hypermobility Extreme mobility of a joint.

hyperpnea Hyperventilation; exaggerated deep breathing that is also more rapid than normal.

hypertension High blood pressure; abnormally high tension.

hyperthermia Abnormally high body temperature.

hypertonic Having a higher osmotic pressure than a comparable solution.

hypertrophy Enlargement of a part caused by an increase in the size of its cells.

hyperventilation Abnormally deep breathing that is prolonged, causing a depletion of carbon dioxide, a fall in blood pressure, and fainting.

hyphemia Bleeding into the anterior portion of the eye.

hypoglycemic (insulin) shock Insulin shock resulting from an abnormally low sugar content in the blood.

hypothermia A body temperature below 33.3° C (95° F).

hypovolemic shock Inability of the cardiovascular system to maintain adequate circulation to all parts of the body.

hypoxia Lack of an adequate amount of oxygen.

I

ICE Ice, compression, and elevation.

idiopathic Cause of a condition is unknown.

incubation period The time between an exposure to an infectious agent and the appearance of symptoms of that infection.

infectious mononucleosis Viral infection characterized by general fatigue and enlargement of organs such as the spleen.

injury Act that damages or hurts.

innervation Nerve stimulation of a muscle.

interosseous membrane Connective tissue membrane between bones.

intertrigo Chafing of the skin.

interval training Alternating periods of work with active recovery.

intracerebral hematoma Bleeding within the brain tissues.

intracranial injury Head injury characterized by disruption of blood vessels, either veins or arteries, resulting in the development of a hematoma or swelling within the confines of the cranium.

inunctions Oily or medicated substances (e.g., liniments) that are rubbed into the skin to produce a local or systemic effect.

inversion of the foot To turn the foot inward; inner border of the foot lifts.

ions Electrically charged atoms.

iontophoresis Using an electrical current to drive a chemical directly through the skin.

ipsilateral Situated on the same side.

ischemia Local anemia.

isokinetic muscle resistance Accommodating and variable resistance.

isometric exercise Exercise that contracts a muscle statically without a concurrent range of motion.

isotonic exercise Exercise that shortens and lengthens a contracted muscle through a range of motion.

J

joint capsule Sac-like structure that encloses the ends of bones in a diarthrodial joint.

juvenile-onset diabetes (type I) Insulin-dependent type of diabetes mellitus usually occurring in children and adolescents.

K

Kehr's sign Pain radiating into the left shoulder that is normally associated with an injury to the spleen.

keratolytic Loosening of a horny layer of skin.

keratosis Excessive growth of a horny layer of skin tissue.

kilocalorie Amount of heat required to raise one kilogram of water one degree Celsius.

kinesthesia Sensation or feeling of movement; the awareness one has of the spatial relationships of the body and its parts.

kyphosis Exaggeration of the normal curve of the thoracic spine.

L

laser A device that concentrates high energies into a narrow beam of visible monochromatic light.

LBW Lean body weight.

leukocytes White blood cells.

liability Legal responsibility to perform an act in a reasonable and prudent manner.

little-league elbow Condition related to excessive throwing that results in swelling of the medial epicondyle of the elbow, i.e., medial humeral epicondylitis.

locus of control People's belief, or lack thereof, of being in control of events occurring in their lives.

lordosis Abnormal curvature of the lumbar vertebrae.

LRI Lower respiratory infection.

luxation Complete dislocation of a joint.

Lyme disease Bacterial infection transmitted by deer tick.

lysis To break down.

M

macerated skin Skin that has been softened through wetting.

malaise Discomfort and uneasiness caused by an illness.

mallet finger Deformity of the distal interphalangeal joint of the finger caused by an avulsion of the tendon of the extensor digitorum muscle from the distal phalanx.

margination Accumulation of leukocytes on the walls of blood vessels at the site of injury during early stages of inflammation.

massage Using the hands to systematically manipulate soft tissues of the body.

mast cells Connective tissue cells that contain heparin and histamine.

menarche Onset of menstrual function.

menisci Fibrocartilaginous structures that are between the hyaline cartilage surfaces in some synovial joints (e.g., the knee).

metatarsalgia A general term to describe pain in the ball of the foot.

microtrauma Microscopic lesion or injury.

modalities Physical agents that help create an optimal healing environment.

mode of transmission The manner in which an infection is spread.

Morton's neuroma A nerve tumor (benign) related to the nerve between the third and fourth metatarsal heads with pain going to the third and fourth toes.

MP Metacarpophalangeal joint.

muscle contracture Permanent contraction of a muscle as a result of spasm or paralysis.

muscular endurance The ability to perform repetitive muscular contractions against some resistance.

muscular strength The maximal force that can be applied by a muscle during a single maximal contraction.

myocarditis Inflammation of the heart muscle.

myoglobin Respiratory protein in muscle tissue that is an oxygen carrier.

myositis Inflammation of muscle.

myositis ossificans Myositis marked by ossification within a muscle.

N

negative resistance Slow, eccentric muscle contraction against a resistance.

negligence The failure to do what a reasonably careful and prudent person would have done under the same or like circumstances, or doing something that a reasonably careful and prudent person would not have done under the same or like circumstances.

nerve entrapment Compression of a nerve between bone or soft tissue.

neuritis Inflammation of a nerve.

neuroma Tumor consisting mostly of nerve cells and nerve fibers.

nociceptor Receptor of pain.

noncontact sport Sport in which athletes are not expected to be involved in any physical contact.

NSAID Nonsteroidal anti-inflammatory drugs.

nuclei A particle that makes up a nucleus of an atom.

nystagmus Constant involuntary movement of the eyeball, which may be back and forth, up and down, or rotary.

O

omission Liability arising when a person fails to perform a legal duty.

orthopedic surgeon Physician who corrects deformities of the musculoskeletal system.

orthosis An appliance or apparatus used in sports to support, align, prevent, or correct deformities, or to improve function of a movable body part.

orthotics Field of knowledge relating to orthoses and their use.

Osgood-Schlatter disease Epiphyseal inflammation of the tibial tubercle.

OSHA Occupational Safety and Health Administration.

osteitis pubis Inflammation of the bones in the region of the symphysis pubis.

osteoarthritis Chronic disease involving joints, especially weight-bearing joints, in which the articular cartilage is damaged and there is a degeneration of the joint.

osteochondral Refers to relationship of bone and cartilage.

osteochondritis Inflammation of bone and cartilage.

osteochondritis dissecans Condition in which a fragment of cartilage and underlying bone are detached from the articular surface.

osteochondrosis Diseased state of a bone and its articular cartilage.

P

PABA *Para*-aminobenzoic acid; the common active ingredient in sunscreen products.

palpation The act of feeling with the hands for the purpose of determining the consistency of the part beneath.

paraplegia Paralysis of lower portion of the body and both legs.

paresis Slight or incomplete paralysis.

paresthesia Abnormal or morbid sensation such as itching or prickling.

patellofemoral joint Articulation (saddle) formed by the posterior surface of the patella and the anterior surface of the femoral condyles.

pathogenic Causing disease.

pathology Area of specialization concerned with the manifestations of disease.

pathomechanics Act of applying mechanical forces to an organism that can adversely affect the structure and function of that organism.

pediatrician Physician specializing in the treatment of children's diseases.

periodization The organization of training into a cyclical structure in order to attain the optimal development of an athlete's performance capacities.

permeable Permitting the passage of a substance through a vessel wall.

pes anserinus tendinitis Irritation of the tibial attachment of the pes anserine associated most often with runners and cyclists.

pes cavus Abnormally high arch of the foot.

pes planus An abnormally flat foot.

pétrissage Kneading type of massage.

phagocytosis Destruction of injurious cells or particles by phagocytes (white blood cells).

phalanges Anatomical name for the bones of both the fingers and/or toes.

phalanx Any one of the bones of the fingers and toes.

pharmacology The science of drugs—their preparation, uses, and effects.

phonophoresis Introduction of ions of soluble salt into the body through ultrasound.

photophobia Unusual intolerance to light.

piezoelectric Production of an electric current as a result of pressure on certain crystals.

PIP Proximal interphalangeal joint.

plantar fasciitis Inflammation of the plantar fascia.

plyometric exercise Exercise that utilizes the stretch reflex to increase athletic power.

pneumonia Inflammation of the lungs.

pneumothorax Collapse of a lung as a result of air in the pleural cavity.

podiatrist Medical practitioner who specializes in the study and care of the foot.

point tenderness Pain produced when an injury site is palpated.

polymers Natural or synthetic substances formed by the combination of two or more molecules of the same substance.

posterior Toward the rear or back.

posttraumatic amnesia Inability to recall events that have occurred from the moment of injury.

primary survey Initial assessment of an injured athlete to determine if the player's life is in immediate jeopardy.

prognosis Prediction as to probable outcome of a disease or injury.

prophylaxis Guarding against injury or disease.

Proprioceptive neuromuscular facilitation (PNF) Stretching techniques that involve combinations of alternating contractions and stretches.

proprioceptor One of several sensory receptors located in muscles, tendons, and joint capsules.

prostaglandins Perhaps some of the most powerful chemicals produced within the body. Related to the inflammatory process, they cause a variety of effects including vasodilation, increased vascular permeability, pain, fever, and clotting.

prosthesis An artificial replacement of an absent body part.

proximal Nearest to the point of reference.

psychogenic Of psychic origin; that which originates in the mind.

purulent Consisting of, or forming pus.

pyoderma Pus-producing infection of the skin.

Q

Q angle Angle made by the rectus femoris and the patellar tendon as they attach to the tibial tuberosity.

quadriceps Four muscles of the anterior thigh: rectus femoris, vastus medialis, vastus intermedius, and vastus lateralis.

quadriplegia Paralysis affecting all four limbs.

R

radiation Emission and diffusion of rays of heat.

radiocarpal joint Articulation (ellipsoidal) formed by the distal end of the radius and three bones of the wrist: navicular, lunate, and triquetral.

radioulnar joints Two articulations (pivot) formed by the proximal and distal radius and ulna, known commonly as the proximal and distal radioulnar joints.

Raynaud's phenomenon Condition in which exposure to cold causes vasospasm of digital arteries.

regeneration Repair, regrowth, or restoration of a part, such as tissue.

residual The remaining amount.

resorption Removal by absorption.

respirator A mechanical device used to assist breathing. In this case it refers to a device used to filter particles from the air.

retrograde amnesia Inability to recall events that occurred just prior to an injury.

retroversion Tilting or turning backward of a part.

revascularize Restoration of blood circulation to an injured area.

rhinitis The common cold.

risk factor Causative agent in a sports injury.

ROM Range of motion.

rotation Turning around an axis in an angular motion.

rotator cuff Group of four muscles of the glenohumeral joint: subscapularis, supraspinatus, infraspinatus, and teres minor.

S

SAID principle Specific adaptation to imposed demands.

scoliosis Lateral and/or rotary curvature of the spine.

secondary survey Assessment of an injured athlete that commences once the primary survey is completed. The objective is to collect as much information about the injury as possible under the circumstances.

seizure Sudden onset of uncoordinated muscular activity and changes in consciousness lasting an unpredictable time.

septic shock Shock caused by bacteria, especially gram-negative bacteria commonly seen in systemic infections.

sequela Pathological condition that occurs as a consequence of another condition or event.

serotonin Hormone and neurotransmitter.

shin splints Medial or posteromedial leg pain brought about by walking, running, or related activities and that decreases with rest.

shoulder pointer Contusion and subsequent hematoma in the region of the acromioclavicular joint.

sign Objective evidence of an abnormal situation within the body.

soft tissue Includes muscles, fascia, tendons, joint capsules, ligaments, blood vessels, and nerves.

spearing A practice in tackle football whereby a player performs either a tackle or a block using the head as the initial point of contact.

spheroid joint A ball-and-socket articulation.

spondylolisthesis Forward slippage of a vertebra, usually between the fifth lumbar and the sacrum.

spondylolysis A defect in the neural arch (pars interarticularis) of the vertebrae.

sports medicine Branch of medicine concerned with the medical aspects of sports participation.

sprain Injury to a joint and the surrounding structures, primarily ligaments and/or joint capsules.

Staphylococcus Genus of gram-positive bacteria normally present on the skin and in the upper respiratory tract and prevalent in localized infections.

stasis Blockage or stoppage of circulation.

static stretching Passively stretching an antagonistic muscle by placing it in a maximal stretch and holding it there.

sternoclavicular joint Articulation (arthrodial) formed by the union of the proximal clavicle and the manubrium of the sternum.

strain Injury involving muscles and tendons or the junction between the two, commonly known as the musculotendinous junction.

Streptococcus Genus of gram-positive bacteria found in the throat, respiratory tract, and intestinal tract.

stress fracture Small crack or break in a bone related to excessive, repeated overloads; also known as overuse fracture or march fracture.

stressor Anything that affects the body's physiological or psychological condition and upsets the homeostatic balance.

subdural hematoma Bleeding below the dura mater.

subluxation Partial or incomplete dislocation of an articulation.

subtalar joint Articulation (arthrodial) formed by the inferior surface of the talus and the superior surface of the calcaneus.

symptom Subjective evidence of an abnormal situation within the body.

syndrome Group of typical symptoms or conditions that characterize a deficiency or disease.

synergy To work in cooperation with.

synovitis Inflammation of the synovium.

synthesis To build up.

systolic blood pressure The pressure caused by the pumping of the heart.

T

tachycardia Rapid or abnormally high pulse rate.

tackler's exostosis Formation of a benign growth projecting from the humerus that is caused by repeated blows to the upper arm region; common in tackle football.

talocrural joint Articulation (ginglymus) formed by the distal tibia and fibula with the superior surface (dome) of the talus.

tapotement Percussion.

TB disease Having the organism that causes TB in the body, in its active state. A person with TB disease usually has symptoms and can transmit the disease to others.

TB infection Having the organism that causes TB in the body, but not having the active disease. A person having TB infection, is asymptomatic and cannot transmit TB unless the organism converts to an active state.

team physician A medical doctor who agrees to provide at least limited medical coverage to a particular sports program or institution.

tendinitis Inflammation of a tendon.

tenosynovitis Inflammation of the sheath of a tendon.

tetanus An acute, often fatal, condition characterized by tonic muscular spasm, hyperreflexia, and sometimes lockjaw.

tetanus toxoid Tetanus toxin modified to produce active immunity against *Clostridium tetani.*

thermotherapy Therapeutic use of heat.

thoracic cage Thoracic vertebrae, their corresponding ribs, and the sternum.

thrombi Plural of thrombus, a blood clot that blocks small blood vessels or a cavity of the heart.

tibiofemoral joint Articulation (bicondylar) formed by the medial and lateral femoral condyles and the medial and lateral tibial condyles.

tinea Group of fungi-related skin infections, commonly called ringworm, which can affect various parts of the body—groin (tinea cruris), feet and toes (tinea pedis), and scalp (tinea capitis).

tinea versicolor Fungus infection resulting in the formation of circular skin lesions that appear either lighter or darker than adjacent skin.

tinnitus Ringing in the ears.

TMJ Temporomandibular joint.

tonic muscle spasm Rigid muscle contraction that lasts over a period of time.

torsion Act or state of being twisted.

tort Harm, other than a breach of contract, done to another for which the law holds the wrongdoer responsible.

training effect Result achieved when stroke volume increases while heart rate is reduced at a given exercise load.

trait anxiety A general disposition or tendency to perceive certain situations as threatening and to react with an anxiety response.

transcutaneous electrical nerve stimulation (TENS) Modality of electrical stimulation typically applied to the body for the purpose of pain reduction.

transitory paralysis Temporary paralysis.

trauma Wound or injury.

traumatic Pertaining to an injury or wound.

trigger points Small areas within a muscle that can become highly irritated.

tunnel of Guyon Anatomic region formed by the hook of the hamate bone and the pisiform bone, whereby the ulnar nerve passes into the hand.

turf toe Sprain of the metatarsophalangeal joint of the great toe.

U

URI Upper respiratory infection.

V

valgus Position of a body part that is bent outward.

varus Position of a body part that is bent inward.

vasoconstriction Decrease in the diameter of a blood vessel resulting in a decreased blood flow.

vasodilation Increase in the diameter of a blood vessel resulting in an increased blood flow.

vasospasm Spasm of a blood vessel.

vehicle The substance in which a drug is transported.

verruca Wart caused by a virus.

vertigo Loss of balance.

vibration Rapid shaking.

viscoelastic Any substance having both viscous and elastic properties.

viscosity Resistance to flow.

volar Pertaining to the palm or the sole.

Volkmann's contracture Contracture of muscles of the forearm related to a loss of blood supply caused by a fracture and/or dislocation of either of the bones in the forearm or the humerus.